THREE PLAYS

Rabindranath Tagore's creative genius needs no introduction. His phenomenal dramatic career alone encompasses more than 60 plays and occupies a prime position in Bengali and modern Indian theatre.

This volume includes three of his plays in translation. While *Red Oleander* (*Rakta-karavi*), a modern classic, protests against man's ruthless use of organization to exploit human and natural resources, *Tapati* is a proto-feminist play that attends to the problems of action and injustice. *Formless Jewel* (*Arup Ratan*) is a play about spiritual beauty and the discovery of God.

Ananda Lal in his introduction helps the reader discover Tagore as a playwright, director, and theatre theorist and discusses the reception of his plays and their themes. With an extensive bibliography and glossary, this volume will appeal to students of literature, performance, and translation studies, as well as to general readers.

Ananda Lal is Professor of English at Jadavpur University, Kolkata.

'His translation … has an authentic ring … he has conveyed the sense of the original as faithfully as possible …'
—*Indian Express*

'With unusual precision and zeal for truthful documentation, Dr Lal tries to correct certain accepted notions on Tagore and his contribution to theatre.'
—*The Telegraph*

RABINDRANATH TAGORE

THREE PLAYS

Translated and with an Introduction
by
Ananda Lal

OXFORD
UNIVERSITY PRESS

OXFORD
UNIVERSITY PRESS

Oxford University Press is a department of the University of Oxford.
It furthers the University's objective of excellence in research, scholarship,
and education by publishing worldwide. Oxford is a registered trademark of
Oxford University Press in the UK and in certain other countries

Published in India by
Oxford University Press
YMCA Library Building, 1 Jai Singh Road, New Delhi 110 001, India

First Edition published by the MP Birla Foundation in 1987
Published by Oxford University Press in 2001
Sixth impression 2015

ISBN-13: 978-0-19-565365-6
ISBN-10: 0-19-565365-3

To Swati
"Bright Star"

RABINDRANATH TAGORE (1861–1941; "Tagore" is the anglicised form of the surname "Ṭhākur") is unanimously respected as the greatest literary figure of modern India. In one way or another, he has influenced the best writers in every Indian language in the present century. His poetry won for him the Nobel Prize in Literature in 1913; he was the first non-European to receive that award. His novels and short stories dealt with social issues realistically; his plays introduced a completely new style of Indian theatre. A composer, director, educator and painter as well, he seemed to master any creative activity that he undertook. Above all, his works reveal a broad humanism that counters the prevailing artistic cynicism of our times. Tagore holds the place of spiritual preceptor in the psyche of Indians, for they know him by the honorific epithet "Gurudev".

PREFACE TO THE SECOND EDITION

Since the first publication of this book, my duties as theatre critic for *The Telegraph* have exposed me to the entire gamut of theatre in Calcutta, encompassing not just local performances in Bengali, Hindi and English, but touring shows from outside in many other languages as well. I maintain a database of my reviews, from which I occasionally unearth fascinating statistics. For instance, I find that among the approximately 1000 productions I have seen in these years, the dramatists whose names recur most frequently include Shakespeare and Brecht, closely followed by Tagore and (curiously enough) Neil Simon, with about twenty productions each. While Calcutta groups account for the majority of the Tagorean and Brechtian stagings, the Shakespeare and Simon shows originate mainly from elsewhere. However, if one adds the huge output of Tagore's dance-dramas—a favourite with Bengali amateur societies, but which I cannot review owing to the technical dominance of dance and music—productions of Tagore soar past those of any rival by far.

Of course, this phenomenon should hardly cause any surprise. Tagore is Bengal's Bard and Calcutta is Bengal's (though not Bangladesh's) capital. We should expect him to preside over the Calcutta stage, like Shakespeare does London's. What does raise eyebrows is the paucity of non-Bengali Tagorean performances and a somewhat disproportionately low corpus of criticism—in any language—on Tagorean drama during this period. The excellent volumes by Sisir Kumar Das in English, and Prasantakumar Pal in Bengali cover Tagore's plays, no doubt, but do not feature drama as their specific subject. Professor Das compiled Tagore's original English works in a three-part anthology with a critical introduction. Professor Pal continues research on what has become Tagore's definitive biography, of which eight volumes have come out so far. In the last dozen years, only Rudraprasad Chakrabarti has focused exclusively on Tagore's plays, publishing, in Bengali, two monographs on their stage history which substantially revise previous scholarship. Visva-Bharati, Tagore's copyright holder, has printed in its journal, *Rabindra-viksha*, several of his draft manuscripts in its possession, separately published *Yogayog*, which he dramatised for Sisir Bhaduri's company in 1936, and issued a variorum edition of *Rakta-karavi*. The two new books in English on Tagore as dramatist, by

R. N. Roy and B. Chakraverty, follow a traditional approach showing no acquaintance with contemporary criticism.

Three English translations of two plays have appeared lately; I have entered them, along with all other new material cited in this preface, in the Addenda to my Bibliography. I should clarify, however, that Krishna Dutta and Andrew Robinson did not translate *The Post Office* anew, but merely touched up the existing Macmillan version without proper acknowledgement. William Radice's translation of the same play metamorphosed unusually under director Jill Parvin. Taking her cue from a 1942 performance in the Warsaw ghetto by Jewish orphans facing death at Nazi hands, she set the production (London, 1 September 1993) in that historical time and place as a play within a play. The printed text retains this metatheatrical structure. The other recent successful foreign staging of Tagore also involved *The Post Office*. Wolfram Mehring directed Martin Kampchen's German translation of it in a minimalist, expressionistic mode (at Chur, Switzerland, 19 January 1989). He then collaborated in Calcutta with director Sunil Das, using the same style, on a Bengali revival which travelled in India, Bangladesh and the UK. Kampchen contrasted the approaches of the British and Swiss productions in an essay illuminated by striking photographs.

Notwithstanding these innovative interpretations, I reiterate that Tagore's plays receive much less theatrical attention outside Bengal than they deserve. This observation applies to both the rest of India and the world, where the message about their worth has clearly not got across. As a result, even the *Cambridge Guide to Theatre* (1990) does not grant Tagore a separate entry. Yet in an age which looks to Peter Brook's intercultural *Mahabharata* as a performatory pathfinder, drama like Tagore's virtually cries out for imaginative treatment. This is precisely why I mention Mehring's *Post Office*, which normally would have stayed out of consideration because this book dealt expressly with the Bengali and Anglo-American contexts. The time to widen our scope to examine the reception of Tagore's plays in other languages and cultures has arrived. The absence of repositories for primary sources had so far hindered any such enterprise. Fortunately, two new books took the first steps toward building up essential indices of Tagoreana in newspaper and periodical literature. *Imagining Tagore: Rabindranath and the British Press (1912–1941)* comprises a near-exhaustive collection of reviews and news items, till then unavailable in any one location; and

Tagoreana in "The Modern Review" lists virtually every reference to Tagore contained in India's pre-eminent English-language journal during the last half of his life. Among the latter, for example, there figure the detailed and valuable comments of the respected art historian Stella Kramrisch on Tagore's 1923 production of *Visarjan*.

As noted in this book, the very first international performance of a Tagore play (significantly, *The Post Office*) took place in neither England nor the US but at the Abbey Theatre in Ireland. The influential Irish dramatist, Padraic Colum, reviewing it for the *Manchester Guardian*, was perhaps the first to connect Tagorean drama with Maeterlinck. Since then, productions have occurred sporadically on every continent, some of considerable interest. In the opinion of Sveto Petrovic, the Croatian National Theatre (Zagreb) staged *Chitra* earlier than anyone else in Europe, to critical acclaim and full houses for three nights in October 1915. The performance of *Chitra* in Munich (1916) caused much controversy in the Anglo-American press; it irritated even the liberal *Daily Chronicle*, London, into titling a news report "The Hun and Tagore" (8 December 1916), which cautioned Tagore about "Prussian" intentions. According to *Modern Review* (January 1925), the Moscow Art Theatre did *The King of the Dark Chamber* as early as 1918, with Madam Germanova as Sudarshana. The illustrious Stanislavsky never mentioned it perhaps because, as Petrovic believes, it came from "a dissident group". The London *Times* (13 November 1920) billed a production of the play in Frankfurt on 27 November as the first "long play by Tagore ... attempted in a European theatre." The celebrated German regisseur, Max Reinhardt, mounted it at the Kammerspiele, Berlin (4 March 1921). The Vienna correspondent of the *Observer* (26 June 1921) recorded that the historic Josefstadt Theatre had successfully staged *The Post Office*, whereas *Chitra* had not received "full justice" but would be repeated the following season at the Raimundtheater. Arabinda Bose translated for *Modern Review* (February 1922) a sensitive German review of a performance of *The Post Office* at the famous Volksbuhne, Berlin, which Tagore had seen; the audience comprising survivors of World War I was touched by this "drama of inner forces which we Westerners have almost lost". Bose says Tagore considered it the best foreign rendition of the play (Tagore also saw a Swedish version in Stockholm earlier on this trip). *Letters to a Friend* corroborates this: Tagore wrote on 4 June 1921, "altogether the whole thing was a success ... the German

interpretation was suggestive of a fairy-story, full of elusive beauty".
A news brief in the *Times* (26 May 1922) announced "*Chitra* and
The King of the Dark Room" on 27 May at the Nouveau Theatre,
Paris, "the first of Rabindranath Tagore's plays to be given in
France". The *Ottawa Evening Journal* (18 February 1924) termed
Chitra by the Drama League Players "one of the great gifts of the
East to the West". Kalidas Nag, eyewitness to the Chinese premiere
of *Chitra* in Tagore's presence (Peking, 8 May 1924, Tagore's
birthday), remarked in his diary on its east–west interface. *Modern
Review* (April 1925) carried trailblazing coverage by "X" of *Sannyasi*
at the Summer Theatre, Sansi Tayuanfu School of Foreign
Languages, China, through a portfolio of 26 photographs, capturing
the performance scene by scene. Melbourne's *The Age* called *Chitra*,
directed by Howard Edie, "a beautiful play" (8 December 1925).
On 13 June 1926, Tagore viewed *Chitra* in Italian at the Argentine
Theatre, Rome. *Modern Review* (1938) recalled that in 1926, *The
Post Office* had played in Dresden and two Prague theatres which
got so crowded as to make entry difficult. Prague had the distinction
of seeing it in Czech and German on consecutive days, with Tagore
as guest (12–13 October 1926; see *Chithipatra*, 3: 43). Another
item in 1931 stated that the Indian Students' Club, Munich, had
staged *Chitrangada* (2 December 1930), the first time in Europe
that actors spoke in Bengali. Local papers had praised the acting of
a "Mr. T. Sen" in the heroine's part, much later identified by Sunil
Bandyopadhyay as the eminent educationist Triguna Sen. Bandyopadhyay's piece in the *Statesman* included a rare performance photo.
The play toured other towns by popular demand.

One reads elsewhere of many radio broadcasts, and other uncon-
firmed or unsubstantiated shows—as in an appendix to the publication *Bilati Yatra theke Svadesi Thiyetar* (which also provides the
information on Canada and Australia cited in the previous paragraph).
The Tagore centenary year, 1961, witnessed a plethora of productions
around the world but the eulogistic nature of the event paradoxically
discounts any great significance we can attach to these tributes. By
far the most important, however, was the off-Broadway *King of the
Dark Chamber* described in this book, on pages 80–84. I should add
here that it travelled to South Africa later, and was viewed by a
consolidated estimated audience of over 50,000 in Durban and Cape
Town. An interesting photograph of *Chitra* that year at the Maison
de l'Unesco, Paris, depicts the princess wearing a mask.

The discovery of several theatre notices—a few in Prasantakumar Pal's seventh volume—enhances my chapter on the British and American responses. The *Manchester Evening News* commended the "atmosphere of mysticism" in the Garrick Society's *Chitra* at Stockport on 10 March 1916. According to the *Chicago Illustrated Journal* (7 October 1916), "The play was acted in Boston earlier, on 8 February 1915, and London saw it played in February of this year." Perhaps the Garrick Society production had reached London. An insertion in the *Los Angeles Examiner* may pinpoint the date of *The Post Office* performed in that city by the Children's Theatre at the Hollywood Library Auditorium (see page 77), to 18 November 1916. On 27 April 1917, the Union of East and West staged *Chitra* at St James' Theatre, London, with Edith Goodall "outstanding" as the leading lady (*Westminster Gazette*, 28 April 1917). A review of the 1918 production of *Sacrifice* (page 77) has surfaced: the *Christian Commonwealth* called it "very successful" and "memorable"; "in dramatic power this play marks an advance on *Chitra*". Tagore watched the enactment of *King of the Dark Chamber* by the Clifton Boarding School for girls in Bristol, 11 July 1920, and referred to it as quite beautiful in a letter (*Chithipatra*, 4: 91). On 3 September 1921, the Union of East and West revived its 1920 production of the playlet "The Farewell Curse", along with two other works, in "an open-air performance ... in the beautiful gardens of Lord Leverhulme's house at Hampstead". The *Morning Post* pronounced that "The piece was played effectively". On 15 September, the Tagore Players debuted in Los Angeles with *Chitra* at the Gamut Club Theatre. Produced by Surendra Narayan Guha, who had previously directed *The Light of Asia*, it starred Marion Frances Bronson and Profulla Kumar Ghosal as the romantic leads. An American critic and self-confessed cynic wrote ecstatically in *Modern Review* (accompanied by uncommon photos, January 1922) about this interracial venture which enshrined the spirit of the East. The Union of East and West then staged the short comedy "Trial by Luck", a translation of *Lakshmir Pariksha*, on 22 October at Wigmore Hall, London, as a curtain-raiser. Two reviewers applauded the acting by English women, though the *Daily Telegraph* observed that "the effect of Indian clothes was to make the actresses look startlingly and uncompromisingly English". While the *Daily Chronicle* commented on Tagore's "simplicity and charm" and "most delicate skill", the *Daily Telegraph* sceptically questioned whether the Union's shows "are really worth the pains and the money expended on them". A quaint picture survives of a sari-clad Ann Firth as the heroine of the playlet "Suttee" (in a Hampstead garden, 30 July 1936), in the *Evening News*. Finally, two small-scale presentations of *Sacrifice* took place in Shoreham and Working Men's College, London, on 4 July 1936 and 27 November 1937 respectively.

Since early reviewers often function as influential standard-bearers, I mention a few extra British notices here to supplement my book-review section. Some of the first commentaries on *The King of the Dark Chamber* persuade me to modify my discussion about press reactions to it. These appeared in the *Observer*, *Globe*, *Daily Chronicle*, *Daily Express* and *Illustrated London News* in June–July 1914. They were so glowingly positive in contrast with the criticism which came later (as in the *Outlook*: "it is only rarely that you would say that Mr. Tagore writes beautiful English—English, that is, completely satisfying in itself"), that I should in all fairness conclude that the drama had a mixed reception. The apogee of approbation remains *The Post Office*; its appreciation in the *Nation* summed up its impact in Britain. Two of the very first reviews of *The Cycle of Spring* and *Sacrifice* came out in the *Manchester Guardian*; readers can consult them as typical of a newspaper sympathetic to Tagore even, as in the latter case, in the midst of a general disillusionment. But as late as 1921, with the Tagore boom over, the *Observer* opined that the playlet "Ama and Vinayaka", in *The Fugitive*, "is equal to the best Tagore has given us in the past".

The text of my first edition remains intact, except for minor corrections necessitated by recent research, notably Rudraprasad Chakrabarti's authoritative reconstruction of the plays' chronology in the theatres. I have also updated my bibliographies. The requirements of a paperback edition, however, entailed that the musical scores and photographic plates had to be omitted. Therefore, readers may please ignore the sentence about appendices containing the transcribed notations of all the songs (page 117). In conclusion, I must thank Professor Swapan Majumdar and Sri Subimal Lahiri for taking personal interest in this second edition and generously helping me with material.

Calcutta, May 2001   ANANDA LAL

ACKNOWLEDGMENTS

This book is substantially the text of my doctoral dissertation submitted to the Department of Theatre at the University of Illinois in May 1986, brought up to date with material available during Tagore's 125th birth anniversary year (1986-87). The dissertation would not have been possible without the support I received from the members on my doctoral committee. I cannot adequately express my gratitude to my advisor and Head of the Department, Professor Robert Graves, for the guidance and encouragement he gave me along every step of the way; I value his friendship, which transcends the purely professional bounds of academia. Professor Burnet Hobgood, director of the Ph.D. program in Theatre, approved unreservedly of the topic for my research when I first mentioned the idea to him, at a time when I still had doubts about the rationale for this project and my abilities to undertake it; I also thank him for the important suggestions he made concerning my translated scripts. Professor Charles Capwell of the School of Music gave generously of his time to educate me on the basics of Western musical notation — without his help the transcriptions of Tagore's songs would not have taken final shape.

I owe a considerable debt to the Library at the University of Illinois because its wide range of holdings, which never ceased to surprise me, covered virtually everything I needed to conduct my research in Urbana. The few items that it did not possess were procured for me from other libraries by the Inter-Library Loans department, whose staff I thank for their prompt and efficient handling of my requests.

I am grateful to the Graduate College of the University of Illinois for awarding me a dissertation research grant which enabled me to enlist the services of Sri V. Balsara in Calcutta, to make the initial transcriptions of the songs into Western notation. My wife Swati prepared the final copies of the transcriptions from Sri Balsara's drafts. The Graduate College also awarded me a fellowship for the Summer 1985 session which greatly facilitated my research by freeing me from assistantship duties.

I also received help from several sources in Calcutta. Among them I am particularly indebted to my parents, Professor P. Lal and Shyamasree Devi, who continued providing me with material directly relevant to my work; to Writers Workshop, for first publishing my translation of *Red Oleander*; to Amita Devi (Tagore) for recording her memories of the first performance of *Tapatī*; to Sri Subhas Chowdhury of Visvabharati for his ready and always dependable assistance; to Sri V. Balsara for the transcriptions; to Dr Subhendusekhar Mukhopadhyay for directing me toward important primary evidence; and to the late Dr Somendranath Bose for some bibliographical information on literary criticism in Bengali on Tagore's plays.

That the M P Birla Foundation chose this work to inaugurate its prestigious "Classics of the East" series is an honour for which I am specially thankful. The Managing Editor, Dr Prithvi Nath Shastri, has helped in its publication in many ways. I also wish to record my gratitude to Sri Jagadindra Bhowmick, Adhyaksha of Visvabharati Publishing Department, for granting permission on behalf of Visvabharati to print these translations.

Although they know the extent of my indebtedness to them, I wish to thank my wife and our daughter for bearing with me patiently throughout the course of my dissertation, especially toward the end. My wife's unfailing enthusiasm for my work boosted my confidence during particularly trying times, and she offered suggestions and improvements on my text too numerous to acknowledge here.

Calcutta, November 1987   ANANDA LAL

CONTENTS

NOTES

PART ONE

Introduction
to
Tagore's Plays

I. PREAMBLE

Critics and detectives are naturally suspicious.
                [Tagore, letter to C.F. Andrews, 15 November 1914][1]

In the Prologue to his play *Phālgunī* Tagore has the poet Kavi-sekhar deride young students of literature, for "they cut up poetry with their logic. They are like the young-horned deer trying their new horns on the flower-beds."[2] Tagore's disenchantment with critics was no secret; I therefore enter the realm of his works with some trepidation, hoping that I shall not unwittingly destroy the abundant flowers Tagore has provided. Nevertheless, in spite of Tagore's opinions on the matter, one wishes that his critics and biographers had been more suspicious sometimes, at least of accepting without independent verification their colleagues' pronouncements about his life and writings. In the present section I propose to briefly delineate the critical misconceptions encountered in a study of Tagore as playwright, and in succeeding sections of this introduction I shall deal with each of the major problems at greater length. While doing so I hope to give the reader a sufficient idea of Tagore's dramatic craft as well.

To begin at a very basic level, we must recognise the fact that substantial misinformation about Tagore as a dramatist circulates in the world of the printed word. The Indian theatre historian Suresh Awasthi writes about Tagore in the *McGraw-Hill Encyclopedia of World Drama*:[3]

> Tagore's career as a dramatist began in 1881 with a musical play, *The Genius of Valmiki (Valmiki Pratibha)*. . . . He later produced this play. . . .
>   The power and theatrical value of Tagore's plays was not discovered until 1954.

The first statement is correct, but gives a reader the impression that Tagore staged his first play quite some time after its publication, when in fact the premiere followed the publication by a mere two weeks. The other sentence I have quoted is incorrect, for the "power and theatrical value" of Tagore's plays was evident to his audiences in Bengal — however select they may have been during Tagore's lifetime — as early as 1916, while most major Indian cities acknow-

ledged the same qualities in Tagore's dance-dramas when he toured
with them in the 1930s. Mr. Awasthi obviously meant to allude to
the revival of interest in Tagore's plays following the acclaimed
1950s productions of Bohurupee, the Calcutta theatre group, but
he should have made the reference clear. These objections may seem
minor, but the misinformation generated forms part of a general
syndrome of misinterpretation affecting the study of Tagore's plays.

Let us consider a couple of other samples of misleading data
about Tagore in some recent reference works in English. Perhaps
the single most indispensable volume that scholars of the theatre
thumb through in search of facts is the *Oxford Companion to the
Theatre*. In its entry on Tagore, we find the following remarks about
his plays:[4]

> The earlier ones were usually in verse or poetic prose, with interludes
> of colloquial speech, and were designed to be played on a bare stage
> with few, but highly symbolic, props. The best known are *Sacrifice*
> (*Visarjana*, 1890), *The King of the Dark Chamber* (*Raja*, 1910), *The
> Post Office* (*Dakaghan*, 1913), *Chitra* (1914), and *Red Oleanders*
> (*Rakta-Karabi*, 1924).

Tagore did not formulate his ideas about symbolist theatre and its
accompanying stagecraft until the first decade of this century, long
after the period of his early verse plays had ended. Actually, his
productions of the nineteenth century featured much of the paraphernalia of the naturalistic stage, hardly classifiable as "a bare
stage with few, but highly symbolic, props." As in virtually all
reference works containing information about Tagore, the dates in
the *Oxford Companion* are inaccurate too. *Dākghar* (not *Dakaghan*)
appeared in 1912, *Chitrāṅgadā* in 1892 (the English translation,
Chitra, was published in 1913).

Oscar Brockett, author of the standard history of theatre recommended to advanced students by most American departments of
theatre, has only one sentence on Tagore in his section on India:[5]

> Of the modern playwrights, Rabindranath Tagore (1861–1941) has
> been most successful in blending Indian and Western traditions in such
> plays as *Chitra* (1894), *King of the Dark Chamber* (1914), and *The Cycle
> of Spring* (1917).

Mr. Brockett has not corrected the misspelling of Tagore's first
name through four editions of his book. He gives the publication

dates of two English translations, but the date for *Chitra* corresponds neither with the year of its Bengali publication nor with that of its English translation. More serious than mere inaccuracy of detail, however, is Mr. Brockett's mistaken notion that Tagore successfully blends Indian and Western dramatic traditions. This statement requires extended discussion because it is one of the critical staples encountered in Tagoreana: a judgment, incidentally, repeated in both the other reference works I have cited so far.

Tagore's knowledge of Western literature, especially that of England, was undoubtedly wide. In particular, he studied Shakespeare diligently, and in his autobiography remembered being enthused by "The frenzy of Romeo's and Juliet's love, the fury of King Lear's impotent lamentation, the all-consuming fire of Othello's jealousy".[6] A devotee of "the passionate emotion in English literature", Tagore admired in the dramatists of the English Renaissance their liberating influence: "man then seemed consumed with the anxiety to break through all barriers to the inmost sanctuary of his being, there to discover the ultimate image of his own violent desire." Not surprisingly, therefore, he patterned his first two full-length plays after Shakespeare. But he soon discarded this imitative mode, gradually coming to believe that "In the Western dramas, human characters drown our attention in the vortex of their passions."[7] Following the period of Shakespearean influence, he wrote several shorter dramatic pieces in the last decade of the nineteenth century which according to some commentators bear similarities with the dramatic monologues of Robert Browning—a plausible debt because Tagore admired the Victorian poet and was familiar with his work.[8] Even so, the resemblances do not run very deep; by this time the Western influence on Tagore's plays was definitely on the wane. Ultimately, the mature dramatic style that he evolved at the turn of the century possessed no discernible connections with occidental models. If anything, its typically musical quality suffused with a characteristic spiritual feeling and the aura of benevolent natural surroundings may recall Indian precedents such as the classical Sanskrit drama or the Bengali folk theatre, both of which we know affected Tagore deeply.

However, the presence of symbolism in these plays sent critics scurrying to Europe for possible sources, and even today many are convinced that somehow or the other Tagore borrowed the

concept of symbolic playwriting from the West: in the words of one
Bengali critic, "There can be no doubt that Rabindranath got the
idea of writing these dramas from the West."[9] The most likely
candidate for the role of Tagore's preceptor in this genre appeared
to be Maurice Maeterlinck. Even the best of critics seem unwilling
to deny that Tagore had anything to do with European symbolist
drama; for instance, while admitting the possibility that Tagore
might have arrived at the symbolic form independently, Niharranjan
Ray believes that Tagore could not help being influenced by prevalent symbolist technique in Europe, even though his themes and
treatment differ markedly from those of Maeterlinck.[10] But
Satyendranath Ghoshal has proved conclusively that Maeterlinck's
most famous play, L'Oiseau bleu, could not possibly have influenced Tagore's first symbolic play, Śāradotsav, since both premiered in 1908.[11] Moreover, Tagore himself did not think very
highly of Maeterlinck's style, for according to him the Belgian playwright made the stage "dark with death and destruction"; besides,
Maeterlinck's world of shadows, indistinct sounds and strange
lights resulted in a rather artificially induced supernaturalism not to
his liking.[12] Tagore may indeed have read Western symbolist
drama, but his characteristic plays come across as entirely Indian,
with no signs whatsoever of the "blend" of Western elements that
Tagore experts so often invoke. Indeed, a Western reader may be
hard put to find anything of Western origin in these plays. Tagore's
Western influences remain confined to his early dramas; none of
them permeates his highly original mature work, which I should
like to suggest is the exclusive product of an Indian genius.
Squarely in the Indian tradition of literature, Tagore's plays dra-
matise the inner quest for fulfilment in man through union with the
universe: quite the opposite of mainstream Western dramaturgy
which, generally speaking, emphasises the individuality of man in
conflict with the physical world, on a realistic and psychological
level.

The obsession with discovering Western sources may reflect an
unconscious desire among some Indian scholars for Western approbation — a literary inheritance of the British raj, according to which
anything Western must be deserving of merit, or at least must make
it more worthy of attention than a purely indigenous product. This
unfortunate legacy of colonial times lingers on in present-day India

and manifests itself in odd ways; some distinguished Indian critics inadvertently lapse into judgments based on Western literary theory that make little sense when applied to Tagore's dramaturgy. For example, M. U. Malkani inexplicably measures Tagore's "deficient" stagecraft by a neo-classical yardstick: "One who has produced Tagore's plays on the stage must have found them particularly wanting in the principles of Time and Place."[13] We even find sympathetic writers falling into the same trap; D.V.K. Raghavacharyulu says of *Muktadhārā* that it "has formal perfection, since it maintains the dramatic unities", while Krishna Kripalani, an otherwise excellent biographer of Tagore in English, states that *Naṭīr Pūjā* "observes all the three classical unities".[14] Even the doyen of Indian literary critics in English, K.R. Srinivasa Iyengar, is not free from this totally inappropriate preoccupation: "Plays like *The Post Office, Mukta-Dhara* and *Natir Puja* also satisfy the strictest demands of the 'unities'."[15] Ignored in all this commentary is the fact that Tagore had no need or reason to conform to the neoclassical norms of playwriting.

As I hope to show, a major segment of available criticism in English on Tagore's drama is deficient if not woefully inadequate. A most disconcerting lack of understanding about Tagore's ideas of theatre has sometimes fuelled commentary of the most destructive kind on the quality of his plays. The noted scholar S.C. Sen Gupta's contention that "he is not a great dramatist"[16] reappears in various forms in recent essays: for instance, "Tagore was not by any means a sophisticated playwright";[17] "it appears rather difficult to claim for Tagore a preeminent position in modern dramatic literature";[18] his medium is "archaic and undramatic" and his later plays "have little relevance to modern life";[19] or "Tagore is not a great dramatist, not even a second best", while his plays are "outmoded by our modern standards".[20] Occasionally attempts are made to sidestep the issue with a left-handed compliment, as in "Rabindranath's dramas unmistakably reveal him as a great man if not as a great dramatist."[21] To be fair, some contemporary critics have praised Tagore's dramatic accomplishments, but their opinions remain in a hopelessly outnumbered minority. Few would share Niharranjan Ray's opinion that "Rabindranath is matchless" in his symbolic plays, much less Satyendranath Ghoshal's belief that "every symbolical or allegorical play of Rabindranath is a

magnificent dramatic work."[22] Few would credit Tagore with even
the bare minimum of a "catholicity of outlook and courage to experiment and create new forms".[23]

What has caused this prevailing lack of awareness about Tagore's
plays? First of all, to borrow a picturesque Indian idiom, Tagore's
plays have received "stepmotherly treatment" in comparison with
his other literary output. His name conjures — to his countrymen
and to knowledgeable foreigners alike — visions of a world-poet,
seer-philosopher, composer, educator, novelist and short-story
writer, even a painter, usually in that order. If the average person
remembers Tagore's capacity as a dramatist at all, he mentions it
last on the list of manifold activities of the Gurudev ("Revered
Guru", the honorific title by which he is commonly known to
Indians). Nearly fifty years after his death, not a single book-length
study exists in English on his plays, whereas his poetry, fiction and
aesthetics have formed the subject of several volumes. Consequently
a reader of English wanting to learn more about his drama must
depend on brief articles or isolated chapters in books about his
literature in general. This state of affairs has not changed much
over the years: consider, for example, the recently published volume
on Tagore in the Twayne's World Authors Series, a series that has
gained a decent reputation for reliability.[24] In a book of approximately 150 pages, the author sets aside only four pages for Tagore's
plays, in a chapter symptomatically titled "The Other Tagore".
In Bengali, too, his plays rank much lower in general esteem than
his poetry, fiction or music.

A second major misconception about Tagore's plays is that they
are unstageable. According to Mary Lago, author of the above-
mentioned Twayne volume, "a number of Tagore's plays . . . were
closet drama, written to be read or given reading performances,
not to be mounted as theatrical productions. Even the political
dramas have this same static quality".[25] Lago's statement could
not have been more false, because Tagore wrote virtually all his
plays for specific theatres and staged most of them too, some of the
productions attaining a high level of artistic success. But even
Bengali literary historians discount their theatrical value as a matter
of course. "Tagore's best dramatic work is to be found in his comedies," says J.C. Ghosh, "In the comedies we meet some real people,
while in the serious plays the characters are almost all of them
mouthpieces for the author's songs and ideas. . . . *Chitra* is delight-

ful ... because of its poetry which makes us forget that it is a play."[26] Sukumar Sen considers *Dākghar*, probably Tagore's most eminently stageworthy play, "not so much dramatic as narrative and there is not much of a story to tell."[27] Echoing this train of thought, Niharranjan Ray terms the symbolic plays as dramatised short stories, not unstageable, but not dependent on stage performance either.[28] The noted Bengali author Pramathanath Bisi employs a colourful metaphor to stress their unfitness for the theatre: Tagore's plays know how to swim — if placed in water they can float, he admits — but it is clear that the shore is their natural habitat.[29] He adds that, unlike Shakespeare, Molière, Ibsen or Shaw, Tagore had no connection with the public stage, hence his drama must remain an incomplete phenomenon. Admittedly the plays never quite established themselves in the repertoire of Bengali professional theatre, but that does not necessarily prove they were in any way inferior as stage-plays.

"Producers shied away from them," writes one theatre historian summing up the objections, because "they were too poetic, too lyrical, too metaphysical, too symbolic and obscure, too unstageable or just plain boring."[30] This statement brings us to the next problem most commentators seem to face in their study of Tagore's drama: his symbolism and perceived inaccessibility has come in for severe criticism at the hands of a host of writers, Bengali, Indian and Western, for being "presented in the most vague and whimsical manner".[31] Many of them appear to have great difficulty in fathoming Tagore's complex levels of meaning in such plays as *Rājā* or *Rakta-karavī*, whereas the plays which offer more easily identifiable symbols, for instance *Chitrāṅgadā* or *Chandālikā*, do not present such obstacles and consequently are more readily accepted. Perhaps as a result of the expectations nourished by naturalistic dramaturgy, there exists a reluctance to accept unrealistic données such as an invisible king or a king who speaks from behind an intricate screen — in *Rājā* and *Rakta-karavī* respectively. Lamentably, therefore, for many critics the best of Tagore's plays came before 1900: straightforward plays like *Visarjan* that provide a direct message which cannot allow ambiguous interpretations and does not force the reader or spectator to exert his mental faculties too much. As an index of this failure to appreciate Tagore's later, more complex work, one can point out that for a long time the only Tagore play read by undergraduate students in the compulsory Bengali course at the University of Calcutta was the early five-act blank verse tragedy *Rājā o Rānī*. An equivalent would be to teach *Titus Andronicus* as the only Shakespeare play in an introductory course on English literature—so remote is the conception of *Rājā o Rānī* from Tagore's later masterpieces.

Another crucial force in formulating current opinion about Tagore's drama was the reaction of English and American reviewers to his plays when they first appeared in English translation, beginning in 1913, the year Tagore became the first non-European to win the Nobel Prize for Literature. Suffice it to say here that the response was hardly encouraging for Tagore; more often than not his plays confused the typical English-speaking reviewer, who moved from an initial position of detached appreciation of an original voice or genuine awe of the exotic novelty of oriental mysticism, through a transitional period of irritability at the perceived repetitiousness of Tagore's themes and style, to a final attitude of exasperation and dismissal of the plays as indulgent or pretentious verbiage. Moreover, the publication by Oxford University Press of two very uneven books by Edward Thompson, at a time when no scholarly studies on Tagore existed in English, only served to compound the problem by crystallising in print many misconceptions about the plays.[32] Thompson's word almost became law, especially to those who could not know any better, namely all readers who did not have access to Tagore in the original Bengali. To this day researchers must confront Thompson's opinions—which I shall discuss in more detail in a later section—in any attempt to analyse Tagore's plays. With just a few exceptions, English and American reviewers never fully understood the spirit in which Tagore created his plays, and their rejection of him provided all the more fodder for unsympathetic readers in his own country to slight the plays as products of inferior inspiration compared to his poetry or fiction.

Finally, the matter of Tagore's English translations of his own plays created several intriguing difficulties in the critical response. Tagore himself translated some plays in the wake of burgeoning interest in his work, which began during his trip to England and America in 1912–13; occasionally he gave the formal nod of approval to translations done by others, which he saw before their submission for publication. Unlike Samuel Beckett, for instance, equally fluent in French and English, Tagore wrote English that

was competent but by no means excellent, especially when it came
to creating a style appropriate for the unusual nature of his plays.
But the initial euphoria in England over his work seemed to give
him some confidence in his own prowess as English interpreter of
his œuvre. Concomitantly this gave his versions a certain measure
of authority; but it has been slowly recognised over the years that his
translations were in general quite weak and dated—precisely one
of the reasons for their ultimate rejection at the hands of critics in
English. Yet few people have undertaken new translations of his
plays; such attempts can truly be counted on the fingers of one
hand. The dilemma of course is as follows: do we judge Tagore's
own translations as translations or as original plays in their own
right, since the author himself converted the originals into English?
If we accept them as translations, then unquestionably we have to
deem them poor, inadequate translations. If we accept them as
independent original works, we must place them in the tradition of
Indian literature written in English; we are then faced with the
prospect of having very few faithful translations of his plays, since
Tagore's versions often differ radically from his originals. There
may appear to be a possible compromise by terming these versions
"transcreations", straddling both worlds—but the indisputable
fact remains that they have done more harm than good to Tagore's
reputation.[33]

The subject of Tagore's translations assumes even greater importance when we realise the extent of the damage he has uninten-
tionally wrought. Most translations of Tagore into other world
languages have actually been based on his own English versions;
it is not difficult to adduce how distant from the original Bengali
these twice-removed works have become through this process. Until
very recently, many translations into other Indian languages too
were directed via his English versions. Thus even the majority of
his own countrymen could read him only in secondhand translations, or in the authorised English renditions. One of the most
curious by-products of this phenomenon was the development—
beginning as early as K.S. Ramaswami Sastri's books on Tagore
published after the Nobel Prize award[34]—of a whole tradition of
Tagore criticism written by non-Bengali Indians in English, founded
exclusively on study of the English texts prepared by Tagore because
the critics did not know Bengali. We should not underestimate the
dangers of such analysis. It is one of the greatest pities of Tagore

studies, therefore, that a definitive, annotated edition of his collected works does not exist in English translation. This critical edition of three Tagore plays is a small attempt to fill part of that vacuum.

II. TAGORE AS DRAMATIST

My compositions are like the cries of a newborn baby, life's answer
in response to the call of the whole universe.

[Kaviśekhar, the poet, in Tagore's *Phālgunī*][1]

Tagore's phenomenal dramatic career, encompassing over sixty
plays in nearly as many years, occupies the prime position in
Bengali and modern Indian drama. In certain ways his dominance
is analogous to that of Ibsen in Norwegian literature: both began
as products of the nineteenth century but ended up having revolu-
tionised their respective literary traditions; both wielded tremendous influence on writers outside their mother tongue—Ibsen on
other European languages, Tagore on other Indian languages; both
tried their hand at a wide variety of dramatic genres and styles
during their careers; and both remained virtually unchallenged as
literary monarchs in the course of lengthy reigns of over half a century each, even if much of their work was widely misunderstood.
"Tagore carried the dramatic tradition of Bengal so much forward
that the people could not equally advance in time", writes Amar
Mukerji;[2] substituting "Ibsen" for "Tagore" and "Norway" for
"Bengal" would not make the statement incongruous. But in order
to appreciate Tagore's farsighted contribution to Bengali drama,
one must very briefly recapitulate the dramatic milieu of his times.

THE BACKGROUND

The indigenous folk-theatre tradition of *yātrā* dates back many
centuries, its precise origins still the subject of much debate.[3]
Perennially fertile, this open-air form of entertainment has always
held its own in rural Bengal, freely mingling stories of myth and
legend with quasi-historical elements and, in recent times, with contemporary social issues. At its best the *yātrā* reflected through the
characteristic originality of a stylised folk idiom the deep religious
fervour of its village audiences; at its worst it degenerated into
crude vulgarities—yet always the genre remained vital and vigo-
rous. With the advent of the British in the eighteenth century, there
also came the attendant social activities for European residents in
the burgeoning port of Calcutta, and the city's first modern theatre,

the Playhouse, was erected in 1753. A second playhouse, the
Calcutta Theatre, opened in 1775; the story goes that David Garrick
assisted by sending a scenic artist and some painted sets.[4]

The most renowned of these early buildings was the Chowringhee
Theatre, founded in 1813 by a number of eminent citizens, among
them Dwarkanath Tagore, grandfather of Rabindranath and a
great patron of theatre in Calcutta. Eventually, in the nineteenth
century, the educated Bengali found access to a repertoire of English
plays that included Shakespeare, naturally, and Restoration and
eighteenth-century dramatists; he also began to look down condescendingly upon the unrefined theatricals of the *yātrā*. One
English newspaper noticed the growing number of "respectable
natives among the audience every play-night", and suggested that
"it indicates a growing taste for the English Drama which is an
auspicious sign of the progress of general literature amongst our
native friends."[5] By mid-century the Bengali segment of the audience had become large enough for one of these playhouses to venture a "Native Gentleman" in a title role: Baishnav Charan Auddy
acted Othello on 17 August 1848 at the Sans Souci Theatre, and the
"debut of a real unpainted nigger *Othello*" understandably set "the
whole world of Calcutta agog".[6]

If we do not count the texts performed by *yātrā* troupes, a fragment titled *Chaṇḍī* written by the poet Bharat Chandra around
1760, and the unperformed play *Chitrayajña* written by a pandit,
Vidyanath Bhattacharya, around 1778, Bengali dramatic literature
did not exist until a Russian bandleader by the name of Herasim
Lebedeff translated into Bengali two obscure English plays, *The
Disguise* and *Love Is the Best Doctor*, and had the former presented
on 27 November 1795 by Bengali actors and actresses at the Bengally
Theatre, which he himself had constructed and "Decorated in the
Bengalee Style".[7] But Lebedeff left the country within a few years,
and the next major development in modern Bengali drama had to
wait another forty years. On 6 October 1835 a play titled *Vidyā
Sundar*, based on a poem by Bharat Chandra, was staged in lavish,
spectacular fashion at the residence of Nabin Chandra Basu, setting
a precedent of performances at so-called "private" theatres, halls
located or built in the houses of aristocratic Bengali families.[8] Not
surprisingly, the Tagores emerged as one of the most important of
such patrons; their "playhouse", in the courtyard of their ancestral
building at Jorasanko, would also serve later as the stage for many

of Rabindranath's plays. They also encouraged the writing of
Bengali plays by offering cash prizes, especially for plays of social
relevance. Gradually the library of Bengali drama began to increase—albeit still mostly translations, including Sanskrit classics
and Shakespeare.

In 1857 Ramnarayan Tarkaratna's *Kulīn-kulasarvasva*, which
attacked the practice among male Kulin Brahmins of marrying
more than once, became the first original Bengali play to reach the
stage.[9] Tarkaratna (1828–86), generally considered the first playwright in Bengali, also won an award of two hundred rupees
announced by the Tagores for a play on the plight of Hindu women,
Nava Nāṭak, produced at Jorasanko in 1867. Two other dramatists
came to the limelight at about the same time. Michael Madhusudan
Dutt (1824–73) broke from tradition by following the model of
European drama, and wrote both serious plays (*Śarmishṭhā*, 1859;
Krishna-kumārī, 1867) and satirical comedies (*Ekei Ki Bale
Sabhyatā?*, 1865; *Buro Śāliker Ghāre Roñ*, 1867). Dinabandhu
Mitra (1830–73) took the drama of social awareness further than
Tarkaratna, with plays like *Sadhavār Ekādaśī* (1868), *Līlāvatī* (1872)
and particularly *Nīldarpan* (1872; performed in Dacca, 1861). The
last-named play had to wait twelve years for a production in
Calcutta because of the sensitive nature of its subject. It dealt in an
uncompromising manner with the ruthless oppression of Bengali
peasants by British indigo planters. Shortly after Mitra wrote it in
1860, Madhusudan Dutt translated it into English and a Reverend
James Long circulated copies of it in England and Bengal, as a result
of which the British government tried Reverend Long, found him
guilty of treason and imprisoned him. Mitra's play also ushered in
the age of the Bengali "public" or professional theatre. On 7 December 1872, the newly-formed Calcutta National Theatrical Society
performed it in the converted annex of a private building, the first
truly public playhouse, and the production received enthusiastic
press notices. It became the banner play for new companies for
decades afterward. In the following year, the Bengal Theatre became
the first company to have its own playhouse, built with the express
purpose of staging drama.

An important historical point was the performance, at the Great
National Theatre on 19 February 1876, of a farce titled *Gajadānanda
and Yuvarāj*, which caricatured a prominent Calcutta lawyer for
entertaining the visiting Prince of Wales—later King Edward

VII—at his home. The police halted further performances and forbade a repeat performance on 26 February under a different name; within ten days the Governor-General of India declared in an emergency ordinance that the state government in Bengal should "prohibit certain dramatic performances which are scandalous, defamatory, seditious, obscene or otherwise prejudicial to the public interest."[10] Not to be so easily undone, the Great National Theatre improvised on stage the following day (1 March) a brief farce called *The Police of Pig and Sheep* (a dig at the then Commissioner of Police, Sir Stuart Hogg, and his Superintendent, Mr. Lamb). Commissioner Hogg responded with a raid on the theatre on 4 March, and arrested ten members of the company. Ironically, they were charged with obscenity in another production; the director and manager were sentenced to a month's imprisonment, but were later acquitted. In December, the Viceroy's Council passed the Dramatic Performances Control Act establishing government censorship, thereby giving themselves the authority to ban a number of plays in the course of the remaining seventy years of British rule over India.

During the 1880s Calcutta theatre proliferated, though the growth of larger, predominantly middle-class audiences tended to direct the drama toward spectacle and sensation. Producers preferred melodramas, farcical comedies, musical entertainments or popular dramatisations of myths and legends because of their box-office appeal. Samples from advertisements in papers of the day should prove their intentions:

SHOOTING ON THE STAGE
Fairy Land [11]
Everything Grand and Wonderful [12]

Magnificent sceneries prepared by Renowned painters, to be presented, with the help of the latest scientific instruments. Electric Light and Electric Fountain playing on the stage; costly wardrobes of pure antique mould; all gorgeous![13]

Sensational Attractions/Railway Train on the Stage![14]

The locomotive on stage apparently was the result of professional rivalry between the Bengal Theatre and the Great National Theatre, in the form of the latter's rejoinder to Bengal Theatre productions in which an actor entered the stage on horseback. Things did not improve much in the heyday of Girish Chandra Ghosh (1844–1912), actor-manager and author of over seventy plays, mostly pseudo-historical or mythological melodramas.[15] Here are some choice phrases from advertisements for some of Ghosh's plays:

A New Sensational Domestic Tragedy
A New Sensational Terrible Tragedy
Vibrates innermost chord of human heart[16]

CANNON AT WORK ON THE STAGE
A rare intellectual and spectacular treat![17]

Soul dissolving songs—where religion and love are harmoniously blended together—will even for the instant inspire confidence and love for God in the heart of the most ungodly!

*   *   *

Please note.—This is that well received play in the *finale* of which marble statues are transformed into living beauties.[18]

Such was the robust state of Bengali theatre when Rabindranath Tagore grew up; it is small wonder that his particular genius disdained the activities on the professional Calcutta stage.

TAGORE'S PLAYS

The penultimate of fifteen children, Rabindranath Tagore was born in 1861 into the gifted and aristocratic Tagore family, one of the most important households in the history of nineteenth-century Calcutta, then capital city of British India. He received an enlightened upbringing at home, in an atmosphere where the spirit of knowledge reigned supreme, where intellectual discussions on international subjects were encouraged and where all members of the large joint family regularly participated in a variety of cultural activities. His career in school was undistinguished—he disliked its institutionalised discipline and often played truant. In any case the education imparted at home in tutorial sessions conducted by his elder brothers was probably more substantial; as was the influence of the personality, scholarship and spiritualism of Debendranath Tagore, his father. In this environment, he wrote his first poem when he was eight years old, and had his first poem published at the age of thirteen.[19] Immediately prior to that, he had translated Shakespeare's *Macbeth* into Bengali verse during the course of Bengali lessons given by his private tutor.[20] At sixteen he made his acting debut, in his elder brother Jyotirindranath's adaptation of Molière's *Le Bourgeois Gentilhomme*. He began writing his first play at the age of eighteen, and at nineteen he had composed and acted the lead role in his first musical drama, *Vālmīki-pratibhā*.[21]

In 1878 Tagore had been sent to England to complete his studies, but with characteristic indifference toward formal education he left University College, London (where he was to study law), and returned home. He brought back the unfinished manuscript of a thirty-four-canto romantic poem in dramatic form, *Bhagna-hriday*,[22] which he had begun in London. This long poem—he insisted it did not qualify as a play[23]—was published in 1881, as well as a historical verse-drama in fourteen scenes by the name of *Rudrachanda*, and the musical drama *Vālmīki-pratibhā*. The last-named boldly refashioned classical Indian ragas into new, unorthodox modes for its songs—an exercise in which Tagore's brother Jyotirindranath initially had the dominant part, but which Rabindranath continued with marvellous ability and effect the rest of his life. The play also bore some influences of Western music, particularly Irish folk melodies, which he had heard during his trip to England. As with his mature musical dramas, virtually the entire play is put to music; the cast therefore had to be accomplished in singing as well as in acting. The successful staging of *Vālmīki-pratibhā* at the family residence encouraged Tagore to compose a second play in the same vein: *Kāl-mrigayā*,[24] published in 1882, was also received favourably. Tagore remembers that "The enthusiasm which went to the making of *Valmiki Pratibha* and *Kal Mrigaya* I have never felt for any other work of mine. In these two the creative musical impulse of the time found expression."[25] But the creative peak of this earliest phase of Tagore's playwriting career came with *Prakritir Pratisodh* (1884),[26] a moving verse-tragedy about an ascetic who finds truth not in renunciation but in affection for an ostracised orphan girl. Tagore himself recognised that this play introduced many of the themes he would return to in his later work: "this has been the subject on which all my writings have dwelt—the joy of attaining the Infinite within the finite."[27]

After his marriage to Mrinalini Devi in 1883, Tagore began working on his first prose play, *Nalinī* (1884), which eventually formed the core of another musical drama, *Māyār Khelā* (1888).[28] In the latter, said Tagore, comparing it to the other musical dramas he had written, "the songs were important, not the drama. In the others a series of dramatic situations were strung on a thread of melody; this was a garland of songs with just a thread of dramatic plot running through."[29] As such, it presaged the technique of the season-plays of his maturity. Despite *Nalinī*, it does not seem that Tagore was ready as yet to use prose as his medium for playwriting. During the interval of 1885–87 he did write a number of slight comic sketches in colloquial prose, subtitling them "riddle plays", later collected under the title *Hāsya-kautuk*.[30] But these were completely at the opposite extreme stylistically from the heightened poetry of his full-length plays. At this stage of development, prose existed for him only as a medium for dramatic work in a lighter vein.

Three major poetic dramas in blank verse followed in quick succession. *Rājā o Rānī* (1889) and *Visarjan* (1890)[31] were elaborate five-act tragedies modelled after Shakespeare, replete with blood-and-thunder declamation, palace intrigues, conflicts of love and duty, subplots involving foil characters, purple poetry spoken by the major roles and plebeian prose by lower-class characters. In fact, these ingredients inadvertently brewed a concoction closer to the heroic drama of the English Restoration than to Shakespearean tragedy, a deviation that Tagore himself seemed to have recognised later on: "our attempts to imitate the blast of a hurricane led us easily into exaggeration".[32] Although both plays still occupy a pre-eminent position in the minds of many Tagorean scholars — and *Visarjan* does mark a considerable advance over its predecessor — they remain in the final analysis derivative, albeit sincere, homages to earlier ideals. Both plays express their ideas forcefully and with conviction, but their technique has yet to display the clear stamp of originality that marks Tagore's mature plays. Their sudden melodramatic endings especially detract from the power of their surcharged poetry. None of these drawbacks characterises *Chitrāṅgadā* (1892), Tagore's lyrical drama about the true nature of love and human beauty, the chimera of physical attractiveness. In 1890 his father had dispatched him to Shelaidaha in East Bengal (now Bangladesh) to oversee the family estates there; that sojourn placed him in intimate contact with rural Bengal and her people. In Shelaidaha he absorbed the natural details that he would use in his writings: the empathetic observation of nature in all its moods, the keen awareness of the simple life of the Bengali peasant, and the mystical bond between nature and man immanent in creation. *Chitrāṅgadā* presented these features for the first time, while simultaneously displaying a mastery of Bengali blank verse and discarding the five-act structure in favour of a few short scenes. The result was the perfect vehicle for Tagore's idealistic thesis about romantic love.

Tagore continued to use prose, though, in progressively more ambitious endeavours. He published his first farce, *Gorāy Galad,*[33] in 1892; although ostensibly a straightforward comedy of errors, it satirised conventional Hindu attitudes toward marriage as well. He returned off and on to exercise his hand at dramatic prose and social satire, in five comic skits published between 1893 and 1901 (later collected as *Vyaṅga-kautuk*[34]), and in the farce *Vaikuṇṭher Khātā* (1897).[35] At the same time, he seems to have decided to dispense with blank verse as a medium for serious plays. Edward Thompson recounts that Tagore told him he had found blank verse "not graceful enough" for drama.[36] In the short one-act dialogue *Vidāy-Abhiśāp* (1894),[37] he introduced rhymed couplets instead and, as usual, perfected the innovation almost immediately. He next applied this new verse technique to a full-length play titled *Mālinī* (1896), the first dramatic expression of his deep respect for Buddhist principles. It also reflects Tagore's change in direction from his earlier multi-plot tragedies to a more simple, direct action that deals with a single situation — a trend to simplify that developed into the standard structural technique for his later plays. The experiment with rhymed couplets concluded successfully with a collection of five poetic plays (including one farce) published in 1900 under the title *Kāhinī;*[38] as with *Vidāy-Abhiśāp* — and *Chitrāṅgadā* before it — Tagore turned to ancient Indian classics and legends for sources for these short pieces, but reworked the original tales to suit his purposes. These exquisitely crafted dramatic miniatures, mostly in the form of dialogues, proved to be his final plays in verse.

The Shelaidaha period came to an end in 1901 when Tagore moved to Santiniketan, a starkly beautiful spot in West Bengal that his father used as a religious retreat. Here he decided to establish his own school, but finances were short and a series of private tragedies beset him. His wife Mrinalini Devi died in 1902, his twelve-year-old daughter Renuka in 1903, his father Debendranath in 1905, and his youngest son Samindranath in 1907. Nothing in the shape of drama emerged during this time. Yet the short story *Karmaphal* from 1903 attests to the fact that the playwriting instinct had not disappeared altogether; although labelled a short story, it consisted almost entirely of conversation and dialogue cast in the form of a play.

For a prolific writer like Tagore, this was indeed a long period away from drama. Finally, in 1908, the dramatic inspiration returned and the publication of *Śāradotsav*[39] heralded new directions, marking the major turning point in his career as dramatist. It was his first significant prose play (henceforth virtually all his dramatic output would be in prose), and also the first of several plays that he composed about the seasons. Almost as if defying through the world of literature the evidence of his personal life, this play conveyed a simple joie de vivre like no other dramatic work of his had done before, singing a paean to autumn, a season of fulfilment in the Bengali calendar. At this time Tagore also began another activity that gradually grew in importance in the second half of his life: he commenced dramatising some of his earlier works of fiction. The novel *Mukuṭ*[40] was dramatised under the same name in 1908, but the first major dramatisation came the following year when he converted his novel *Bau-ṭhākurānīr Hāṭ* into the play *Prāyaśchitta.*[41] Tagore had started participating in nationalistic protests against the British, and although he soon withdrew from active political life, this play exists as an example of his sagacious political vision since it introduces a personage who prefigures Mahatma Gandhi and propagates the doctrine of satyagraha, nonviolent noncooperation against a repressive regime, years before Gandhi arrived in India from South Africa.

There followed a most productive period in Tagore's dramatic career, during the course of which he published three of his finest plays, one each year between 1910 and 1912. The first of them, *Rājā*, critically regarded as one of his masterpieces, also garnered for him the reputation of being a symbolical or allegorical playwright. The theme of man's realisation of the true nature of divinity proved difficult for his readers, even in his mother tongue. The second play, *Achalāyatan,*[42] parodied in thinly-disguised language the rigid and often unjust orthodox beliefs of Hinduism, consequently receiving in turn severe denunciation from conservative Hindu Bengalis. The final play in this sequence, *Dākghar,*[43] eventually became Tagore's best-known play, not only in India, but internationally as well. In its English translation as *The Post Office* it gained a wide audience of both readers and viewers, impressing W. B. Yeats sufficiently for him to write a preface to the published translation. The play was widely translated and produced in other languages, often by eminent writers, the most renowned among them perhaps being André Gide.[44] The accessibility of this direct and touching play, increased by its appealing simplicity and the absence of Tagore's characteristic use of songs, makes it the ideal entrance into the dramatic world of Tagore's maturity.

In 1912 Tagore undertook another trip to the West. While in London he showed his acquaintance the painter William Rothenstein a few English translations he had made of his poems; through Rothenstein's good offices, the India Society of London published these exercises as the English volume titled *Gitanjali (Song Offerings)*, which Macmillan issued the following year in a commercial edition. Meanwhile Tagore had travelled further west to the United States, accompanying his son Rathindranath, who had graduated from and wished to complete a doctorate at the University of Illinois. Tagore spent the winter of 1912–13 in America, lecturing in several cities. The announcement late in 1913, after his return to India, that *Gitanjali* had won for him the Nobel Prize made him an instant celebrity all over the world. For the rest of his life his presence was in such great demand that he went on a dozen foreign tours of Europe, England, North and South America, Russia, the Far East, Southeast Asia, and the Middle East. Yet his literary output did not decrease. In 1915 came his next play, *Phālgunī*,[45] which continued the cycle of season-plays that *Śāradotsav* had begun. Although simple in matter — it celebrated joyously but not with any special profundity the continuity of life and nature as reflected in the defeat of winter (death) by the arrival of spring (life) — the play introduced several new items in Tagore's repertoire, including a play-within-a-play setting and the innovation of generic lines of dialogue, unassigned to specific characters.

Tagore's next dramatic project was the reworking of several earlier plays into what he called "stageworthy" versions. The reasons for this decision could have been many, aside from the ostensible purpose of condensing or improving the texts for new performances, which occurred with fair regularity at his school in Santiniketan. Although no evidence exists to support such a theory, it is possible that the critical response (both Bengali and English) to his plays influenced Tagore to think of radically revising the originals. However, Tagore's characteristic method of writing also involved repeated returns to a composition until he had convinced himself he had done justice to the theme. Sometimes these changes merely took the shape of revised later editions which superseded previous ones; sometimes the alterations were substantial enough to warrant being titled differently, assuming the guise of altogether new plays. The latter course finds fruit in *Guru* (1918), *Arūp Ratan* (1920) and *Riṅśodh* (1921),[46] "stageworthy" versions of *Achalāyatan*, *Rājā* and *Śāradotsav* respectively. In between, Tagore also published a short comedy called *Svarga-marta* (1919),[47] dealing satirically with the schism in relations between gods and men.

In spite of all his commitments — by now he was also actively engaged in running the university he had established in 1918 in Santiniketan — the prodigious flow of his writing carried on unabated. The last two decades of his life were particularly productive in the field of drama. He surprised those who thought his creativity had passed its prime by writing two of his finest "symbolical" plays in close succession, *Muktadhārā* (1922) and *Rakta-karavī* (1924).[48] Both had similar messages: powerful indictments of political oppression of subjugated people and unfeeling exploitation of the earth's resources, and espousals of the spirit of self-sacrifice for a noble cause embodied in the protagonists. In the intervening year Tagore produced *Vasanta*,[49] a play about spring, his plays about the seasons becoming progressively more musical, with more songs and less dialogue; and *Rath-ýātrā*,[50] a short play arguing against the entrenched inequalities of the Hindu caste system.

Several dramatisations of his own fiction followed. *Grihapraveś* and *Śodhbodh*,[51] both published in 1925, were stage adaptations of two short stories, specifically written for production by a professional company, Calcutta's Art Theatre Limited. Despite the sentimentality of their conclusions, they possess the realistic detail of much of Tagore's fiction, a tone quite different from the heightened poetic tone customary in his major drama. Another adaptation for the professional stage appeared the next year, several months after its premiere by the Art Theatre: this time it was a dramatisation of the novel *Prajāpatir Nirbandha*, which became the social comedy *Chirakumār-Sabhā*,[52] perhaps Tagore's most popular play among Bengalis on account of its sparkling humour. Significantly, he made concessions to the tastes of public audiences by adding the roles of two clowns. Also in 1926, Tagore revisited the realms of Buddhism in the play *Naṭīr Pūjā*.[53] The fundamental equality preached by the

Buddhist faith appealed to Tagore deeply, and in this work he contrasted the demands of institutionalised Hinduism as opposed to the reforms of the Buddha's movement. The first edition of the play was also historically important in that it contained no male characters — a revolutionary idea in the Indian theatre of its time, where women could not even perform without their morals coming into question.

New plays on the seasons continued to come out at regular intervals: *Śesh Varshan* and *Sundar* in 1926,[54] *Natarāj* and *Rituraṅga* in 1927.[55] Gradually this Tagorean genre became indistinguishable from song-sequences; each "play" became really only a compendium of Tagore songs on a specific season or theme, linked by minimal dialogue and occasional recitative or prose commentary. The pervading effect, though, remained one of unity and interdependence between man and nature, expressed through rejoicing in the cycle of the seasons. Meanwhile Tagore produced some more scripts for the professional theatre in Calcutta. He converted the farce *Gorāy Galad* into a "stageworthy" version entitled *Śesh Rakshā* (1927),[56] for performance by Sisir Bhaduri's Natyamandir Limited; and he revised *Prāyaśchitta*, renaming it *Paritrāṇ* (1927),[57] for the Art Theatre. In 1928 he wrote a short dramatic dialogue called *Śiver Bhikshā*.[58] The following year, he undertook perhaps his most ambitious project of revision, completely recasting his old tragedy *Rājā o Rānī* into a more typically Tagorean play, *Tapatī*.

During his later years Tagore grew more and more fascinated with the incorporation of dance into drama. For some time he had experimented along these lines by adding dance sequences to plays such as *Naṭīr Pūjā*, *Natarāj* and *Rituraṅga*. Many of his musical dramas now began to include dances as a matter of course; among them were *Navīn*,[59] a season-play on spring, and *Śāpmochan*,[60] based on the *Rājā* legend (both 1931). As with his use of music, his implementation of dance in his plays resulted from a drive to liberate classical Indian styles from strict conformity and an emphasis on mere virtuosity to a heterogenous lyrical form that stressed appeal to the emotions. Purists of both music and dance traditions naturally disapproved of Tagore's breaking classical norms or concocting hybrid forms, and many still do. Tagore himself could not be concerned with the rigid requirements of man-made regulations; he was interested foremost in expressing the aesthetic values of his plays, through whatever media he found appropriate.

Revisions also continued to appear: *Naṭarāj Riturangaśālā* (1931)[61] combined the earlier plays *Naṭarāj* and *Riturangā*; *Kāler Yātrā* (1932)[62] contained new versions of *Rath-yātrā* and *Śiver Bhikṣhā* under new titles.

1933 brought several original plays. *Chaṇḍālikā*, dealing with an untouchable girl, reprised once again Tagore's recurrent concern with Buddhism and the promise of equality it held for the downtrodden classes. *Tāser Deś*,[63] in a less serious and more satirical vein, poked fun at the fossilised conservatism and orthodoxy of the "Land of Cards", Hinduism. These plays reveal an intense social motivation at work, an earnest desire to rid Indian society of its rigidities and prejudices. The preoccupation with society pervades *Bānśari* too, an ironic examination of the foibles of urban uppercrust Calcutta, where witty conversation takes the place of genuine warmth and feeling. Tagore also adapted his novel *Mālañcha*[64] for the stage in the same year. In 1934 came the last of his plays of the seasons, *Śrāvaṇ-gāthā*,[65] a musical drama about the monsoons. In 1936 he abridged *Visarjan* for the benefit of a performance done by the schoolchildren at Santiniketan.

In the final years of his life Tagore, never one to stagnate, went in search of even newer paths. Furthering his interest in dance to the utmost, disenchanted by what he considered to be the limitations of the spoken word, he began composing dance-dramas based on his earlier plays. Much impressed by what he had seen of Javanese and Balinese dance on a trip to Indonesia, he created a stylised dramatic form that borrowed liberally from diverse traditions — mostly Manipuri and Kathakali,[66] but also Bharata-natyam and Kathak, various folk styles, and even other sources from abroad such as the Kandyan dance of Srilanka. Critics frequently make the mistake of taking it for granted that Tagore set out to create his own dance style; in fact, he viewed these final works primarily as drama, not dance, and he used with the greatest catholicity whatever dance idioms he found suitable to convey the ideas and images in these plays. While both these and his earliest musical dramas are set to music, the difference between them lies in the central focus given to dances in the later works. The actors and actresses no longer sing themselves (a chorus on stage accompanied by musicians would sing the entire text), but express the play through dance. A series of these dance-dramas appeared — *Chitrāṅgadā* (1936), *Pariśodh* (1936, though Tagore did not call it a dance-drama),[67]

Chaṇḍālikā (1938), *Māyār Khelā* (written 1938), *Śyāmā* (1939, a revision of *Pariśodh*) — and encouraged by positive reactions, Tagore even took some of the productions on tour. In between, in 1938, he published a dramatisation for the professional stage titled *Muktir Upāy* based on his short story of the same name,[68] and revised *Svarga-marta* under the title *Svarge Chakraṭebil Baiṭhak*.[69]

Tagore's health, which had slowly begun to deteriorate during this period, eventually broke down in 1940 and he died in 1941, at the age of eighty. His use of symbolism in the later plays and invention of genres such as the dance-drama and season-drama had perhaps altered the direction of his repertoire toward "art" theatre, but in so doing he had also eliminated much of the derivative quality of early Bengali drama and offered a serious alternative to the frequently escapist fare produced by his contemporaries in the Bengali commercial theatre. In addition, he presented his countrymen with viable and original dramatic forms belonging to the Indian tradition. Over sixty years ago K. S. Ramaswami Sastri remarked about Tagore: "More than everything else he has shown the way, both in respect of ideals as well as of methods, by which the soul of India could be realised and revealed in the realm of dramatic creation and representation."[70] Tagore's drama was no cul-de-sac: as a playwright, he was the pathfinder of modern Indian drama.

III. TAGORE AS THEATRICIAN

It needs to be kept in mind that this play is to be seen and heard, but
not read.

[Tagore, Introduction to the dance-drama *Chaṇḍālikā*, 1st ed.][1]

In his autobiography, Tagore said nearly the same thing about
his very first play: "*Valmiki Pratibha* is not a composition which
will bear being read. Its significance is lost if it is not heard sung
and seen acted."[2] This is a dictum true not only of his musical
dramas, but of his plays in general. Commentators make a grave
mistake when they accept the printed text of a Tagore play as the
final incarnation of his inspiration. It must be stressed that one of
the most important aspects of Tagore's productions was the
flexible nature of the playscript, which he changed constantly
during rehearsals. Not only did he alter the text between rehearsals,
recalls his son Rathindranath, but sometimes even after opening
night: "Father's creative mind could never find pleasure in repetition. Invariably he would make alterations and additions to the
plays whenever they were about to be performed. Such modifications would continue till the last day of the rehearsals and even in
between successive nights of the performance much to the consternation of the actors."[3] Publication did not make the script
sacrosanct; Tagore typically revised the text for any revival and,
depending on the extent of the changes, published the later version
either as a new edition or as a new drama.[4] Consequently, in a
Tagore play the printed words form merely a skeleton to which any
director must add flesh and blood; like Shakespeare or Molière,
Tagore rarely gives us stage directions, precisely because he desires
that the play come to life on stage.

TAGORE'S PRODUCTIONS

When *Vālmīki-pratibhā* premiered on 26 February 1881 at the
private theatre in the family residence at Jorasanko, Calcutta, it
did not take long for the invited audience to recognise the advent
of an original dramatic talent. Several luminaries of Bengali literature and society were present in this gathering, among them the
great novelist Bankim Chandra Chatterjee, who said of the per-

formance later that nobody who had witnessed it could ever forget Tagore's depiction of the birth of poetic inspiration in Valmiki. The play affected at least one other member of the august assembly, Gurudas Banerjee, later Vice-Chancellor of the University of Calcutta, who was so moved as to compose a poem announcing the arrival of a literary genius.[5] Reviewers too were suitably impressed; one of them pointed out a historically significant aspect of the production not usually remembered these days: "a maiden from a respectable family acted before the public" for the first time.[6] Tagore's pioneering work in this sphere continued with *Māyār Khelā* — at its opening night on 29 December 1888, the women of the Tagore family played all the parts, including those of men.[7] According to many viewers, this production surpassed the musical plays that had preceded it; in his memoirs Tagore's nephew Abanindranath, later to become a famous painter, termed it one of a kind: an invaluable contribution to musical drama, a perfect marriage of word and music.[8]

Yet, as far as scenic qualities went, these early performances showed little inventiveness for their time. Tagore obeyed the concept of stage illusion in them by striving for naturalistic settings. Tagore's niece Indira Devi Chaudhurani, who acted in these plays, says that in pursuit of their ideal, to imitate reality as far as possible, their make-up and stage design mainly followed British practices of the period.[9] Abanindranath Tagore refers to one production of *Vālmīki-pratibhā* featuring stuffed deer, birds made of cotton perched on real branches, and a painted backdrop of a forest scene with a boar hidden behind the trees; he mentions a later performance in which one of the actors made his entrance leading a horse, while "rain" was made to fall on stage via a tin waterpipe overhead; and for the premiere of *Kāl-mṛigayā* they let loose a pet deer on stage.[10]

For the next ten years or so, till the end of the century, Tagore did not appear to alter his ideas of theatre very much. His five-act tragedy *Rājā o Rānī* drew predictably large audiences over this period during its stints in the professional Calcutta theatres, done in the grandiose commercial style we have referred to earlier; but Tagore himself had no hand in these productions. Then, quite unexpectedly, there appeared in 1902 an essay by him titled *Raṅga-mañcha* ("The Stage") which indicated that a complete volte-face had occurred in his thoughts about the theatre. Because of its revolutionary place in Tagore's thoughts on dramaturgy, passages from it deserve to be quoted at some length here:[11]

In the *Natyashastra* of Bharata is a description of a stage, but no mention of scenes. It does not seem to me that this absence of concrete scenery can have been much of a loss.

*   *   *

To my mind it shows only faint-heartedness on the actor's part to seek their help [of scenery]. The relief from responsibility which he gains from the illusion created by pictorial scenes is one which is begged of the painter. Besides it pays to the spectators the very poor compliment of ascribing to them an utter poverty of imagination. . . . Why all this paraphernalia of illusion to delude the poor trusting creatures who have come with the deliberate intention of believing and being happy? They have not surely left their imaginations at home under lock and key. They have come to co-operate, not quarrel, with the interpretation of the drama.

King Dushyanta hidden behind the trunk of the tree is listening to the conversation of Sakuntala and her companions. We for our part feel our creative faculty quite equal to imagining the tree trunk, even though its image be not bodily there . . . what is the difficulty about imagining a few trees, a cottage, or a bit of a river? To attempt to assist us even in regard to these with painted canvas hangings is only to betray a woeful mistrust in our capacity.

That is why I like the *Jatra* plays of our country. There is not so much of a gulf separating the stage from the audience. . . .

If the poet who created Sakuntala had to think of bringing concrete scenes on his stage, then at the very outset he would have had to stop the chariot from pursuing the flying deer. . . . The stage that is in the Poet's mind has no lack of space or appurtenances. There scenes follow one another at the touch of his magic wand. . . .

*   *   *

I have elsewhere said that the European wants his truth concrete. He would have imaginative treats, but he must be deluded by having these imaginings to be exact imitations of actual things. He is too much afraid of being cheated, and before accepting any representation of imaginative truth with some amount of enjoyment he must have a sworn testimony of its reality accompanying it. He will not trust the flower until he sees the earth of the mountain top in which it has its roots. . . . The cost which is incurred for mere accessories on the stage in Europe would swamp the whole of Histrionic Art in famine-stricken India.

*   *   *

The theatres that we have set up in imitation of the West are too
elaborate to be brought to the door of all and sundry. In them the creative richness of poet and player are overshadowed by the wealth of the
capitalist. If the Hindu spectator has not been too far infected with
the greed for realism and the Hindu artist still has any respect for his
craft and his skill, the best thing they can do for themselves is to regain
their freedom by making a clean sweep of the costly rubbish that has
accumulated round about and is clogging the stage.

Within a few years Tagore commenced writing plays that suited
the new principles he had delineated in theory. It might be emphasised at this point that he always wrote plays to fit the actors and
actresses available to him. Most of his nineteenth-century dramatic
output revolved round the thespian talents of members of his large
joint family and the demands of staging in the family theatre at
Jorasanko. After he moved to Santiniketan, the plays he produced
there reflected the change in the casting pool. In its early years his
school at Santiniketan had only boys on its roster; as a result the
first couple of plays written for performance there, *Śaradotsav*
(1908) and *Mukut* (1908), contained no female roles, the former
additionally allowing for a large group of merry-making boys in
its cast. The ratio of males to females in the next play, *Prāyaśchitta*
(1909, staged 1910), rose to eleven to four, while *Rājā* (1910,
staged 1911) had three major women's roles. But *Achalāyatan* (1911,
staged 1914) featured no parts for women, *Dākghar* (1912, staged
1917) only one small girl, and *Phālgunī* (1915) none. Sizeable
crowds of "Boys" or "Students" or "Youths" figured prominently
in several of these plays. Not until much later in the history of
Santiniketan did the number of female students surpass that of male
students, and when that happened Tagore also responded appropri-
ately: *Natīr Pūjā* (1926) gave the women full scope by eschewing
male roles altogether, while *Chandālikā* (1933) brought in a man
only in its final scene. Meanwhile, by casting women alongside
men, Tagore had also persistently chipped away at the social convention that decent, respectable women did not participate in theatrical
activities.

A guest at the ashram, William Pearson, has recorded the school's
novel approach to dramatic productions in its early years:[12]

At the end of each term arrangements are made for staging one of
the poet's plays. The teachers and boys take the different parts. . . .

The poet coaches the actors himself, first reading the play aloud, and then reading it over with those who are to take part. During the days when the play is being rehearsed there are not many classes held, for the boys of the whole school are always present at the rehearsals. . . . To this [the dress rehearsal] the boys are not admitted, as it would take away the freshness of the play if they were able to see a too nearly perfect presentation of it beforehand. But when it begins . . . the songs and dances reveal the spirit of the play to the delighted audience. In this way the ideas of the poet are assimilated by the boys, without their having to make any conscious effort.

In his memoirs Rathindranath Tagore corroborates the above account of the educational experience inherent in this production process. "Father himself selected the actors after putting them through hard tests. In those days he preferred to hold the rehearsals in an open place and did not mind the whole Asrama looking on and listening. As a result, the rehearsals of plays and of music were of great educative value to the whole community and not to the participants only."[13]

From the technical standpoint the beginnings of theatre in Santiniketan were quite rudimentary. Rathindranath tells us that the stage began as a "ramshackle shed behind the Library, used as the dining hall", where only "a few rickety bedsteads" sufficed to create the necessary platform. Soon, however, a spacious hall in a newly constructed dormitory became the site of performances, though Rathindranath concedes that "It was not much of a hall, with its low ceiling".[14] This hall, named the Natya-ghar ("Theatre Room"), witnessed the premieres of many of Tagore's Santiniketan plays. Even as late as 1911, though, a viewer of *Rājā* recalls that there was nothing resembling a stage or set except for a raised platform with a "drop scene" bearing the painted image of Nataraj, Siva in his manifestation as cosmic dancer; the audience sat Indian-style, on the floor.[15]

Yet these productions delighted spectators. Rathindranath relates how the first audience of *Śāradotsav* was "charmed with the spontaneity and *joie de vivre* that characterised the acting."[16] In his opinion its success, and that of *Prāyaśchitta*, encouraged Tagore—no doubt to proceed along these new theatrical paths, using more challenging themes. Despite their difficulty in comprehending the meaning of *Rājā*, the viewers on its opening night were "enthralled by the artistic nature of the performance." Rathindranath compares the

spirit of the company at that time to that of the Moscow Art Theatre
and the Abbey Theatre: "In both of these enterprises, as at Santiniketan, it was not the individual artist so much as the effect produced
by the spirit that moved the whole group of actors which impressed
the audience and convinced them of the sincerity of the effort and
gave them complete artistic satisfaction."[17] Others confirm this
view too; the noted actress and singer Sahana Devi, speaking of
Tagore's 1923 production of *Visarjan* in Calcutta, testified to "a
wonderful understanding and easy relation between the director
and the actors. Rarely . . . have I seen such a singleminded devotion
and team work."[18]

The Santiniketan style of acting is usually described as very
natural, the paramount influence upon it being Tagore's own
superlative acting which various writers have eulogised as "natural
and elevating",[19] "supremely natural" and "sheer beauty".[20]
Sahana Devi summed up the reactions of many eyewitnesses by her
remark that Tagore's acting "opened another world before my
eyes—an inner world of beauty and truth."[21] Even Edward
Thompson, not the most perceptive critic of Tagore, waxed eloquent
when describing a performance of *Visarjan* (presumably the 1923
production mentioned above): "How moving he can be as an actor
only this generation can realize. I can only assure those who will
follow us, *Vidi docentem; credite, posteri*."[22] Tagore himself ex-
postulated on acting—a subject about which he regrettably never
wrote much—while analysing the performances of Henry Irving
in *Hamlet* and *The Bride of Lammermoor*, which he had seen in
London in 1890.[23] Acting, he said,

> . . . has the responsibility of drawing apart the curtain of naturalism
> and reveal [*sic*] the inner reality of things. If there is too much emphasis
> on imitative naturalism the inner view becomes clouded. To express
> the emotional turmoil of a character the actor very often takes recourse
> to violent gesture and declamation . . . he aims at imitating truth in-
> stead of expressing it. Like the false witness he has to exaggerate . . . in
> England . . . I saw the most glaring example of this. . . . I was struck
> dumb. The unrestrained exaggeration of his [Irving's] acting completely
> spoiled the clarity and inner beauty of the plays. It moved one's senses
> but acted as an insurmountable barrier to one's entering into the heart
> of the matter.

After his return from the England-America trip in 1913, Tagore
continued producing new plays at Santiniketan. However, the dis-

tance from Calcutta delimited the possibilities of gaining a wider audience. Except for a few cognoscenti among his friends who travelled between Calcutta and Santiniketan, people outside the small school community remained blissfully ignorant of Tagore's theatrical advances. This state of affairs had to change sooner or later, and an important milestone in the stage history of Tagore's plays came with the performance of *Phālgunī* in Calcutta on 29 January 1916. The play had premiered the previous year in Santiniketan on an open-air "set" that became a common fixture for many of Tagore's seasonal plays and festivals: "The setting was an elaborate garden with real trees, flowers and rustic seats with a swing thrown in."[24] Yet it created the general impression, according to Tagore's biographer, of a simple, unadorned set shorn of all artificiality.[25] It must have seemed only natural to enact plays about the seasons under the open sky.

Tagore then revamped the play for a benefit at the Jorasanko theatre to aid famine victims in Bankura, Bengal, and the result was an enormous success, both critical and commercial, aptly described by the historian Sukumar Sen as "the most remarkable event in the history of Bengali stage . . . in the current century."[26] Edward Thompson, present at the "unforgettable first night", found it "too ravishing for words. It was a complete musical and scenic success."[27] Another important critic, Ajit Kumar Chakravarty, stated that "The playgoers of Calcutta were convinced that a play without action and characterisation, without any stage preparations, without that 'tawdry overdressing' as the poet calls them in condemnation, could be interestingly represented and enjoyed. This was an important advance in the history of the Bengali stage."[28] Nevertheless, we do have the evidence of a contemporary review that "stage preparations" were not exactly nonexistent: "The back drop was a blue curtain with hints of green. It was as if the forest and the sky had blended. A few stars . . . A faint crescent moon . . . A few branches of a tree . . . A swing was attached to one of them. A few creepers, few tufts of grass".[29] The same reviewer praised Tagore's acting as something "to be felt through one's whole being and to be remembered for one's whole life." In Edward Thompson's enthusiastic words, Tagore's "interpretation of Baul reached a height of tragic sublimity which could hardly be endured. Not often can men have seen a stage part so piercing in its combination of fervid acting with personal significance. It was almost as if Milton had acted his own Samson Agonistes."[30] He also observed Tagore breaking the convention of stage illusion on one occasion, by garlanding an actor "for no reason but affection."[31]

After this landmark event it became fairly routine for a Tagore play to open in Santiniketan and transfer at a later date to Calcutta for a few performances. *Dākghar* followed this course, and its staging in Jorasanko on 10–11 October 1917 proved such a huge success that it had to be repeated several times by popular demand. Rathindranath thought the production perfect: "no other play so far attempted ever gave such complete satisfaction to the author, the producers, actors and the audience."[32] The scene design by Tagore's nephew Gaganendranath, also a famous painter, gathered considerable acclaim—an unusually detailed box set of a village hut with thatched roof and three bamboo walls. The auditorium was arranged so as to allow only about 150 people since, as Rathindranath remembers, "Many of the delicate nuances . . . would have been lost in a less intimate atmosphere." The general effect once again enchanted all comers, Indira Devi recalling that they had never seen such a beautiful stage design before.[33] As photographs of the production reveal, the trappings of naturalistic scene design — real straw for the roof, furniture and bric-a-brac inside, plants and foliage on the outer edges—had evidently not disappeared altogether; and the artistic beauty of the set must have evinced from the audience feelings equivalent to the applause that used to greet elaborate scenes in the West. However, one must hasten to add that the designs of Abanindranath and Gaganendranath approximated more closely to an impressionistic style rather than a naturalistic one, though the intricate detail they used may suggest a superficial concern with realism. We do not know if Tagore grew to regard this aspect of the productions as an obtrusive distraction, but we do know that later productions dispensed with detailed settings too. Tagore appreciated the work of Gordon Craig, which he had seen while in England; as early as 1912, he wrote in a letter that the landscape of Urbana (home to the University of Illinois) "reminds me of Mr. Craig's arrangement of the stage where materials are few and simple and unaggressive."[34]

During the 1920s Tagore began to develop a greater interest in stylised theatrical forms. One of the earliest manifestations of this trend was the mime performance of *Arūp Ratan* in Calcutta on 15 September 1924, about which one viewer writes:[35]

The musicians and narrators sat in a half-circle near the wings, and down-stage were the actors miming in time with them. The threefold combination of narration, recitation and miming produced a novel and remarkable effect on the stage.

... Tagore could not fail to note the favourable effect produced by the small element of dance that it carried.

Later in the year, during his visit to Argentina, Tagore elaborated his views on the "wealth of language in movement" in the course of conversations with his friend Leonard Elmhirst. He praised the practice of Japanese actors, who use their entire bodies in performance, and pointed to the natural ability to move inherent in all children:[36]

The best actors will always be those who have been trained to use the whole body as a tool for the expression of thought, of emotion or of sentiment. Words, to convey the full perfection of their message, must be accompanied by the appropriate bodily movement. If our schools were run on the right lines, boys and girls would never lose their natural gifts of bodily expression, making use for that purpose of all their limbs.

Unfortunately, today, in civilized communities, expression through movement is repressed and is no longer looked upon as quite proper....
We pay actors, therefore, to cultivate their natural gifts, and to give us the chance of experiencing the joys we crave, but can no longer achieve....

... I advise you to make the practice of drama and of the histrionic arts compulsory for all children.

Towards the end of the decade, Tagore provided his readers with further definitions of what he called the "new theatre". In an article in the Bengali theatre magazine *Nāchghar* he criticised the lack of aesthetic sense in Bengali professional theatre and suggested that the artistic "new theatre" might follow the ideals of "what is known as 'Little Theatres' in the Western countries."[37] In the same place he indicated that a small auditorium best suited the purposes of such a theatre, and claimed that "A true artist's soul is bound to get deadened" by the long run. While preparing the script for *Tapati* in 1929, he wrote a Preface to the play which reiterated in stronger terms much of what he had already stated in his essay on the stage in 1902; now he denounced the elaborate scenery employed in European theatres as "childishness", "impertinence" and a "pestilence".[38]

Without a doubt, Tagore's new ideas on stagecraft had been strengthened by the presence in Santiniketan of the painter Nandalal Bose, who later became one of the most famous exponents of the "Bengal School" of art. He had joined the fledgling university in 1919 and had assisted in establishing its department of fine arts. Soon afterwards, he developed a method of scene design which gradually evolved into standard procedure for future productions. Nandalal employed a scheme using the three primary colours, blue, yellow and red. The backdrop was always indigo. About four feet downstage he placed a pair of wings coloured deep yellow, followed by a pair of blue wings four feet further down; a third pair of wings, bluish-purple in colour, stood five feet away, with a final pair of red wings three feet further downstage. Above each set of wings there was a short border drop of the corresponding colour hanging from the flies. Occasionally cloth pieces of varying sizes featuring traditional Indian designs were attached to the wings or backdrop for decorative effect. Lighting patterns closely matched the scene design. Hung from the flies behind the first pair of wings upstage was a row of blue lights, behind each of the next two pairs of wings a row of white and faint yellow lights, and behind the front pair of wings white and red lights. Footlights were arranged in a row, in the colours of white and light yellow. Spotlights stood in the wings on both sides. The prevalent mood of a scene, passage or song dictated the choice of colours for that sequence in the lighting design; Santidev Ghosh speculates that colour selection probably adhered to the norms laid down in classical Indian aesthetics as regards the appropriateness of certain colours for certain moods.[39]

The set designs for Tagore's productions during the 1920s witness this trend toward minimalisation and simplification. In the highly acclaimed revival of *Visarjan* at Calcutta's Empire Theatre, 25–28 August 1923, the stage contained only a square altar with a lamp-stand and flower-tray upon it and two steps leading up to it.[40] The premiere of *Tapatī* at Jorasanko on 26 September 1929 occurred against the by-now ubiquitous blue backdrop; when the characters needed to sit, they did so on a couple of stools wrapped in embroidered cloth.[41] Amita Tagore, who played the title-role of the queen Sumitra, remembers also that the costumes were not elaborate because Tagore felt that such glitter distracted attention from the actors' facial expressions.[42] In general, according to Niharranjan Ray, "Rich, flashing dresses are avoided, and so are avoided very

dazzling colors; the more dominant colors that Tagore would use
are white, red ochre, yellow, red and blue, but always in subdued
tints and tones."[43] Amita Tagore had to change costumes just once
in *Tapatī*, for the last scene where her otherwise blue and black dress
scheme gave way to pure white. As in most of Tagore's later productions, the cast no longer sang themselves the songs assigned to
characters; a chorus of singers offstage fulfilled this function. Anti-
illusionistic practices such as this increased in number and importance, and in the later season-plays and dance-dramas Tagore constantly broke the illusion of reality by himself sitting in a prominent
position on stage throughout the performance, usually in a down-
stage corner, driving home their primary identity as works of art
supervised by a human director.

Marjorie Sykes, who taught in Santiniketan between 1939 and
1942, describes a performance of the dance-drama *Chitrāṅgadā*
there—probably one of the last under Tagore's direction—which
captures succinctly the final phase of Tagore's theatrical work:[44]

> The play takes place out of doors, the open verandah in front of the
> library of the *ashrama* being used for the stage. The audience sits on
> carpets, or on the grass, under the stars, for the performance cannot
> begin till after night has fallen. The musicians with their instruments
> sit on one side of the stage, together with the choir which is to sing the
> songs; and on the stage in the opposite corner sits the drummer who ac-
> companies the dancing. There is no curtain to be lowered or raised; the
> stage is lighted and the action begins.
>
> There is no scenery, but we are to know that the scene is a forest. A
> hunter enters, and dances a hunting scene to the accompaniment of
> male voices singing a hunting song. We picture the trees, the birds, the
> lovely surroundings. The hunter's work in the play is done, when he
> has called up the scene in our imagination.

Whether open-air in Santiniketan or before indigo backdrops in
Calcutta and elsewhere, Tagore's productions had by this time
begun to draw virtually unanimous critical approval.[45] No doubt
some of the plaudits derived from the author's unassailable stature
as world-renowned poet, but there is no reason why we should
question their sincerity—the fact remains that the dance-dramas
overwhelmed most reviewers and spectators with their sheer artistry.
P. Guha-Thakurta commented during Tagore's lifetime that "He
has not written plays for the public but has rather created a public
for his plays."[46] Indeed, Tagore almost single-handedly moulded the

tastes of a significant section of his audience, leading to an arguably
more congenial milieu for serious dramatic expression, without
sacrificing Indian theatrical traditions. Perhaps it is the resemblance,
however slight, between the classical Sanskrit drama and the work
of this distant descendant that prompts even a non-Bengali playwright such as Balwant Gargi to accept Tagorean drama as possibly
the beginning of an original, national Indian theatre.[47]

PRODUCTIONS BY OTHERS

Concerning the stage history of Tagore's plays not directed by the
author himself, two episodes need special attention: the first during
the 1920s, when Tagore collaborated briefly with two professional
companies in Calcutta by preparing new scripts for them, and the
second during the years between 1954 and 1964 when a Calcutta
group theatre by the name of Bohurupee staged several of Tagore's
"unstageable" plays with sensational success.

Tagore generally avoided contact with the Bengali professional
stage because it really had nothing to offer him; its dependence on
commercial success precluded any attempts at experimentation,
and Tagore justifiably had no wish to compromise his dramatic
principles. Some of his plays did do well professionally, though —
notably the comedies and *Rājā o Rānī* — but Tagore took no part
in the productions. Finally, in 1925, encouraged by the formation a
few years earlier of the Art Theatre, a company which declared an
interest in staging new plays, Tagore presented them with the dramatisation of one of his novels, the comedy *Chirakumār-Sabhā*.
The play opened at Calcutta's Star Theatre on 18 July, its music
and sets including substantial input from members of the Tagore
family, who regularly attended rehearsals. The play went on to
become a box office hit, a rare distinction for a work by Tagore.
The author himself saw a later performance and came away highly
pleased with the outcome, particularly the acting.

The somewhat unexpected popular welcome given to that play
must have urged Tagore to attempt further forays into the world of
professional theatre: he quickly adapted two of his short stories
into plays, and the Art Theatre produced them without delay. But
predictably, neither of these more serious later exercises could
match the phenomenal success attained by the preceding comedy.
Grihapraveś, which opened at the Star on 5 December 1925, created

minor theatrical history on account of Gaganendranath Tagore's set, which depicted for the first time on the Bengali public stage two adjoining rooms, the action flowing swiftly from one half of the stage to the other. The production satisfied Tagore's own aesthetic sense, but did not impress audiences. *Sodhbodh* (23 July 1926 at the same theatre) garnered even less popular attention, though the press reviewed it favourably. Tagore's final work written for the Art Theatre, *Paritrāṇ*, a revision of an earlier play, took the stage at the Star Theatre on 10 September 1927, and did not distinguish itself in any way.

By this time the focus of innovative work in the professional theatre had shifted to the Natyamandir company run by Sisir Bhaduri at the Cornwallis Theatre. Tagore held Bhaduri's talents as director and actor in special regard, and at the latter's request he revised one of his earlier farces, renaming it *Sesh Rakshā*, for performance by Natyamandir. Bhaduri's production on 7 September 1927 was a spectacular event, notable historically for the first use of audience participation on the Bengali stage: Bhaduri broke the proscenium barrier between stage and auditorium, and in the final scene invited the spectators to join the wedding festivities in the play. The house responded with great enthusiasm, singing along with the marriage songs and intermingling with the cast on stage in celebration of the happy ending. Inspired by this smash success Bhaduri tried his hand at a complex Tagore play, *Tapatī*, staging it on 25 December 1929. However, he learnt the same hard lesson that the Art Theatre had learnt previously—namely, the average Bengali theatre-goer loved Tagore's comedies, but could not appreciate his serious plays. *Tapatī* proved a commercial failure, though a critical success on account of the splendid acting performances.

Apart from a few other instances in later years when Tagore provided professional companies with scripts he himself had prepared from his own fiction, he withdrew from active association with Calcutta's public theatres. The short-lived dalliance may have begun positively, but eventually ended in disillusionment. A polarisation set in—the professionals looked upon Tagore's plays as too high-brow, comprehensible only to the intellectual elite or the select coterie of people connected with Santiniketan; for their part, Tagore's disciples educated at Santiniketan more or less ignored the public stage or looked down upon it with traces of condescension. The twain have rarely met since. Meanwhile the myth grew that

only those who had been trained at Santiniketan could perform
Tagore's plays: without their expertise these plays were unplayable.
This mental block finally dissipated only in the mid-1950s when a
group called Bohurupee, in the vanguard of the Calcutta group
theatre movement, started producing one "unplayable" Tagore
play after another with astonishing facility.

The brainchild of director Sombhu Mitra, Bohurupee commenced
its assault upon the prevailing neglect of Tagorean drama with one
of the most difficult plays, *Rakta-karavī* (10 May 1954). Critics in
Calcutta referred to the production as one of "haunting beauty".[48]
Even outside Bengal the impact did not diminish. The Delhi reviewer L. M. Thapalyal found that it "stood out like a grand
symphony which overwhelms and sweeps you off your feet", more
so when compared to an atrocious Hindi version that he saw in
which the Raja's lines caused unintended laughter.[49] In a play that
had been avoided so far as too symbolical, viewers discovered
characters who "live, talk and move like people we know in real
life."[50] Shiv Kapur noticed that the Bohurupee production re-
frained from emphasising any symbolism: "No postures were
struck" and "no stylisation of character", instead of which "there
were living people on the stage."[51] He singled out Tripti Mitra's
excellent acting as Nandini and Sombhu Mitra's performance as
the Raja, who spoke in "a voice of human anguish: lonely and
divided in his arrogant power." He objected only to the gimmickry
in a scene of workers "being spat out" to a mechanical sound,
though other critics approved of this insertion.[52] In an earlier review the same writer had described Khaled Chowdhury's sets and
Tapas Sen's lighting in some detail:[53]

> They used austere, highly suggestive sets which fell into an overall
> geometric pattern. The palace of the King ... suggested malignant
> strength. This effect was heightened by the use of two lights in the
> facade which glowed red to herald the King's invisible entry on the
> stage. ... The lighting was experimental and was given a liquid life
> of its own which rose and sank with the mood of the lines. ... Its re-
> lationship with the sets was more organic and was used to create ab-
> stract silhouettes on the cyclorama. The overall effect was to enlarge
> the arena of action and of audience-participation into an extra semi-
> abstract dimension of shadows. ... Here poetry and drama were fused
> in a harmony that lightly walked the thin dividing line between fantasy
> and reality.

Bohurupee staged other important Tagore plays at fairly regular intervals: *Dākghar* (24 February 1957), *Muktadhārā* (15 December 1959), *Visarjan* (11 November 1961) and *Rājā* (13 June 1964). Under Mitra's capable direction even *Visarjan* was prevented from becoming "a crude blood-and-thunder affair".[54] Their last major Tagore play, *Rājā*, "brilliantly produced" in the words of the historian Kironmoy Raha, showed little decline in the abilities of the group.[55] Once again the Delhi critic Shiv Kapur provides a good summary:[56]

> Sombhu Mitra's production took the play as a processional, as a journey, and made of it a profoundly moving experience. The production combined the sophisticated with folk elements. It emphasised the poetic quality of myth making in multiple images of sight and sound. Colour glinted upon the stage, alternating with engulfing blackness. The false gods strutted, men walked dressed in saffron, the colour of spiritual seeking; women played holi, men clashed at arms; voices went aloft in song; watchmen cried out in the night; a madman danced; drums pulsed, the voice of humanity, and its anguish, filled the universe.

Mitra's eye for the particular had been noticed previously: L. M. Thapalyal calls him "a master of the small detail which makes a great artist . . . every shade of meaning, every nuance of character seemed to stand out in clear tone and colour".[57]

One cannot underestimate Sombhu Mitra's contribution to the revival of interest in Tagore's plays—not just in Bengal but, as evidenced by the wide range of reviews, in the rest of India too. He himself recalls modestly, "it has been my good fortune to be told by hundreds of people after they saw *Raktakarabi* or *Dak Ghar* . . . that they realised then and for the first time what a great playwright Tagore was."[58] He believes that "Tagore's major plays grapple with the fundamentals and as such the characters have an archetypal quality about them." But he also finds that Tagore's characters "assume individual identities while retaining at the same time their universal, archetypal and symbolic qualities. . . . And it is because they have such individual personalities that the plays become eminently actable." Elsewhere he expands on the theatrical difficulties issuing from this juxtaposition of the universal with the particular, the real with the unreal:[59]

> Tagore's plays do not use realistic characters, yet when we do these plays we feel they are real. He doesn't use common everyday language.

In *Raktakarabi* Kishore says: "I often dream of dying one day for
your sake, Nandini." Most of our actors find it difficult to perform
these words. They feel that even if Kishore feels this, he would express
it in a different way. The words sound pretentious, they say. Consequently, even today is it [*sic*] difficult to perform Tagore's language.

So Mitra conceived of a less naturalistic, more "subjective" style of
acting attuned to Tagore's poetic prose, "in the way in which it was
once so natural for Hamlet to move into a soliloquy." While per-
fecting this technique he discovered that his group had "hit upon a
distinctive form of theatre."[60] This theatre was sui generis, yet
clearly Indian to the core, contemplative instead of active. Sombhu
Mitra came to these conclusions: "Only Tagore has been able to
establish a connection with our Golden Age," and "a Bengali
theatre of the future must first pass through Tagore."[61] We might
broaden this latter thesis to include all of Indian theatre, for it
seems clear that a sensitive Indian director cannot afford to ignore
the legacy that Tagore has left behind.

IV. TAGORE'S THEMES

"What is Art?" It is the response of man's creative soul to the call of
the Real.

[Tagore, lecture delivered at the University of Oxford, 1930][1]

Tagore's statement above obtains primary importance with
respect to any discussion of his drama, because of the common
accusation that his plays contain little realism and overmuch
symbolism. Consider, for example, two representative critical
opinions: Sujit Mukherjee finds Tagore's drama "constantly in
danger of letting its symbols proliferate and obscure the human
significance"; S.K. Desai alleges that Tagore "creates 'prisons' of
symbols" without "genuine vitality and life, which is the primary
criterion of literature."[2] According to such criteria, plays such as
Rājā or *Rakta-karavī* can only be regarded as dreary or lifeless,
and—as charged by many critics—worked backwards from the
idea or allegory. Thus we have K.P.K. Menon saying that "plays
like *The King of the Dark Chamber* and *Red Oleanders* are unintelligible to the readers who seek only the surface meaning"; he also
confronts "frequent obscurity and absurdity in *The King of the
Dark Chamber* and *Red Oleanders*, which could not, therefore, be
termed successful plays of ideas."[3] Yet Tagore repeatedly issued
disclaimers about the symbolism of his plays, constantly asserting
that he based them on reality, on the lives of real people. The answer
to this apparent conundrum lies in the fact that what Tagore considered real is considered unreal by most critics, and vice versa.
When Nirmal Mukerji criticises Tagore by pointing out that "The
allegory, in fact, seems to be more real than reality",[4] she unwittingly identifies the motif at the heart of Tagore's drama: namely,
that superficial reality is in fact unreal. Realism in art, Tagore
believed, is not achieved by depictions of external circumstances
alone, however truthful, but by the presentation of inner truth, the
inner life of man.

Tagore clarified his views on reality many different times. He
always insisted that "the world is what we perceive it to be . . . our
mind itself is the principal element of creation."[5] Arguing therefore
that reality is necessarily relative, he set scientific reality and mental
reality at two separate poles, in mutual opposition. Science, he

theorised, subjects God to analysis "in the laboratory of reason outside our personal relationship, and then describes the result as unknown and unknowable."[6] But he believed, on the contrary, that such a relationship is indeed comprehensible, that one cannot know a book by merely counting its pages, analysing its paper, or measuring and weighing its dimensions.[7] Asking why, for example, "we look upon Shakespeare's portrayal of extraordinary and powerful feelings as more truthful than the exact portrayal of everyday life", he supplied his own answer with a comment made in 1892 that we find in Shakespeare "the perennial man . . . not merely the surface man."[8] Almost forty years later, in a letter written during his trip to Indonesia in 1927, he expressed the opinion that if a person laughs at the apparent unrealism of Javanese dances, "he needs must also laugh at Shakespeare, whose heroes not only fight in metre, but even die to it."[9] So he did not allow his own plays to be dictated by the common man's standards of reality. He wrote with regard to the translated play *The King of the Dark Chamber* that "the human soul has its inner drama, which is just the same as anything else that concerns Man, and Sudarshana is not more an abstraction than Lady Macbeth".[10]

Consequently the realism in Tagore's plays is a realism of the mind, not so much of exterior physical action as of emotional or spiritual action. It does not depict external conflicts as much as internal conflicts of the mind and spirit. It depicts realistically fluctuations in mood and feeling, the progress of awareness and consciousness. It does not emphasise the development of a plot, but rather develops a pattern of symbols which reflect those fluctuations in great detail. In fact, "paradoxically enough, Rabindranath achieves his most intense realism when his symbolism is most complex", writes Hirankumar Sanyal.[11] But few commentators realise the basic truth that "The symbol may enhance rather than diminish the sense of reality by pointing to areas of experience which we ordinarily tend to overlook."[12] Additionally, in Guha-Thakurta's words, Tagore "enables us to grasp reality not so much through a process of reasoning as through feeling".[13] Tagore's technique in creating this almost tangible mood in each of his plays shows delicate artistry. "What he aims at is to build up," observes Niharranjan Ray, "out of suggestions and associations and emanations of the total atmosphere, a world whose existence cannot be perceived by any of the senses but only felt as a realisation."[14] And, according to the same author, "this infinite suggestiveness makes the symbolist plays truly immortal."[15] Unquestionably, this indefinable aura in Tagore's dramas partially accounts for their having, "on our first contact with them, an overpowering effect on us."[16]

Before analysing the issues in the three plays translated in this volume, we might briefly identify how some of Tagore's general thematic concerns arise from this view of reality. Amar Mukerji outlines as follows the dramatic progress of a typical Tagore protagonist:[17]

> ... a human being because of the narrow barriers of selfhood that he has woven round himself, continues for a while to thrive within that barrier till "the touch of the eternal" or, in other words, the sense of an impending realisation comes to him (mostly through an innocent girl or apparently some such ineffective character) and makes him victorious over his previous infinities [sic]. While undergoing this process, hesitancy first appears in him; he then sees the first glimmer of the true knowledge and then the struggle intensifies till he is able to defeat the selfhood in him.

This movement toward true knowledge and self-awareness (and the concomitant self-negation) we find in the characters of the Raja in *Rakta-karavī* and Sudarshana in *Arūp Ratan*, while we expect that it overcomes Bikram at the tragic ending of *Tapatī*. They are aided in this journey from darkness to light by their interaction with the agents of good in each play: Nandini in *Rakta-karavī*, the Raja in *Arūp Ratan*, and Sumitra in *Tapatī*. In each play, suffering occupies a central position in this development by precipitating the conclusion, because of Tagore's belief that it cleanses the spirit and enables man to see with true clarity. In *Tapatī* suffering climaxes in death, while Tagore has made it clear in his commentaries on *Rakta-karavī* that death concludes it too, though the play itself does not end so explicitly. Death recurs frequently in Tagore's plays, always resulting in transformation or self-realisation in other characters. "To know life truly," said Tagore, "one must see life introduced through death."[18] He agreed with Hinduism that "Out of destruction rises the path of creation",[19] finding support for his faith in the regenerative annual cycles of nature. Therefore death in his plays rarely is just a cause for mourning, leading as it does to a victory of the spirit.

Although Tagore makes his protagonists relinquish their self-centredness on the spiritual level through the process of suffering, on the social level he consistently espoused the causes of individualism. The dichotomy between the individual and the organisation pervades his drama, Tagore constantly choosing the former over the latter. As he put it, "All our spiritual teachers have proclaimed the infinite worth of the individual. It is the rampant materialism of the present age which ruthlessly sacrifices individuals to the blood-thirsty idols of organization."[20] He distrusted the concept of organisation since it distracted and dehumanised mankind: "Because men have been building up vast and monstrous organizations they have got into the habit of thinking that this turning-out power has something of the nature of perfection in itself."[21] Tagore hoped that these leviathan systems would go the way of the dinosaurs, who had similar "gigantic muscles" and made similar "mighty efforts".[22] Thus we discover images of claustrophobia crowding his plays, as individuals longing for freedom of one kind or another try desperately to extricate themselves from the meshes of unfeeling organisation.

Tagore held that civilisation had begun to ignore the individual too by becoming totally masculine in nature, thereby generating more wars and strife among people. He had a great respect for the feminine principle; in his opinion woman had a sensitivity, a sympathetic quality, an innate spirituality and a freshness of mind that eclipsed the more earthly desires and attributes of the opposite sex.[23] "In our country," he writes, "woman is accepted as the symbol of strength in every aspiration of man."[24] It comes as no surprise, therefore, to find women such as Nandini or Sumitra in Tagore's plays completely dominating the stage with their gentle yet powerful personalities. The other omnipresent force in his drama is an unseen one, that of the natural world. Following in the heritage of Sanskrit poets, Tagore points out in an essay aptly titled "The Religion of the Forest" that "in all our dramas which still retain their fame . . . Nature stands on her own right, proving that she has her great function, to impart the peace of the eternal to human emotions."[25] Although he admits that Shakespeare's natural backgrounds sometimes uncover "a secret vein of complaint against the artificial life of the king's court", in the tragedies Shakespeare presents Nature as malignant or ambivalent or absent altogether.[26] On the other hand, Tagore's Nature is a perennially beneficent and healing power; by neglecting it or divesting ourselves of its influence we close our eyes to the world around us, and cut ourselves off from the unity of the universe.

In the final analysis, Tagore's drama reveals a strong underlying current of optimism. The affirmative attitude to life, the broad humanism, the conviction about the inviolable relationship between man and his maker, the deep faith in woman and the beauty of nature, all contribute to the pervasive sense of harmony and the invincible spirit of hope in his plays.

RAKTA-KARAVĪ ("RED OLEANDER")

Rakta-karavī is a difficult play for even the best of critics. Niharranjan Ray, judging that it does not possess dramatic *rasa* although its lyricism may qualify it as a dramatic poem, calls it "thin and unconvincing as a drama."[27] Sujit Mukherjee complains, "nowhere is there a sustained effort at full statement."[28] Tagore's subtle and unconventional handling of the theme, in a manner that suggests rather than states outright, has unfortunately created much critical consternation. Nevertheless, a careful second reading seems to have clarified problems in at least one illustrative case. In 1968 S. K. Desai felt "completely dazed and bewildered" by the intermingling of realism and symbolism in the play, especially at the end.[29] But ten years later he terms it a "superb poetic play . . . yielding levels of meaning at each successive reading. It is a classic".[30] He concludes percipiently that "The reader/spectator is *supposed* to ask: 'What is the meaning of this?'"[31]

The confusion surrounding the meaning of *Rakta-karavī* dates back to its publication. In fact, Tagore felt so disappointed at its critical reception that he thought himself duty-bound to serve as interpreter of the play on several occasions. Since he has voiced his opinion substantially on this subject, and since his word regarding his intentions should count as preferred evidence, I trust readers will forgive me for quoting him at length in this section. "In daring to sit in judgement upon *Red Oleanders*," he said, "we are not judges, we are the accused."[32] In the play, "The habit of greed — greed for things, for power, for facts, with all the ramifications that greed is able to set up between man and man — is arrayed against the explosive force of human sympathy, of neighbourliness, of fellowship and of love, the force which we may term good. Good is here arrayed against the dehumanizing force of mammon, of selfishness, of evil; of that which separates us from our fellows against that which cements us together, of that which, because it divides us, is untruth, is a lie." The thesis stated in bald terms, Tagore then explicates the rest of the play:

The background, then, is a world based upon the principle that each must fight the other, oppress or be oppressed, in order not merely that the ordinary simple needs of life may be satisfied, but that piles of accumulation may be set up. This is a world where, with every available means in his power, the Great King exploits the resources of the underworld, of nature, of the mind, of science and of human physique and intelligence, using all the weapons of organization and the elaborate machinery of a highly centralized bureaucracy in order to add to his wealth. This wealth he measures in gold, or in souls or in facts, or in human bodies, so that men are men no longer but numbers. The King sits fascinated as he watches this hive where everyone is busy, but no one content, where all are piling cell to cell, adding honey to honey, guarding the stores of accumulated wealth with efficient death-dealing stings, or casting out the human wastage, the drones, men who have been broken, or exploited. Into his hive flies the butterfly, armed with no sting, equipped with no power to gather or to store, but clothed in beauty, loving the light of day and life, asking all to share in her sunshine revels. . . . Like strings on an untuned instrument they respond to her touch, and though the instrument had long been thrown on one side, still here and there music and harmony come struggling forth, toils and troubles are forgotten, memories are aroused of the old scents and sounds, of the simple artistic colour and variety of nature, of the co-operative life of the village, where all were not numbers but neighbours, where there was music and beauty and life. But we have become numbers, with numbers on our doors, our telephones, our cars, our factories, our restaurants, our votes, and our tickets at sports or theatre. . . .

Nandini then is this touch of life, the spirit of joy in life. Matched with Ranjan, the spirit of joy in work, together they embody the spirit of love . . . they walk fearlessly into this world of getting, and, being independent of it, they break down its barriers, even though in the process they are broken themselves, — but such sacrifice is the price which must always be paid in the effort to break down the wall of the darkness, of untruth and to flood the world with light. . . .

So it is that, when men make use of men . . . they crush and mutilate not merely their victims but the humanity which is in themselves. They prefer to think in terms of empire, of organization in factory or field or workshop, in politics or church or sport, and to satisfy their craving for power or survival. . . .

... men use men as tools, as a means to some further end in which these tools have no part, lot or interest, and . . . they fail to recognize in their fellow beings a common inheritance of a common humanity.

Tagore then makes an interesting comment which throws some light on the significance of the screen that obscures the Raja from everyone's vision in the play:

Such is the complication of life today that most of our money, which is the measure of our power over our fellows, "changes hands" as we say, without those hands ever coming into civil much less friendly contact. We sign cheques, we drop money into slots, and we push it through pigeon holes, where a hand but no face takes charge of it . . . we hurt ourselves at the same time as we deprive others of their self-respect, and deny to them their own human significance.

Against this picture of society Tagore depicts "Nandini, the embodiment of that light that is beauty and love." As he proceeds to explain, this spirit of love can have many altruistic manifestations:

So it is that, according to the measure in which we fail to reach this relationship of love in our relations with our fellow men, our life is incomplete. . . .
The problem is simple, the cure is simple, so simple that we have grown clever enough not to see it. The highest goal of all is love; a love that each of us is still able to recognize and appreciate. . . .
The diggers, the King, the Governor, these were men who had no love for the medium in which they worked, for the soil that they were bent upon exploiting. . . . Yet the law of love holds good in the world of nature as well as in the world of man. It is through love for the soil, and for the cherishing of it, that the soil responds to our touch. . . . In mutilating the soil, that source of beauty that is also wealth, we mutilate ourselves.

Some time later, Tagore sent a letter to the *Manchester Guardian* in response to the discombobulated reactions of English reviewers to *Red Oleanders*. In this correspondence he issued a severe indictment of the covetousness and inhumanity of Western colonialism as a further message of the play:[33]

To-day another factor has made itself immensely evident in shaping and guiding human destiny. It is the spirit of organisation, which is not social in character, but utilitarian. . . . Naturally, in all organisations, variation of personality is eliminated, and the individual members . . .

give expression to a common type and very little to their uniqueness of individuality.

... The world has became [*sic*] the world of Jack and Giant—the Giant who is not a gigantic man, but a multitude of men turned into a gigantic system.

... I can say, on behalf of inarticulate Asia, what a terrible reality for us is the West, whose relation to ourselves is so little human. The view that we can get of her, in our mutual dealings, is that of a titanic power with an endless curiosity to analyse and know, but without sympathy to understand; with numberless arms to coerce and acquire, but no serenity of soul to realise and enjoy.

It is an organised passion of greed that is stalking abroad in the name of European civilisation. ... Such an objectified passion lacks the true majesty of human nature; it only assumes a terrifying bigness, its physiognomy blurred through its cover of an intricate network,—the scientific system. It barricades itself against all direct human touch with barriers of race pride and prestige of power.

Tagore thus defended his motives in writing the play: "Therefore it should cause no surprise to anybody if a poet, belonging to a continent swallowed by the menacing shadow of Europe, gives a prominent place among the *dramatis personae* of his play to an apparition which now so powerfully occupies the imagination of a vast world consisting of non-Western races." Once again, he ends with a portrait of Nandini, epitomising his concepts of ideal womanhood as an alternative to the evils of twentieth-century civilisation:

Nandini is a real woman who knows that wealth and power are *māyā*, and that the highest expression of life is in love, which she manifests in this play in her love for Ranjan.... I have a stronger faith in the simple personality of man than in the prolific brood of machinery that wants to crowd it out. This personality ... has its last treasure-house in woman's heart. Her pervading influence will some day restore the human to the desolated world of man.

In the wide range of issues that it covers, *Rakta-karavī* forms almost an apogee of Tagore's dramatic work, but in recent years critical interpretation of the play has focused mainly on its socialistic import. As we have seen, Tagore made its political implications quite clear, but the thinly disguised condemnation of British rule had not escaped readers either; one contemporary reviewer had hailed the play, predicting that for future generations "it will be a momentous landmark in the history of their country's political regeneration."[34] In more recent times one notices that the play has lent itself quite easily to leftist doctrine; the Czech critic and translator of Tagore, Dusan Zbavitel, praises it for attacking "capitalist exploiters".[35] After the success of Bohurupee's production it became fashionable to see Yakshapuri (the social microcosm in the play) as Sombhu Mitra did — an industrialised city siphoning people away from surrounding villages.[36] This interpretation derives of course from Tagore, who said on one occasion: "The artificial lights of the town are ablaze — lights that have no connection with sun, moon or star — but the humble lamps of the village are dead. The siren of the factory lures men away from the peaceful refuge of their community."[37] Yakshapuri breaks natural rhythms and tempts men with gold; fear, intimidation and depersonalisation on the one hand, and power, organisation and totalitarianism on the other, characterise such a society.[38] No doubt Tagore intended to suggest the dichotomy, but to stress such polarisations might actually make the conflict in the play too simple and two-dimensional. We must also remember that Sombhu Mitra's Raja spoke in a voice "charged with the agonised pathos of a soul in torment".[39] The Raja is human, perhaps even the second half of the split personality of man, the other half of which is Nandini: he joins hands with her at the end of the play to overturn the depressing status quo. Tagore's methods were inclusive, not denying, and in any performance or analysis we must do our best to preserve the all-encompassing nature of suggestiveness in *Rakta-karavī*; we must not isolate only some aspects of it.

TAPATĪ ("TAPATĪ")

One of the most common critical fallacies with respect to *Tapatī* is the unnecessary application of western theories of tragedy in judging the quality of the play — naturally it falls short of meeting the requirements of a conventional tragedy, because Tagore did not intend it to fit the tragic mould although he had followed Shakespearean ideals in composing his popular earlier play with the same plot, *Rājā o Rānī*. This tendency among critics is not, of course, limited to *Tapatī*. For example, Kanak Bandyopadhyay applies concepts of tragedy much too eagerly to Tagore's later plays (such as *Rakta-karavī*); his analysis is excellent on its own terms, but ultimately without foundation because Tagore no longer cared to follow western modes of playwriting.[40]

The main problem with critics' approaches to *Tapatī* lies in their reluctance to accept it as a play better than, or even equal to, *Rājā o Rānī*. This trend flourishes despite Tagore's own embarrassment with *Rājā o Rānī* and his conviction that he had improved it by writing *Tapatī*.[41] Most major Bengali scholars (*Tapatī* is unavailable in English translation) do not believe that Tagore fulfilled his claim and, to paraphrase Santikumar Dasgupta, they consider it only proper to view *Rājā o Rānī* as the superior play.[42] Srikumar Bandyopadhyay offers one extreme rationale for doing so, by arguing that revision and adaptation indicate an immature and un-selfconfident dramatic craftsmanship; he thereby arbitrarily dispenses with all Tagore revisions, including *Tapatī*, as deficient compared to their respective originals.[43] Apart from such inexplicable criteria, the reasons for rejecting *Tapatī* are varied. Upendranath Bhattacharya prefers the earlier tragedy because it contains at least some traces of the "illusion of reality" which, according to him, forms the chief attraction of drama.[44] I have already suggested, however, that such standards are meaningless when applied to Tagore's plays. Other critics seem uncomfortable with the conclusion to *Tapatī*: its ambiguity does not satisfy Kanak Bandyopadhyay, who wishes to know for certain whether Sumitra's suicide has converted Bikram or not.[45] Love does not conquer in *Tapatī* as clearly as it does in *Rājā o Rānī*, but in my opinion this openendedness does not detract from the play. It is not essential for a drama to provide solutions to a problem or to tie up all its loose ends in an acceptable denouement; its job is done as long as the problem has been presented forcefully.

Despite its beautiful poetry, *Rājā o Rānī* has major structural shortcomings that ruin it as drama. It develops powerfully the tension between the two protagonists, Raja Bikram and Rani Sumitra, but then after reaching a point midway the role of the heroine Sumitra gradually dissipates into the background. As if that were not enough, the focus on the hero shifts markedly from Bikram to Kumarsen, Sumitra's brother, a character who enters as late as III.ii. By the end of the play we have the tragic love-story of Kumarsen and Ila taking precedence, decidedly undermining the story of Bikram and Sumitra. In addition, the subplots of two other couples, Chandrasen and Rebati, and Debdatta and Narayani, gain in treatment at the further expense of the main plot. Above all, the gory and sensational last scene in which Sumitra enters carrying Kumarsen's severed head, then collapses and dies, is totally uncharacteristic of Tagore. But in *Tapati*, Tagore has concentrated on the fate of Sumitra throughout the drama, the secondary love interest between Naresh and Bipasha functioning as a subsidiary foil without ever diffusing the primary narrative.

Even Tagore, who thought in a letter after completing *Tapati* that he had written a play "beautiful in all aspects", admitted in another letter while supervising its rehearsals about a month later that it was a difficult play.[46] The grim, unrelenting nature of its theme makes it hard for readers or viewers to assimilate, though the plot—relatively easy to understand—develops along more conventional lines than Tagore's symbolic plays. The concept behind the play is itself not a difficult one: ideally, according to Tagore, love should free, not possess. Mere passion driven to obsession eventually destroys the person whom it attempts to secure—an idea embodied in the story of Bikram and Sumitra. As in several other Tagore plays, pride and the ego must be vanquished in Bikram, and self-centredness must give way to humility. Also as typical in Tagore, suffering becomes a purifying agent which helps in the attainment of humility and the realisation of truth.

On several earlier occasions Tagore had made comments on the works of Kalidasa (one of his prime influences) that actually appear to clarify *Tapati*. For instance, Tagore writes of *Śakuntala* that Kalidasa "has rescued the relation of the sexes from the sway of lust and enthroned it on the holy and pure seat of asceticism."[47] It seems that Tagore aimed for a similar effect in *Tapati*. He presents his unusual interpretation of the development of Kalidasa's play from "matter into spirit" as follows:[48]

> In truth there are two unions in *Sakuntala*; and the *motif* of the play is the progress from the earlier union of the First Act, with its earthly unstable beauty and romance, to the higher union in the heavenly hermitage of eternal bliss described in the last act. This drama was meant ... to elevate love from the sphere of physical beauty to the eternal heaven of moral beauty.

Of course the happy ending that concludes *Śakuntala* is conspicuously absent in *Tapati*, which terminates in the death of the title character; nor, in fact, does the play begin with a portrayal of

romantic, sensual love as in the first act of Kalidasa's play. But in
its essentials *Tapatī* conforms with Tagore's hypothesis about its
illustrious predecessor. For example, Tagore's views on Sakuntala's immature early love correspond exactly with his depiction of
the king, Bikram: "When Sakuntala forgot her duty of tending
guests, when her husband became all the world to her,—then her
love ceased to be beneficent. The wild love which forgets everything
except the loved one, succeeds in rousing against itself all the laws
of the universe."[49] Instead of this kind of passion, which negates
the world, Tagore advocates a humanitarian love such as Sumitra's:
"The love that is self-controlled and friendly to general society,
which does not ignore any one, great or small, kindred or stranger,
around itself,—the love which, while placing the loved one in its
centre, diffuses its sweet graciousness within the circle of the entire
universe,—has a permanence unassailable by God or man."

Tagore also reminds his readers of the Hindu myth that Parvati
tried to win Siva through penance, meditation, asceticism and religious austerities;[50] and the reader of *Tapatī* can instantly make
the connection with Sumitra's method of responding to Bikram's
emotions, excepting for the fact that Bikram in no way resembles
Siva, the supreme ascetic. However, Tagore might have seen some
resemblances between Bikram and one of Kalidasa's other heroes,
the king Agnimitra in *Mālavikāgnimitra*, since Tagore reflects elsewhere that Agnimitra symbolises "the destructive force of uncon-
trolled desire" in a play which expresses "the ugliness of the trea-
chery and cruelty inherent in unchecked self-indulgence."[51]
Interestingly enough, the queen Dharini in the same play signifies
to Tagore attributes which may recall those of Sumitra, such as
"the fortitude and forbearance that comes from majesty of soul"
and "the infinite dignity of love, purified by a self-abnegation that
rises far above all insult". But above all, Tagore's appraisal of the
characterisation of Sakuntala could just as well suit his own portrayal of Sumitra. Kalidasa, he writes, "has developed her into the
model of a devoted wife, with her reserve, endurance of sorrow, and
life of rigid spiritual discipline . . . at the end we see her deeper
feminine soul,—sober, patient under ill, intent on austerities,
strictly regulated by the sacred laws of piety. With matchless art
Kalidas has placed his heroine on the meeting-point of action and
calmness".[52]

Several of Tagore's later plays share themes similar to that of

Tapatī. In *Chaṇḍālikā* the title character falls in love with Ananda, disciple of the Buddha, and becomes so obsessed with him as to convince her mother to employ magic to make Ananda love her. In the end she realises her mistake, and the Buddhist monk's severely tested spiritual discipline remains unscathed. The heroine of *Bānśarī* is told by a guru that passionate love undermines the sense of duty in man, and so he arranges a marriage of passionless love between Somsankar, the man Bansari loves, and another girl. Somsankar himself tells Bansari that his love for her may prove to be a weakness, diverting him away from his duties. Thus in one case too much romantic attachment detracts from spiritualism, in the other it detracts from dutifulness; in both cases Tagore associates it with selfishness. All three aspects are present in *Tapatī*. In spite of his oft-repeated credo "Deliverance is not for me in renunciation",[53] in his later works Tagore did grow more sympathetic to asceticism and the force of sublimated love. However, he never embraced these ideals to the exclusion of all else, for he always maintained that "The two peculiar principles of India are the beneficent *tie of home life* on the one hand, and the *liberty of the soul* abstracted from the world on the other."[54] Totally estranged from each other, at opposite poles of sensuality and asceticism respectively, Bikram and Sumitra cannot have any aspirations to the former principle. But Sumitra attains liberty of the soul through suicide, as a means to restore internal peace to her husband's kingdom, perhaps achieving in death, the supreme act of renunciation, what she could not while alive—namely, Bikram's return to benevolent home rule.

ARŪP RATAN ("FORMLESS JEWEL")

The play *Rājā* was a favourite of Tagore's. As he put it in a letter to his friend William Rothenstein, "I do want the message embodied in this particular play to reach your people. This play has come out of my innermost experience, almost unconsciously almost inspite [*sic*] of myself ... I have an almost impersonal love for it."[55] *Arūp Ratan* represents the final published incarnation of *Rājā*, altered mainly in the shape of compression, but close enough to the original drama to make thematic analyses of both virtually interchangeable. I do not, therefore, distinguish between the two plays here.

When K. S. Ramaswami Sastri terms the play "peerless in its

spiritual beauty and depth of vision", he does not exaggerate.[56] To put it plainly, the play is allegorical: it cannot be comprehended on simple realistic terms. As such, it has received many different readings. A beautiful woman, disgusted by the sudden sight of her ugly suitor whom she has never seen before, spontaneously rejects him but ultimately comes to the realisation that true beauty does not lie in physical appearances—this fable has universal counterparts, and indeed, the German scholar Heinz Mode traces Tagore's play to the archetypal folk legend of beauty and the beast.[57] But the most common view correctly holds that the play depicts the spiritual journey of man in relation to his creator, demarcating a progress that quite literally leads the protagonist from darkness into light. To quote Tripti Mitra, who played the heroine in the Bohurupee production of *Rājā*, "I was terrified of the role of Rani Sudarshana, for how does one remain a human individual on stage while portraying the spiritual travail of mankind in all its time."[58] Sudarshana, then, stands for everyman while her husband, the nameless and invisible Raja, symbolises supreme godhead. Tagore also peoples his play with a fairly representative cross-section of humanity running the gamut from the sceptics to the faithful, the ignorant to the empiricists.

With this cast, Tagore follows through the course of this play the spiritual maturation and enlightenment of humankind from a one-dimensional conception of God to an all-inclusive one. Man's originally innocent or myopic vision of life and divinity as happy and benign is usually shattered at some point by a confrontation with the harshness and pitiless cruelty of reality, which leads him immediately to question God and negate life, sometimes as a result embracing false ideals — as exemplified in this play by the impostor king, Subarna. Experience makes man mature, bringing him to a complete understanding that life and divinity are simultaneously terrible and beautiful, eventually reconciling him with God. The spiritual allegory of growth from the state of innocence through experience to the state of full acceptance is by no means original, but Tagore's treatment of it shows a characteristically simple and unfettered purity.

The play presents two basic themes: that man becomes too attached to the artificial glitter of the material world, and that he cannot accept the fact that God can permit the process of living to bring with it tragedy as well as happiness. Both concepts stem from the premise that man in his ignorance sees superficially, which leads inevitably to his suffering and disillusionment, which in turn contribute finally to the recognition of truth. The view of the world as maya or illusion forms, of course, a central tenet in Hinduism, and Tagore adopted this philosophy unquestioningly. Men get entangled in the magic web of maya, enticed by the allurements of physical beauty and material possessions and selfish aggrandisement, forgetting meanwhile the prime mover of the universe. Thus in Tagore's play we find Sudarshana temporarily infatuated with the king manqué Subarna (the name literally means "gold"), before she becomes aware of her transgression. In an essay Tagore applied the analogy of Sudarshana's predicament to what he saw as the materialistic West: "The western Sudarshana captivated by the beauty of the false king 'Gold' has chosen him by mistake."[59]

In addition, men misunderstand the nature of God, rarely recognising — in the words of a Tagore song — that "In one hand he has a sword,/In the other a garland."[60] Tagore believed that we should accept the duality of God, who for him was fundamentally benign but could also be cruel and terrible, the preserver as well as the destroyer. The apparent ugliness of Tagore's Raja has troubled some critics, but as S.C. Sen Gupta perceptively remarked, the average person considers "his appearance repulsive, because God is formless and the human eye cannot stand the presence of the formless."[61] Other writers periodically object to the allegorical interpretation of the relationship between the Raja and Sudarshana. S.K. Desai, for instance, argues that an association between God and the human soul "cannot be narrowed down to the husband-wife relationship", and K.P.K. Menon agrees that "when the God-Soul relationship and the wife-husband-lover relationship are mixed up, the result is confusion and chaos."[62] But these critics ignore the time-honoured tradition in Indian art and literature which depicts relations between God and the individual in terms of love between the sexes, the best illustration of which is obviously the legend of Krishna and his lover Radha, a motif which dominates the popular Hindu mind.

Tagore offers in his play definite directions for the initiate entering these two relationships, one with the world and the other with God. He believed in the notion of immanence, an Upanishadic doctrine that God pervades all things in life: "The world," says the *Īsā Upanishad*, "is swaddled in the glory of God."[63] Thus in the second

scene of *Arūp Ratan* a Guard, when requested by travellers to show
them the road to the Raja's festival, replies "Here all roads are the
road."[64] And soon after in the same scene, when the subject of the
Raja's invisibility arises, the wise Thakurda suggests that the whole
country is filled with the Raja. Of the three plays in this volume,
Arūp Ratan best illustrates Tagore's conviction about the presence
of God in nature. For all its conflict of the soul, the play centres on
a festival of spring and celebrates the rejuvenation of life—not only
spiritual but natural. An atmosphere of benevolent nature permeates the work, Thakurda and his young disciples repeatedly
bringing it to our attention through their songs and dances. Tagore
implies that we should not ignore the physical world around us, for
it can provide the deepest and clearest insights into divinity if we
seek or are receptive to the unity underlying its marvellous diver-
sity.

Sudarshana's conversion at the end of the play typifies man's
ideal reconciliation with God. She prostrates herself in front of the
Raja in the dark room of the final scene, declaring with complete
humility "I'm a servant at your feet".[65] Man must surrender his
self-centredness and self-consciousness, and approach God in
total submission. Tagore explains why in an essay titled "The
Problem of Self":[66]

> Everything has this dualism of *māyā* and *satyam*, appearance and truth.
> . . . Our self is *māyā* where it is merely individual and finite, where it con-
> siders its separateness as absolute; it is *satyam* where it recognizes its
> essence in the universal and infinite, in the supreme self, in *paramātman*.

A poem in *Gitanjali* throws more light on this recurrent theme in
Tagore's writings, as well as on his use of the image of the king:[67]

> The king has come—but where are lights, where are wreaths? Where
> is the throne to seat him? Oh, shame, Oh utter shame! Where is the
> hall, the decorations? Some one has said, "Vain is this cry! Greet him
> with empty hands, lead him into thy rooms all bare!"

One must relinquish all attachments to the material world, believed
Tagore, and welcome God with "empty hands". In the play *Muktadhārā* the anchorite Dhananjay touches upon this point by observing
that "He who gives all, keeps all. . . . What you set free is yours for
ever. Clutch at it, and it is gone."[68] Thus, stripping oneself of the
ego and of materialistic ties can help man attain union with God.

There may appear to be a minor paradox in Tagore's support of renunciation on the one hand and glorification of the physical world on the other. But if we return to the line from the *Īśā Upanishad* quoted earlier we find that Hinduism does not consider these incompatible in the spiritual life of man:[69]

> The world is swaddled in the glory of God.
> But it changes!
> Renounce it,
> Enjoy the wealth of the world with dispassion.

By enjoying the mutable world dispassionately—thereby not allowing oneself to form any attachments to things transient — man can remain steadfast in his devotion to and vision of God, the one immutable being pervading all of existence. The noted scholar Abu Sayeed Ayyub defined Tagore's religion as threefold: to find God in mankind (and nature), to be detached (and renounce), and to act dutifully against injustice.[70] At the risk of over-generalisation, we may identify each of the three plays in this collection with one of these three quests: *Arūp Ratan* with the discovery of God, *Tapatī* with detachment and renunciation, and *Rakta-karavī* with action against injustice.

V. TAGORE'S RECEPTION IN ENGLAND AND AMERICA

I am an interloper whose intrusions into your literature must not be too often, and in my unseemly greed I should not let your warm welcome of a guest degenerate into sullen tolerance or what is worse into angry hostility.

[Tagore, letter to William Rothenstein, 15 June 1914][1]

Particularly interesting in a study of Tagore is the response of the West to his work. Several scholars have already dealt with this aspect at length, but none has isolated the plays for detailed treatment. In doing so here, I have confined my research to the writings of major English and American reviewers in reaction to the English editions of his plays. In this context one should mention the fact that different countries welcomed Tagore differently. The Germans, for instance, adulated him in a manner not unlike that accorded to contemporary rock musicians, replete with women fainting and people being trampled in stampedes.[2] The English and Americans received him less whole-heartedly, and an analysis of the graph of Tagore's literary fortunes in these two countries offers fascinating insights into cross-cultural relations, providing a perfect case-history of the English-speaking world's initial acceptance but ultimate rejection of the stereotypical wise man from the Orient. Tagore's fears quoted at the head of this section were prophetic, bearing an uncanny resemblance to the actual stages of his English reputation. Many reasons led to this disaffection with Tagore, but above all this survey will expose a real lack of understanding about India (or the Orient, for that matter) as the main cause behind the inability to fathom Tagore. Cultural differences — and often a perceived cultural superiority — created insurmountable barriers. The blame frequently falls on Tagore's symbolism, which in truth could not have been too much more of a problem than the symbolism of Strindberg or Maeterlinck.

Historically speaking, the passage of Tagore's comet through English literary skies came to an end at about the same time that the First World War did. His works in English published after 1918 hardly attracted the phenomenal attention given him earlier. A combination of several secondary factors contributed to this abrupt decline of his reputation. As with most literary fads, the opening euphoria over Tagore was bound to suffer a letdown eventually; the appeal of exoticism has a limited life at best, based as it is on the ephemeral charm of novelty. While the fascination with the bearded mystic from the East wore off, the deluge of substandard translations also took its toll. No dramatist can be expected to survive the publication of so many plays translated so inadequately in so short a span of time: it has been said (perhaps unkindly) that Macmillan, Tagore's publisher, killed the goose that laid their golden eggs. But at the same time, some of the responsibility rests with Tagore himself for churning out many poor renderings in rapid succession despite his awareness of his own imperfect English. To compound the problem, his editors issued the plays without introductions or explanatory notes. Then again, poetic tastes also changed. The mysticism that critics identified Tagore with may have had adherents around the fin de siècle or in the early years of the Georgian period, but the horrors of the War and subsequent European cynicism brought such movements as Imagism to the fore, and Tagore's English versions were ill-prepared to fit these new moulds. Eliot's *Love Song of J. Alfred Prufrock* ushered in a new poetic age in 1917, by the standards of which Tagore's translations soon became passé. Last of all, the rejection of Tagore also resulted from political reasons. The publication by Macmillan of his book of lectures titled *Nationalism* (1917), which advocated pacifism and criticised jingoism, could not have come at a time more inopportune for Tagore's popularity: the West obviously had no patience for anti-war sentiments at this stage of the World War. Moreover, Tagore's resignation of his knighthood in 1919, to protest the killing of unarmed Indians at Jalianwala Bagh by British troops, led in England to a cooling of interest in this "native" who had dared to rebuff the honour bestowed on him by His Majesty.

BOOK REVIEWS

The first Tagore play published in English was *Chitra* (*Chitrāṅgadā*), and it received considerable critical attention because it appeared soon after the announcement of Tagore's Nobel Prize in 1913. Reviewers stressed the point — whether as an echo or independent finding it is impossible to tell — that the play had "a direct and powerful bearing on the question of the emancipation of women."[3] The *New York Times*, under the heading "Tagore's Ideal Woman", paid the author a left-handed compliment: "We did not look for an Oriental, even though a seer, to write a book that might serve as evangel to the most advanced among modern Occidental women". It needs mentioning, perhaps, that this paper had previously caused quite a stir by its racist remarks on the Nobel award to Tagore.[4] Among other periodicals the *American Review of Reviews* commented, in words that might outrage women today, that the play

> ... answers with gravely beautiful symbolism the puzzling questions of feminism, — is woman really the equal of man? Can she share the great duties of his life and retain both her womanliness and his love?

Current Opinion, writing about this "strange Hindu poet", predicted that Chitra "distinctly partakes of the type of the New Woman. Her troubles are those that will beset the next generation when suffrage has borne its fruit." And Abraham Sinberg of the *Colonnade* asked incredulously:

> it cannot be disputed that the idea that, in a true love-union, woman is a loyal partner rather than a beautiful dependent, savors a good deal more of the West than of the East. What can we take this phenomenon to mean, this unmistakably Western major harmony, making a full close to a development built up on weird Oriental scales? Has the feminist movement overcome India? We have no word of such a state of affairs.

Sinberg decided that the explanation lay in Tagore's "Western training".

The critics agreed on another point too, one that would become a commonplace of Tagore criticism. The play was "an allegory rich in suggestiveness", said the *Athenaeum*. But "The discovery of spiritual meanings in every sentence which he pens," warned the London *Nation* in a prophetic utterance, "will end by obscuring the true merit and character". E. M. Forster, who made a gaffe by writing that the play was "to be acted by villagers in India", echoed this observation while stating:

> the play is not the least spoilt by the symbolism. An allegory may be as lame as it likes if it walks quietly, and Tagore's always do that. ... But to drag the allegory from its retirement, and proclaim it has importance in itself is to brutalize the atmosphere and pay no real honour to the author.

The *New York Times* concurred:

> It is an allegory, of course, but not one of those crude modern-mediae-
> val moralities under that name which our western public loves as it
> would any other bright-colored mechanical toy. It is constructed in ac-
> cordance with the theory that the life of each individual repeats in little
> the life of the race.

Ironically, few critics later heeded these early notes of caution not
to over-emphasise the symbolical elements in Tagore's plays, so he
rapidly became typecast as a symbolic dramatist, and ultimately
neglected because of it.

When words of praise came, they were lavish. The reviewer for
the London *Nation* called the play "a beautiful work of art" and
said of its author, "his genius is the genius of the true creator of
beauty, not merely of the ethical or religious teacher deliberately
giving to his doctrine a poetic form." But later, critics would
question Tagore's creative inspiration and accuse him of presenting
ideas as literature. Forster, not one for easy accolades, thought
"The story is told with faultless delicacy and grace." The *New York
Times*, admitting that it had become difficult to discuss Tagore
without hyperbole, offered its own poetic simile: "It is at once as
clear and as profound as a mountain pool." The critic for the *Little
Review* showed an extreme reaction: "Nothing is more irritating to
a really modern critic than to have to join in a chorus of universal
praise," began Arthur Davison Ficke; "this reviewer, who was
about to send the book back with a refusal to review any work of
Tagore, found, after reading a few lines, that he was forced to go
on". He eventually ended up finding it "so perfect a work" that
"the very lifeblood of our own hearts seems quivering with the
intimations of a better-than-godlike beauty." Henry Baerlein of
the London *Bookman* called the play "Simple and beautiful and
grand," avowing that "The beauties of this small book are almost
inexhaustible."

But a few reviewers remained sceptical. The *Times Literary
Supplement* set out with a rationalising thesis to prove Tagore's
dependence on Christian ideals, and considered *Chitra* "disap-
pointing". The reviewer for the New York *Nation* could only allow
that "It is a pretty situation, prettily worked out", and discovered
"something piquant in the combination of the old Hindu metaphorical style, half mystical in allusion, with what is really a plea

for the emancipation of women." The unfamiliar style presented a problem for the *Athenaeum* too: "the prevalence of more or less conventional imagery becomes to the Western mind at times distinctly cloying." Walter de la Mare, writing for the *Westminster Gazette*, applauded Tagore's "astonishing mastery of English" but pointed out occasional phrases "destructive of illusion". The London *Nation* too voiced reservations about the quality of the translation, "which does not appear to be Mr. Tagore's own work", and doubts about its stageability, a theme that became another staple with critics:

> "Chitra" is primarily a poem: from the point of view of Western criticism, more truly poem than play. There is in it much atmosphere, but little action.

The *Boston Evening Transcript*, calling it an "unimpressive piece of work", explained that "it does not seem to take hold of one's imagination", and expressed the opinion that if Tagore had been first introduced to the West through *Chitra* "he would hardly have caused a ripple of interest." And Forster, in order to ensure that Tagore-worshippers do not turn bardolatrous, overstated the case somewhat by insisting that "He is not a seer or a thinker. He is not to be classed with Nietzsche or Whitman".

Tagore's reputation as playwright reached its peak with the publication of *The Post Office* (*Ḍākghar*) in 1914. It comes as a relief to know that even book reviewers on occasion can wax poetic unanimously.[5] A few examples should suffice. Thus, the *New York Times* had this to say:

> Wholly unornamented, artless as the actual speech of a sick child, the a b c of pathos, it yet leaves the reader with the sudden catch of the breath at its abrupt close, the suspense, and the quickened imagination that follow, like a wind, the passing of genius.
> . . . It is not only as "simple as all mysterious things," but, to transpose Mr. Le Gallienne's line, it is as mysterious as all simple things . . . and . . . gives us the threefold clue to freedom — love, purity, and simplicity. If we hold to that clue and follow it, it will lead us out of darkness into starlight.

Comparing the play with *Chitra*, the *Boston Evening Transcript* regarded it as "a much more beautiful and appealing piece of dramatic work . . . there is the essence of the striking symbolism and mystery that has imbued the best work" of Tagore. The normally tight-lipped *Times Literary Supplement* almost grew ecstatic:

> It shows in Mr. Tagore a gift of drama. To read it is to want to have it acted . . . all the time the story is trembling on the edge of allegory, as dawn trembles on the edge of sunrise. And at the end allegory breaks in with its full light of consolation and peace.

The *Athenaeum* contrasted it favourably with Tagore's other plays, where

> characters and situations alike groaned under the weight of the ill-concealed transcendentalism. Here . . . while the symbolic idea is not obtruded, and does not, as we apprehend it, assume inappropriate definiteness, the purely human interest is exquisitely sustained.
> . . . the effect is one of singular unity and beauty.

Almost immediately, though, the reaction set in. Macmillan published *The King of the Dark Chamber* (*Rājā*) shortly after *The Post Office*, and the meaning of the more complex new play confounded most reviewers.[6] The *Athenaeum*, incorrectly identifying it as a play written in Hindustani, considered it "the least successful" of Tagore's works, and remarked fallaciously that "it even bears some signs of having seemed less interesting than the others in its author's eyes" (this about one of Tagore's favourite plays). The *Guardian* chose phrases such as "curious drama" and "strange performance" to describe it—"something from the East not easily appreciated by us Westerns." The reviewer seemed grudgingly resigned to the realisation that "We have to learn from them as they from us." According to the *Manchester Guardian*, "finer memories are to be gained from Mr. Tagore's other works". The *Nation* expressed its "distinct feeling that each fresh volume from that fertile pen is a step downwards" and that the play "will probably do a good service by putting an end" to eulogies of Tagore's work; the *Independent* believed that "its detail may seem trivial to Western readers"; the *Dramatist*, in a somewhat baffled (and baffling) review, discovered in it "something of the mystery and dreaminess of the land of indirection—the land of India." Homer E. Woodbridge, of the *Dial*, found it "refreshing" to turn to an anthology of French drama which he reviewed together with Tagore's play:

> Here is no recondite or symbolical meaning, no prophet or lyricist dis-

guised as a playwright. We go back with a certain sense of relief to the
good old triangle.

Woodbridge's reservations summed up the objections to the
play. Firstly as an allegory it was obviously difficult to accept. "It
suffers principally from the fact," wrote the *Athenaeum*, "that
almost before we have begun to read we have divined the meaning
of the chief symbols, and that the action never unrolls rapidly
enough to anticipate our interpretation of the subsidiary ones."
This paper also questioned "Whether a play can be effective in which
the chief personage often speaks, but never appears". Baerlein of
the *Bookman* found that "the lyrical beauties, which are the great
merit of the 'Gitanjali,' are in 'The King of the Dark Chamber'
somewhat cloaked by the mysticism". The reviewer for the *Manchester Guardian* charged that "the symbolic figures—they are not
characters—are all too anxious to act as Chorus to the play."
Woodbridge constructed his own rather simplistic analysis of the
symbolism by following a similar argument:

> the characters could by no possibility be mistaken for real persons. . .
> the play is an allegory of the conquest of the soul (the Queen) by Love
> (the King), with the help of Humility (Surangama), and the discomfiture of the King's chief rival, Practical Sagacity or Efficiency (Kanchi).

There followed, of course, the inevitable comparison of Tagore's
style and symbolism with that of Maeterlinck.

The second criticism was levelled at the play's theatrical potential. The *Athenaeum* asserted:

> Mr. Tagore is emphatically a lyric, and not a dramatic, poet. . . .
> Drama, as he here presents it, affects us like cumbrous harness fitted
> to the translucent wings of an imago.

Reiterating a common thought, the *Nation* wished to "be allowed
to enjoy the really charming lyrics of our Hindu poet" instead of
plays like this one. "It is not a play which could well be acted,"
claimed Baerlein, "because the flitting to and fro of a number of
characters seems to be governed by no dramatic, but by a loftier
sense." The *Dramatist* echoed this view: "From this single specimen
it would not seem that Rabindranath Tagore possessed any dawning
sense of the dramatic." The *Manchester Guardian* could not even
decide what term to use: "Drama the play is not; poem it is not;
true allegory it is not. It lives only by the lyric flames which destroy

it." With the latter sentence Woodbridge agreed; "There is a good deal of the material of poetry floating around in a rather nebulous state," he said, granting that "there are some pretty lyrics". Curiously enough, the truncated songs in the play came in for some praise from the critics; on the other hand, the prose often did not agree with them. Thus, in the opinion of the *Athenaeum*, words such as "awfully" succeeded in "ringing false in his deliberate chill diction." Baerlein admonished Tagore for frequently using "slang or unpoetic expressions which are at variance with the atmosphere". And the *Guardian* remarked with tongue in cheek that the play "shows that the natives of India can master English colloquialisms."

A few exceptional reviewers remained loyal. The *Times Literary Supplement* praised Tagore's "steady vision into the profound secrets of the spirit" and the "passages of exquisite beauty" in the play, and contended:

> the refreshment of coming into contact with a mind like Mr. Tagore's, is a privilege for which this age in the West should be especially grateful. . . . He that had mastered all that *Chitra* and *The King of the Dark Chamber* had to tell him, would have no lack of intelligence in love.

Alice Henderson wrote in *Poetry* that "Tagore indeed records a joy that it is impossible for many of us of the western mold of faith to attain". She recounted an incident that occurred in Cambridge, Massachusetts, during Tagore's reading of the play there—to the "complete mystification" of the audience—which well illustrates the misconceptions about its theme. Apparently one lady courageously ventured her opinion, addressing Tagore:

> "I suppose that by the King of the dark chamber you mean the spirit of evil. And I suppose, that in your eastern, oriental way, you mean that we should not struggle against it, but give in to it, be reconciled; but that," drawing herself up proudly, "that is not our western way, Mr. Tagore—*we fight!*"

The *New York Times* responded positively as well, perhaps to some degree obliged to do so, in order to continue to compensate for its insensitive comments when Tagore won the Nobel Prize. In the leading article on the front page of the book-review section, Helen Bullis recognised that "all the poems and dramas Tagore has so far given us in English deal with the adventures of the soul", and congratulated him on his handling of allegory, "a form of which Tagore is the greatest living master; probably because he never submerges the artist in the preacher; the moral is not crammed down the reader's throat." She also perceptively connected the play with Tagore's translations of the fifteenth-century Indian mystic poet Kabir.

Late in 1916 the American branch of Macmillan issued a special ten-volume collection of previously published Tagore works named the Bolpur Edition, after the town in Bengal where Tagore established his school and later his university. The edition did not contain anything new, so most periodicals ignored its appearance. The notable exception once again was the *New York Times*, which reserved the entire front page of its book-review section for a notice.[7] The critic singled out *The Post Office* for praise:

> the humor and the tender fancy shown in this play must be personal, and must flow from the personality of a great artist. We contrasted "The Post Office" with a European play on the same theme, with Hauptmann's "Hannele," and then began to realize the significance for us that was in the work of the Indian artist.

The review concluded with a paean to Tagore:

> if he is not the greatest secular figure in the world, he is the one that is most worthy of our attention and our reverence today. At a time when man and man, nation and nation, ideal and ideal is so tragically divided he comes forward to tell us that not in power but in comprehension is the fulfilment of man's existence.

Tagore's next play available in English, *The Cycle of Spring* (*Phālgunī*), was widely reviewed after its publication in 1917. Ironically Bengali critics had panned the original version as a relatively trivial exercise; but what had seemed merely simple to the Bengali reviewer must have appeared easily understandable to his English counterpart. Consequently, as had happened earlier with *The Post Office*, several writers approved of the play no doubt precisely because its ideas were accessible and uncomplicated.[8] The *New York Times* took the lead: "it proclaims the immortality of spirit, the ever-recurring rebirth of life into youth and hope for the saving of the world." According to the *American Review of Reviews*, "Poetry, philosophy, and the beauty of youth live in every scene of the play." Reginald Buckley wrote in the *Bookman* that "one has an almost perfect art-form, simple enough to be played by boys, yet a very malleable medium for poetry." *Theatre Arts Magazine*, in its second year of existence, seemed impressed by "the delicacy of his feeling." But the reviewer continued:

> the volume as a whole seems the least important of his works so far published in this country. If drama implies action in the American sense, this is indeed leisurely drama—if drama at all. . . . It is musical in expression, philosophically interesting, and at times lyrically beautiful; but it is not a theatre-play.

While the observation about its importance is correct, the final judgment is questionable: many writers have testified to its entrancing charm on the Bengali stage, and the *New York Times* attested to its "essentially dramatic quality" too. Critics also noticed an element in this play hitherto in short supply in Tagore: "humor bubbles through it," noted the *New York Times*, "and every now and then it sparkles with wit, wit that sometimes is sharply barbed for a thrust at some meanness in human nature." The *Catholic World* pronounced that "It is pungent . . . with a growing spirit of irony".

Clearly, however, approbation of the play was by no means a consensus, as it had been in the case of *The Post Office*. Buckley apologised for its defects in a roundabout way: "translation, and the absence of music, may be responsible for an unsatisfied feeling that the play is what lawyers would call 'inchoate.'" Others were less kind. The critic for the *Nation*, O.W. Firkins, at least remained consistent in his rejection of Tagore:

> I am alive to something half-celestial in the daintiness, the sleekness, and the pliancy of its wavy and murmurous English. But my heart remains hard; I do not like books that put up their mouths to be kissed.

He had no patience for scenes that "flutter and twitter with a band of young Hindus who want neither to ask nor answer, neither to teach nor listen, but simply to merge themselves in the gayety of the world as it reveals itself in mellowing sky and opening leaf-bud." The *Independent* commented sharply:

> Tagore's greatly overestimated wit, wisdom, mysticism, pleasantness, cast again their glamor. Considered as a play *The Cycle* lacks, however, complicating forces, and, therefore, development, characterization, interest, climax. It is chaotic art. . . . Here is not a tithe of the

atmosphere of Maeterlinck's "Pelleas and Melisande" ... Yeats and ...
Francis Jammes have incomparably more intimacy with both humanity
and nature than is here or elsewhere yet shown in Tagore. Still the
world will always crown glamour, renunciation, the sentiments and
the exotics.

The *Catholic World* gently relegated the play to a lesser category
by stating "it is likely to delight the *habitués* of those exotic 'little
theatres' springing up on all sides."

In spite of the mounting critical impatience with Tagore, new
translations kept arriving. The anthology titled *"Sacrifice" and
Other Plays* (1917) included four plays from Tagore's nineteenth-
century output, generally less complex than his twentieth-century
work and therefore more easy to comprehend.[9] Nevertheless,
reviews sharply declined in number; it seemed that the Tagore
craze, a brief phenomenon at best, had finally subsided.[10] Hardly
any notices appeared in British journals: the *London Quarterly
Review* reported noncommittally, "These plays seem to take
Western readers into a new world." Moreover, positive commentary now became the exception, and when it came, it subtly implied
the cultural superiority of the West. Thus, the *American Review of
Reviews* suggested that "the teachings are more forceful, and
emerge from the philosophy of the East in sharp, definite outlines
which are satisfying to the Western mind." *Theatre Arts Magazine*
began with praise, then followed it up with cultural comparisons
not entirely benign:

> Exquisitely worded, studded with philosophical observations, and
> pretty in legend, any one of the four plays here collected might stand
> as representative of the talents and genius of the great Indian poet-dra-
> matist. The action is elusive, and there is a total lack of the drive, the
> directness and the compactness which with [*sic*] Western playwrights
> spell the essence of drama. For this very reason, to show our loss as
> well as our gain, we hope that some of the experimental theatres in
> America will bring these delicate studies to their stages.

Other reviewers put their objections in stronger language. Padraic
Colum of the *Dial* stated, not without some truth in the first sentence below:

> Not one of the plays given in the volume is at all on a level with "The
> Post Office," or "The King of the Dark Chamber," or "Chitra." The

persons in these five [sic] plays have the indistinctness of character that
is in romances composed by children. And the dooms meted out to these
persons are just such dooms as imaginative children would be touched
by. For each of the plays there is a philosophic setting, but then the
children of a philosophic people might lisp in such terms.

As usual, O.W. Firkins did not have complimentary things to say,
but he did analyse the plays individually. *Sacrifice* did not appeal
to him at all, because of "the dramatic futility of the busily idle
succession of scenes, shrill with quarrel and sibilant with conspiracy,
in which the play rummages for the plot it cannot find." *Malini*
"contains both ideas and situations, which consume thirty-five
ineffectual pages in the vain quest of a rendezvous." As for *Sanyasi*,
"The sketches of common life in this play surprise us a little by
their incisiveness. The cynicisms of a sentimentalist . . . are often
his sanities and perspicacities, and the imponderable Tagore, in
seeking the vulgar, attains the human." Finally, "The highest
promise and the worst disappointment" comes in *The King and the
Queen* which, "turning aside to insignificant and uninteresting
things, concludes with a *coup de théâtre* the flashiness of which is
as incontestable as its brilliancy."

Translations of Tagore's dramatic dialogues appeared in an
anthology titled *The Fugitive* (1921).[11] Critics did not receive it
very warmly; one review bore as its title "Moonshine from the
East", and another reverted to the standard stereotype of Tagore,
reviewing the book along with one by the Japanese poet Yone
Noguchi under the heading "Two Wise Men from the East".[12]
There was no longer any attempt to appreciate Tagore. The *Manchester Guardian* remarked frankly, "We treasure the volume as we
treasure a Persian carpet or a Japanese print; the colour is good,
but we do not understand the thoughts of those quaint figures".
The *Saturday Review* found Tagore deficient in vision compared
to William Blake, commenting with a tinge of sarcasm that "even
nothing, said by Tagore, is sure to be said very smoothly, very
felicitously;" it criticised Tagore's lavish use of metaphors, which
usually "slide like skating-beetles along the smooth levels of the
obvious." Fillmore Hyde of the *Literary Review* repeated the same
allegation, and his charges developed at times into pure vitriol:

Tagore's mind is Oriental in its belief that the only knowledge worth
acquiring is the knowledge that can never be acquired. He pecks for-
lornly at meaning. . . .

. . . Alas! he "sells" himself badly. He is guilty of writing stuff that is
bad prose and is certainly not poetry. . . . His crimes against metaphor
are countless. But the fact remains that few people think so sweetly. . . .

It is in a sense unfortunate that life is too short to warrant our
seeking out a wonderfully sensitive and percipient man who does not
know how to show himself. . . . We have no time for Orientalism. We
have no time for a man who is no friend to us. We Occidentals, when a
poet maintains that nonsense means something, can hardly be expected
to forgive him a criticism so terribly caustic.

Equally damaging in its own way was the sugary praise of the *Dial*:

> In this volume is to be seen the rare, shimmering beauty typical of
> Tagore, a glow as of remote sunsets, of sea-sand glittering on far-off
> beaches, of snow on the peaks of dawn-flushed mountains, and of
> music heard in a dream . . . pervaded with a faint dreaminess, . . .
> they have the vagueness of wind-blown perfume, yet there is a rich
> spiritual beauty in them all.

The *Manchester Guardian*, too, caught "gleams and jewels of vision-
ary beauty" but refused to fall under their spell: "as we know his
incense more we like it less". The critic for the *Sunday Times* must
have astonished everybody with his contention that Tagore "never,
in our judgment, has surpassed this". But even he could not avoid
the usual cliches of orientalism: "it is a world of shadows, and at
any turn there may open glimpses of the reality, for which the
Eastern seers for ever hunger." The only reviewer who actually
mentioned the plays in the book, Richard Le Gallienne of the
New York Times, surprisingly recommended them: "The most
striking portions . . . are the little symbolic dramas . . . simply
written, they have the qualities of a fairy tale and a 'morality' combined, and they are stark in outline and relentless in their irony as
Ibsen."

The nadir of Tagore's reputation as a dramatist in English came
with the publication of *Red Oleanders* (*Rakta-karavī*) in 1925.
Reviews agreed unanimously on its demerits.[13] One of the first,
in the *Times Literary Supplement*, summed up the new attitude:

> it is frankly difficult to make anything of the symbolism . . . Tagore
> seems to depend on the very vagueness of his style for whatever meaning
> the drama can support. For the greater part of the time, it is quite im-
> possible to discover what is happening . . . there is not the faintest at-
> tempt to present the few scattered and mysterious events in a logical

sequence . . . the characters of the play are sufficiently lifeless to com-
pel one to wonder what intellectual or moral purpose they can possibly
serve. . . .

The most acute of Tagore's literary failings is perhaps a rather un-
bridled passion for metaphor. In "Red Oleanders" the profusion of
metaphor is particularly trying. . . . Tagore has been far more occupied
with mere words than it is the business either of the dramatist or the
poet to be. The entire dialogue is persistently sententious. But it is not
profound.

A reputed scholar like Gilbert Norwood found strange consola-
tions in the play:

> though the purport of the whole escapes a Westerner . . . the dialogue
> ever and anon shows wonderful beauty and piercing wisdom: the play
> is a haystack full of needles. . . . As a drama in any European (even the
> Maeterlinckian) sense *Red Oleanders* is out of the question. . . . But
> this kind of work provides the best means whereby we Occidentals may
> understand Russian literature. Dostoevsky and Tchehov stand half-
> way between the mercilessly clear thinking, the moral lucidity, the sense
> of structure which are our dramatic ideals, and the lovely plangent
> elusiveness of Tagore.

A similar opinion was expressed by the *Saturday Review of Literature*, which regarded the play as

> almost unintelligible to the definite, more matter-of-fact Anglo-Saxon
> mind. We confess to a steadily growing sense of baffled bewilderment
> as we read page after page of "Red Oleanders." There were times when
> Truth did seem about to poke its head out of the maze and Reality to
> be just around the corner, but never once did either come out and stand
> fairly and squarely in the open for all to see. This doesn't seem to be
> playing quite fair with readers. . . . Why write in the play form if one
> never expects to make one's people real enough to be able to appear
> on any stage . . . ?

The writer conceded that many of the lines "are full of poetical
beauty" and often "philosophically illuminating". But on the
whole, "the reader wallows in a kind of heavy, sleep-provoking
sweetness in which the mind becomes gradually inactive." The
Bookman offered the lone comparatively sympathetic review: "the
interest is not dramatic, but philosophic. . . . The drama is really a
drama of ideas, and as such it certainly deserves to be called a
drama." The reviewer commended the "satirical and poetic thought

which is condensed with great clarity and suggestiveness".

Understandably, Tagore never published any other play in English translation in the West after this disaster. Eleven years later Macmillan released his *Collected Poems and Plays* ("Selected" would have been a more accurate appellation). Perhaps because of the intervening gap during which Tagore had virtually disappeared from the world of English literature, critics gave this collection warmer notices.[14] Vincent Engels in the *Commonweal* called the plays "beautiful", compared *The Post Office* with Chekhov and observed that the prelude to the "lively" *Cycle of Spring* was "better than Gilbert and Sullivan." For the *Boston Evening Transcript*, Barrett Parker opined that "it is of the keenest spiritual and intellectual interest to consider the character and writings" of Tagore. He credited Tagore's literary achievements, preferring the plays to the poetry, and lamented the absence of any editorial commentary accompanying the selections:

> Although much of the translation is in prose, Tagore nevertheless writes in English in a style sparkling and flexible, having in it the song of the birds and the touch of the texture of firm earth. He speaks to us with the wisdom of the ages . . . the plays, dealing more simply and directly with the life of the people, are firmer in continuity, more complete in motivation.
>
> It is to be regretted that this volume . . . should be edited without introduction, foreword, or preface of any kind, and without notes on deletions or on any of the translations.

Robert Keighton of the *Crozer Quarterly* discovered in the book

> a soft, diffused feeling of beauty and truth. Here and there is a veritable gem, but one does not hasten to reach them, nor does one search for them alone; every page has its quieting assurance or encouraging inspiration.

Theatre Arts generously commented that "It is simple, fluid, gracious in style, wise and sane in philosophy . . . a source of contentment in the days of exaggerated imagery, incomprehensible free verse, immature pseudo-philosophizing, bleak pessimism". Yet the response in England still remained cool. In the *London Mercury* Hugh Fausset complained of Tagore's "mellifluous musing", but condescendingly approved of the fact that "an Eastern poet has attained such fluent mastery of the English tongue." He continued:

Certainly his plays provide some relief. Yet there is more of lyrical meditation in them than there is of drama or of character, while the scenes tend to be as loosely connected and to succeed each other with as little inner necessity as the sections in his prose poems.

After Tagore's death hardly any new translations of the plays reached the English-reading public outside India. The few that did attracted little attention from reviewers. The situation remains unchanged today. We may believe nowadays that time has made the average Western reader more empathetic, more amenable to non-Western literature and the cultural differences that raise obstacles in understanding it. Lest we become too complacent in that assumption, however, I conclude this survey with the following remark by George Cloyne from the London *Times* of 1961:[15]

I have been reading *The King of the Dark Chamber*, and a thinner piece of hocus-pocus in English would be hard to find. Yet we must take the experts' word for it that the original text trembles with meaning.

PLAY REVIEWS

The first Tagore play performed in English was *The Post Office*. Even before the original Bengali version was staged or the English translation published, it had its world premiere at the Abbey Theatre in Dublin on 17 May 1913, under the direction of W.B. Yeats and Lady Gregory. The production moved to the Court Theatre in London in the summer on a double bill with Synge's *The Well of the Saints*, and the reviews in London papers became the first critical responses in England to Tagore's plays.[16] The opening sentence of the review in the *Times* struck the note that would henceforth dominate most criticism of his drama, by calling it a "dreamy, symbolical, spiritual play". Other critics categorised it as a "dream play" (the *Standard*) or an "allegory which is barely definable" (the *Evening Standard*). That the *Times* reviewer — like so many others after him — did not quite know what to make of this new dramatist is evident in the following comment: "It is a curious play, leaving to a certain extent a sense of incompleteness, since it ends before its climax, rich in poetical thought and imagery, as well as in a kind of symbolism that must not be pressed too closely." That the reviewer himself may have pressed the symbolism too closely is apparent in his next observation, "The King . . . is presumably the King of this country." As early as this notice, the awkwardness of English translations of Tagore's plays becomes clear: "such expressions as 'awfully,' 'jolly good,' and 'shut up' contrast strangely with the beauty of most of Mr. Tagore's language".

The critic also noted that most of the actors, "though they did their best to represent Indian natives, remained always Irishmen." An American spectator corroborated this view in a letter; "I don't think the Irish Players the best ones to have produced it", wrote Harriet Tilden Moody, wife of the poet William Vaughn Moody.[17] In his book on Tagore Ernest Rhys recorded a similar impression: "even with the drawback of having a partly Irish, instead of an Indian, characterisation of its village humours, it proved moving and particularly effective in the stroke of tragedy redeemed at the close."[18] Regarding individual performers, the *Era* reported that "This delicate and mystic little piece was admirably acted . . . Lilian Jagoe giving a very impressive and pathetically beautiful portrayal of little Amal, . . . one that will long linger in the memory." The *Stage* followed suit, commending her performance as a "tearfully wistful and delicately fanciful and poetical impersonation", and praising the "sweet simplicity" of Lennox Robinson's sets:

> it consisted merely of a screen or framework, with backing of contrasted hue. Thus, the exterior of Madhav's house was shown as white, with jet-black background, and the interior as of crimson colour, with deep green to represent the opening beyond.

Robinson himself later referred to the sets as "Gordon Craig Screens".[19]

Other critics were not particularly impressed. The *Westminster Gazette* looked down upon the production with a patronising tone:

> it is one of those elaborate attempts to be simple and elemental which are favored by those who by non-commercial drama mean drama that nobody would pay to see . . . no doubt it is a creditable attempt by an Indian gentleman to write a play. But it was all on one note and never moved one inch; and . . . I cannot remember anything said by anybody to cause it to go on even for the short time that it lasted. And what induced these Irish players to take it up I cannot guess.

The reviewers for the *Globe* and the *Standard* raised doubts concerning its theatrical potential, the former bluntly stating that "Play is scarcely the right name for 'The Post Office,' which is really a poetic and conversational fragment, with no pretence to anything approaching drama."

One should mention the fact that Tagore frequently read from his plays in the course of his foreign tours, but these public readings fall outside the strict purview of this study; moreover, they are not well documented.[20] Paucity of documentation also hinders attempts to reconstruct the productions of some Tagore plays which occurred during the years of the World War. On 8 June 1915 the Indian Dramatic Society gave a "costume recital" of *Malini* at Grafton Galleries in London, for the benefit of wounded Indian soldiers.[21] Writing in 1917, William Chislett observes that the "divine *Chitra*" and the "exquisite *Post-office*" were performed "unforgettably" in Los Angeles, but does not specify the date, place or occasion if any.[22] According to the records of Allardyce Nicoll a production of *Sacrifice*, again by the Indian Dramatic Society, took place at King George's Hall in London on 9 February 1918, but apparently no reviews appeared.[23]

On 12 February 1919 the Indian Art and Dramatic Society presented at the Comedy Theatre in London a matinee bill of two plays, one of them Tagore's *The King and the Queen*.[24] The *Era* found the characterisation "very strong", especially the parts of Vikram ("surely the Indian Hamlet") and Sumitra. The production played in front of "a beautiful setting of black curtains, against which the superb garments of the East were in violent, but most effective, contrast." However, the reviewer for the *Stage* noticed several obvious defects, particularly the "over-violent transitions". Tagore disappoints us, he felt, because "the Queen fades away into becoming merely a weak . . . woman, instead of developing into a Joan of Arc, a Queen Elizabeth, or a Maria Theresa". The subplot involving Ila shifts interest "in a most unexpected manner", and the Queen's entrance at the conclusion "bearing, in gruesome Eastern fashion, the wrapped-up head of her brother" contributes to an "unsatisfactory inconclusive end". Despite able performances by the British actor and actress in the titular roles, the overwhelming impression was of "a strange play". This reviewer had, in fact, pinpointed the shortcomings of the original Bengali script, magnified in the telescoped translation which additionally made "motives insufficiently clear" and the King's transformation "extraordinarily rapid".

Nicoll mentions a performance of *Autumn Festival* (Tagore's translation of *Śāradotsav*) by the Union of East and West at Wigmore Hall in London on 6 March 1920, of which no reviews seem to have survived. Under the auspices of the same organisation, the Indian Art and Dramatic Society staged *Sacrifice* and *Chitra* at the Prince of Wales' Theatre on 4 May. It proved to be one of the very few Tagore productions in English that have gathered generally positive critical reactions.[25] In the opinion of the *Daily Telegraph*, *Sacrifice* "was all true, human, and moving", containing "dignity and . . . wealth of imagery"; and *Chitra* "is a beautifully-told story . . . splendidly cast," featuring the "best acting of the afternoon." The *Stage* praised Frederic Sargent's firm grip over the role of Raghupati the priest in *Sacrifice*, given the "sudden change" in his implacable character, though the *Daily Telegraph* accused him of spoiling the effect "by allowing himself to rant most uncomfortably" at the end of the play. Both the latter paper and the *Observer* applauded the singing of Marjorie Gordon as the girl Aparna, which "helped considerably in creating the atmosphere". They congratulated John Foulds on his music, but the *Observer* did not take too kindly to the orchestral setting of "Butterfly" before the curtain and "Samson" afterwards. The *Observer* also described the effective absence of scenery: "two pairs of curtains and unlimited lighting" gave a "convincing" representation, particularly in the "beautifully played" *Chitra* where the dark curtains had the "advantage of concentrating attention on the two actors".

When Tagore visited England later in the year, he helped in rehearsals for a performance of his newly translated dramatic dialogues by the Union of East and West at Wigmore Hall on 28 July. His son remembers that the plays, conforming to Tagore's ideals, "were given . . . without elaborate stage effects, with only a simple background of blue curtain and some pot plants and two spot lights."[26] He thought the production was "on the whole very effective", citing in particular the dumb show before "Kacha and Devayani" suggested by his father to set the mood. He regretted, however, that the plays had not been offered earlier in the season, as "all the best people" had left town. "Still the hall was filled," he recalls, "and I could feel that the audience was appreciative."

Nicoll gives the names of the plays as follows —"The Mother's Prayer", "The Farewell Curse", "The Deserted Mother", "The Sinner", "Suttee"—presumably the working titles before their publication the following year in *The Fugitive*.

The Union of East and West next tried its luck across the Atlantic, staging *Sacrifice* and *The Post Office* at the Garrick Theatre in New York on 10 December the same year. How far the climate for Tagore's work had changed in America can easily be assessed from the reviews.[27] Alexander Woollcott of the *New York Times* regarded it as a production which "at its best, is merely oratorical and, at its worst, unbelievably grotesque." He acknowledged that *The Post Office* "is a beautiful and gently pathetic work which can tug at the heartstrings", but considered the performance "obfuscating and singularly deterrent". He specifically attacked Lilian Jagoe's impersonation of the little boy Amal — a curious objection, since she had acted the same role at the premiere and received praise for it:

> To see this part played not by a little boy but by an adult woman is to witness a monstrous perversion of the play . . . to watch her translating the boyish wistfulness and shyness into an extremely feminine, incorrigibly fliratious [*sic*] cajolery.

Woollcott dismissed *Sacrifice* as having "little . . . to commend it", and protested its clumsy presentation, "which would never be tolerated in the much-derided commercial theatre and which achieved its deepest impressions with an Indian General rigged up to look quite killingly like the late Queen Victoria". O.W. Firkins, drama critic for the *Weekly Review*, disapproved of the performances too. Although he appreciated Jagoe's "incomparable" voice, he did not like the sombre tone of the production and concluded:

> One feels that a lancet applied to the veins of these people would extract nothing more formidable than gelatine or metaphor. The fact that all the actors mouth or globe their lines with a gusto far too solemn to be serious increases the believer's difficulties.

Undoubtedly the production as well as the translation may have possessed flaws, but one can also sense the new antipathy towards Tagore by reading between the lines.

The plays in *The Fugitive* were revived by the Union of East and

West in London, on 24 and 26 July 1924, "in the open in the charming gardens of The Hill, Lord Leverhulme's Hampstead residence,
which afforded a delightful setting."[28] Only some photographs of
this production survive, which bear testimony to the unusual
picturesque surroundings; if nothing else the setting must have
helped evoke the right atmosphere for Tagore's dramas. Nicoll
records also that a play titled "The Farewell"—no doubt a version
of "The Farewell Curse"—was staged at the Devonshire Park
Theatre in Eastbourne on 4 September the same year. These productions marked the beginning of a long hiatus of nearly thirty
years during which period no important performances of Tagore's
plays occurred in England; the interval was even longer in America.

After the Second World War major productions of Tagore plays
have reached England and America just twice, once in London and
once in New York, both significantly done by Indian directors.
In May 1952 the East and West Drama Society staged *Sacrifice*
and *The Post Office* as the first event in an international drama
festival at the Irving Theatre, London. According to the London
Times, Tarun Roy directed "with great simplicity so that the im-
plicit message of each play can make its effect unmarred by elaborate stage effects."[29] But immediately came the by-now predic-
table cautionary note: "Both plays are symbolic and they seem,
to western eyes, to be more essays in literary allegory than subjects
for drama as we see it." The critic did observe that *Sacrifice* is
much abridged, which "may well explain why it seems here awkward
and unconvincing." During the course of the Tagore centenary
celebrations in 1961 several American university theatres produced
his plays, but the special nature of the occasion unfortunately sets
them aside as curiosities; none of them made any significant impact.[30]

If these performances did not receive much attention, the one
of *The King of the Dark Chamber* in New York compensated
amply.[31] The director, Krishna Shah, had first staged it at Iowa
State University in 1960, then entered it in the Midwest Colleges
Drama Conference where it had taken honours.[32] It started an off-
Broadway run at the Jan Hus House in February 1961, and continued for quite a few months at several shows each week, with
full or near-capacity houses each time.[33] The production was a
minor sensation. Howard Taubman of the *New York Times* termed
it "a striking amalgamation of mime, song, dance and poetry. Its

appeal is to the mind as well as the senses." Evidently inspired, Robert Brustein wrote in the *New Republic* that the play

> more than compensates for off Broadway's recent failures, for it fulfills the highest function of the minority theatre. This 20th Century Indian masterpiece, with its allegorical fairy-tale atmosphere and its highly charged poetic intensity, is a stunning theatrical work. . . . Clearly an inspired dramatic artist, Tagore manages to exploit all the various resources of the stage—music, mime, chorus, lyrical speech, song, declamation, gesture, makeup, costume—in a completely original manner. For in his hands, the conventions of Eastern theatre are liberating devices rather than restrictions, freeing his imagination to an extent almost unequalled in modern Western tradition. Tagore's dramatic world is so multifarious that elements of broad farcical humor, sinister melodrama, and metaphysical soul-drama can jostle each other with no apparent friction; and his dramatic action is so multi-leveled that it becomes fairy tale, metaphor, and philosophy all at once.

One indeed wonders if this is the same Tagore to whom critics reacted ambivalently half a century previously. Like Taubman, Brustein spoke of the "charming and child-like naïveté" in Tagore's play—a "ceremony of innocence that Yeats (in his *Plays for Dancers*) and Brecht (in his *Caucasian Chalk Circle*) tried to restore to the Western theatre as a necessary antidote to the cliches of an exhausted realism". Theophilus Lewis, the reviewer for *America*, said "Tagore's mystical drama is the most beautiful production of the season." In the *Christian Century* Tom Driver commented, "The universalism of Tagore's play will not be questioned." In more popular terminology, *Life* magazine called it "Fantastic and sensual, but astir with spiritual overtones, a poetic play by a wise man of India". Most of the reviewers complimented the deep baritone of Brock Peters as the Voice of the king, and the graceful performance of Surya Kumari as his queen.

Howard Taubman was affected deeply enough to write a second piece two months later comparing the themes of Tagore's play and Dylan Thomas' *Under Milk Wood* (playing at the Circle in the Square), a comparison which coincidentally Tom Driver also made. Taubman found that "Tagore affirms his faith in the possibilities of man." However, Driver stumbled slightly: ı

> both plays are to some extent influenced by Christian thought. . . . One sees in these works the Christian ethic of love, and even Christian

sacramentalism, absorbed into non-Christian mysticism . . . the as-
sertion that man has within him all that he needs to have and that no
change at all is needed in his society . . . cuts short the historical realism
of the West. It is our Western genius that we take particulars seriously.
. . . We have much to learn from the East . . . but we dare not forget
the wisdom of our own past.

But he did point out the "allegory of the soul" in the play, and he
considered the scenes in the dark chamber, done in silhouette,
"especially moving because of their bold use of the language of
erotic love to express the soul's love of God." As for the layman's
reaction to the theme, Theophilus Lewis probably expressed it
most honestly:

> The play is full of symbols and mystical allusions which your reviewer,
> who was never good at solving puzzles, did not attempt to decipher. He
> was amply rewarded by the exotic beauty of the performance and
> staging.

Exoticism may indeed have been an important element in the
production's success. The reviews dwelt more upon the sensuous
— especially the visual — aspect of the performance rather than the
thematic. In explaining to his readers about Shah's use of mudras,
Taubman wrote:

> It is doubtful that on initial acquaintance a Westerner will absorb all
> the levels of communication . . . .
> [But] There is an immediacy of communication in the rhythms of
> speech, chanted verse, song and dance, which bridge the gulf of remote-
> ness.

He concluded with the belief that "this production speaks a language of the theatre that willing eyes and ears can appreciate."
Lewis added perceptively:

> As a series of stage pictures, the play will appeal to connoisseurs of
> lacquer and jade.
> . . . Still, one wonders if Tagore's ghost, wandering into the Jan
> Hus, would be pleased with a production that distracts attention
> from the mystical import of the play.

In this light, Taubman's remark that the show projected "an
atmosphere that charms and diverts" gains an extra dimension.
Writing for the *New Yorker*, Whitney Balliett confirmed the
superficial appeal of the production:

It is not so much Tagore's thought that entrances one, however, as the play's heady visual fragments -- the wicked kings with their towering gold-and-white templelike hats and garish clown faces; a dancer, bare to the waist, moving slowly toward the back of the stage, his arms straight out and waving like seaweed, his back muscles revolving incredibly in opposite directions; and the terrible King himself, whom we never see, gliding in a tall, muscular silhouette through the dark chamber toward his tiny, quivering Queen.

And as a guide to the average theatre-goer's response, *Life* magazine provided the crucial bit of evidence:

the play has the air of old-fashioned allegory. But for many playgoers this is redeemed by its jingling dancers, exotic Hindu melodies and parades of myth-begotten potentates.

It is perhaps unfortunate that Krishna Shah did not live up to his own intentions, spelt out in his programme notes:[34]

It is vital that the factor of novelty not become the keynote of the production. The exotic flavor of the Orient should not be unduly stressed to the detriment of the basic thesis of the play. Whatever "spectacle" is natural to the play should be aesthetically conceived. The director should attempt to recreate the lyrical and exciting theatre that Tagore intended.

Yet he interpolated sequences in the performance that the original play did not warrant. Some of these may certainly have been legitimate and inventive theatrical devices, such as the elaborate use of classical Indian mudras, or of a *yātrā*-style chorus which also physically functioned as trees, lamps, doors and flames. But other intrusions, like the gorgeously decorated set, the role of a "King's Cosmic Dancer" and particularly the danced battle in which the king defeats his enemies, may indeed have contributed unwittingly to a spectacular production that inadvertently subverted the theme. Undeniably, however, Shah deserves lavish praise for exposing American audiences to a representation of Tagore's drama more authentic than anything before or since.

There was the rare dissension, though, among the critics, and this time it came unexpectedly from the reviewer for *Theatre Arts*, Alan Pryce-Jones:

I have been amazed by the reaction of my fellow critics . . . turning their prayer wheels in ecstasy ever since this really terrible piece of

tushery oozed (rather than burst) upon the unlikely surroundings of the
Jan Hus House. . . . This is a very, very slow Indian drama full of
Implications rather than Symbols. . . . All this takes a very long time,
much of it in darkness, and the spoken words are in a kind of Poona
prose poetry.

We come almost full circle again; although a definite exception to
the rule, Pryce-Jones proves that even in recent times there will
always be some who dismiss the unfamiliar as inferior. His comments remind one of the Australian reviewer who wrote in 1925
about a performance of *Chitra* in Sydney:[35]

Bernard Shaw would have made a modern social comedy of it and
carried more conviction. These poetic romances are better in their
natural setting, chanted by a solitary loin-clothed spokesman to the
thumping of a drum while a posse of dancing-girls makes sensuous
explanatory movements.

The difference lies only in degree.

BOOKS AND ARTICLES

Although several articles on Tagore appeared in English and
American periodicals at the height of his popularity in the West,
only a couple had anything significant to say about his drama;
both were written by American women and published in American
journals in 1914.[36] Mary Carolyn Davies, profoundly moved by the
plays, believed "There is a certain grandeur in Tagore's dramatic
work that Shakespeare never attained". Alice Corbin Henderson
displayed critical acumen much ahead of her time by placing
Tagore's work against the proper backdrop of their Indian dramatic
heritage, thus pre-empting adverse criticism about their unsuita-
bility for the stage; she even discussed the plays individually. But
these two surprisingly sensitive and laudatory essays were clearly
atypical. Among the few early books written in English on Tagore
and published outside India, only the one by Ernest Rhys — editor
of Everyman's Library — contained serious material on his plays.
Rhys devoted a full chapter to Tagore as playwright, making occasionally astute observations and unambiguously defending their
lyrical quality: "as if in great drama, in Aeschylus, in Sophocles, in
Shakespeare, in Goethe's *Faust*, there was not any attempt to find
lyrical alleviation on the road to the dramatic climax."[37]

The first major breakthrough in dramatic criticism on Tagore in English came with the publication by Oxford University Press in 1926 of a book by Edward Thompson, a British missionary and author who had served as Principal of Wesleyan College in Bankura (Bengal) and later taught Bengali at Oxford University.[38] He became the first English critic to base his opinions on readings of Tagore in the original Bengali. Thompson reminded his readers that Tagore had written comedies and musical dramas in addition to his available English work, provided them with much background information on Tagore's development beginning with his juvenilia, and quoted extensively from private conversations with Tagore. He made pertinent critical remarks about individual plays and their English editions, often resorting to translating passages more faithfully to show how Tagore departed from the originals in constructing English versions.

Thompson's critical judgments, however, created more problems than they solved. By arbitrarily classifying Tagore's plays into three categories—the early verse plays, the short dramas in rhymed couplets, and the later symbolical prose plays—he gave undue prominence to the small second group and trivialised the importance of the third, while ignoring the musical dramas. Moreover, Thompson's realistic bent of mind could not appreciate what he termed Tagore's "mist of symbolism" (p. 220); regrettably, therefore, a scholar who had little sympathy for Tagore's mature plays ended up writing the first ostensibly authoritative critical work on them. "Whatever fire of human interest was present in the earlier plays is fading out", said Thompson of the later dramas (p. 287). His bias in favour of the verse dramas came out very clearly, having the unfortunate ricochet of influencing the reactions of critics who followed him. The literary and theatrical establishment has still not shaken off the effects of his damaging verdicts, such as "We tire of these mysterious kings" in the plays (p. 224), or the statements that he "wearies of the incessant and unprovoked singing" which goes against dramatic realism (p. 219), and wearies of Tagore's "monotony" and "deadening sameness" (p. 291). Thompson's arguments were also quite uneven; what he disliked in one chapter or paragraph frequently became a praiseworthy item in another, leading to contradictory viewpoints, particularly in his "Epilogue" which often conflicted with what he had suggested earlier.

Most readers remain unaware of Tagore's own feelings about

Thompson's book, for which reason alone they deserve quoting. We must remember that Tagore rarely expressed anger or displeasure in his correspondence, but in a long letter to William Rothenstein he called Thompson's work "one of the most absurd books that I have ever read . . . he has never allowed his readers to guess that he has a very imperfect knowledge of Bengali".[39] Among other things, Tagore referred to Thompson's "pompous spirit of self confidence" and his missionary training which "makes him incapable of understanding some of the ideas that run all through my writings". Coming from the normally polite Tagore, who also knew Thompson personally, these were harsh words indeed. In at least one respect Tagore was correct; Ramananda Chatterjee attested to Thompson's little Bengali in an early review article, a devastating attack on Thompson's scholarship which cited many inaccuracies in his book as well as pointed out his deficient knowledge of Bengali.[40] Surely any writer who translates the title of the play *Arūp Ratan* as "The Ugly Gem" (p. 314) needs to have his credibility questioned. Nevertheless, this book still retains its position as a standard text of Tagore criticism in English. As recently as 1976, for instance, a noted Tagore scholar such as William Radice termed it a "good" book.[41]

Strangest of all, when Thompson revised the book for a second edition published in 1948, he added hardly anything of critical substance in the one chapter that supposedly brought the study up to date. The final twenty years of Tagore's life — almost one-third of his literary career, in which he had remained as prolific and innovative as ever — received such short shrift from Thompson that he did not even mention a masterpiece like *Rakta-karavī* (which at least had merited one cursory sentence in the earlier edition), or most other later works including the season-plays and dance-dramas. Yet from all appearances it purported to be a complete study. The "revisions" consisted mostly of deletions of a few critical superlatives which Thompson probably later regarded as embarrassing or unrestrained. The additional chapter mainly detailed Tagore's foreign tours. This second edition remains an extremely misleading and quite incomplete book, of considerable danger to the novice reader who approaches it wishing to know more about Tagore's work.

Thompson has effectively maintained a virtual monopoly on book-length Tagore criticism in English, indubitably helped by the fact that he had been published by perhaps the most august press in England in the field of literary scholarship. Before Tagore's death only two other writers published books in English outside India that had relevance to his plays; these volumes did not gather much attention probably because their authors were not Englishmen. The first of these, P. Guha-Thakurta's history of Bengali drama (1930), faced the additional disadvantage of dealing with an esoteric subject.[42] Himself a Bengali, Guha-Thakurta reserved three chapters for Tagore in his study, which contained several inaccuracies and spent too much space summarising the plots of the plays, but treated the symbolical dramas with great understanding and offered a chapter on Tagore's dramatic art which still stands as a model of sensitive and empathetic analysis on the subject. The other book was on Tagore, written in Czech by Vincenc Lesný, professor of Indology at Charles University in Prague; it was translated for English publication in 1939.[43] Lesný had translated Tagore into Czech as early as 1914. His work did not contribute anything particularly new, but it did briefly comment on most of the later plays which Thompson completely ignored.

The almost total critical disinterest in Tagore in England and America after his death is conclusively proved by the amazing statistic that, besides a handful of isolated articles in journals and reprint editions of Indian books in English, Mary Lago's volume on Tagore in the Twayne's World Authors Series (1976) exists as the sole original work of literary criticism. And as I have indicated before, that study contains merely four pages on Tagore's plays. Few authors of Tagore's stature have met with such appalling neglect.

VI. PREVIOUS ENGLISH TRANSLATIONS

I was recently going through my translations. I wonder if they are my
own writings. Why did I present myself in this fashion? This is self-
mockery.

[Tagore, letter to Amiya Chakravarty, 7 March 1935][1]

The existing English translations of Tagore's plays present several
problems which require discussion. At the outset, one must recognise the fact that fewer than half of his plays have been translated
into English, although these do include his major works. Moreover,
the available translations give readers in English a lopsided view of
Tagore's dramatic canon, because they concentrate on just two
or three genres in which he wrote, neglecting the others. The best
represented style among the English versions is Tagore's verse
drama: all of the short pieces and five of seven full-length verse plays
exist in English redactions. Of course, as we have seen, Tagore
himself rejected verse drama in his later years. When we come to
his mature prose plays, we find that not even half have been converted into English, though this number does contain the more
important ones. The percentage of translations plummets as one
goes further down the list, for among Tagore's comedies only one
(the shortest) of five full-length plays has been Englished, while just
four of the twenty-plus comic sketches have appeared in English,
three of them as recently as 1983. Only two of Tagore's dance-
dramas have found their way into print in English, one in a little-
known, now-defunct journal, the other hidden in a volume of
original poems by its translator. Finally, not one among Tagore's
early musical plays or later season-plays has appeared in English.

The problem, however, is not solely one of quantity. Tagore, who
himself did or supervised most of the translations, remained per-
petually uncertain about their quality. His letters periodically
betray his concern about the subject. On two separate occasions in
1913, within a year after he began translating his plays, he wrote
"I do not feel equal to expressing myself in English" and "one
cannot quite translate one's own works."[2] Towards the end of his
life he had even reached a frame of mind in which he almost dis-
owned his own translations: "I regret it and am ashamed of it", he
confessed, as well as "It occurs to me that I can never attain a com-

plete knowledge of the language of the Europeans. . . . To trespass
into that territory therefore involves not only failure but indignity".[3]
Tagore seemed fully aware, not only that he lacked a full command
of colloquial English, but also that he was often guilty of writing
faulty English. As early as February 1914 he wrote to William
Rothenstein:[4]

> your language is not easy for me to use. I know I am apt to make a mess
> of your prepositions and in my blissful ignorance I go on dropping
> your articles in wrong places or dropping them out altogether. Then
> I do not know set phrases which greatly economise trouble in sentence
> making and very often I do not know how to write simple matter of
> fact things in English . . . little learning is a dangerous thing.

Even if we concede a good share of humility to these remarks, they
may at first be hard to believe, because Tagore's nonfictional
English prose reads perfectly well, and some passages from his
English poetry can stand their own against the best of poetry in the
English language. But these passages are the exception, not the
rule; and in terms of literary craftsmanship a good writer of prose
does not necessarily make a good poet or dramatist.

In a pioneering essay Shyamal Kumar Sarkar has examined
Tagore's translating practices. To begin with, most translators work
from a less familiar language to a more familiar one, but Tagore
worked in the opposite direction.[5] We have on the authority of
Amiya Chakravarty, Tagore's personal secretary for many years,
that "his English was just as true, but it was rather in the grand
manner. He never quite grasped the conversational" and "just
missed the modern touch" since he hardly encountered spoken
English used on a "nonintellectual" level.[6] Furthermore, according
to Sarkar's findings, Tagore rarely spent premium time on translation. He started translating poems as a diversion (resulting in
Gitanjali), but also translated for therapeutic reasons — when he
felt mentally tired, for instance — and when under public pressure
to produce samples of his work in English, as for example during
his 1912–13 trip to England and America.[7] Sarkar points out in
addition that Tagore took full advantage of his unusual position as
author as well as translator; as creator of his works, he possessed
the liberty to do whatever he pleased in recreating them in translation, which the normal translator is inhibited from doing. Again
from his letters we learn the following facts: "When I write in

English I give way to the subconscious", and "I cannot translate, I have to write almost anew."[8] Consequently Tagore never did translate; he attempted to "transcreate", however, and often derived great joy from this exercise.[9] Although this method worked successfully in producing some excellent poems in *Gitanjali*, it understandably bore erratic results in his much longer dramatic compositions. Tagore admitted ruefully later on, "I have done great injustice to my own writings in translating them — There was much slackness and so much impudence perhaps because they were my own writings."[10]

The first play that Tagore translated was *Chitra*, while in England in 1912.[11] It appeared under the imprint of the India Society the next year, and is one of his better efforts at translation. Some of the original beauty of language and much of the wonderful imagery comes across in English, but it also displays Tagore's typically bad translating habits. Without exception, he converted his verse plays into plain prose, and greatly condensed the original texts. The eleven scenes of the original play thus become nine scenes in *Chitra*. Such methods make it impossible to treat any of Tagore's English recensions as faithful. Also characteristic of Tagore's English is the use of "thou", "thee" and their variants, a common feature in his translated poetry, which not only makes his language rather dated but also injects a formal note absent in the Bengali. One modern scholar explores the relation to characterisation of Tagore's "you" and "thou" in *Chitra*, proving the danger of taking his English too seriously, because Tagore clearly employed the pronouns without any definite pattern.[12] Tagore also had the English-language *Malini* ready in 1912, but it did not appear in print until 1917. Like all his translations, *Malini* was much abridged, leaving too little room for development and making changes in character seem too abrupt.

Two Bengali students living in England translated the next couple of plays in 1912, Tagore having the final say in revising them before their publication in 1914. Devabrata Mukerjea prepared the script of *The Post Office*, but apparently Tagore did not like his work very much. Mukerjea had inexplicably titled the translation "The Message Office", and Tagore felt "His style was flamboyant and I had to tone it down. Even after that I am not satisfied."[13] More than flamboyance, the basic problems with *The Post Office* were its awkward and inconsistent attempts at overcoming regional and cultural differences by using words such as "hummingbird" (there

are no hummingbirds in the Old World) or "tabor" (with its associations of Morris dancing) and interjections such as "By Jove" or
"Well, I'm jiggered".[14] The worst example is the translation of
Thakurda ("Grandfather") as "Gaffer", an almost archaic British
term which has in fact confused some readers into thinking of it as
the character's given name. In spite of these flaws, compared to
Tagore's own work the rendition is on the whole faithful. Concerning the shortcomings of Kshitish Chandra Sen's translation of
The King of the Dark Chamber we shall have more to say later in
this section, since it relates specifically to one of the plays translated
in this volume.

After perusing the manuscripts of the English versions available
in 1912 Charles Whibley, a reader for the publishing firm of Macmillan, reported to his employers that "there are a certain number
of plays or dramatic dialogues which . . . are of undoubted interest."[15] The company followed his suggestions and undertook
to publish them, but strangely enough issued none of the plays until
1914. It may be unwise to speculate about the reasons for this delay,
yet one cannot help wondering whether uncertainties about the
quality of the translations prevented Macmillan from publishing
them earlier. We know that several influential literary figures who
had read the manuscripts in 1912–13 had in private correspondence
expressed doubts about them. Consider, for instance, John Masefield's opinion:[16]

> I doubt if we have a sufficiently delicate instrument for them on our
> stage; they would need the most subtle handling . . . I fear that they
> would lose so much, if done in the accustomed London way, that the
> production would be a failure. . . .
> . . . the plays are short and difficult to do fittingly, . . . written for a
> stage and an audience strangely unlike our own; a great deal of the
> Chitra play would have to be cut. Our people could not get effects out of
> dialogue of that kind; the plant won't transplant.

Masefield's criticism implicates British theatrical practices and
theatre-going audiences more than it does Tagore's translations,
but his opinion of *Chitra* is revealing. W.B. Yeats, who read the
plays soon afterwards, extended this view to cover *Malini* and *The
King of the Dark Chamber* too, writing to Rothenstein that neither
could play well for Western audiences; and Rothenstein explained
the matter to Tagore as follows: "Yeats thinks The Post Office a

masterpiece . . . he thinks the other plays need more knowledge &
understanding than an English or Irish audience is likely to possess."[17] T. Sturge Moore did not like *The King of the Dark Chamber*
either, because "It is all symbolist the whole way through and I am
very doubtful whether it can be possible to produce the best effects
with that method."[18] The only steady champion of Tagore's plays
seemed to be Rothenstein, who wrote to Tagore several times
praising his dramatic output.[19] Given the responses of Masefield,
Yeats and Sturge Moore, it is not impossible that Macmillan
independently hesitated about publishing the plays for the same
reasons. The Nobel Prize (in late 1913) may have finally coaxed the
company into going ahead with prompt publication, for the award
had made Tagore an instant celebrity and popular demand for his
books had spiralled.

In early 1917 appeared *The Cycle of Spring*, on the introductory
portion of which Tagore had received considerable help from
C.F. Andrews and Nishikanta Sen, colleagues in Santiniketan. The
presence of two collaborators may indeed have been a blessing, for
their final product ranks among the better English versions credited
to Tagore. It did not delete substantial portions of the original and,
in fact, added stage directions to make visualisation of the play
easier.

Later in 1917 Macmillan published the collection titled *"Sacrifice" and Other Plays*, which consisted of *Malini* (ready since 1912)
and three other verse plays translated by Tagore in May 1916 on a
ship to Japan. *Sacrifice* and *The King and the Queen* bring Tagore's
truncated renditions to a head. Typically, he cut extensively from
the second halves of his plays in translating them; but in *Sacrifice*
he dropped entire scenes (III.i, III.ii, IV.iii, V.ii and V.iii). Consequently, Raghupati's change of heart at the end seems much too
sudden. An illustration of Tagore's technique of compression might
clarify matters: Jayasingha's crucial soliloquy in II.iii, conveying
his doubts and dilemma, takes up fifty lines of blank verse in the
Bengali, interspersed with a song. Tagore shortened this speech to
ten prose sentences and dropped the sight of Aparna in the distance, which in the original had added to Jayasingha's indecision.
The only positive element in Tagore's changes in *Sacrifice* appears
to be the implementation of one continuous scene, which corresponds more closely to his mature theatrical ideals.[20] In *The King
and the Queen* he provided the ultimate instance of brevity in

translation, compressing five acts into two by retaining just the basic plot. But as a result, this severely telescoped recension bears little resemblance in impact to that of its source — a full-length, full-blown romantic tragedy has turned into a skeletal structure without vitality, the saving grace of the original. The volume also contained *Sanyasi, or the Ascetic*. Here, in reducing sixteen scenes to four, Tagore got rid of several songs and large chunks from the middle of the play involving the Sanyasi and the Girl. While this method removed most of the melodramatic passages, it dispensed with the Sanyasi's moving soliloquies too. The conclusion also became very weak. The translation has a woman report the Girl's death to the Sanyasi, who responds in three unconvincing lines; in the Bengali he himself had discovered her dead and the play had ended with his heartfelt lament.

In 1921 Macmillan brought out *The Fugitive*, an anthology of Tagore's poetry that also included five of his short verse dramas. Characteristically, he transformed the Bengali rhymed couplets into English prose, and paraphrased many lengthy conversations into a few lines. Virtually all the plays suffered indiscriminate cuts at their close. In "The Mother's Prayer", besides excising much of the dialogue between Gandhari and Dhritarashtra — the central figures — Tagore omits everything after Gandhari's soliloquy, thus denying the reader in English a fifth of the play. "Ama and Vinayaka" whittles down the concluding exchanges in the original, probably to minimise the depiction of forced sati. The effect of "Somaka and Ritvik" is diminished by the removal of Dharma's final benediction and the compression of the final sequence of speeches into one sentence per speaker. In "Kacha and Devayani" Tagore needlessly drops Kacha's blessing at the end to Devayani, which in the Bengali had introduced a subtle variation to the hero's character. Tagore's last play to be published by Macmillan, in 1925, was *Red Oleanders*, which I shall examine in more detail later in this section.

Several of Tagore's translations never made it to the Macmillan catalogue. The first of these was "Autumn-Festival", prepared by Tagore in Illinois over the New Year, 1912–13, and eventually published by the *Modern Review* of Calcutta in 1919. It shows the same major flaw as his other translations: unnecessary condensation. Unhappily, for a play in which the lyrics provide so much of the mood and theme, Tagore eclipsed most of the songs in his

English version. Another major play, *Muktadhārā*, also appeared in the *Modern Review*, under the title "The Waterfall" in 1922. It was followed by "The Dancing Girl's Worship" (*Naṭīr Pūjā*), printed in the journal founded by Tagore, the *Visva-Bharati Quarterly*, in 1927. Both translations featured the usual compression in the middle and toward the end, and left out about half the songs in each play. But these two versions read more smoothly than Tagore's earlier work for Macmillan, somehow being relatively free from the awkwardnesses and convolutions of expression found in the Macmillan texts. Other English renditions by Tagore not published outside India comprise two shorter plays: "The Trial" (*Lakshmīr Parīkshā*) in the *Modern Review* for 1920, and "The Car of Time" (*Rath-ẏātrā*) in the *Visva-Bharati Quarterly* for 1924.

In the early twenties two Englishmen tried their hand at translating two of Tagore's short plays. In "The Foundling Hero", published in the second issue of the artsy, short-lived magazine titled the *Golden Hind* in 1923, T. Sturge Moore determined to put in metre Tagore's English "Karna and Kunti" from *The Fugitive*. An admirable attempt by an accomplished poet to restore the piece to its original metrical form, its lush style may nevertheless sound too cloying to a reader today. A much superior work was Edward Thompson's *The Curse at Farewell*, a translation of *Vidāy-Abhiśāp* which appeared in 1924. Thompson knew just enough Bengali to go to the original and — despite some glaring errors[21] — produce a more faithful translation than Tagore's own English version, "Kacha and Devayani". He used rhymed couplets to approximate the Bengali verse better, wrote an introduction containing background information, and provided ample notes, a helpful guide to pronunciation and transliteration, and an appendix on the source of the plot. He also alerted his English readership to the translation deficiencies existing in Tagore's own renditions:[22]

> At present he has no notes, and often slurs over difficulties by rendering Indian thought and mythology as if they were colourless imitations of Western thought and mythology. Thus, Kāmadeva becomes Cupid, calling up one cannot say what pictures of late Latin triviality and Elizabethan conceits; the Indian *kokil* becomes the cuckoo . . . if I have used such a word as "nymphs," I have made amends by a note.

However, this testimony conflicted with Thompson's judgment in

the book on Tagore he wrote later, namely that "it is critical
maturity that in his translations is working over again the output
of his creative youth".[23] Generally speaking, Thompson's comments in this latter book comparing Tagore's translations with
their originals favoured the translations for being more direct,
swift and straightforward.[24]

During the late thirties Tagore's biographer in English, Krishna
Kripalani, translated three plays for the *Visva-Bharati Quarterly*.
"Kach and Debjani", printed in 1937, was a new prose translation
of *Vidāy-Abhiśāp*; it improved upon Tagore's version by restoring
more of the original text, though not as fully as Thompson had in
The Curse at Farewell. Kripalani then created the English "Chandalika" in 1938—a good job considering the state of translations
so far, but like Tagore he preferred to discard the lyrics of songs, in
this case transferring only one from Bengali to English. Finally,
in 1939 he Englished *Tāser Deś* as "Kingdom of Cards", the only
translation of this late satirical drama. Unfortunately, Kripalani's
script deviated considerably from the second edition of the play,
which Tagore published the same year. In this standard edition the
scenes are arranged differently, and much of the present Bengali
text has no equivalent in Kripalani's translation. But from a
historical standpoint Kripalani's achievements must be commended
because he effectively proved—through more than just one translation—that Tagore's plays could be rendered into better English
than Tagore or the Macmillan volumes offered. Besides, he must
have had Tagore's approval of his endeavours because he worked
in close association with Tagore.

The next step toward accurate English editions of the plays came
with Marjorie Sykes' work over the forties, ultimately collected in
an anthology titled *Three Plays* (1950), consisting of *Mukta-dhara*,
Natir Puja and *Chandalika*. At long last a reader in English had
access to competent translations of major Tagore plays. As a rule
Sykes, an instructor at Santiniketan, remained faithful to the
originals while producing eminently readable versions. Still, her
work was not perfect. One cannot justify the division of *Mukta-
dhara* into three acts to "indicate the intervals which would be
found desirable in stage production."[25] We must remember that
Tagore resisted such artificial breaks in his plays of that period.
But if we judge the fidelity of translations of Tagore's plays by
their inclusion of the original songs, Sykes' *Mukta-dhara* and *Natir*

Puja would receive high marks, for she provides generally excellent translations of the lyrics and excludes only one song in each play. However, her rendition of *Chandalika* omits many songs because she deemed them "not dramatically necessary", unquestionably an arbitrary opinion.[26] One must also complain about her utilisation of the ubiquitous "thou" and "thee" found in English versions of Tagore, vocabulary barely pardonable in the early twentieth century but inexcusable in 1950.

Restoration work continued during the fifties. The prominent novelist Bhabani Bhattacharya Englished the short verse drama *Narakvās* as "A Sojourn in Hell" (1955), still in prose like Tagore's "Somaka and Ritvik" but truer to the Bengali in retaining the full conclusion previously telescoped by Tagore. Birendra Nath Roy published *Chitrangada* (1957), the only complete translation of the play to date, courageously prepared in verse which, however, is occasionally not felicitous and full of terms such as "Amen" and "nymph" that only perplex the modern reader. India's Minister of Cultural Affairs, Humayun Kabir, made slight textual modifications in his rendering of "Karna and Kunti" (1959), but successfully moulded it into blank verse and presented a more complete version, the best so far.

Tagore's birth centenary in 1961 brought among many other things a surge of interest in translating his plays. Shakuntala Rao Sastri's contribution with the unappealing title of *Devouring Love* still remains the only full translation in English of *Rājā o Rānī*, albeit in prose. It is a fairly accurate rendition, although Sastri omits several passages in the concluding scene for no apparent reason. Shyamasree Devi's "transcreation" called *The Court Dancer* supersedes both earlier translations of *Natīr Pūjā* by virtue of its straightforward yet lyrical style and relatively complete text. Amiya Chakravarty edited two Tagore anthologies which contained new renderings of plays. The English *Chandalika* attributed to Robert Steele and Donald Junkins, who based it on the earlier translations, adds stage directions and makes the play more readable, but usually at the expense of faithfulness. Sometimes the footnotes are misleading or inaccurate, for instance misplacing the positions of some songs. The version of *Grihapraveś* titled *The Housewarming* (1965), by Mary Lago, Tarun Gupta and Amiya Chakravarty, is a fine piece of work important as the only English translation of that play.

Few translations have appeared of Tagore's other dramatic enterprises, such as the dance-dramas or comic skits. Shyamasree Devi prepared "Chandalika", adapted from the dance-drama, for the *Orient Review and Literary Digest* in 1956. The script, however, was converted to prose and much abbreviated toward the end. The adaptation also left out a few songs and did not distinguish between the second scene and the next, final scene, thereby losing some of the climactic effect. In 1971 P. K. Saha authored "Shyama", a verse translation of the dance-drama by the same name; originally published in the magazine *Thought*, the author later incorporated it in a volume of his original poetry. Well-written on the whole, it nevertheless contained omissions, especially of choral comments sung by the heroine's companion, and unnecessarily created new scenes within existing scenes (twelve in place of the original four), which interrupts the flow of action. Tagore's short comic sketches remained unavailable in English until Prithvindra Chakravarti "transcreated" three of them under the title *Three Riddle Plays* in 1983. Good examples of "transcreation", these pieces transform the Bengali puns and in-jokes into intelligible English equivalents. On rare occasions the technique does not work satisfactorily, notably in "The Reception" (*Abhyarthanā*).

A minor dramatic work by Tagore, *Svarga-marta*, has curiously had the honour of being translated thrice, perhaps because Tagore placed it in a book of prose poems. Bhabani Bhattacharya's "Heaven and Earth", from 1932, dropped the last section of the playlet as well as two songs; Indu Dutt in 1969 employed the same English title for a fuller translation; and Aurobindo Bose's version from 1978, in two parts titled "Heaven and Earth" and "Indra's Heaven", is the best of all—complete, written well, with explanatory notes.

Although marginally better over the years, recent translations have still not done justice to the wealth of Tagore's drama. Apart from the many plays that remain unavailable in English versions, translators have shied away from re-translating plays that already exist in English, perhaps wishing not to rival Tagore's Macmillan editions. Consequently, for over twenty years no major Tagore play has appeared in a new English translation.

The King of the Dark Chamber

Concerning the relationship between Tagore and Macmillan over Tagore's copious writings in English, Mary Lago has made a general statement to the effect that "There were too many translators, too many editors, and too little communication between them and the author, and the author was much too willing to dispense permissions without reference to prior agreements with his publisher."[27] She goes on to exemplify the situation as follows:[28]

> A member of the firm would be informed that certain works were being translated by Tagore, or by one of his relatives, or by an associate at Santiniketan, or by any one of a number of other persons. One day a draft, with or without Tagore's final revisions, would appear on a Macmillan desk.

One Macmillan executive even commented in amazement about the speed at which manuscripts arrived from Tagore. For all of Tagore's faults, however, an equal portion of the blame for swamping the market with Tagore's works must go to Macmillan, especially in the early stages of his fame; Rothenstein put it quite bluntly to Tagore: "everything which now bears your name is gold to Macmillan".[29] The most embarrassing example of this disregard for the author is the history behind the publication of *The King of the Dark Chamber*.

Shyamal Kumar Sarkar, in an investigative study of six extant manuscripts and typescripts of the English version, made some startling discoveries that reflect poorly on almost everybody concerned and offer chastening glimpses into a case history of bungled translation and publication.[30] A Bengali student of Cambridge University, Kshitish Chandra Sen, undertook to translate *Rājā* in 1912 when Tagore was in England. We know from Tagore's letters that Sen had finished his work by 18 October 1912.[31] What we did not know until Sarkar's essay appeared was how Sen had translated the play. In a letter, Sen informed Sarkar that he had been studying for an examination at that time, and was occupied for only seven days on the translation; he even "dashed off lines of the concluding portion" while waiting for a train at a railway station.[32] Sarkar found in his analysis of Sen's manuscript copy that he had inserted ellipses whenever unsure of the right word to use, and had excluded all but one of the songs.

Tagore probably had little time to look over Sen's work before he set sail for America on 19 October. But he did blue-pencil lines and passages in the first five scenes of the manuscript, add twelve songs in translation, and consistently change "thou" into "you" in the latter three-fourths of the play. Then, as Sarkar reconstructs it, two typescripts based on this corrected manuscript were prepared, one of which stayed in England in the care of Rothenstein. The other copy remained with Tagore who, while in America, hurriedly went through another incomplete revision of this script after receiving a request from the Chicago journal *The Drama* for a contribution. In general, he excised some lengthy passages, mostly from three specific scenes, reduced the play from twenty to nineteen scenes, and brushed up the language. This version eventually appeared in the May 1914 issue of *The Drama*. Meanwhile, the typescript in England was circulating; as I have noted previously, Rothenstein liked the play whereas Yeats did not, both after reading it in November 1912. Not much else happened regarding *The King of the Dark Chamber* for more than a year, except that after Tagore's return to England in April 1913, he read the play to select private gatherings in May and June, and Macmillan vetoed a proposal later in the year to publish it as a supplement to the London *Nation*.

Back in India in October 1913, Tagore got to work again on the typescript in his possession. He completed another draft featuring even more compression: the omission of scenes 9 to 14 and the integration of the essential matter in them into two new scenes now left the translation with only fourteen scenes. Two later typescripts also exist, which consist mainly of revisions in language. Then, in June 1914, came a bolt from the blue. Macmillan sent Tagore copies of *The King of the Dark Chamber*, fresh from the press. Rothenstein, unaware that Tagore had not sanctioned this publication — indeed, had not even seen the proofs — wrote letters congratulating him on its appearance and reaffirming his own deep appreciation of its theme.[33] Characteristically understating this unexpected turn of events, Tagore replied that he was "rather surprised" to receive the books. He continued:[34]

> The manuscript that you had with you was the first draft and in the later ones the translation had undergone such a vast deal of alterations that it is quite a different thing now. So I was rather put out at the sudden appearance of this book with all its crudities ... the worst of it is that I am not the translator — it was an Indian student, Kshitish Chandra Sen,

who translated it for me. I have cabled to Macmillans to make correct
announcement — please see that it is done properly.

Except in some publicity material, however, Macmillan never
acknowledged Sen's role as translator, notwithstanding the fact
that it issued several reprint editions; the translation was credited
to Tagore on the title-page. But the mess does not end there.
Rothenstein wrote back, explaining that in their haste to publish
something by Tagore, Macmillan had got hold of the typescript in
his possession; he added with hindsight, "the slang and other
weaknesses of the translation always worry me a little."[35] The other
weaknesses that had entered into print were unforgiveable —
Rothenstein's typescript had grammatical errors, misspellings of
proper names, dropped lines, all of which were carried over into
published form. Even the ellipses — which Sen had put in and
Tagore had not the time to substitute with words — did not escape
print. The book caught everyone by surprise, including the New
York branch of Macmillan, who consequently could not publish
the American edition until September. To this day we do not know
who read the proofs.

Thus we have in *The King of the Dark Chamber* the ironic — if
not unique — case of an unauthorised publication issued by the
writer's authorised publisher, a book that should have been with-
drawn immediately. Few people realise this fact, though, and the
play continues to be treated respectfully as an authorised translation like the other Macmillan volumes.[36] Sarkar believes that
Tagore may have persuaded C.F. Andrews to undertake a revision
of the printed text in 1914.[37] But would this revision or Tagore's
own earlier abridged version have been any better? At least one
song interpolated (perhaps by Andrews) in a copy of the book
preserved in the archives at Santiniketan suggests that it would not
have improved matters, and I reproduce it here in full:[38]

> In my glad heart, in my mad heart, who is dancing?
>> Ding a ding dong, ring a ting tong, ding a ding dong.
> Where no fears are, joy and tears are ever glancing,
>> Ding a ding dong . . .
> Where the music rises higher, like a fire,
> Now advancing, all entrancing, joy enhancing
>> Ding a ding dong . . .
> Pain and gladness, smiles and sadness, toil and leisure

Night and morning, light and dawning, full the measure
    Ding a ding dong . . .
Oh the pleasure, oh the pleasure, oh the pleasure
Of our dancing, ever glancing, all entrancing
    Ding a ding dong . . .
Like the ocean in its motion waves are
Fears are groundless, freedom boundless, life is waking
  With our dancing, ever glancing, joy enhancing
    Ding a ding dong, ring a ting tong, ding a ding dong.

Such a translation can only provoke laughter. The meticulous attention paid to rhyme and metre replicates the original Bengali technique but does not possess any vitality of its own, and the jejune refrain kills whatever little life the song had. Comparisons are odious, but out of necessity I quote below my own translation of this song, in which I have tried to attain textual fidelity above anything else:[39]

    Who dances in my heart the dance eternal?
    What mridanga beats with it incessantly?
Smiles and tears, emeralds and diamonds, swing in fate,
Good and bad vibrate to the rhythm, keeping time,
Birth and death dance at one another's heels.
What happiness, what happiness, what happiness,
  For freedom and confinement dance all day and night
I flow with those waves, joyful, at their heels.

I have deliberately omitted the refrain since any English counter-part would certainly be bathetic; instead I have glossed its significance in a footnote. Another translation of a song inserted in the same copy has a similar problem, beginning thus:

My head's a whirl   Taran Tara
I would unfurl   Taran Tara
My sails and more, on waves of love.

One must be thankful for small mercies, that these renderings never made it into print.

Still, the process of judging translated songs is very subjective. An essay by William Radice, translator of the recently published Penguin selection of Tagore's poetry, proves this point. Radice praises the following version of a song from *Rājā*, translated by Arthur Geddes for the Tagore centenary festival in Edinburgh, 1961:[40]

O the gateways of the South
Are opening—let fling
For the flaming of the Spring!
  Come away, come away, O my Spring!
With the swing of my heart, you shall swing,
In the whispering of the leaves,
In the blossoming o' the trees,
    Come Spring!
  Come away, come away, O my Spring!
With sighs of joy
To the pipe of a boy
See the breeze, in tipsy swirls,
Sway the saris of girls!
  Come away, come away, O my Spring!

Radice admits the compression and the liberties taken, "but has the charm and form of a Tagore song ever been so masterfully recaptured?" he asks, stating that "an *equivalent* form has been found." But mere versification alone does not make for a good translation; in this particular case, it imparts to the song a preciousness absent in the original. The music and the content of a Tagore song are of paramount importance, not so much its lyric form — technique may have to be sacrificed, if necessary, to preserve the ideas in the words. My own translation therefore reads as follows:[41]

The southern gate is open now —
  Oh come, oh come, oh come, my spring.
In my heart's cradle you will swing,
  Oh come, oh come, oh come, my spring.
On a new chariot, green and beautiful
Come on the path strewn with *bakul*,
Come playing the eager flute,
Wearing the pollen of *piyāl* flowers,
  Oh come, oh come, oh come, my spring.
Come to the dense clusters of leaves
  Oh come, oh come, oh come.
Come to the wild *mallikā* groves
  Oh come, oh come, oh come.
With a soft, sweet, intoxicating smile
Come to the land of maddened winds,
Free your impatient scarf
Letting it fly into the sky,
  Oh come, oh come, oh come, my spring.

Why should the flute become an ordinary "pipe", or specific Indian flowers lose their beautiful names to a generalised "blossoming o' the trees"? Why should the invocation "Oh come" be transformed into the quaint "Come away", reminding one of medieval fays and elves? Worst of all, why should the wind have to "Sway the saris of girls"? Nothing in the original song justifies this misinterpretation.

RED OLEANDERS

Since I have translated *Rakta-karavī* anew in this volume, I shall devote some space here to a detailed dissection of Tagore's version, titled *Red Oleanders*, which may also serve as a case-study of his inadequate workmanship when it came to translation. The deficiencies in his methods exposed here are fairly typical of his translating work elsewhere in his plays; in fact, *Red Oleanders* figures among Tagore's more accurate translations which, as we shall see, does not say very much. Before we begin I should observe that *Red Oleanders* may have been Englished by Kshitish Chandra Sen, at least in the early stages — in a letter from 1923 Tagore writes that he might give the play to "Kshitish" for translation.[42]

To take up minor matters first, one must mention the odd assortment of vocabulary used in the English recension, ranging from the archaic ("whither") to the exotic ("Jinn") to the distinctly British ("parish"). Concerning the last-named element, it is particularly disconcerting to hear Indian characters spout such typically British exclamations as "I say", "Bless my soul", "Good heavens", "Dear me", "my dear fellow" or even "Ah misery me". Furthermore, without the useful scholarly aid nowadays of apparatus like the footnote, it became virtually impossible for Tagore to translate the numerous cultural concepts such as maya, mythological references such as the aquatic monster *makar*, literary allusions such as the "illusory deer" or *māyā-mṛiga*, and lexicographical marvels such as the word *rasa* with its many shades of meaning. More often than not, therefore, Tagore skipped such difficulties. But they should not excuse the unnecessary inaccuracies that Tagore perpetrated, for example turning simple items like rice into "corn", pomegranates into "grapes" and a python into a "boa-constrictor".

Frequently, Tagore generalised very specific Bengali lines into obscure or abstract English ones, no doubt confusing readers. Vagueness in his choice of words led to incomprehensibility, parti-

cularly true of the Raja's often cryptic speeches. "The dance
rhythm that plays on the flute of the universe" becomes "The dance
rhythm of the All" (p. 29).[43] At one point the Raja says, in Tagore's
words:

> I must either gather or scatter. I can feel no pity for what I do not get.
> Breaking is a fierce kind of getting. (p. 89)

In the original this statement reads much more lucidly:

> Either I possess, or I destroy. I cannot feel kindness for one whom I
> cannot possess. Even the act of crushing him is really one way of posses-
> sing.

Let us select another character. The matter-of-fact excavator named
Phagulal speaks very directly yet picturesquely, for instance:

> If a bird gets released in a forest it can fly; if you give it freedom in a
> cage it knocks its head about and dies.

This line is transformed into the following:

> Freedom itself was enough for the holidays in our village. The caged
> bird spends its holiday knocking against the bars. (p. 34)

Phagulal's joke about goats "crying 'baa' in front of the chopping
block" gets cleaned up into goats "bleating when butchered"
(p. 35). The convoluted English of Phagulal's "Please to speak
plainly, Bishu, otherwise it becomes positively annoying!" (p. 63)
was originally quite terse: "Brother Bishu, talk clearly, otherwise it
angers me." Similar treatment mars the speeches of the poet-
singer Bishu. He says of the town Yakshapuri,

> ... there's no path at all except the path going into its belly. Today
> I'm digested inside that hopeless lightless belly.

Tagore sanitises this as follows:

> ... the one road that remains open leads withinwards. Now I am
> swamped in that interior without hope and without light. (p. 46)

Bishu's self-portrait given to the Raja—"I'm Ranjan's other side,
the side on which light doesn't fall—I'm the night of the new
moon"—gets obfuscated into "I am the obverse side of Ranjan,
on which falls the shadow" (p. 79). The Sardar's snide remark to
Bishu on seeing him alone with Nandini, "you have love for just
about everyone", loses its sexual innuendo when Tagore changes

it to "you seem to be making friends with everybody" (p. 76).

Besides making the particular general, Tagore freely discarded details which make the Bengali text vivid. The Professor's theory that "The naked is without a credential, it's the made-up clothes that define us" (p. 7) originally contained examples to illustrate the point: "The naked have no means of introduction; made-up clothes alone make someone a raja, someone a beggar." Nandini's conviction about Ranjan's impending arrival, "Through the same way that brings news of the coming Spring" (p. 11), omits in English the examples she subsequently gives to support her belief: "the colours of the sky, the games of the breeze." Similarly, Bishu's "we can only say the words, — they put in the meaning" (p. 50) drops his picturesque metaphor that follows: "So, no one knows which charcoal speck of a word sets fire to which thatch roof." Nandini's "Look over there—what a piteous sight!" (p. 107) preceded a poignant question, "Have the doors of the city of the dead opened?", left out of the English version. The Raja's appeal, "You will come with me, Nandini?" (p. 170), excludes his evocative picture of her as "my lamp-flame on the path to doomsday". The Headman's complaint about Ranjan, "Nothing seems to fasten on to him" (p. 98), replaces a much more elaborate description of Ranjan's elusive nature:

> he had been tightly bound with chains. A little later I see he has slipped out somehow — nothing can hold fast to his body. And, he frequently changes his appearance by changing outfits.

The Gosain's admonition to Nandini for talking of things she should not, "these discussions ill become your lips" (p. 122), does not retain the tone of finality and forewarning present in the original, where he adds that her discussions "grate harshly on our ears, we don't like them." The exchange between Phagulal and Bishu regarding their respective numerical designations —

PHAGULAL: It's painted on the clothes on my back, I'm 47-P.
BISHU: I'm 69-U. In the village I was a person, here I've become one square in the game of 10-25. Gambling continues upon my chest.

—is whittled down into the following, bereft of any colour:

PHAGULAL: I'm No. 47V.
BISHU: I'm 69Ng. (p. 47)

Several times, words that clarify gestures or incidents on stage are deleted from Tagore's translation. In response to the Gosain's

enquiry concerning the next district he should visit, the Sardar indicates "Over there", a physical gesture dropped by Tagore (p. 57).
In the final scene, Phagulal stumbles on Nandini's bracelet:

> And, see there, her bracelet of red oleanders rolls in the dust. It has
> slipped off some time from her right hand.

But Tagore's rendering, "Here is her wristlet of red oleanders"
(p. 180), provides no clue to reader or actor where Phagulal got the
ornament.

Omissions therefore form a major defect in the authorised translation. I do not deny the possibility that judicious cutting can often
improve upon the originals, but in Tagore's case the deletions
serve no positive purpose; they strike one as being random and
arbitrary. The tone is set by the very first stage direction, which
in the Bengali goes as follows:

> *The town in which these dramatic events are set is named Yakshapuri.
> Its band of labourers is employed in underground mining for gold. Its
> Raja lives behind an extremely complex screen. That netted screen of
> the palace is the only scene in this play. The entire action occurs on the
> outer portion of that screen.*

In comparison, Tagore's single English sentence is cursory and
singularly unhelpful:

> *The Curtain rises on a window covered by a network of intricate pattern
> in front of the Palace.* (p. 1)

Many of the omitted passages fulfil crucial functions in the original
text, especially providing information important for an understanding of the characterisation. I list below some of the more
significant among these deleted lines, all of which offer insights
into the personalities of either the speakers or the subjects of the
speeches:

(a) NANDINI: ...I want to open the dark lid to those tunnels of
    yours and pour light into them; so also do I want to tear down
    that ugly screen and liberate the man inside.
(b) CHANDRA: Is that so? So they believe in gods and deities?
    PHAGULAL: Haven't you seen that their drinking-house, armoury
    and temple exist side by side?
(c) VOICE [THE RAJA]: I crush the Creator's intelligence.
(d) HEADMAN: His [Ranjan's] following becomes larger every moment.
    Some day he'll excite even us into dancing.

(e) PROFESSOR: He [the Raja] wants to appropriate the means to know just everything, all that there is to know in the world.

(f) PROFESSOR: I don't have the courage, Nandini.

(g) SARDAR: Precisely for the sake of duty toward the Raja we have to deceive the Raja, have to stop the Raja too.

Tagore's excisions affect also the rare instances in this play where he employs humour. Chandra's tirade against the drinking habits of Phagulal and Bishu loses repartee such as "There's no end to God's kindness for drunks-from-birth like you. He has overturned the wine pitcher!" In the long sequence between the Sardar and the ingratiating Headman of Section E, the latter's obsequious requests for favours on behalf of his endless relatives includes one even for his "father-in-law's brother-in-law", a phrase which gets considerably watered down in Tagore's rendition, "a distant connection of mine by marriage" (p. 142).

Sometimes Tagore added words and expressions in the English that seem quite unnecessary. Nandini calls Kishor "my boy" (pp. 2, 130) without any reason whatsoever. Similarly, she calls Bishu by various sugary epithets, such as "Singer of my heart" (pp. 131–32), "dear heart!" (p. 133) and "my heart's Joy!" (p. 134), also without any basis in the Bengali text other than her nickname for him in the second instance, and the affectionate term *āmār bhāi* ("my brother") in the last. If "dear heart" was meant as a substitute for the nickname, Tagore has not used it consistently either. Some additions, like the Professor's line "The privilege of wasting time proves one's wealth of time" (p. 8), are generalised maxims absent in the Bengali. Other additions are totally out of character, for example Nandini's curt and antagonistic dismissal of Gokul, "You'll die digging" (p. 16).

Finally we come to the songs, which Tagore truncated and translated very inadequately throughout his English works. A side-by-side comparison of sample selections from *Red Oleanders* will make this point clear. Here is one of Bishu's songs in my translation:

The spirit of your life runs dry,
So fill the cup with the spirit of death.
It is squeezed from the fire of the funeral pyre,
    Relieves the pain of suffering,
It colours all the emptiness with loud laughter.

> Your sun's embedded in dense clouds;
> Your day has died in useless deeds,
> So allow that dark, deepening night to arrive,
>   Lost oblivion's last companion,
> To cover your tired eyes with veiled, devious darkness.

And this is Tagore's version, fuller than usual for his English songs:

> My life, your sap has run dry,
> Fill then the cup with the wine of death,
> That flushes all emptiness with its laughter.
>
> Thy sun is hidden amid a mass of murky cloud.
> Thy day has smudged itself black in dusty toil.
> Then let the dark night descend
>   the last comrade of drunken oblivion.
> Let it cover thy tired eyes with the mist
>   that will help thee desperately to lose thyself. (pp. 41–42)

Another of Bishu's songs, addressed to Nandini, runs as follows:

> You keep me awake so that I sing you songs,
>   O destroyer of sleep.
> So that's why you call me and startle my breast,
>   O awaker of grief.
>   Comes darkness around,
>   Birds come to their nests,
>   Boats come to the shore,
> But only my heart cannot find any rest,
>   O awaker of grief.
>
>   For while I worked
> You never let the swells of weeping cease.
>   After you touched me,
>   Filled life with nectar,
>   Moved away later,
> Perhaps you still stand in the shade of my pain,
>   O awaker of grief.

But Tagore's rendering condenses this lyric substantially, discarding the second half:

> You keep me awake that I may sing to you,
>   O Breaker of my sleep!
> And so my heart you startle with your call,
>   O Waker of my grief!
> The shades of evening fall,

the birds come to their nest.
The boat arrives ashore,.
   yet my heart knows no rest,
   O Waker of my grief! (pp. 66–67)

Compression of songs was a characteristic trait of Tagore's English. He even converted one of the songs in *Red Oleanders* into straightforward prose speech. Bishu's short song —

O moon, the tide of tears now strikes the sea of sorrow,
The whispers reach the brim of this shore and the other.
My boat was on known banks, its moorings came untied,
The breezes took it to the edge of some unknown.

— became one line of dialogue spoken by him: "My boat was tied to the bank; the rope snapped; the wild wind drove it into the trackless unknown" (pp. 68–69). Several of Tagore's versions also suffer from the dated vocabulary he habitually used; take for instance the very first song in *Red Oleanders*, which at the end of the play also functions as a coda:

Hark 'tis Autumn calling, —
   Come, O come away!
The earth's mantle of dust is filled with ripe corn!
   O the joy! the joy! (p. 181)

There can be little doubt that such obsolescent phraseology mars Tagore's translations, leaving readers and prospective directors no choice but to set these works aside as curious museum pieces.

VII. THE PRESENT TRANSLATION

There is no such thing as a 'good' translation in the sense of re-expressing what is said in the original. A translation may be a re-incarnation but it cannot be identical.

[Tagore, interviewed by *Musical America*, 27 November 1920][1]

One cannot find fault with Tagore's statement above, yet the first principle I have adopted in translating the three plays in this volume is fidelity to the original Bengali text. In introducing his version of Brecht's *The Caucasian Chalk Circle*, Eric Bentley proposed a rule of thumb ideal for the business of translation: "Perhaps all good foreign plays should be published first in a very literal translation and subsequently in various attempts at a true equivalent, even, if necessary, in 'adaptations.'"[2] Because Tagore's own renderings hardly qualify as literal ones, faithful English translations of these plays do not exist; I elected therefore to fill this vacuum. I hope that future translators might prepare freer versions or adaptations, but for now it seems essential for readers in English to have as close an approximation to the originals as possible. The translations in this volume present for the first time in English the full texts of these plays.

Fidelity can, of course, suggest many different things. I have attempted firstly to maintain a scrupulously close correspondence between Bengali and English, certainly sentence for sentence, and in many instances even word for word. For better or for worse, I have not excised a single line of dialogue. This procedure obviously raises major difficulties, not the least of which is the problem Tagore hinted at in the comment quoted as epigraph to this section. Tagore's reservations about "literal" translations stemmed from the truism that, as he put it in the same interview, "the sound of a word has a significance utterly apart from its meaning . . . as you cannot take the sound of a word but only its meaning into another language, just so you can never really translate from one language into another." No translation, therefore, can be really faithful; yet this realisation need not discourage translators from the aim of fidelity. In my choice of words I have always paid attention to the Bengali sounds as an important guide, albeit more in terms of general sound patterns than in attempting to match the sounds of specific words — the latter a clearly futile task.

Then again, Tagore conjures a certain atmosphere by his use of the Bengali language which can only be described somewhat ineptly as the aura created by the words. Many savants despair of coming to grips with this ineffable element in the plays, helplessly pointing to Tagore's apparent incommunicability; others offer insufficient explanations. Among those who have delved a little deeper into this matter, Dhurjati Prasad Mukerji finds that "In his dramas, there are two levels; one, that of the people, where the language is simple, responses the stock ones and the technique of presentation fairly firm, and the other, that of ideas of which the language is poetry, the interactions subtle, and the presentation sophisticated."[3] However, these tiers are by no means as discrete as Mukerji indicates; often they merge inextricably, the simple cadence of the common man conveying by itself the subtle and sophisticated themes. One of Tagore's better translators, Marjorie Sykes, analyses his handling of language more accurately: "he has united in the closest harmony the homeliest and most familiar language of daily life with that of the most exalted mystical experience, so that the very words which on one man's lips are prosaic, on the lips of another are instinct with poetry."[4]

I believe that a proper transference into English of the flavour and particularly the rhythm of the Bengali can recapture to some degree this evanescent aspect of Tagore's language. Consequently I have tried to preserve in my translations the speech-rhythms of Tagore's characters, perhaps even to a fault: I have occasionally pushed correct syntax to its limits in order to achieve what I thought was the right word-order; I would like to believe that I have not overstepped any boundaries or transgressed into bad English. Some examples of typical Bengali usage may illustrate my practices. In Bengali, the emphatic suffix -i is often used to stress a word or phrase, so I have generally added an emphatic word (such as "too", "only", "very", "certainly") to match the tone of the original, even though the translated English sentence does not demand it at all. Bengali speech frequently features superfluous expressions inserted at random within a sentence, a common interposition of this kind being *to* (which usually has no meaning); I have added in my text a word such as "well" which functions in a similar manner in spoken English. Bengali also regularly utilises constructions in which adjectives such as *tomār* ("your") and *oi* ("that") both immediately precede a noun; I convert such phrases into an equivalent structure, "that — of yours", in my bid to retain some of the flavour of Bengali. The language is also an effusive one, freely doubling or tripling imperative verbs or negative responses where in English a single "Go!" or "No" suffices. I have deliberately sacrificed the restraint and economy of English in favour of the more luxuriant Bengali in such cases.

My second consideration in preparing these translations, equally important as fidelity, has been their stage potential. Since Tagore did not write closet drama and always intended to have his plays staged, I have taken pains to construct versions which could serve as performance scripts. The peculiar demands of language on the stage made the job of translation more difficult than it may seem. My primary guideline in this respect has been whether the English reads well, *aloud*; I hope that for the most part the translations fulfil this criterion of stageworthiness. The reader should therefore keep in mind that I have made no attempt to refine the texts so as to suit narrowly literary norms and sensibilities: these versions must be judged not by what the reader finds in them, but by what a spectator finds in performances of them. I am a firm believer in the doctrine that a play comes to life on the boards, not on the page, and fully agree with Peter Arnott who — writing of Greek drama — averred that "Actor and director may often, by a process akin to mysticism in religion, attain to an intuitive appreciation of a difficult line or passage which defies analysis on paper."[5] More than most dramatists, Tagore has gained a good deal of notoriety for eluding the grasp of literary critics; I feel that actors and directors possess the innate capacity to slice through the morass of interpretation and present, without over-simplification, the cruxes of his difficult lines and passages.

I also hope that prospective directors and actors treat these translations uninhibitedly as performance scripts. I prefer the term "script" for these translations because I visualise a theatrical team dissecting them with an eye on production, cutting and rearranging to fit their designs. By no means should these versions be regarded as sacrosanct texts, the more so because of their very nature as translations. A play-script always changes from one performance to the next, and we have the additional authority of Tagore himself, who significantly altered his own plays whenever he revived them.

I harbour no doubts that he would approve of editing the plays if necessary to attain effects truer to his goals. The director must act as Tagore's surrogate to make sure these goals are accomplished, and together with the actor, should feel free to add to, subtract from, and reorder the lines in this volume to suit their purpose. Obviously I do not justify editing that might alter substantially the themes or characterisation of the plays; but reasonable and legitimate changes should include such things as the rephrasing of words or sentences with which actors feel awkward or uncomfortable, and the judicious cutting of lines the significance of which may be lost on specific regional audiences.

This brings us to my third and final concern in these translations, the question of their readership. One school of thought argues pointedly that Tagore's plays can never be truly appreciated by Western audiences and therefore should never be staged for their benefit. Opposition of this kind ranges from mere queries raised by scholars such as Sujit Mukherjee, who doubts whether "his concept of drama is suitable for expression in foreign theatre", to explicit denials of their suitability such as that of Mary Lago, who supports John Masefield's contention of sixty years earlier that their "staging would require a delicate touch beyond the abilities of Western directors."[6] Most of these dissenters find Tagore's "philosophy rather enigmatic to the Western mentality, and thus Tagore's symbolic dramas are more suitable to Eastern audiences".[7] I do not subscribe to this notion and in fact have based my translations partly upon the conviction that Western theatre can indeed express Tagore's dramaturgy and philosophy, if not perfectly, at least quite satisfactorily.

Therefore, in an arguably too ambitious attempt, I have tried to use an English idiom acceptable both to Western and Indian audiences of English theatre, without having to Indianise it excessively on the one hand, or on the other hand to compromise too much with the average Westerner's unfamiliarity with Indian customs and culture. This intention has necessitated the lavish use of footnotes—an unfortunate hindrance to smooth reading, but essential to elucidate many details of Indian life and thought to the Western reader. Because my desired audience includes Western members, I have also had to employ vocabulary that could not be regarded by them as too esoteric. Thus, as far as possible, I have chosen words or terms in common English usage instead of Indian words which could have been readily understood by English-speaking Indian spectators. To provide a simple example, I have consistently used "brother" in place of *bhāi* ("brother") or *dādā* ("elder brother"), familial terms with which Bengalis (and other Indians) address not just relatives, but male acquaintances and even strangers. I expect that in an Indian performance the actor would return to the original Bengali word, since it is more natural. In order to ensure that the actor always has this choice, my footnotes present the Bengali words in such instances.

As a reference guide to current English usage I have relied on *Webster's Ninth New Collegiate Dictionary*, but have studiously tried to avoid particularly American idioms (or British ones, for that matter). Since my translations need to function as play-scripts, the spoken language in day-to-day expression assumed more importance for me than the written or literary language. *Webster's Ninth* met my requirements perfectly because of the emphasis it places on descriptive rather than prescriptive lexicography, and because of its very recent publication; hence I did not deem it necessary to consult the larger, more authoritative Webster's or Oxford dictionaries. It may be of special interest to note that *Webster's Ninth* contains many words of Indian origin (for example "maya", "pipal", "raja", "sardar", "yuga"), and I have selected them whenever appropriate, naturally not italicising them or burdening them with diacritical marks. But whenever I have had to resort to other Indian or Bengali terms in the text of a play, I have italicised them, and in an accompanying footnote done my best to suggest a performance substitute in English for the benefit of the Western actor. I hope that this methodology will offer optimum satisfaction to the largest number of readers.

Of course in the final analysis it is not Tagore's words so much as their evocative subtext that remains the enduring vocabular feature of his plays. Whether Western or Indian, the actor must have a sensitivity to this aspect of Tagore—the heightened prose that does not necessarily demand a sing-song delivery, that surcharges the play with a dominant mood resembling the *rasa* of Sanskrit aesthetics. K. R. Srinivasa Iyengar notices this connection between Sanskrit theory and Tagore's drama:[8]

> the music of ideas and symbols is the 'soul' of this drama. Not the apparent meaning but its echoing cadence of suggestion—*dhwani*, as

the Sanskrit rhetoricians called it; in other words, the richness of the undertones — is what matters, for this alone kindles the sluggish soul to a new awareness.

If my translations succeed in recreating to some extent this "feeling" within Tagore's plays, I shall indeed be gratified.

THE MUSIC

The special nature and function of Tagore's songs in these plays require some comment. Music was very dear to Tagore's heart, and he was often fond of foretelling that future generations would remember him more for his songs than for anything else. Nearly fifty years after his death, his prophecy has come true: his songs have certainly become more popular among Bengalis than any of his other compositions; through the services of accomplished vocalists and the radio network, hundreds of Tagore's two thousand songs have reached the general populace and implanted themselves in the cultural ethos of Bengal. As a measure of their strong popular appeal, one can point to the fact that both India and Bangladesh chose as their national anthems songs by Tagore.

Even in the sphere of theatre, music literally circumscribes Tagore's dramatic career, which began in 1881 and ended in 1939 with plays that he set to music. Once again one must permit Tagore to speak for himself, about the origins of his interest in amalgamating music and drama which led to his first play, *Vālmīki-pratibhā*:[9]

> I had read in some work of Herbert Spencer's that speech takes on tuneful inflexions whenever emotion comes into play. It is a fact that the tone or tune is as important to us as the spoken word for the expression of anger, sorrow, joy and wonder. Spencer's idea that, through a development of these emotional modulations of voice, man found music, appealed to me. Why should it not do, I thought to myself, to act a drama in a kind of recitative based on this idea? The *Kathakas* of our country attempt this to some extent, for they frequently break into a chant which, however, stops short of full melodic form.

Later he began constructing his own theories about the relationship between lyrics and melodies:[10]

> The song being great in its own wealth, why should it wait upon the words? Rather does it begin where mere words fail. Its power lies in

the region of the inexpressible; it tells us what the words cannot.

So the less a song is burdened with words the better ... our music, though professedly in attendance only, ends by dominating the song.

... the words had no means of reaching by themselves the region into which they were borne away by the tune.

In Tagore's plays, songs have additional duties as well. They contribute significantly to the almost tangible atmosphere of each play, to which I have so often referred. Structurally, they build toward dramatic intensity, provide lyrical relief, offer choric commentary, and even present the climax: according to the musicologist Beerendra Bandyopadhyaya, "Not only their theme but the culmination of the plays depends on the songs."[11] Each of the three plays in this volume concludes with a song, proof enough of this view. In *Tapatī*, the final song is also followed by two Vedic hymns and a chanted Upanishadic mantra, without any intervening dialogue. As for the first part of Bandyopadhyaya's thesis, we may turn to *Arūp Ratan* as a case in point. Pervaded with songs — twice as many as in *Tapatī*, a much longer play — this work really celebrates through its music the spiritual progress of the protagonist from ignorance to knowledge. The songs themselves form the play in miniature, a paean to the spiritual awakening of the soul. The irritated response of some critics to these songs is astonishing, to say the least; for instance, Nirmal Mukerji thinks that the play "reels under an abundance of music much of which is not integrated at all. Characters are always bursting forth into song for no rhyme or reason."[12]

Tagore composed the music to his own songs. He had a thorough background in Indian classical music, and his early songwriting displays a penchant for inventiveness within the field of traditional ragas and talas. But as he grew older he found himself attracted to folk songs, and gradually his musical compositions too gravitated in the direction of simplicity and directness, leaving behind the intricacy and sophistication of his classical heritage. He developed especially deep feelings for the Bāul, a common figure in Bengali villages — an itinerant minstrel-bard belonging to a religious sect that follows the *sahajiyā* ("simple", "instinctive") tradition, which practises a personal relationship with God and disdains the rituals of organised religion. The Bāul's heartfelt devotional songs, characterised by metaphysical themes couched in plain colloquial

language on the easily comprehensible level of human love, influenced Tagore's thought greatly and strengthened his belief in the
reciprocity between the finite and infinite worlds. Tagore regularly
made room for the brief entrance of a Bāul in his plays, as in *Arūp
Ratan*, and he also borrowed typical Bāul tunes and form for many
of his own songs. Moreover, the characters in his plays who do
most of the singing usually reveal in their own lives the power of a
personal, intuitive relationship with God which Tagore so admired
in the Bāul, and they communicate this deep and true faith through
their songs: we may find this special spiritual trait in the "mad"
Bishu in *Rakta-karavī*, Surangama and Thakurda in *Arūp Ratan*,
and to some extent even Bipasha in *Tapatī*.

Speaking of Bāul songs, Tagore once wrote that "the best part
of a song is missed when the tune is absent; for thereby its movement and its colour are lost, and it becomes like a butterfly whose
wings have been plucked."[13] He reiterated this point in his autobiography: "That is why I am always reluctant to publish books of
the words of songs, for therein the soul must needs be lacking."[14]
For this reason, I have decided to include the original Bengali music
to the three plays in the appendices to this volume. The question
obviously arises, how should the music be integrated into a performance in English translation, particularly in the West? I personally
do not favour setting my English lyrics to the original music,
because Tagore's songs have received this treatment before and the
result has sometimes proved ludicrous, though this may have been
largely due to very poor translations. Besides, such an endeavour
must demand from major members of the cast fairly competent
singing prowess in the Indian style of music, where modes are
singularly important, quite different from normal Western vocal
technique. Extrapolating from Krishna Shah's experience in producing *The King of the Dark Chamber* off-Broadway, directors may
find it more pragmatic to have the lyrics chanted while the music
plays on instrumentation in the background:[15]

> the most effective technique is to chant the songs in English with the
> beats of the Indian meters. In this way, both the original meaning and
> function of the songs could be preserved.

Alternatively, the songs may be performed by a chorus or solo
vocalist, either offstage or at one side of the stage—a practice which
Tagore frequently employed in his later productions, as in the case

of Bipasha's songs in *Tapatī*. Another, more ambitious, possibility
is to write new scores for the English lyrics, perhaps based upon
Tagore's own music. The most convenient solution of course
would be to exclude the songs altogether, which would be a pity,
but some directors may have no other recourse. I therefore leave
the decision on music up to the individual director.

It might help the director, however, to conceive of productions
of Tagore's plays in terms of musical compositions. "There is a
deeper connection between Tagore the composer and Tagore the
dramatist than what appears on the surface", observes Dhurjati
Prasad Mukerji correctly.[16] Tagore's mature plays resemble nothing
more closely than symphonic compositions or, to use an Indian
analogy, the complete elaboration of a raga. They unfold as does a
raga in the hands of an Indian classical maestro, slowly developing
themes and variations, improvising along the way; progressing
from the *ālāp* ("introduction") of the expository beginning to the
climactic crescendo at the end, which achieves calm of mind all
passion spent.

TRANSLITERATION

In transliterating Bengali words into English I have used a modi-
fied version of the standard Sanskrit-English system of transliteration. My rationale for adopting the Sanskritic convention is that its
relatively widespread currency (both in India and the West) will
enable readers conversant with it to recognise Bengali words easily
by their spelling, which does not differ radically from the methods
of spelling in Sanskrit or Hindi, whereas Bengali pronunciation
does deviate considerably from that of languages like Sanskrit or
Hindi which utilise the Devanagari script. If I had employed a
phonetic pattern of transcription it probably would have confused
more readers than helped others — the words would have been
most readily identifiable to Bengalis, for whom these translations
are not primarily intended anyway. However, in order to facilitate
the process of pronunciation I provide below a transliteration chart
of the Bengali alphabet, together with the corresponding English
letter or letters, a general phonetic description, a key to pronunciation, and an example from my text for each character. I ought to
forewarn readers that a few Bengali letters have no equivalent
sounds in the English tongue: blank spaces in the column on pronunciation identify these characters.

Bengali	English	Description	Pronunciation	Example

VOWELS

| অ | a | The "inherent vowel", the vowel-sound that accompanies a consonant when the consonant is not followed by any other vowel | (1) a as in "all"
 (2) o as in "go" | Arūp

 Agni |

[When two successive syllables carry a vowels, the first one is often pronounced as in (1), and the second one as in (2): e.g., Rakta-karavī = Raktokarovī, Ratan = Raton, Tapatī = Tapotī]

| আ | ā | International Phonetic Alphabet (IPA): [a] | a as in "car" | ektārā |

| ই | i | IPA [i]; theoretically, ī is longer than i, but in spoken Bengali there is no discernible distinction between the two | i as in "ski" | Indra |
| ঈ | ī | | | Tapatī |

| উ | u | IPA [u]; theoretically, ū is longer than u, but in spoken Bengali there is no discernible distinction between the two | u as in "flu" | Viśu |
| ঊ | ū | | | pūjā |

| ঋ | r̥i | Liquid vowel, resembling somewhat the French r | ri as in "grip" | Mr̥ityuñjay |

[The standard transcription is r̥, but this often causes confusion because the Bengali retroflex flap is also commonly transcribed as r]

| এ | e | IPA [e] | e as in "melee" | devī |

[Sometimes e is also pronounced as the a in "mat"]

| ঐ | ai | The diphthong [o] + [i] | | Kailās |

| ও | o | IPA [o] | o as in "bone" | aśok |

| ঔ | au | The diphthong [o] + [u] | | Gaurī |

| ং | ṁ | IPA [ŋ]; see also the velar nasal consonant | ng as in "sing" | Siṁhagar |

| ঃ | ḥ | Aspirated vowel | | śāntiḥ |

| ঁ | n̐ | Nasalised vowel, resembling the French n; always in conjunction with another vowel, the n sound not being enunciated | n as in "manqué" | ān̐chal |

Bengali	English	Description	Pronunciation	Example
		CONSONANTS: VELAR		
ক	k	Voiceless velar stop	*k* as in "kid"	Kumārsen
খ	kh	ʌspirated *k*	*kh* as in "khaki"	Khetulāl
গ	g	Voiced velar stop	*g* as in "go"	Gokul
ঘ	gh	Aspirated *g*	*gh* as in "ghat"	Maghā
ঙ	ṅ	Velar nasal; the IPA [ŋ], it is now virtually identical with *ṁ* and they are often employed interchangeably	*n* as in "sink"	Śaṅkar
		CONSONANTS: PALATAL		
চ	ch	Voiceless palatal stop	*ch* as in "chin"	Chandrā
ছ	chh	Aspirated *ch*		*chhi*
জ	j	Voiced palatal stop	*j* as in "joy"	Jālandhar
ঝ	jh	Aspirated *j*	[not used in my text]	
ঞ	ñ	Palatal nasal, the IPA [ɲ], almost always in conjunction with another palatal consonant	*n* as in "inch"	Rañjan
		CONSONANTS: RETROFLEX		
ট	ṭ	Voiceless retroflex stop	*t* as in "toe"	Naṭarāj
ঠ	ṭh	Aspirated *ṭ*		Ṭhākurdā
ড/ড়	ḍ/r	(1) Voiced retroflex stop	*d* as in "did"	Chaṇḍī
		(2) Retroflex flap, carrying an *r* sound following the *ḍ*		Kubergaṛ
ঢ/ঢ়	ḍh/ rh	(1) Aspirated *ḍ*	[not used in my text]	
		(2) Aspirated *r*		Āshāṛh
ণ	ṇ	Retroflex nasal; in common speech virtually indistinguishable from the dental *n*	*n* as in "no"	Suvarṇa

Bengali	English	Description	Pronunciation	Example
		CONSONANTS: DENTAL		
ত	t	Voiceless dental stop; resembles the soft *t* in Italian		*tāl*
থ	th	Aspirated *t*	*th* as in "thick"	*aśvattha*
দ	d	Voiced dental stop; resembles the soft *d* in Italian		Devdatta
ধ	dh	Aspirated *d*	*dh* as in "dharma"	Dhruva
ন	n	Dental nasal; in common speech virtually indistinguishable from the retroflex *ṇ*	*n* as in "no"	Nandinī
		CONSONANTS: BILABIAL		
প	p	Voiceless bilabial stop	*p* as in "put"	*praṇām*
ফ	ph	Aspirated *p*		Phālgun
ব	b	Voiced bilabial stop	*b* as in "baby"	Bāul
ভ	bh	Aspirated *b*	*bh* as in "bhakti"	Bhairav
ম	m	Bilabial nasal	*m* as in "me"	*makar*
		LIQUIDS AND CONTINUANTS		
য়/য	y/ẏ	Continuant; but pronounced as a *j* when it begins a word, and is often silent when it follows a consonant in conjunct form or intervenes between two vowels	(1) *y* as in "yard" (2) *j* as in "joy" (3) silent	Udaypur *ẏātrā* *piyāl*

[In conjunct form, *y* slightly modifies the sound of a syllable: e.g., *yā* after a consonant is pronounced as the *a* in "mat"; *y* also tends to double the value of the preceding consonant, as in *satya*-yuga, where the *tya* would sound more like *tto*]

| র | r | Liquid | *r* as in "red" | Rudra |
| ল | l | Liquid | *l* as in "low" | Lakshmī |

Bengali	English	Description	Pronunciation	Example
ব	v	Continuant; always pronounced as a *b*, but when following a consonant in conjunct form it becomes silent (at the beginning of a word) or doubles the value of the preceding consonant	(1) *b* as in "baby" (2) silent (3) doubles preceding consonant	Vikram Jvālāmukhī Ratneśvar

SIBILANTS AND ASPIRATE

Bengali	English	Description	Pronunciation	Example
শ	ś	Palatal sibilant; in normal speech indistinguishable from the other sibilants, but as a conjunct has a different sound	(1) *sh* as in "shy" (2) *s* as in "say"	Kiśor śruti
ষ	sh	Retroflex sibilant; in normal speech indistinguishable from the other sibilants	*sh* as in "shy"	Paush
স	s	Dental sibilant, retaining its distinct sound only in conjunct form, when preceding another consonant; otherwise identical to the other sibilants	(1) *s* as in "say" (2) *sh* as in "shy"	smṛiti Sumitrā
হ	h	Aspirated consonant	*h* as in "hat"	Hari

All aspirated consonants in the velar, palatal, retroflex, dental and bilabial groups — *kh, gh, chh, jh, ṭh, ḍh, ṛh, th, dh, ph* and *bh* — should be pronounced with a strong expulsion of breath following the initial consonant. Their pronunciations should approximate the *kh* in "brick-house", *chh* in "thatch-house", *th* (not the Bengali *th*) in "anthill", *ph* in "uphill", and so on, keeping in mind that these are single sounds in Bengali, not two distinct sounds as in these English words. Also, several English consonants carry some amount of aspiration, but the speaker should take care not to expel any breath while pronouncing the unaspirated stops in Bengali which correspond to these English letters, such as *k, g, p* and *b*. Like all languages Bengali too has occasional vagaries of pronunciation (the conjunct letters *ksh* and *jñ*, for instance, are pronounced *kh* and a nasalised *g* respectively), but I do not think it necessary to dwell upon them here. However, I should point out that the stress system in Bengali is considerably weaker than in

English. Non-Indians sometimes assume that the accent in Bengali falls on the second syllable of a word, but it is usually the first syllable that carries a slight stress.

I should also add that in my transliteration of proper nouns — for example the names of mythological figures or deities — I have frequently adhered to standard Indian spelling for the convenience of readers, although Bengali pronunciation often drops the last inherent vowel *a* from words which end with a single consonant (thus I have retained "Rama", "Siva", "Yama", and so on, instead of omitting the terminal "a"s). Furthermore, I have not deployed diacritical marks on names that have gained currency in the English language and are included in *Webster's Ninth*, such as Brahma, Vishnu, Siva, Krishna and Rama. I have also hyphenated compound words like *Rakta-karavī*, which in Bengali would be written as one word. Finally, I have capitalised first letters of words according to the norms of English — the Bengali language does not have separate upper and lower case alphabets. I hope these minor changes make the texts slightly easier to read.

PART TWO

The Plays

RED OLEANDER

(Rakta-Karavī)

NOTE ON THE PLAY

Tagore began this play under the title *Yakshapurī*, in the summer of 1923 while vacationing in Shillong, Assam. Later in the year he changed the title of the play—still in manuscript—to *Nandinī*. In late 1924 the full text was published in the journal *Pravāsī*, the title altered a second time to *Rakta-karavī*.[1] Pramathanath Bisi recounts the incident that apparently prompted Tagore to change the name: years after its publication Tagore told one of his colleagues, Kshitimohan Sen, of an oleander plant near his house that had been crushed under a heap of discarded iron pieces. He thought the plant had died. A few days later he saw that an oleander branch had emerged from the debris, proudly sporting a single red flower "as if created from the blood of its cruelly pierced breast." It seemed to say, "Well friend, I haven't died, were you able to kill me?"[2] Simultaneously with the Bengali publication, an English translation named "Red Oleanders" appeared as a special issue of the *Visva-Bharati Quarterly*. No major play of Tagore's had consumed so much creative time between conception and publication. Moreover, the Bengali original was not printed as a book until December 1926, more than a year after Macmillan had issued the English translation in book-form.

Leonard Elmhirst, close friend of Tagore's and indefatigable pioneer at Tagore's rural reconstruction centre at Sriniketan, tells us about the genesis of the play. According to him, Tagore completed it during their trip to western India late in 1923:[3]

> Day by day, as we travelled, he would spend his spare hours reading, or dreaming about the new play he was then busy writing. When we arrived at the State of Limbidi he began to complain sadly that he had come to the last scene of the last act of his latest play and that having lived so long on such intimate terms with the characters of his invention, he could not bear to bring the play to a sudden end or say to these people his final farewell. "I have delayed the guillotine for one more day," he would say, "but fall it must."

Elmhirst goes on to say that Tagore hinted it was the friendship among both of them and a certain girl they knew in Santiniketan (who remains unnamed) that gave him the idea for the play. Elmhirst also narrates how, one morning after their return to the Jorasanko house, Tagore confirmed his nephews' suspicions when they started teasing him about the source of his inspiration:[4]

"She even begged of me that this new drama should be dedicated to her. I told her, Never, you have had nothing to do with it. But she knew, and I know, that she is the figure around whom the whole theme revolves. For goodness sake, Gagen, don't breathe a word of this to your wife or the news will be round Calcutta like wild fire."

Everyone, it seems, took great pleasure in noticing a resurgence of the "old fire" in Tagore's most recent poems and play, and the author himself delighted in joining the fun.

However, it took nearly ten years for this work to see the lights of a stage. Before the play was published, Tagore had given Sisir Bhaduri exclusive permission to stage it, but the production never materialised. In August 1924 the Bengali theatre magazine *Nāchghar* anticipated with eager interest the upcoming production of *Rakta-karavī*; in March 1925 it asked, "What happened to the staging of the play *Rakta-karavī*?"[5] Apparently a suitable Nandini could not be found.[6] As late as November 1927, Tagore wrote in a letter that he had finalised the cast for a production, including himself as the Raja, but this endeavour too was stillborn.[7] Eventually, the Tagore family staged the play at Natya Niketan on 6 April 1934, and Tagore attended the performance.[8] The difficulties in getting the play produced led to popular doubts about its stageworthiness, and it was not until Bohurupee's trend-setting production in Calcutta on 10 May 1954 (under the direction of Sombhu Mitra) that its reputation as a closet drama was finally laid to rest.[9]

INTRODUCTION[10]

This play is based in reality. Readers will be deceived if the responsibility of collecting evidence to prove whether the event has occurred anywhere is placed upon historians. Suffice it to say this much, that according to the poet's knowledge and belief it is completely real.

It is possible that geographers will have differences of opinion regarding the actual name of the place of occurrence. But everybody knows its nickname is Yakshapuri.[11] Pandits say that the Puranic Yakshapuri contained the golden throne of Kubera, the god of wealth. But this play is not at all of Puranic times, it cannot even be called an allegory. A Yaksha treasure is buried underground in the place about which we are speaking. The treasure having been detected, the excavation of tunnels continues in the underworld, and for this reason alone people have affectionately named it Yakshapuri. In due course in this play we will be introduced to the tunnel-excavators of this place.

Nobody expects agreement of opinion among historians concerning the actual name of Yakshapuri's Raja. This much we know, that he has a nickname — Makar-raja.[12] The reason for this nomenclature will be understood in due time through the mouths of the people.

On the outer wall of the Raja's residence is a screen window. From behind that screen Makar-raja serves men to the degree he pleases. We do not know any more about his reasons for such strange behaviour than the meagre conversation and discussion on it that the characters provide.

The sardars of this state are worthy people and what is known as "experienced". They are the Raja's intimate counsellors.[13] By virtue of their careful arrangements the excavators find no opportunity for relief in work and Yakshapuri's endless prosperity continues. The headmen here were at one time excavators; their promotions and titles have accrued through their own merit. In their devotion to work they surpass in many respects the sardars. If, in the poet's language, Yakshapuri's laws can be termed the full moon, then the responsibility for its dark spots falls chiefly on the headmen.

Apart from these, there is one Gosain-ji;[14] he takes the name of

God but takes food from the sardars. Through him many benefits occur to Yakshapuri.

Sometimes aquatic creatures of the inedible variety accidentally get caught in fishermen's nets. Not only do they not suit the work of filling stomachs or filling pockets, in the process they tear the nets too. A girl named Nandini has arrived in a similar manner in the story-net of this play. This girl, it seems, will not allow the barrier behind which Makar-raja stays to endure.

At the very beginning of the play we shall meet this girl on the verandah outside the Raja's screen window. It would be impossible to describe very clearly what kind of window it is. Only those who are its artisans understand its artifice.

All of the dramatic incidents that we witness occur on the verandah outside this screen window of the Raja's residence. We get to know very little indeed of what happens inside.

[Rabindranath Tagore]

CAST OF CHARACTERS

Nandini (Nandinī)
Kishor (Kiśor), a boy excavator
The Professor
Gokul (Gokul), an excavator
Phagulal (Phāgulāl), an excavator
Chandra (Chandrā), Phagulal's wife
Bishu (Viśu)
The Sardar
The Gosain (Gosāiṅ)
A Headman
An Assistant Sardar
A Puranic Scholar
A Wrestler
A Guard
A Doctor
The Headman of Section E
The Deputy Sardar
Four Groups of People
The Raja

This translation of *Red Oleander* was first staged by Myriad Productions at Camden People's Theatre, London, in July 2006, directed by Kevin Rowntree.

*The town in which these dramatic events are set is named Yakshapuri.
Its band of labourers is employed in underground mining for gold. Its
Raja lives behind an extremely complex screen. That netted screen of
the palace is the only scene in this play. The entire action occurs on the
outer portion of that screen.*

Nandini and Kishor, a tunnel-excavator boy

KISHOR: Nandini, Nandini, Nandini!

NANDINI: Why do you call me so many times, Kishor? Can't I hear?

KISHOR: I know you can hear me, but I like calling out your name.
Do you need any more flowers? If so I'll go bring some more.

NANDINI: Go, go, return to your work immediately, don't be late.

KISHOR: All I do the whole day is dig up lumps of gold. I'd be relieved
if I could take a little time off from it to find flowers for you.

NANDINI: Oh Kishor, if they find out they'll punish you.

KISHOR: But you said you must have red oleanders.[16] I'm happy
that red oleanders can't easily be found here. After a lot of
searching I've found in one place just one tree, behind some
rubbish.

NANDINI: Show it to me, I'll go myself and pick up the flowers.

KISHOR: Don't say such things. Nandini, don't be cruel. Let that
tree remain as my only secret. Bishu sings you songs, they are
his own songs. From now on I'll bring you flowers, they will
be my very own flowers.

NANDINI: But the beasts here punish you, and it breaks my heart.

KISHOR: That pain makes my flowers blossom all the more as mine.
They are the treasures of my sorrow.

NANDINI: But how can I bear this sorrow which all of you suffer?

KISHOR: What sorrow? One day I'll give my life for you, Nandini,
I think about this so often to myself.

NANDINI: You have given me so much, what can I give you in
return — tell me, Kishor?

KISHOR: Make me this promise, Nandini, that you will accept
flowers only from my hand every morning.

NANDINI: All right, I promise. But do be a little careful.

KISHOR: No, I will never be careful, never! I will bring you flowers
every day, right in the face of their beatings.

Exit

Enter Professor

PROFESSOR: Nandini! Don't go away, look back.

NANDINI: What, Professor?

PROFESSOR: Why do you dazzle us like that every now and then, and go away? Since you touch the heart so, you may as well answer before you leave. Wait a bit, let me tell you a couple of things.

NANDINI: What need do you have of me?

PROFESSOR: If you speak of need, look over there. Our band of excavators is emerging like worms from the tunnels, on their heads loads of "need" torn from the breast of the earth. In this Yakshapur all the wealth we have is the wealth of that artery of dust—gold. But beautiful one, the gold you are made of is not that of dust, it's the gold of light. Who could tie it into bonds of need?

NANDINI: You say those same words to me time and again. Why do you marvel so much at seeing me, Professor?

PROFESSOR: There is no marvelling at the light that comes to a forest of flowers in the morning, but the light that comes through a crack in a solid wall is another thing altogether. In Yakshapur you are that sudden flash of light. What do you yourself think of this place, tell me.

NANDINI: I'm amazed to see the entire town submerge its head underground and grope its way in the dark. You are unearthing the Yakshas' treasure from the tunnels dug in the underworld. But it is the dead treasure of many yugas, which the earth had left buried.

PROFESSOR: Well, we participate in occult communion with that dead treasure. We want to harness its spirit. If we can capture the ghouls[17] in the piles of gold, we will have the world in the palm of our hand.

NANDINI: Then again, you've kept your Raja hidden behind this strange screen wall, fearing that it will be discovered he is human. I want to open the dark lid to those tunnels of yours and pour light into them; so also do I want to tear down that ugly screen and liberate the man inside.

PROFESSOR: As the spirit of our dead treasure possesses awesome force, so does our Raja, strained of humanity, possess equally fearsome might.

NANDINI: All these are tales made up by you people.

PROFESSOR: Made-up indeed. The naked have no means of introduction; made-up clothes alone make someone a raja, someone a beggar. Come to my house. Making you understand philosophical matters gives me great pleasure.

NANDINI: Day and night you continue digging holes into your books just like your excavators continue lowering themselves into the ground while working the mines. Why would you spend your time wastefully with me?

PROFESSOR: We are stupid insects in a dense hole, engrossed in heavy work; you are the evening star in the sky of free time. Our wings become restless on seeing you. Come to my house, let me waste some time with you.

NANDINI: No, no, not now. I have come to see your Raja inside his house.

PROFESSOR: He lives behind the screen, he won't allow you to enter his house.

NANDINI: I disregard the barrier of the screen, I have come to enter the house.

PROFESSOR: Do you know, Nandini, I too am behind a screen? Only the pandit in me is awake, excluding the rest of man in me. Our Raja is so formidable, and I'm just as formidable a pandit.

NANDINI: You are joking with me. You don't seem formidable at all. Let me ask you one question: they have brought me here, why didn't they bring Ranjan too?

PROFESSOR: Their procedure is to bring everything piece by piece. But still I ask you, why do you want to bring the treasure of your life into the midst of the dead treasure here?

NANDINI: If my Ranjan is brought here their hearts will dance inside their dead ribs.

PROFESSOR: Nandini alone has created consternation among Yakshapuri's sardars. What would happen to them if Ranjan was brought too?

NANDINI: They don't know how odd they are. If God laughs a loud laugh in their midst, only then might their reverie be broken. Ranjan is that laughter of God's.

PROFESSOR: A god's laughter is the light of the sun — it will melt ice, but won't move stone. To move our sardars one needs physical strength.

NANDINI: My Ranjan's strength is like your Śaṅkhinī river. Like that river, he can laugh as well as he can crush. Professor, let me tell you a secret I learnt today. I shall meet Ranjan today.

PROFESSOR: How did you know?

NANDINI: We will, we will, we will meet. The news has come.

PROFESSOR: By which path can news arrive, yet escape the eyes of the Sardar?

NANDINI: The same path by which news arrives that spring is coming. Attached to it are the colours of the sky, the games of the breeze.

PROFESSOR: That means a rumour has arrived in the colours of the sky and the games of the breeze.

NANDINI: When Ranjan comes I'll show you how a rumour in the air came down to earth.

PROFESSOR: If the subject of Ranjan crops up Nandini's mouth doesn't want to stop! Well, I have my science of physics, let me retreat into its cave to study—I dare no more now. (*Moves away slightly, then returns*) Nandini, let me ask you one question: don't you feel afraid of Yakshapuri?

NANDINI: Why should I feel afraid?

PROFESSOR: Animals fear an eclipsed sun, they don't fear the full sun. Yakshapuri is a town eclipsed. The Rāhu[18] of the golden pits has bitten into it. It isn't whole itself, it doesn't want anyone else to remain whole. I'm telling you, don't stay here. If you go away those pits will open their mouths wider in front of us; still I tell you, escape! Live happily with Ranjan in a place where the people don't plunder and rip mother earth's *āṅchal*[19] into little shreds. (*Moves further away, then returns*) Nandini— that bracelet of red oleanders on your right hand—will you loosen a flower from it and give it to me?

NANDINI: Why, what will you do?

PROFESSOR: I have thought many times that there must be some kind of meaning in your wearing those red oleander ornaments.

NANDINI: I don't know of any such meaning.

PROFESSOR: Perhaps your destiny knows. In this blood-red lustre lies a fearful mystery, not merely beauty.

NANDINI: Fear within me?

PROFESSOR: God has placed a blood-red brush in the hand of beauty. I don't know what it is you have come to write in red. The *mālatī* was there, the *mallikā* was there, there was the *chāmeli*;[20] why did you select this flower, rejecting all the others? Do you know that man unwittingly selects his fate in this manner?

NANDINI: Ranjan sometimes calls me "Red Oleander" affectionately. I don't know, I feel somehow that the colour of the love
between Ranjan and myself is red. That colour I've worn on
my neck, on my breast, on my hands.

PROFESSOR: Well, give me one of those flowers, only as a temporary
gift. Let me try to comprehend the essence of its colour.

NANDINI: Here, take it. Today Ranjan will come; in that happiness
I give you this flower.

Exit Professor

Enter Gokul, a tunnel-excavator

GOKUL: Let's see you turn your face once this way — I just can't
understand you. Who are you?

NANDINI: I am nothing else besides what you see. What need do you
have of understanding me?

GOKUL: When I can't understand I feel uneasy. For what work or
purpose has the Raja brought you here?

NANDINI: For some useless purpose.

GOKUL: You possess a spell of some sort. You've thrown everybody
into a trap. You will bring destruction. Those who see that
lovely face of yours and forget will die. Let me see — what's
that hanging in the parting of your hair?

NANDINI: A cluster of red oleanders.

GOKUL: What does it mean?

NANDINI: It has no meaning at all.

GOKUL: I don't believe you. You've plotted a conspiracy of some
sort. You will create some kind of calamity before the day is
done. That's why such an elaborate outfit. Monster, O you
monster!

NANDINI: Why do you feel my looks are so terrifying?

GOKUL: Looking at you makes me feel you are a torch of red light.
I must go, convince the fools, "Beware, beware, beware!"

Exit

NANDINI: (*Knocking on the screen door*) Can you hear me?

VOICE FROM BEHIND THE SCENE: Nandā,[21] I can hear you. But don't
call me repeatedly; I don't have time, none at all.

NANDINI: My heart feels full today in happiness. I want to go into
your house with that happiness.

VOICE: No, not inside the house, speak from outside whatever you
have to say.

NANDINI : I have thread a garland of jasmine,[22] and brought it covered in lotus leaves.

VOICE : Wear it yourself.

NANDINI : It doesn't suit me, my garland is of red oleanders.

VOICE : I am like the summit of a mountain, bareness itself is my splendour.

NANDINI : Waterfalls flow down the chest of that peak; so also will garlands from your neck. Open the screen, I must go in.

VOICE : I won't let you come in; tell me quickly what you have to say. There is no time.

NANDINI : Can you hear that song in the distance?

VOICE : What is the song about?

NANDINI : A song of Paush.[23] The crop has ripened, it has to be harvested — that is its cry.

Song

> Paush is calling for you — oh, come along.
> Her basket's full with ripe harvest today.

Can't you see the Paush sun spreading the gracefulness of the ripe rice across the skies?

> Intoxicated by the winds
> The spirits[24] rise in the rice fields,
> The gold of sunlight streams upon the *añchal* of the earth.

Come out, you too, Raja, let me take you to the fields!

> The sky is delighted on hearing the flute of the fields —
> Who would remain in their houses today? Open the doors!

VOICE : I go to the fields? What work will I do?

NANDINI : Work in the fields is much easier than the work in your Yakshapuri.

VOICE : The simple task to me is always difficult. Can a lake dance like a waterfall wearing anklets of spray? Go, go, don't talk any more, there's no time.

NANDINI : Your power is strange! The day you allowed me to enter your treasury I wasn't at all surprised to see your piles of gold. But I was fascinated by seeing the immense power with which you were effortlessly arranging them into a mound. Still I say, can lumps of gold answer to the wonderful rhythm of those hands of yours, as can fields of rice? Well Raja, tell me, don't you feel afraid to handle day and night these dead treasures of the earth?

VOICE: Why, what should I fear?

NANDINI: The earth herself gives us the substance of her heart, happily. But when you rip open her breast, and snatch up the bones calling them wealth, you bring from the dark the curse of a blind *rākshas*.[25] Can't you see, everyone here seems to be angry, or suspicious, or afraid?

VOICE: A curse?

NANDINI: Yes, the curse of bloodshed and robbery.

VOICE: I don't know of any curses. I do know that we bring power. Are you pleased with my power, Nandin?[26]

NANDINI: I feel very pleased. That's why I say come out into the light, place your feet on the ground, let the earth be pleased too.

> The joy of light awakens with
> The dew upon the stalks of rice,
> The joy of earth knows no restraint, look there — it over-
> flows.

VOICE: Nandini, do you know that God has kept even you behind an illusion of beauty, apparently wonderful? I want to snatch you away from there and keep you within my fist, but I can never catch you. I want to see you from all aspects, and if I cannot I want to break you into pieces.

NANDINI: Oh, what are you saying?

VOICE: Why am I unable to distil the glow of those red oleanders of yours and wear it as collyrium around my eyes? A few mere petals cover you with an *āṅchal* and obstruct me. A similar obstruction lies within you — difficult because so delicate. All right Nandini, what do you think of me, tell me openly.

NANDINI: I'll tell you that another day. Today you don't have any time, today I'll go.

VOICE: No, no, don't go; tell me. Say what you think of me.

NANDINI: How many times have I told you, I think you're wonder-ful. Tremendous strength swollen up in enormous arms, like the clouds heralding a storm — my heart dances on seeing you.

VOICE: Your heart also dances on seeing Ranjan, is that too —

NANDINI: That talk can wait, you don't seem to have the time.

VOICE: There is time, just tell me the answer and go.

NANDINI : The beat of that dance is different, you won't understand
   it.

VOICE : I will understand. I want to understand.

NANDINI : I can't explain everything clearly, I'll go.

VOICE : Don't go. Tell me whether you like me or not.

NANDINI : Yes, I like you.

VOICE : Just like Ranjan?

NANDINI : You always return to the same theme. You don't understand these matters.

VOICE : I understand some of it. I know what the difference is
   between Ranjan and myself. Only strength lies within me, magic
   lies within Ranjan.

NANDINI : What do you call magic?

VOICE : Shall I explain? In the earth's lower level are lumps and
   lumps of stone, iron, gold; therein lies the icon of strength.
   At the upper level grass grows, flowers blossom on a little bit
   of fresh turf—therein lies the game of magic. I bring diamonds, rubies, from the impenetrable; but I cannot wrest
   that bit of life's magic from the accessible.

NANDINI : You have plenty, why do you still talk so much like a
   greedy man?

VOICE : All that I have is a burden. Gold hoarded away still doesn't
   become the touchstone—however much I increase my power
   it hasn't arrived at youth. So I want to bind you by keeping
   guard over you; if I had youth like Ranjan's I could have left
   you free yet bound you. My time's been spent in knotting
   thus the ropes of your confinement. Ah, but all else may be
   captured, only happiness can't.

NANDINI : Well, you've tied yourself up in a screen, so I don't
   understand why you behave so restlessly.

VOICE : You won't be able to understand. I am an enormous desert—
   I extend my hand toward a small blade of grass like you, saying,
   "I am burning, I am empty, I am weary." Consumed by the fire
   of thirst, this desert has lapped up many fertile regions, so that
   its extent ever increases. Yet it cannot make part of itself the
   life within that tiny fragile blade of grass.

NANDINI : Looking at you it doesn't seem at all that you're so weary.
   I can see only your great strength.

VOICE : Nandin, one day in a distant country I saw a weary mountain
   just like myself. From the outside I just couldn't make out that

all its rock pined inwardly. Late one night I heard a horrifying noise, as if some demon's long-suppressed nightmare had suddenly broken. In the morning I saw that the mountain had sunk underground from the force of an earthquake. I understood from seeing that mountain how the burden of power crushes itself, unknown to itself. And, in you I see something— which is its opposite.

NANDINI: What do you see in me?

VOICE: The dance rhythm that plays on the flute of the universe.

NANDINI: I don't understand.

VOICE: By that rhythm the immense burden of the elements becomes light. By that rhythm the troupes of stars and planets dance about the skies like poor minstrel boys. By that dance rhythm alone, Nandini, have you become so simple, so beautiful. Compared to me you are diminutive, yet I envy you.

NANDINI: You have separated yourself from everyone, depriving yourself; why don't you reveal yourself easily?

VOICE: By keeping myself hidden I have set out to steal the rich substances in the world's large warehouses. But the strength of my entire body cannot take me near that gift enclosed within the palm of God's hand, which your finger like a champak bud can reach freely. I must open that closed fist of God's.

NANDINI: I can't understand very well all this talk of yours, I'll go.

VOICE: All right, go — but I'm extending this hand out of the window, place your hand upon it once.

NANDINI: No, no, I feel afraid if a hand appears suddenly without the rest of yourself.

VOICE: Just because I want to hold with one hand everyone runs away from me. But if I wanted to hold you with all of me, would you allow it, Nandin?

NANDINI: You didn't even let me enter the house, so why are you saying all this?

VOICE: I don't want to bring you to my house against the current, into my lack of leisure. The auspicious moment for the song of welcome[27] will strike the day that you arrive effortlessly, sail spread to the wind. Even if that wind happens to be the gale of a storm, it will be fine. The time hasn't come yet.

NANDINI: I'm telling you, Raja, Ranjan will bring the wind for that sail. Wherever he goes he brings freedom with him.

VOICE: Don't I know who keeps that freedom that your Ranjan

carries around filled with the honey of red oleanders? Nandin, you've only given me news of a hollow freedom, where will I find the honey?

NANDINI: I should go now.

VOICE: No, answer this question and then go.

NANDINI: "How is freedom filled with honey?" You will find its answer as soon as you see Ranjan. He is really beautiful.

VOICE: Only beauty can hear the answer of beauty. When anti-beauty wants to snatch the answer away, the strings of the vina do not sound, they snap. No more, go, go away — otherwise trouble will arise.

NANDINI: I'm going, but I tell you before I go, my Ranjan will come today, he will, he will — nothing will be able to prevent him.

Exit

Enter Phagulal, an excavator, and his wife Chandra

PHAGULAL: Where did you hide my drink, Chandra, bring it out!

CHANDRA: What kind of talk is that! Drinking right from the morning?

PHAGULAL: Today's a holiday. Yesterday they observed a vow to the goddess Chandī.[28] Today's the Flag-*pūjā*, with it the Weapons-*pūjā*.[29]

CHANDRA: Is that so? So they believe in gods and deities?

PHAGULAL: Haven't you seen that their drinking-house, armoury and temple exist side by side?

CHANDRA: So just because you've got a holiday you want to drink? But when we were in the village, on festival days you —

PHAGULAL: If a bird gets released in a forest it can fly, if you give it freedom in a cage it knocks its head about and dies. In Yaksha-pur, a holiday's a bigger curse than work.

CHANDRA: Why not leave your job, why don't we return home?

PHAGULAL: The way home is blocked, don't you know that?

CHANDRA: Why blocked?

PHAGULAL: There isn't any profit for them in our home.

CHANDRA: Are we tightly glued to their needs, like husk to grains of rice? Nothing extra left over?

PHAGULAL: Our madman[30] Bishu says, to remain whole is essential only for the goat; those who eat it, do so by throwing away its bones and ribs, hooves and tail. In fact, they even object to the goats' crying "baa" in front of the chopping block, saying it's excessive. There's mad Bishu, singing along as he comes.

CHANDRA: His songs suddenly burst forth over the last few days.

PHAGULAL: That's what I see.

CHANDRA: He's possessed by Nandini; she pulls at his heart, at his songs too.

PHAGULAL: And what's surprising about that?

CHANDRA: No, there's nothing surprising at all. But be careful, some day she'll bring out songs from your voice too — what will be the state of people in the neighbourhood on that day? The enchantress knows magic. She'll make trouble.

PHAGULAL: Bishu's trouble hasn't begun today, he knew Nandini long before he came here.

CHANDRA: Brother[31] Bishu, listen, listen. Where are you going? You may find a few listeners for your songs here too, it won't be a complete loss.

Bishu's entrance and song

Who are you, boatman of my dreams?
　　The drunk wind strikes the sail,
　　The wild soul sings along.
Make me forget
By your swaying,
Carry me to your distant shore.

CHANDRA: Then there's no hope, because we're too near.

BISHU:
　　My worries are all false,
　　My all remains behind.
　　Remove your veil,[32]
　　Lift up your eyes,
　　Cover my soul with your warm smile.

CHANDRA: I know who the boatman of your dreams is.

BISHU: From the outside how would you know? You haven't seen her from the middle of my boat.

CHANDRA: I'm telling you, that Nandini of your desires will sink your boat one day.

Enter Gokul

GOKUL: Look Bishu, I don't feel good about that Nandini of yours.

BISHU: Why, what has she done?

GOKUL: Doesn't do a thing, that's why I have misgivings. Why did the Raja unnecessarily have her brought here? I don't understand her ways at all.

CHANDRA: Brother, this is our place of sorrow. She just goes around here being beautiful twenty-four hours a day, which we can't stand.

GOKUL: We trust appearances of a plain, ordinary type, quite solid in bearing.

BISHU: The air of Yakshapuri breeds contempt for beauty, that's precisely the danger. There's beauty in hell too, but no one there can understand beauty; that's the greatest punishment of all for those living in hell.

CHANDRA: All right, fine, maybe we are the idiots, but even the Sardar here can't bear to see her, you know that?

BISHU: Careful, Chandra, that the Sardar's eye infection doesn't touch you, otherwise your eyes will become red on seeing us as well. —All right, what do you say Phagulal?

PHAGULAL: To tell you the truth, brother, when I see Nandini, I feel ashamed to look at myself. I can't speak in front of her.

GOKUL: Brother Bishu, your mind's gone astray having seen that girl, that's why you can't see what an ill omen she has brought along. It won't be too late before you find out, I tell you.

PHAGULAL: Brother Bishu, your sister[33] wishes to know why we drink.

BISHU: By the Almighty's own mercy wine has been allotted across the four corners of the world, even in those sidelong glances from you women. By these arms of ours we supply work, by the embrace of your arms you supply wine. In this world we have to work, and we have to forget work too. If there wasn't wine what would make us forget?

CHANDRA: Is that so? There's no end to God's kindness for drunks-from-birth like you. He has overturned the wine pitcher!

BISHU: From one direction hunger whips us, thirst whips us; they inflict pain—they say, do your work. In the other direction the forest's green spreads maya, the sun's gold spreads maya; they ignite intoxication—they say, freedom, freedom.

CHANDRA: These things are called wine, are they?

BISHU: The wine of life; the intoxication is fleeting, but it attracts day and night. Look at the proof. I came to this kingdom, got to work burglarising the underworld, the ration of natural wine was stopped. That's why my inner spirit now revels in the liquors of the bazaar. When normal breathing is obstructed, then only does man draw his breath by panting.

Song

The spirit[34] of your life runs dry,
So fill the cup with the spirit of death.
It is squeezed from the fire of the funeral pyre,
   Relieves the pain of suffering,
It colours all the emptiness with loud laughter.

CHANDRA: Come on, brother, let's escape.

BISHU: Under that blue canopy, in the open wine-haunt! The path's closed. That's the reason for so terrifying an attraction to illicit liquor in this prison. We have neither the sky, nor the time; so we've distilled the essence of all the laughter, songs and sunlight of twelve hours into one sip of liquid fire. The denser the slavery the darker the freedom.

Your sun's embedded in dense clouds,
Your day has died in useless deeds,
So allow that dark, deepening night to arrive,
   Lost oblivion's last companion,
To cover your tired eyes with veiled, devious darkness.

CHANDRA: Whatever you say, brother Bishu, it's you men who have lost yourselves after coming to Yakshapuri. But nothing's changed in us women.

BISHU: Hasn't it? Your flowers have dried up, now your soul gasps "gold, gold".

CHANDRA: Certainly not.

BISHU: I say "yes". That miserable Phagu, after the usual twelve hours, adds another four hours to die working, for a reason Phagu himself doesn't know, you too don't know. But God knows. Your dream of gold lashes him inside, a lashing harsher than that of even the Sardar.

CHANDRA: All right, fine, then why don't we go, let's leave here and return home.

BISHU: The Sardar has not only closed the path of return, he has blocked the desire as well. Even if you go home today you won't

be able to stand it; by tomorrow you'll come running back
intoxicated by the gold, like an opium-fed bird returns to its
cage even after being released.

PHAGULAL: All right brother Bishu; but once you used to ruin your
eyes reading books, why did they hand you a spade to join
fools like us?

CHANDRA: We've been here so long, but have never succeeded in
getting the answer to this question from our brother.

PHAGULAL: Yet everybody knows the reason.

BISHU: What, tell me.

PHAGULAL: They kept you as a spy to gather information about us.

BISHU: If all of you knew, why did you keep me alive?

PHAGULAL: We also know that this job couldn't be done by you.

CHANDRA: Couldn't even stick to such a comfortable job, brother?

BISHU: Comfortable job? To stick like an open sore to the back of a
body full of life! I said, "I'm going home, my health is very
bad." The Sardar said, "Oh, with such bad health how will
you go home at all? Still, try and see." I tried. Finally I saw
that if you enter the mouth of Yakshapuri its jaws close; now
there's no path at all except the path going into its belly. Today
I'm digested inside that hopeless lightless belly. Now the
difference between you and me is that the Sardar disregards me
even more than he does you. More than the torn banana leaf
man despises the broken claypot.[35]

PHAGULAL: Why the sadness, brother Bishu? We've raised you
upon our shoulders.

BISHU: As soon as it's discovered I'll be dead. Where your affections
fall, there too falls the Sardar's vision. However excitedly the
golden frog welcomes the toad with its croaks, they reach the
ears of the viper.[36]

CHANDRA: In how many days will you people finish your work?

BISHU: The calendar doesn't show the end of our days. After day
one comes day two, after day two day three; I still continue
digging the tunnel, yard one followed by yard two, yard two
followed by yard three. I bring up piles and piles of gold, after
the first pile the second, after the second pile the third. In
Yakshapur figures follow figures continuously in rows, never
reaching any total. That's why for them we're not people,
we're only numbers. Brother Phagu, what number are you?

PHAGULAL: It's painted on the clothes on my back, I'm 47-P.

BISHU: I'm 69-U. In the village I was a person, here I've become one square in the game of 10-25.[37] Gambling continues upon my chest.

CHANDRA: Brother, they've collected a lot of gold, what need do they have of more?

BISHU: There's an end to things of need. There is need to eat, it can be ended by filling the stomach; there is no need for intoxication, so no end to it either. Those piles of gold are wine, our Yaksha-raja's[38] solidified wine. Can't you understand?

CHANDRA: No.

BISHU: With our cup of liquor we forget we are tied within the bounds of fate. We think we have unrestricted freedom. With the lump of gold in his hand the master of this place feels the same illusion. He thinks the gravitational pull that affects all common people doesn't reach him; he flies the sky of the uncommon.

CHANDRA: In villages all over preparations are being made because the time for the harvest festival[39] has come. I fall at your feet, let's go home. If we went to the Sardar once —

BISHU: Your feminine intelligence hasn't yet understood the Sardar, has it?

CHANDRA: Why, he appears to me quite —

BISHU: Yes, quite dazzling. The teeth of a *makar*, dovetailing very neatly as they bite you. Makar-raja himself couldn't loosen them even if he wished.

CHANDRA: There's the Sardar.

BISHU: That's done it. He must have heard our words.

CHANDRA: Why, we haven't said any such thing that would —

BISHU: Sister, we speak the words, but they provide the meaning. So, no one knows which charcoal speck of a word sets fire to which thatch roof.

Enter Sardar

CHANDRA: Sardar, grandfather![40]

SARDAR: What, grand-daughter, everything all right I hope?

CHANDRA: Give us leave to go home.

SARDAR: Why? That place I've given you is really excellent, much better than your home. Even a watchman has been hired at the government's expense. Well now, 69-U, seeing you among these people makes me think that a crane has come to teach a group of herons to dance.[41]

BISHU: Sardar-ji, your joke doesn't amuse me. If I had the strength
in my feet to make others dance I would have run away from
here immediately. I've seen many examples in your territory
of how dangerous the business is of making people dance, so
much so that the feet tremble to walk even in a normal manner.

SARDAR: Grand-daughter, there's one bit of good news. To make
these people hear the good word I've had Kenaram Gosain
brought here. The tributes realised from these people will
defray the cost. From Gosain-ji every evening they will—

PHAGULAL: No no, that won't do, Sardar-ji. Now at the worst we
go wild after drinking in the evenings; if he comes to preach
advice there'll be murder.

BISHU: Quiet, quiet, Phagulal.

Enter Gosain

SARDAR: Here he is, just as we were speaking of him. Master, my
praṇām.[42] The weak minds of these, our workers, sometimes
become restless. Present some peaceful mantras to their ears—
it's highly necessary.

GOSAIN: You're speaking of these people? Ah, but they are the
Tortoise-avatar himself.[43] It is because they have weighted
themselves under their burden that the whole world functions.
To think of it makes me have gooseflesh. My son 47-P, notice
carefully, this mouth that sings holy *kīrtans*[44] is the same mouth
to which you all bring food; the same holy wrap[45] that purifies
this body by being worn has been manufactured by yourselves
through the sweat of your brow. Is that a mean task? I bless you
that you may always remain unperturbed, since only then will
the mercy of the Lord too remain undisturbed upon you. My
sons, free your voices just once and say "Hari, Hari".[46] May
all your burdens be lightened. The chant of Hari must be the
beginning, the middle and the end.[47]

CHANDRA: Ah, how sweet. Father, I haven't heard such words in
many days. Please, please, allow me some dust from your feet.

PHAGULAL: I've been unmoved so long, but I can't continue any
more. Sardar, why such a great waste of money? If you want to
receive tributes we're willing, but we won't stand for fraud.

BISHU: Once Phagulal gets mad there's no saving us—quiet, quiet.

CHANDRA: Are you set on ruining both this life and the next? What

will be your fate? You never had such intentions before; I can
see quite well, that Nandini's influence has touched all of you.

GOSAIN: Whatever you say, Sardar, such simplicity! They speak
exactly what they feel; will we teach them or will they educate
us? You understand?

SARDAR: Sure, I understand. I also understand where the disturbance originated. I'll have to take charge of these people myself.
Meanwhile, Honourable Master, spread the holy name in that
section, the woodcutters there seem to have become a little
irritable.

GOSAIN: Which section did you say, Sardar, my son?

SARDAR: Over there, in sections T/1 and T/2. 71-T is the headman
there. That section ends to the left of where 65 of N/1 lives.

GOSAIN: My son, although section N/2 is still unstable, the N/1s of
late are virtually subdued in pleasant spirits. That's because
their ears are ready to receive mantras. Still it's good to keep
forces in that section a few more months. The reason is, Pride
Goeth Before a Fall.[48] The pride is vanquished by the pressure
of your forces, after which it's our turn. Well, I shall depart.

CHANDRA: Master, bless us, that these people here come to their
senses. Don't take offence.

GOSAIN: Fear not, mother Lakshmī,[49] they will be completely
pacified.

Exit

SARDAR: Hey 69-U, I notice something about the mood of that
section of yours!

BISHU: That may be. Gosain-ji called them the Tortoise-avatar,
but according to *śāstra*[50] the avatars change. The Tortoise
suddenly turns into the Boar; instead of armour there emerges
teeth, instead of patience obstinacy.

CHANDRA: Brother Bishu, stop for a little while. Sardar, grandfather, don't forget my request.

SARDAR: Certainly not. I've heard it, I'll keep it in mind too.

Exit

CHANDRA: Ah, did you see? The Sardar is such an excellent person.
He speaks smilingly with everyone.

BISHU: The *makar*'s teeth begin with a smile, end with a bite.

CHANDRA: Where does the bite come in here?

BISHU: Don't you know, they've decided that from now on the workers can't bring their wives here with them?

CHANDRA: Why?

BISHU: We find place in their account books in the form of numbers, but the mating of the figures of women with numerical figures doesn't balance in their mathematics.

CHANDRA: Oh no! Are there no wives in their own homes? What do they say?

BISHU: They too are swooning with the wine of gold lumps. In their addiction they surpass their husbands. Their eyes don't even notice us.

CHANDRA: Brother Bishu, you had a wife at home, what happened to her? I haven't had news of her in many days.

BISHU: So long as I filled the high position of spy, she would get summons to play cards in the mansions of the sardars' wives. When I joined the band of Phagulal and the others, her invitations to that section stopped. Because of that humiliation she left me and went away.

CHANDRA: *Chhi*,[51] can anyone commit such a sin?

BISHU: As punishment for this sin she will be born in future lives as a sardar's wife.

CHANDRA: Brother Bishu, look, look there, people going in such grandeur. Rows and rows of peacock-shaped palanquins, do you see the fringes on the elephants' howdahs? They sparkle! What marvellous cavalrymen! They look as if they're each carrying a piece of sunlight pinned to the tips of their spears.

BISHU: That's them, the sardars' wives, going to the feast of the Flag-*pūjā*.

CHANDRA: Oh, what splendid costumes! What appearances! Tell me, brother, if you hadn't left the job, would you too have gone out in their group with such splendour? And that wife of yours—

BISHU: Yes, we too would have been in that condition.

CHANDRA: Now there's no way to return? Not at all?

BISHU: There is, through the gutter.

VOICE OFFSTAGE: My mad brother![52]

BISHU: What, mad one?

PHAGULAL: There's the call of your Nandini. For today we won't be able to have brother Bishu any more.

CHANDRA: Don't have any more hopes for your brother Bishu.

Through what happiness has she charmed you, tell me, brother?

BISHU: Charmed me through sorrow.

CHANDRA: Brother, why do you speak so contradictorily?

BISHU: You people won't understand. There are such sorrows from which no sorrow can charm you.

PHAGULAL: Brother Bishu, talk clearly, otherwise it angers me.

BISHU: I'm telling you, listen; the sorrow of desiring that which is near belongs to animals, the sorrow of longing for what is remote belongs to men. That distant light of my perpetual sorrow has found expression in Nandini.

CHANDRA: I don't understand all these words, brother; one thing I do understand is that the less you people understand a girl the more she attracts you. We are simple, our price is low, yet whatever happens we take you people along the straight path. But today I tell you, that girl will drag you on the path to disaster, in the noose of her garland of red oleanders.

Exit Chandra and Phagulal

Enter Nandini

NANDINI: My mad brother, this morning they were singing the songs of Paush as they went along the distant road to the fields, did you hear them?

BISHU: Is my morning like your morning, that I'll be able to hear songs? It is just a swept-away leftover of the weary night.

NANDINI: In my happiness today I thought I'd climb to the top of our ramparts and join in their singing. I couldn't find a way anywhere, so I've come to you.

BISHU: But I'm not a rampart.

NANDINI: You *are* my rampart. When I come to you I can climb high and see the outside.

BISHU: I feel surprised hearing these words from your lips.

NANDINI: Why?

BISHU: All this time, since I entered Yakshapuri, I used to think I'd lost the sky from my life. I used to think they had ground me under a husking pedal into a thick heap with the other fragmented people here. Within it there were no openings. At that time you came and looked at my face in such a way, I understood light could still be seen within me.

NANDINI: My mad brother, inside this closed fortress a piece of sky

survives only in the middle between you and me. Everywhere
else is shut.

BISHU: Only because that sky is there can I sing you songs.

Song

You keep me awake so that I sing you songs,
 O destroyer of sleep.
So that's why you call me and startle my breast,
 O awaker of grief.
 Comes darkness around,
 Birds come to their nests,
 Boats come to the shore,
But only my heart cannot find any rest,
 O awaker of grief.

NANDINI: My mad Bishu, you call me "awaker of grief"?

BISHU: You are a messenger from the inaccessible coast of my
ocean. The day you came to Yakshapuri, you arrived on a
saltwater breeze that buffeted my heart.

 For while I worked
You never let the swells of weeping cease.
 After you touched me,
 Filled life with nectar,[53]
 Moved away later,
Perhaps you still stand in the shade of my pain,
 O awaker of grief.

NANDINI: Let me tell you one thing, madman. I did not know
beforehand about the sorrow of which you sing.

BISHU: Why, what about Ranjan?

NANDINI: No, he holds two oars in his hands and takes me across
the cyclone-struck river; he holds the mane of a wild horse
and races me through the forest; he shoots an arrow between
the eyebrows of a leaping tiger and blows away my fear with
loud laughter. Just as he upsets the current of our Nāgāi
river after jumping into it, so does he continue to disturb
me. He stakes everything, including his life, playing to win in
a game of gambling. He's even won me in that game. Well, once
you were in it too, but for some reason you went away alone
from the betting crowd. At the time you left you looked at me

in such a way I couldn't understand — afterwards I had no
news of you for so long. Tell me, where did you go?
BISHU:

Song

O moon, the tide of tears now strikes the sea of sorrow,
The whispers reach the brim of this shore and the other.
My boat was on known banks, its moorings came untied,
The breezes took it to the edge of some unknown.

NANDINI: Who pulled you away again from that edge of the unknown to the work of digging tunnels here in Yakshapuri?
BISHU: A certain girl. Just as a flying bird drops to the ground when
suddenly hit by an arrow, so has she thrown me in this dust; I
had forgotten myself.
NANDINI: How was she able to touch you?
BISHU: When the hope of finding water to quench thirst has passed,
mirages deceive easily. After that the lost self can't be found any
more. One day I was watching through the western window
the golden city of the clouds, and she was watching the Sardar's
golden spires. She told me through a sidelong glance, "Take
me over there, let's see how great your powers are." I dared to
say, "I'll take you." I brought her beneath the golden spires.
Then the illusion I was under broke.
NANDINI: I've come, I'll take you out, away from here. I'll break
the golden chains.
BISHU: Since you've caused even the Raja of this place to waver,
what's going to stop you? Tell me, aren't you afraid of him?
NANDINI: From outside this screen one feels fear. But I've gone
inside and seen him.
BISHU: What did you see?
NANDINI: I saw a man, but gigantic. The forehead like the gateway
of a huge seven-sectioned building. The two arms the iron bolts
of some unapproachable fort. It seemed like somebody from
the *Rāmāyaṇa* or *Mahābhārata* had come down.
BISHU: What did you see when you entered the room?
NANDINI: A falcon sat upon his right arm; he set it on a perch and
kept staring at my face. After that, just like he'd been running
his fingers down the falcon's wing, he took my hand in the
same way and began stroking it gently. A little later he asked
suddenly, "Don't you fear me?" I said, "Not one bit." Then

he held my open hair in his hands and for some time sat with eyes closed.

BISHU: How did you feel?

NANDINI: I felt good. Shall I tell you in what way? He was like a thousand-year-old banyan tree, I like a small bird. If I swing a little while on the tip of one of his branches, surely he feels happy down to his marrow. I wish to give this bit of happiness to that lonely soul.

BISHU: After that what did he say?

NANDINI: At one point he started up and, placing his gaze like a spearhead on my face, suddenly said, "I want to know you." My body shivered involuntarily. I said, "What is there to know? Am I your manuscript?" He said, "I know all that there is in manuscripts, I don't know you." After that he spoke somewhat eagerly, "Tell me about Ranjan. In what way do you love him?" I said, "Like the rudder in the water loves the sail in the sky — the song of the wind strikes the sail, and the dance of the waves awakes the rudder." Like a big greedy boy he kept staring and listened silently. Suddenly he startled me by saying, "Can you give your life for him?" I said, "Right now." He seemed angry as he roared out, "Certainly not." I said, "Yes I can." "What would you gain out of it?" I said, "I don't know." Then he said restlessly, "Go, go from my room, go, don't ruin my work." I couldn't understand the meaning.

BISHU: He wants to know the clear meaning of every word. That which he cannot understand makes his mind impatient, and because of that he gets angry.

NANDINI: My mad brother, don't you have pity for him?

BISHU: The day God has pity for him, that day he will die.

NANDINI: No, no, you don't know how desperate he has become because he wants to live.

BISHU: This very day you'll be able to see what is meant by his living; I don't know if you'll be able to bear it or not.

NANDINI: Look there, my mad brother, that shadow. I'm sure the Sardar has heard our words secretly.

BISHU: But here the Sardar's shadow lies in all directions, where's the opportunity to evade it? — How do you like the Sardar?

NANDINI: I haven't seen anything as dead as him. Like a cane cut and brought from a cane-forest. No leaves, no roots, no sap in its pith, so dried up it's withered.

BISHU: The unfortunate man has given his life just to repress life.

NANDINI: Quiet, he'll hear you.

BISHU: But he hears even the keeping quiet, which increases the danger further. When I'm with the excavators, I toe the Sardar's line in conversations. That's why they call me worthless and have kept me alive through sheer contempt. They don't touch me even with their rod. But my mad girl, in front of you the mind becomes courageous, it seems to scorn caution.

NANDINI: No, no, don't call upon trouble. Look there, the Sardar has arrived.

Enter Sardar

SARDAR: Well hello 69-U, you have love for just about everyone, don't you discriminate?

BISHU: So much so that it had begun with you too, but it was my discrimination that created an obstacle.

SARDAR: What's the discussion all about?

BISHU: We're having a conference about the ways in which we can get out of your fortress.

SARDAR: What did you say? Such audacity! Aren't you afraid of even admitting it?

BISHU: Sardar, surely you know about it all in your mind. The caged bird pecks at the bars, he certainly doesn't caress them. What if this matter is admitted or not?

SARDAR: That he doesn't caress is well-known; but that he doesn't fear to admit it has become evident over these few days.

NANDINI: Sardar-ji, you had said that you'd bring Ranjan today. Well, won't you keep your word?

SARDAR: You'll be able to see him this very day.

NANDINI: That I knew. But since you've given me hope, may victory be yours, Sardar, take this garland of jasmine.

BISHU: *Chhi, chhi*, you wasted the garland. Why didn't you keep it for Ranjan?

NANDINI: There is a garland for him.

SARDAR: Of course there is, I suppose that one dangling from your neck? These jasmines are a victory laurel, for they are a gift of the hands—and those red oleanders are a welcome garland, they are a gift of the heart.[54] Good, good, the gift of the hands should be handed over promptly, otherwise it'll dry up; the gift of the heart, the longer it waits the more its value increases.

Exit

NANDINI: (*Near the window*) Can you hear me?

VOICE: What do you want to say, tell me.

NANDINI: Come and stand near the window once.

VOICE: Here, I've come.

NANDINI: Let me go inside the room, I have many things to say.

VOICE: Why do you keep repeating a futile request? The time hasn't come yet. Who's that with you? Ranjan's twin or what?

BISHU: No, Raja, I'm Ranjan's other side, the side on which light doesn't fall — I'm the night of the new moon.

VOICE: What need does Nandini have of you? Nandini, who is this person to you?

NANDINI: He's my companion, he teaches me songs. He's the one who has taught me —

Song

"I love, I love,"
To this tune plays the flute, both near and far, at sea, on land.

VOICE: That's your companion? What would happen if I separated him from your company right now?

NANDINI: Why has the tone of your voice become like that? Please stop. As if you didn't have any companion.

VOICE: My companion? Does the midday sun have any companion?

NANDINI: All right, let's stop that talk. Oh my, what's that in your hand?

VOICE: A dead frog.

NANDINI: What will you do with him?

VOICE: One day this frog got inside a crevice in a rock. Under that cover he existed for three thousand years. From him I was learning the secret of how to keep existing in this manner; he doesn't know how to keep living, though. I didn't like it any more today, I smashed the rock cover, I gave him freedom from endless existing. Isn't that good news?

NANDINI: For me too, your stone fortress will open up today from all directions. I know I'll meet Ranjan today.

VOICE: I would like then to see the two of you together.

NANDINI: You won't be able to see through your glasses, from behind the screen.

VOICE: I'll seat you inside the room and see you.

NANDINI: What'll follow from that?

VOICE: I want to know.

NANDINI: When you speak of knowing, I feel a kind of fear.

VOICE: Why?

NANDINI: I think you have no sympathy for something that can't be known by the mind but can be understood by the heart.

VOICE: I dare not believe it, in case I'm deceived. Go, don't waste time. No, no, wait a bit. Give me that bunch of red oleanders which has fallen near your cheek from your hair.

NANDINI: What'll you do with this?

VOICE: I see that bunch of flowers and I think, the blood-red light of my own Saturn[55] has arrived there in the form of flowers. Sometimes I want to snatch them from you and tear them up; then again I think, should Nandini some day with her own hands adorn my head with that cluster, then —

NANDINI: Then what will happen?

VOICE: Then perhaps I'll be able to die with ease.

NANDINI: One person loves red oleanders, with him in mind I've made those flowers my earrings.

VOICE: Then I say, those are my Saturn as well as his Saturn.

NANDINI: *Chhi, chhi,* what kind of talk is that? I'm going.

VOICE: Where will you go?

NANDINI: I'll sit near your fortress gates.

VOICE: Why?

NANDINI: When Ranjan arrives by that path, he'll be able to see I'm waiting for him alone.

VOICE: If I crush Ranjan, mix him with the dust, and he can't be recognised at all?

NANDINI: What's happened to you today? Why are you frightening me for nothing?

VOICE: Frighten for nothing? Don't you know I'm frightful?

NANDINI: Why is your mood like this all of a sudden? People fear you, is that the only thing you love to see? Śṅkaṇṭha, in our village, plays the *rākshas* in the *yātrā*[56]—when he takes the stage he feels very pleased if the children get scared. You too are in the same condition. Shall I tell you truthfully what I think? You won't get angry?

VOICE: Let's see what you have to say.

NANDINI: The business of people here is to frighten. That's why they have surrounded you with a screen and dressed you up so strangely. Aren't you ashamed to stay dressed up like this, a voodoo doll?

VOICE: What are you saying, Nandini!

NANDINI: Those you have been frightening for so long will one day be ashamed of feeling afraid. If my Ranjan were here, he would have snapped his fingers in your face and died for it, still he wouldn't have felt afraid.

VOICE: Your impudence isn't slight, is it? I feel like making you see, standing you on the peak of the mountain heaped with all that I have smashed to pieces all these days. After that—

NANDINI: After that what?

VOICE: After that I would do my last act of crushing. Like pomegranate seeds squeezed so that their juice seeps through the openings between the fingers, so will I take you in these two hands—go, go, escape right now, at once.

NANDINI: Here I remain standing. Do what you can do. Why do you roar in such an ugly way?

VOICE: I feel like making it apparent to you through all the proof available how uncommonly cruel I am. Haven't you ever heard cries of pain from inside my room?

NANDINI: I have, what cries were they?

VOICE: I crush the Creator's intelligence. I want to snatch all that is hidden in the heart of the world— it's the weeping of all those ripped-up lives. In order to steal fire from a tree it has to be burnt. Nandini, inside you too there is fire, red fire. One day I shall bring it out by burning, before then there's no deliverance.

NANDINI: Why are you cruel?

VOICE: Either I possess, or I destroy. I cannot feel kindness for one whom I cannot possess. Even the act of crushing him is really one way of possessing.

NANDINI: What's that, why do you bring your hand out like that, with fist clenched?

VOICE: All right, I remove my hand; run away, like the pigeon flies on seeing the falcon's shadow.

NANDINI: All right, I'm going, I won't anger you any more.

VOICE: Listen, listen, you come back here. Nandini! Nandini!
NANDINI: What, tell me.
VOICE: In front there's the game[57] of life on your face and eyes,
and at the back the stream of your black hair is the still waterfall of death. That day these hands of mine had found within
it the ease of death by drowning. I have never felt in such a way
the sweetness of death. I wish very much to sleep with my face
covered by those clusters of black hair. You don't know how
tired I am.
NANDINI: Don't you ever sleep?
VOICE: I feel afraid to sleep.
NANDINI: Let me finish singing my song for you —

"I love, I love,"
To this tune plays the flute, both near and far, at sea, on land.
In someone's breast, in the sky
There beats a dull pain,
On the horizon, someone's black eyes overflow with tears.

VOICE: Enough, enough, stop, don't sing any more.
NANDINI:
To that tune, on the shore of the sea
Restraint set free
A deep wailing arises and sways.
To that tune, plays in the mind
Unreasonably
Words of forgotten songs, tears and smiles of forgotten days.

Look there, my mad brother, he has dropped the dead frog
and long since run away. He feels afraid to hear songs.
BISHU: The old frog inside his breast which shuns contact with all
kinds of melody wishes to die when it hears songs. That's why
he feels fear. — My mad girl, I see in your face today a certain
light, won't you tell me what thought has dawned in your mind?
NANDINI: News has arrived in my mind that Ranjan will surely come
today.
BISHU: From which direction did the sure news come?
NANDINI: Listen then, I'll tell you. Every day a blue jay[58] comes and
sits on the branch of the pomegranate tree in front of my window. As soon as evening falls I *praṇām* and tell the pole star,[59]
if a feather from its wing comes and falls inside my room then

I'll know my Ranjan will come. Today, in the morning as soon
as I woke up, I saw a feather carried by the north wind lying
on my bed. Here, see, it's in my *āṅchal* over my breast.

BISHU: That's what I see, and I see you've worn on your forehead
today a mark of saffron.[60]

NANDINI: When I see him I'll place this feather in his crown.

BISHU: People say the feathers of a blue jay have the auspicious
omen of a victorious journey.

NANDINI: Ranjan's victorious journey lies through my heart.

BISHU: My mad girl, I'll go now to my own work.

NANDINI: No, I won't let you work today.

BISHU: What shall I do, tell me.

NANDINI: Sing.

BISHU: What shall I sing?

NANDINI: The song of waiting expectantly and eagerly.

BISHU:

Song

Throughout the yugas I believe he wanted me.
Can it be him who sits beside my path today?
  But why do I remember now,
    The time when through the corner of my eyes
    I saw him in the evening indistinct,
It seems it's him who sits beside my path today.
Tonight the songs of light will welcome over there the moon,
The darkness on the face of night will vanish at a sign.
    And in that light of the white night
    The two of us will meet, for in a blink
    All veils will crumble and will fall away.
It seems it's him who sits beside my path today.

NANDINI: Madman, when you sing I always think, much was due
to you but I haven't been able to give you anything.

BISHU: I will wear that nothing-to-give of yours on my temples and
go away. I won't sell my songs for the price of a-little-to-give.
— Now where will you go?

NANDINI: To the side of the path down which Ranjan will come.
There I'll sit and hear your song again.

Exit both

Enter Sardar and Headman

SARDAR: No, it won't do at all to allow Ranjan to come to this section.

HEADMAN: It was to keep him far away that I had taken him to work in the tunnels of Vajragar.

SARDAR: So what happened?

HEADMAN: We weren't able to at all. He said, "I'm not in the habit of obeying orders to work."

SARDAR: What's the harm in beginning the habit right now?

HEADMAN: We made that attempt. The Chief Headman came with the police. The man knows no form of fear. When the slightest tone of discipline touches our voices he immediately bursts out in loud laughter. If questioned he says, "Solemnity is the mask of stupidity, I have come to take it off."

SARDAR: Why didn't you make him join the crowd in the tunnels?

HEADMAN: I did, thinking that under pressure he'd obey authority. The opposite happened; it seemed the excavators too felt the pressure upon them had decreased. He made them excited, and said, "Today we shall have an excavating dance."

SARDAR: An excavating dance? What does that mean?

HEADMAN: Ranjan began a song; they said, "Where do we get drums?" He said, "If there aren't drums, there are spades." Spades started falling with the beat; what a game of catch there was with the lumps of gold! The Chief Headman himself came and said, "What kind of working method of yours is this?" Ranjan said, "I've opened the ropes of work. we won't have to pull it along, it'll dance along."

SARDAR: I see the man is mad.

HEADMAN: Completely mad. I said, "Hold your spade." He says, "More work than that will result if you bring me a *sārengi*."[61]

SARDAR: You people had taken him to Vajragar, how did he come to Kubergar[62] from there?

HEADMAN: I don't know, my lord. For he had been tightly bound with chains. A little later I see he has slipped out somehow — nothing can hold fast to his body. And, he frequently changes his appearance by changing outfits. Amazing are his abilities. If he stays here a few days the excavators too won't heed restraints.

SARDAR: What's that? Isn't that Ranjan going down the road

singing a song? He's managed to get a broken *sārengi*. Look
at his impudence, not even the slightest attempt to hide.

HEADMAN: That's right. When did he cut through the prison walls
and escape? He knows magic.

SARDAR: Go, take this opportunity to catch him. Make sure he is
never able to meet Nandini in this section.

HEADMAN: His following becomes larger every moment. Some day
he'll excite even us into dancing.

Enter Assistant Sardar

SARDAR: Where are you going?

ASSISTANT SARDAR: Going to tie up Ranjan.

SARDAR: Why you? Where's the Deputy Sardar?[63]

ASSISTANT SARDAR: His Honour is so amused on seeing him that
His Honour doesn't want even to lay hands on him. His Honour
says, "I can understand when I see his smile how strange we
sardars have become."

SARDAR: Listen, you don't have to tie him up; send him to the
Raja's room.

ASSISTANT SARDAR: But he doesn't even want to obey the Raja's
command.

SARDAR: Go tell him, the Raja has kept his Nandini as a concubine.[64]

ASSISTANT SARDAR: But if the Raja—

SARDAR: You don't have to think anything. Come, I'll go myself.

Exit all

Enter Professor and Puranic Scholar

PURANIC SCHOLAR: Tell me, what's this terrible disturbance going
on inside? It's a horrifying noise!

PROFESSOR: The Raja has probably got angry with himself. So he's
shattering something of his own creation.

SCHOLAR: It seems like huge pillars are crumbling down.

PROFESSOR: We had a lake surrounding the foot of that hill, water
from the Śaṅkhinī river used to come and collect in it. One day
the mound of rock at its left tilted and fell over, the stored
water rushed out like a madman's roaring laughter and went
away. I think, after observing the Raja for several days, that
the rock around his hoarded reservoir is being pushed out-

wards, and the bottom has eroded within.

SCHOLAR: Physicist, what is this place you've brought me to, and for that matter what have you brought me to do?

PROFESSOR: He wants to appropriate the means to know just every-thing, all that there is to know in the world. He has virtually exhausted my knowledge of physics; off and on now he gets angry and says, "Your science has only broken one wall with a burglar's tool to discover another wall behind it. But where is the inner chamber of the life-spirit?" I thought, let's distract him now for a few days by discussing the Puranas—my bag has been shaken empty, now let the pickpocketing of antiquity follow. Can you see who's going by over there?

SCHOLAR: A girl wearing green clothes the colour of rice-fields.

PROFESSOR: She has pulled around her entire body the joy of the earth, full of life; that is our Nandini. In this Yakshapur there are sardars, there are headmen, there are excavators, there are pandits like me, there are policemen, there are executioners, there are cremators, all have blended quite well. But she is completely incompatible. In all directions is the clamour of the market, she is the tuned tambura. On certain days just the breeze of her passing by tears up the web of my study of physics. Through the gap the attention flies away and escapes with a whoosh, like a wild bird.

SCHOLAR: Well what do you know, are your seasoned bones affected by such knocks and blows?

PROFESSOR: As soon as the attraction of life becomes greater than the attraction of knowledge, the inclination to escape from school can't be restrained.

SCHOLAR: Now tell me, where will I meet your Raja?

PROFESSOR: There's no way of meeting; the conversation will take place through that screen.

SCHOLAR: What are you saying? Through this screen?

PROFESSOR: If not that, what else? It's not the kind of witty love-talk that can occur through a veil, it's absolutely clear dialogue. The cows in his cowshed probably don't know how to give milk, they give butter right away.

SCHOLAR: To reject the false and realise the true is certainly the pandit's objective.

PROFESSOR: But not God's. He has created true things in order to rear false things carefully. He gives respect to the fruit's seed, but gives love to its pulp.

SCHOLAR: I see at present that your physics is galloping straight toward the green colour of rice-fields. But Professor, how do you tolerate this raja of yours?

PROFESSOR: Shall I tell you the truth? I love him.

SCHOLAR: What are you saying?

PROFESSOR: You don't know, he is so great that even his faults cannot destroy him.

Enter Sardar

SARDAR: Hey physicist, so you handpicked and brought this man! As soon as our Raja heard the description of his subject he flew into a rage.

PROFESSOR: In what way?

SARDAR: The Raja says, there is no such thing as the ancient.[65] It's just the present time that extends continuously.

SCHOLAR: If the ancient isn't there then how is anything there? If the back doesn't exist can the front then exist?

SARDAR: The Raja says: the future proceeds by revealing the new in front, the pandit suppresses that fact and says the future moves along by carrying the old on its back.

PROFESSOR: Every instant the Raja can see the illusory deer[66] of newness in the shaded vista of Nandini's intense youthfulness; but he cannot catch it, and gets angry at my physics.

Enter Nandini, hurriedly

NANDINI: Sardar, Sardar, what's that! Who are they!

SARDAR: Hello Nandini, when I wear your garland of jasmine it will be late at night. When in the dark three-fourths of me becomes indistinct, then perhaps a garland of flowers might suit even me.

NANDINI: Take a look, what a horrifying sight that is! Have the doors of the city of the dead[67] opened? Who are those going with the guards? There, they are coming out through the back door of the Raja's building.

SARDAR: We call them the Raja's leftovers.

NANDINI: What does that mean?

SARDAR: One day you too will understand the meaning, let it be today.

NANDINI: But what shapes are all these? Are they men? Is there anything inside them, flesh, marrow, mind, life?

SARDAR: Perhaps not.

NANDINI: Was there ever any?

SARDAR: Perhaps there was.

NANDINI: Where is it gone now?

SARDAR: Physicist, explain if you can, I'm leaving.

Exit

NANDINI: What's that, among all those shadows I see known faces. That is surely our Anup and Upamanyu. Professor, they are people from our neighbouring village. The two brothers were as strong as they were tall, everyone called them the *tāl* and *tamāl* trees [68] On the fourteenth of Āshārh[69] they would come to take part in the boat-race on our river. I can't bear it, who placed them in such a condition? There I see Śaklu, he would win laurels in swordplay before everyone else. Anu—p, Śaklu—, look this way, it's me, your Nandin, Nandin of Īśānīpārā.[70] You didn't raise your heads to look, your heads have been lowered for all time. What's that, it's Kaṅku! Oh, oh, it seems even a boy like him has been chewed up like sugarcane and thrown away. He was very shy; he used to sit on the sloping bank near the ghat where I'd go to bring water, pretending as if he had come to pluck reeds in order to make arrows. How much embarrassment I've caused him by my teasing. O Kaṅku, look back at me. Ah, the one whose blood used to dance at a sign from me, doesn't even answer my call. They've gone, all the lights in our village have gone out. Professor, the iron has eroded, only the black rust remains! Why did this happen?

PROFESSOR: Nandini, your sight today falls only on that direction in which there are ashes. Look once toward the flame, you'll see its flashing tongue.

NANDINI: I can't understand your words.

PROFESSOR: You've seen the Raja, haven't you? I hear that your mind's been captivated on seeing his appearance?

NANDINI: Of course it has. For he's a figure of extraordinary power.

PROFESSOR: That extraordinariness is the credit side for the person whose debit side is this grotesquerie. Those small ones continue becoming ashes, and that great one continues burning as a flame. This is the essence of becoming great.

NANDINI: But that's the essence of a *rākshas*.

PROFESSOR: It's pointless to get angry over essences. They are neither good, nor bad. That which happens, happens; if you go against it, you'd go against being itself.

NANDINI: If this is the way to be a man, then I don't want to be — I'll go away with those shadows, show me the way.

PROFESSOR: When the day comes to show us the way, these people themselves will show it; before then there's no such evil called a way. See now, the Puranic Scholar has long since quietly removed himself, thinking he'll be saved by escaping. He'll understand after advancing just a little bit that the wire fence is tied post by post, beginning from here up to many miles away. Nandini, you're getting angry. The bunch of red oleanders on your cheek looks today like the clouds of twilight on doomsday.[71]

NANDINI: (*Pushing the window*) Listen, listen!

PROFESSOR: Whom are you calling?

NANDINI: Your Raja, covered by the mist of the screen.

PROFESSOR: The inner door has closed, he won't be able to hear your call.

NANDINI: My mad Bishu, my mad brother!

PROFESSOR: Why are you calling him?

NANDINI: Because he hasn't returned yet. I feel afraid.

PROFESSOR: But I just saw him with you, only a little while ago.

NANDINI: The Sardar said, he had been called in order to identify Ranjan. I wanted to go with him, they wouldn't let me — whose cry is that?

PROFESSOR: It's probably that wrestler's.

NANDINI: Who is he?

PROFESSOR: He's the world-famous Gajju, whose brother Bhajan dared to come to wrestle with the Raja; afterwards we could not find even a torn thread from his loincloth anywhere. Angered by that, Gajju came with a challenge. I had told him at the very beginning, "Come to this kingdom if you want to dig tunnels, you'll at least stay alive a few days while dying. But if you want to show off your manhood he won't tolerate it for one moment. This is a very cruel place."

NANDINI: Can they remain good even slightly, by guarding these traps for catching people day and night?

PROFESSOR: The word "good" doesn't figure in this, only the word "remaining" does. That "remaining" of theirs has expanded so terribly that unless they put pressure on lakhs of people, who will support their burden? That's why the net just continues expanding. Because they *must* remain.

NANDINI: *Must* remain? If indeed one has to die in order to remain a human being, what's the fault in that?

PROFESSOR: Again that anger? That blaze of red oleanders? Very sweet, but what's true is true. If you find happiness in saying that one has to die in order to remain human, then say it. But they only remain who say that one has to kill in order to remain. You people say this creates a lack of humanity; in the heat of your anger you forget this alone is humanity. Tigers don't grow up by feeding on tigers, it's only men who swell up by feeding on men.

Enter Wrestler

NANDINI: Ah, look there, how he staggers as he comes. Wrestler, lie down here. Professor, why don't you see where he's been hurt?

PROFESSOR: You won't even be able to see the marks of hurt from the outside.

WRESTLER: Merciful God, may I get strength once in my life, if only for one more day.

PROFESSOR: Why, hm?

WRESTLER: Just to break that Sardar's neck.

PROFESSOR: What has the Sardar done to you?

WRESTLER: He's the one who has caused just about everything. For I didn't want to fight. Today he's spreading it around that it's entirely my fault.

PROFESSOR: Why? What's his motive?

WRESTLER: They feel safe only when able to make the whole world powerless. Merciful Hari, may I be able to gouge his eyes out one day, may I pull out his tongue.

NANDINI: How are you feeling, Wrestler?

WRESTLER: I feel my inside has become hollow. Where are these demons from, they know magic! They suck out not only strength, but even hope. —If once through some way—O gracious Hari, ah, if once—when you have mercy anything can happen. If once I could set my teeth on the Sardar's chest.

170 THE PLAYS

NANDINI: Professor, hold him, let's take him to our place together.

PROFESSOR: I don't have the courage, Nandini. That would be an offence according to the laws here.

NANDINI: Wouldn't it be an offence to let the man die?

PROFESSOR: The offence for which there is nobody to punish may be a sin but not a crime. Nandini, come away completely from all this. The tree does its work of removing and absorbing by spreading its hand of roots under the ground, but it doesn't make its flowers blossom there. Flowers blossom on the branches above, toward the sky. O red oleander, don't come to enquire about us below the ground; we look upward so that we can see you swing on the breeze above. —There's the Sardar. Then I must move. He can't tolerate it when I speak to you.

NANDINI: Why so much anger at me?

PROFESSOR: I can guess. Inwardly, you have pulled at the strings of his mind; the more the notes don't match, the more sharply the discord screams out.

Exit

Enter Sardar

NANDINI: Sardar!

SARDAR: Nandini, when Gosain-ji saw that jasmine-garland of yours in my room his eyes—here he comes himself. My *praṇām*! Master, Nandini had given me that garland.

Enter Gosain

GOSAIN: Ah, the offering of a pure heart, the pure jasmines of God. Their purity has not dimmed even after falling into the hands of a worldly man. In this alone I can see the power of virtue and hope for the salvation of sinners.

NANDINI: Gosain-ji, make an arrangement for this man. How much more is there left of his life?

GOSAIN: After considering all aspects, our Sardar will certainly keep him alive exactly to that degree of living which is necessary. But dear girl, all these discussions from your mouths grate harshly on our ears, we don't like them.

NANDINI: So in this kingdom there are decisions made as to the degree of keeping one alive?

GOSAIN: Of course there are. Since earthly life is limited. That's why its apportionment into shares must be made under proper calculation. God has placed an unbearable responsibility upon people of our class; if we are to carry it life's essence must fall on our shares to a much greater degree. They can get by with very little living too, because we do the living on account of their reduced burdens. Is this small relief for them?

NANDINI: Gosain-ji, what severe burden of doing good to these people has God unloaded on you?

GOSAIN: There is no need at all for quarrels among one another about the distribution of shares in the life that is not limited; we Gosains have come to show the way toward that very life. We shall be their friends just as long as they remain contented with this.

NANDINI: Then will this man with his limited life remain lying in this kind of half-dead state?

GOSAIN: But why should he remain lying anyway? What do you say, Sardar?

SARDAR: That's absolutely correct. Why should we let him remain lying? From now on he won't even need to move on his own strength. We'll move him around with our strength alone. Hey, Gajju.

WRESTLER: What, master?

GOSAIN: Hari Hari, already the voice has become quite a bit softer; I think I can pull him into our group that sings holy *kīrtans*.

SARDAR: Your quarters are in the headman's building of sections H-K, go there.

NANDINI: What kind of talk is that? How can he move?

SARDAR: Look Nandini, our very business is making people move. We know, when a man comes somewhere and falls flat on his face, he can go a little more if given a strong push. Go, Gajju.

WRESTLER: As you command.

NANDINI: Wrestler, I'm going to the headman's building too. There isn't anybody at all to look after you there.

WRESTLER: No, no, let it be, the Sardar will get angry.

NANDINI: I don't fear the Sardar's anger.

WRESTLER: I fear it, I beg of you, don't increase my troubles.

Exit

NANDINI: Sardar, don't go, tell me where you've taken my mad

Bishu.

SARDAR: Who am I to take him away? The wind takes the clouds away; if you think that's wrong, enquire about who gave the wind a push.

NANDINI: Oh, what disastrous country is this? You yourselves aren't men, and those whom you move aren't men either? You're the wind, they're the clouds? Gosain, you certainly know where my mad Bishu is.

GOSAIN: I certainly know, that wherever he is it's all for the best.

NANDINI: For whose best?

GOSAIN: That you wouldn't understand. —Ah, let go, let go, those are my prayer-beads. There, they've got torn. Hey Sardar, is this the girl you people—

SARDAR: Who knows how, she has found a home inside a loophole in the laws here. Our Raja himself—

GOSAIN: Hey, this time she'll tear my holy wrap as well. You've put me in danger. I'm leaving.

Exit

NANDINI: Sardar, you *have* to say where you've taken mad Bishu.

SARDAR: He's been called to the court — there isn't any more to say. Let go of me, I have work.

NANDINI: Because I'm a woman you don't fear me? Indra[72] sends his thunderbolt in the hand of a beam of lightning. I have carried that thunderbolt here, it'll smash the golden spire of your leadership.

SARDAR: I'll tell you the truth then and go. You yourself have created danger for Bishu.

NANDINI: Me!

SARDAR: Yes, yourself. All these days he had been burrowing under the ground silently like an insect; you yourself have taught him to spread the wings of death, O fire of Lord Indra. You'll attract many, after which the final confrontation will be between you and me. Not much later.

NANDINI: So be it, but tell me one thing before going, will you let Ranjan meet me?

SARDAR: Certainly not.

NANDINI: Certainly not! I'll see where you get your ability. My union with him *will* come, it *will*, it will *today*. This I say to you.

Exit Sardar

NANDINI: (*Knocking at the window*) Listen, listen, Raja. Where is your court? I'll break this hiding-place of your screen. Oh, who's that! It's Kishor! Tell me, do you know where our Bishu is?

Enter Kishor

KISHOR: Yes Nandini, you'll meet him right now, keep your mind prepared. I don't know why the chief of guards took pity on seeing my face. At my request he agreed to take Bishu away down this path.

NANDINI: The chief of guards? Then is —

KISHOR: Yes, there they come.

NANDINI: What's that! Handcuffs on your wrists! My mad brother, where are they taking you like that?

Enter Guard, with Bishu

BISHU: Never fear, don't fear anything. My mad girl, after so many days I have my liberty.

NANDINI: I can't understand what you're saying.

BISHU: When fearfully step by step I used to tide over danger I was free. That freedom-like bondage exists no more.

NANDINI: What fault have you committed that they should take you away tied up?

BISHU: After so many days I had spoken the truth today.

NANDINI: What is the fault in that?

BISHU: None at all.

NANDINI: Then why tie you up like this?

BISHU: But what's the harm in it either? I've found liberty in truth — these bonds will remain the true witness to that.

NANDINI: They take you down the road tied up like an animal, don't they feel ashamed of themselves? *Chhi, chhi*, after all they are men too.

BISHU: But inside there is a huge animal — their heads aren't lowered by indignities to man, the inner beast's tail starts swelling, starts swaying.

NANDINI: Ah my mad brother, have they beaten you? What made these marks on your body?

BISHU: They whipped me, the whip with which they beat dogs. The cord that makes this whip is exactly the same cord whose

thread makes their Gosain's prayer-beads. When they tell
their beads in the name of God they forget that part, but God
is aware.

NANDINI: Let them tie me up too and take me with you like this,
my brother. If I too don't receive some of these beatings you
got, then from today food will not suit my mouth.

KISHOR: Bishu, if I try surely they will take me instead of you. Ask
them permission for that.

BISHU: These words of yours are like a madman's.

KISHOR: But punishment won't hurt me, I am young, I'll be able to
bear it gladly.

NANDINI: Ah, no Kishor, don't say those words.

KISHOR: Nandini, I have avoided work, they are aware of that.
They have set hounds after me. This punishment would save me
from those indignities they will do me.

BISHU: No Kishor, it won't do as yet for you to be caught. There's
one dangerous job to do. Ranjan has come here; you have to
find him through whatever means possible. It won't be easy.

KISHOR: Nandini, then I take your leave. When I meet Ranjan what
message of yours will I give him?

NANDINI: None at all. If you just give him this bunch of red oleanders all my words will have been said.

Exit Kishor

BISHU: May your union with Ranjan occur this time.

NANDINI: There won't be any happiness for me in the union. I will
not be able to forget this fact, ever, that I sent you away empty-
handed. And there, that boy Kishor, what did he too get from
me?

BISHU: All the treasure in his heart has come to light, by the fire
that you have lit in his mind. What else could we want? Do you
remember, you have to place that blue jay's feather in Ranjan's
crown?

NANDINI: Here it is, in the *āṅchal* on my breast.

BISHU: My mad girl, can you hear that harvesting song?

NANDINI: I can hear it, my soul cries out.

BISHU: The game of the fields has ended, the owner of the land is
taking the ripe crop home. Come, Guard, no more delaying —

Song

Reap the crop of the last harvest now, bind it in sheaves,
Let the rest that's not for use turn in the dust to dust.

Exit all

Enter Doctor and Sardar

DOCTOR: I saw. The Raja has become irritated with himself. This illness is not external, it's of the mind.

SARDAR: What's the remedy for this?

DOCTOR: A shock of a big nature. The fomenting of a disturbance either with another kingdom, or among his subjects.

SARDAR: In other words, if not allowed to harm someone else, he will harm himself.

DOCTOR: They are big men, big babies, they play games. When they get irritated at one game, if you don't supply another game they break their toys. But be ready Sardar, there isn't too much time.

SARDAR: After seeing the signs I have already kept everything ready. But ah, what a pity. Our golden city had filled up with such manner of wealth as has not happened ever, then just at this time — all right, go, I'm thinking it over.

Exit Doctor

Enter Headman

HEADMAN: Sardar-maharaja, did you call? I'm Headman of Section E.

SARDAR: You're 321, aren't you?

HEADMAN: What powers of memory my master has! He doesn't forget even a worthless person like me.

SARDAR: My wife's coming from the country. The post will change near your section; I want you to bring her here quickly.

HEADMAN: There's a cattle-plague in the section, a shortage of bullocks to pull carts. No matter, the excavators can be pressed into service.

SARDAR: You know where you have to go, don't you? To the garden-house, where there's the sardars' feast.

HEADMAN: I'm going, but let me tell you one thing before I go. Please pay a little heed to it. That 69-U, whom people call mad Bishu, the time has come to correct his madness.

SARDAR: Why? Does he disturb you people?

HEADMAN: Not through spoken words, through attitude and behaviour.

SARDAR: Don't worry any more. Understand?

HEADMAN: Is that so? In that case, good. Another thing, that 47-P, he associates a bit much with 69-U.

SARDAR: I've noticed that.

HEADMAN: My master's observation is sharp indeed. But after all you have to keep your sight on several directions — one or two may even slip notice. Take a look, if you please, at our 95 — since we come from the same village we call ourselves relatives,[73] he is my father-in-law's brother-in-law — ready to make clogs from the bones of his ribs for my Sardar-maharaja's sweeper; his virtuous wife herself lowers her head in shame on seeing his devotion to my master, yet till today —

SARDAR: His name has entered the Great Register.

HEADMAN: Well, service for so long has succeeded. We will have to tell him the news carefully, he has epilepsy too, what if suddenly —

SARDAR: All right, that'll be done, now go immediately.

HEADMAN: I have to tell you the story of one other man — although he is my own brother-in-law, after his mother died my wife raised him with her own hands, still when my lord's benefit —

SARDAR: We'll have his story tomorrow, you run along, go.

HEADMAN: Here comes the Honourable Deputy Sardar. Please say a couple of words to him on my behalf. His Honour doesn't look favourably upon me. I believe when 69-U used to frequent the masters' residence, he spread against my name during that very time —

SARDAR: No, no, I haven't heard him even mention your name any day.

HEADMAN: But that's his shrewdness. Indeed, to kill a man who is renowned you only have to suppress his name. Because it's not wise to intrigue by deceit and gesture. Our 33 has that disease. For I see he has no other work at all, just going on entering and leaving the masters' private estate at any hour. I fear what he may concoct against somebody's good name. Yet if the news from his own house —

SARDAR: There's no more time today, go immediately.

HEADMAN: Then I make my *pranām*.[74] (*Returning*) One word, that section's 88 began work only the other day at a salary of thirty; even before two years are over his income today including perquisites is if nothing else quite certainly a thousand to fifteen hundred a month. The masters have pure minds, like gods they are deceived by empty eulogies alone. As soon as they see the spectacle of a man fully prostrating himself to make his *pranām* —

SARDAR: All right, all right, we'll have that talk tomorrow.

HEADMAN: I do profess the virtue of charity, I'm not speaking of depriving him of his bread; but please think about whether it's doing good to keep him at the treasury. Our Vishnudatta knows everything there is to know about him. By calling for him —

SARDAR: I'll call for him this very day, you go.

HEADMAN: Master, my third son has come of age. He had come to *pranām* you, but has returned after three days of repeated visits on foot without being granted an audience. He suffers really great mental anguish. My daughter-in-law cooked with her own hands, as an offering for my master, a green pumpkin—

SARDAR: All right, tell him to come day after tomorrow, he will see me.

Exit Headman

Enter Deputy Sardar

DEPUTY SARDAR: I've seen the dancing girls and musicians off to the garden.

SARDAR: And, how far has that Ranjan business —

DEPUTY: This sort of job can't be done by me. The Assistant Sardar took a liking to it himself and has taken the responsibility. By this time his —

SARDAR: Has the Raja —

DEPUTY: The Raja surely couldn't have understood. Ten people were grouped with him as he — but really I don't think it's our duty to deceive the Raja like this.

SARDAR: Precisely for the sake of duty toward the Raja we have to deceive the Raja, have to stop the Raja too. That obligation is mine. But this time without delay that girl must —

DEPUTY: No, no, don't talk about all this with me. The headman upon whom the responsibility has been placed is a worthy man, he doesn't fear any kind of dirtiness whatsoever.

SARDAR: Does Kenaram Gosain know Ranjan's story?

DEPUTY: By guessing he knows just about everything, he doesn't
   want to know explicitly.

SARDAR: Why?

DEPUTY: Should the way to say the words "I don't know" be closed.

SARDAR: So what if it is?

DEPUTY: Don't you understand? We have only one appearance, the
   appearance of Sardars. But he has on one face a Gosain, on the
   other face a Sardar. If the holy wrap gets torn just a little it
   becomes a noose. That's why he has to nourish the creed of
   leadership stealthily by himself, so that it doesn't interfere too
   much at the time of telling beads.

SARDAR: Well, he could have dropped the telling of beads altogether.

DEPUTY: But whatever his blood may be, his mind on the other
   hand is God-fearing. That's why he stays healthy if he can tell
   his beads explicitly and play the sardar implicitly. Only because
   he exists does our deity exist with ease, its tarnish covered up,
   otherwise the image wouldn't look good.

SARDAR: Deputy Sardar, I have seen that your blood hasn't agreed
   with the blood of sardars either.

DEPUTY: The hope still exists that the harm won't remain once the
   blood dries up. But even today I can't stand that 321 of yours.
   When in the midst of an assembly you have to clasp to your
   chest and address as friend the person whom you would
   loathe to touch even by a pinch from a distance, then you
   don't feel yourself cleansed after bathing in any pilgrimage
   waters. —There's Nandini coming.

SARDAR: Come along, Deputy Sardar.

DEPUTY: Why? What are you afraid of?

SARDAR: I don't trust you; I know Nandini's spell has touched
   your eyes.

DEPUTY: But you don't know that in your eyes too the colour of
   duty has mixed somewhat with the colour of red oleanders;
   indeed that's what has made their redness so terrifying.

SARDAR: That may be, the mind doesn't know even the mind's own
   thoughts. You come along with me.

                                                    Exit both

                        Enter Nandini

NANDINI: Within moments today's twilight has reddened with

vermilion[75] clouds. Is that the colour of our union? The vermilion in the parting of my hair seems to have spread over the entire sky. (*Knocking at the window*) Listen, listen, listen. I'll remain lying here day and night, as long as you don't listen.

Enter Gosain

GOSAIN: Whom are you prodding?

NANDINI: That python[76] of your people who remains in hiding and swallows men.

GOSAIN: Hari Hari, when God destroys the small He does so indeed by placing big words in their small mouths. Look Nandini, be assured, I think about your welfare.

NANDINI: That won't make my welfare.

GOSAIN: Come to my prayer-room, I'll sing you the holy name.

NANDINI: What'll I do with just a name?

GOSAIN: You'll find peace of mind.

NANDINI: If I find peace, then shame, shame, shame on me. I'll remain sitting at this door waiting.

GOSAIN: You have more faith in man than in God?

NANDINI: That god of yours on the flagstaff — he will never ever become gentle. But will the man behind a screen remain forever tied in its net? Go, go — go. Your business is to tear man's life away and delude him with names.

Exit Gosain

Enter Phagulal and Chandra

PHAGULAL: Bishu came with you, where's he now? Tell us truthfully.

NANDINI: They have taken him away as prisoner.

CHANDRA: *Rākshasī*,[77] you have handed him over. You're their spy.

NANDINI: How could you say such a thing?

CHANDRA: Otherwise what's your work here? You just move around bewitching everyone's minds.

PHAGULAL: Everyone here suspects everyone else, but still I came trusting you. In my heart of hearts you — let that thought be. But today somehow feels bad.

NANDINI: May be, that may be. He fell into trouble only because he came with me. He used to stay safely with you people, even said as much himself.

CHANDRA: Then why did you charm him away? Shameless destructive woman!

NANDINI: He said that he wanted freedom.

CHANDRA: Great freedom you've given him.

NANDINI: But I couldn't understand all his words, Chandra. Why did he tell me, freedom comes after drowning at the bottom of danger? Phagulal, how can I save the man who wants freedom from the beatings of safety?

CHANDRA: I don't understand all that talk. If you cannot bring him back, you'll die, die. I'm not bewitched by seeing that seemingly beautiful face of yours.

PHAGULAL: Chandra, what's done by futile scolding? Let's collect and bring followers from the workers' section. We'll break the prison to pieces.

NANDINI: I'll go with you.

PHAGULAL: Go to do what?

NANDINI: Go to break.

CHANDRA: Oh no, you've done a lot of breaking, enchantress. No more work for you.

Enter Gokul

GOKUL: Before anyone else that witch must be burnt to death.

CHANDRA: Kill her? That won't be punishment for her. Destroy that beauty, the beauty with which she causes disaster. Weed out her beauty, in the same way that grass is weeded, with spuds.

GOKUL: That I can do. Once this hammer's dance—

PHAGULAL: Careful! If you lay hands on her body then—

NANDINI: Phagulal, stop. He's cowardly, he fears me so he wants to kill me. I don't fear his blows. Let the coward do what he can do.

GOKUL: Phagulal, you still haven't come to your senses! You know only the Sardar as the enemy! That may be, I respect the enemy who is a straightforward enemy, but that sweet-talking beauty of yours—

NANDINI: Your respect for the Sardar! Just like the respect of the mud under the feet for the soles of the feet. Can he who is a slave ever feel respect?

PHAGULAL: Gokul, the time has come to show your manliness. But not to a girl. Come with me.

Exit Phagulal, Chandra and Gokul

Enter a Group of People

NANDINI: Hey, where are you going?
FIRST PERSON: We're going with the offering for the Flag-*pūjā*.
NANDINI: Have you seen Ranjan?
SECOND PERSON: I had seen him once five days ago, haven't seen him since. There, ask them, maybe they can tell you.
NANDINI: Who are they?
THIRD PERSON: They are taking wine to the sardars' feast.

Exit this Group

Enter Another Group

NANDINI: Hey, you with red caps, have you seen Ranjan?
FIRST PERSON: I saw him that night at Headman Śambhu's house.
NANDINI: Where is he now?
SECOND PERSON: There, those going with decorations to the feast for the sardars' wives, ask them, they can hear many things that don't reach our ears.

Exit this Group

Enter Another Group

NANDINI: Hey, do you know where these people have kept Ranjan?
FIRST PERSON: Quiet, quiet.
NANDINI: Surely you know, you *have* to tell me.
SECOND PERSON: What enters through our ears doesn't escape through our mouths, that's why we stay alive. There, those coming with the load of weapons, ask them.

Exit this Group

Enter Another Group

NANDINI: Hey, stop a while, tell me where Ranjan is.
FIRST PERSON: Listen, I'll tell you, the auspicious moment has arrived. The Raja has to come out for the Flag-*pūjā*. Ask the Raja himself. We know the beginning, we don't know the end.

Exit

NANDINI: (*Knocking at the window*) The time has come, open the door.
VOICE: Again you've come at a wrong time. Go immediately, go.

NANDINI: There's no time to wait, you *have* to hear my words!

VOICE: Say from the outside what you have to say, and go away.

NANDINI: From the outside the sound of words doesn't reach your ears.

VOICE: Today's the Flag-*pūjā*, do not distract my mind. The *pūjā* will be interrupted. Go, go! Go immediately.

NANDINI: My fear has ended. You won't be able to drive me away like that. Even if I die it's fine; I won't move until I have the door opened.

VOICE: I take it you want Ranjan? I have told the Sardar, he'll have him brought immediately. Don't remain standing at the door at the time I go to the *pūjā*. Trouble will follow.

NANDINI: God has no lack of time, he can wait yugas for a *pūjā*. But man's sorrows want contact with man. His time is short.

VOICE: I'm tired, very tired. I'll remove the weariness at the Flag-*pūjā* and return. Do not weaken me. If you obstruct me now you'll get crushed under the chariot wheels.

NANDINI: Let the wheels roll over my breast, I won't move.

VOICE: Nandini, from me you've received indulgence, that's why you don't feel fear. Today you have to feel fear.

NANDINI: I want you to threaten me too in the same way that you go about threatening everyone. I scorn your indulgence.

VOICE: Scorn it? I'll crush your arrogance. The time has come to reveal myself to you.

NANDINI: I'm just waiting for the revelation, open the door. (*The door opens*) What's that! Who's lying there? It seems, looks like Ranjan!

RAJA: What did you say? Ranjan? Never, not Ranjan.

NANDINI: Yes, oh, but this is my Ranjan.

RAJA: Why didn't he tell me his name? Why did he come so defiantly?

NANDINI: Wake up Ranjan, I've come, your friend. Raja, why doesn't he wake up?

RAJA: Tricked. These people have tricked me. Disastrous! My own machine doesn't obey me. Call, you people, call and bring the Sardar, bring him tied up.

NANDINI: Raja, wake Ranjan up, everyone says you know magic, wake him up.

RAJA: I've learnt magic from Yama,[78] I can't awaken. I can only destroy consciousness.

NANDINI: Then lull me into that same sleep. I can't bear it. Why did you cause such ruin?

RAJA: I have killed youth — in all these days I've just killed youth with all my power. The curse of dead youth has touched me.

NANDINI: Didn't he say my name?

RAJA: He said it in such a way, I could not tolerate it. Suddenly it seemed fire burned through my veins.

NANDINI: (*To Ranjan*) My hero, I place this blue jay's feather in your crown. Your victorious journey has begun from today. I'm the vehicle for that journey. — Ah, here is that cluster of my red oleanders in his hand. But then Kishor met him. Where did he go? Raja, where is that boy?

RAJA: Which boy?

NANDINI: The boy who had brought this cluster of flowers to Ranjan.

RAJA: He was a strange boy. His tender face like a girl's, but his speech insolent. He had dared to come to attack me.

NANDINI: After that? What happened to him? Tell me what happened. You have to tell me, don't keep quiet.

RAJA: Like a bubble he has vanished.

NANDINI: Raja, the time has come now.

RAJA: Time for what?

NANDINI: My battle with you, with all my power.

RAJA: You will battle with me! But I can kill you this very moment.

NANDINI: From then on that killing of me will kill you at every moment. I don't have weapons, my weapon is death.

RAJA: If that's so, come near. Do you have the courage to trust me? Come with me. Make me your companion today, Nandin.

NANDINI: Where will you go?

RAJA: To battle against me, but keeping your hand in my own hand. Can't you understand? That battle has begun. This is my flag, I break its staff, you tear its banner. Let your hand come into my own hand and kill me, kill, utterly kill, only that will be my salvation.

MAN FROM THE GROUP: Maharaja, what deed is this? What madness is this? You broke the flag! Our deity's flag, whose invincible pole has pierced earth with one end and heaven with the other, that most sacred flagstaff of ours! What a deadly sin on the day of *pūjā*. Come, let's give the sardars the news.

Exit

RAJA: There's still a lot of breaking left, but will you too go with me Nandini, my lamp-flame on the path to doomsday?

NANDINI: I'll go.

Enter Phagulal

PHAGULAL: They will not on any account release Bishu. Who is this? So this is the Raja? Witch, you are consulting with him! Traitor!

RAJA: What's happened to you people? What have you come out to do?

PHAGULAL: To break the prison doors; we may die but we won't turn back.

RAJA: Why should you turn back? I too go on the path to break. That is its first sign. My broken flag, my last achievement.

PHAGULAL: Nandin, I cannot understand well. We're simple people, be kind, don't trick us. For you're a girl of our own family.

NANDINI: But brother Phagu, you people have resolved to death itself, you have not left anything at all to trick.

PHAGULAL: Nandin, then you too come along with us.

NANDINI: But that's the only reason I am alive. Phagulal, I had wanted to bring Ranjan amongst all of you. Look there, my hero has come, treating death with contempt.

PHAGULAL: Utter ruin! Is that Ranjan! Lying down silent!

NANDINI: Not silent. For in death I can hear it, his unconquered voice. Ranjan will come alive—he cannot ever die.

PHAGULAL: Ah poor Nandini, my beautiful girl! Was it only for this you had been waiting all these days in this dark hell of ours?

NANDINI: I'd been waiting because he'd come, and he came. I'll prepare for him to come again, he'll come again. —Where's Chandra, Phagulal?

PHAGULAL: She's gone with Gokul to plead with the Sardar. They have unlimited faith in the Sardar. —But Maharaja, surely you haven't misunderstood? We've come out to break your own prison.

RAJA: Yes, my own prison. Both you and I will have to work together. It's not your work alone.

PHAGULAL: As soon as the sardars get the news they'll come to stop us.

RAJA: My battle is with them.

PHAGULAL: But the soldiers won't obey you.

RAJA: I'll fight alone; you people are with me.

PHAGULAL: Will you be able to win?

RAJA: At least I'll be able to die. After so many days I've been able to see the meaning of death — I've been saved.

PHAGULAL: Raja, can you hear the roar?

RAJA: There I see the Sardar coming with the soldiers. How was it possible so quickly? He was prepared quite in advance, only I alone did not know. They've tricked me. They've tied me with my own power.

PHAGULAL: And my followers still have not arrived.

RAJA: The Sardar must have prevented them. They won't ever arrive.

NANDINI: I had thought they would bring my mad Bishu to me. Will that not happen, ever?

RAJA: There's no way. I haven't seen anybody like the Sardar for blocking means of passage.

PHAGULAL: If that's so, come Nandini, we'll keep you in a safe place and return, after which what will be will be. If the Sardar sees you there'll be no defending you.

NANDINI: You'll send just me, alone, to an exile of safety? Phagulal, the Sardar is better than you people, he himself has opened the path for my victorious journey. Sardar, Sardar! — Look, he has hung my garland of jasmine in front of his spear. I'll go and make that garland the colour of red oleanders with the blood of my breast. — Sardar! He has seen me. Victory, victory to Ranjan.

Quick exit

RAJA: Nandini.

Exit

Enter Professor

PHAGULAL: Where are you running, Professor?

PROFESSOR: Someone said, the Raja has come out after so many days having discovered the greatest heights of life — I left my books and papers and came to join him.

PHAGULAL: But the Raja has gone there to die, he has heard Nandini's call.

PROFESSOR: She has torn his screen. Where's Nandini?

PHAGULAL: She has gone before everyone. We won't be able to catch up with her any more.

PROFESSOR: This time indeed we'll be able to. She cannot avoid me
    any more, I'll catch her.

Exit

Enter Bishu

BISHU: Phagulal, where's Nandini?

PHAGULAL: How did you come?

BISHU: Our workers have destroyed the prison. There they go to
    fight. I came to find Nandini. Where's she?

PHAGULAL: She has gone ahead, before everybody.

BISHU: Where?

PHAGULAL: To final freedom. —Bishu, can you see who is lying
    there?

BISHU: But that's Ranjan!

PHAGULAL: See that line of blood in the dust?

BISHU: I understand, that's the bloodied *rākhī*[79] of their supreme
    union. Now my time has come for the lonely journey to death.
    Perhaps she'll want to hear songs. My mad girl! Come my
    brother, let's go now to the battle.

PHAGULAL: Victory to Nandini.

BISHU: Victory to Nandini.

PHAGULAL: And, see there, her bracelet of red oleanders rolls in the
    dust. It has slipped off some time from her right hand. She
    emptied her hand today and went away.

BISHU: I had told her, I wouldn't take anything from her hand.
    This I have to take, her final gift.

Exit

Song in the distance

Paush is calling for you — oh, come along.
The dust's *āṅchal* is full with ripe harvest today.

TAPATI

(TAPATĪ)

NOTE ON THE PLAY

Tagore wrote his five-act verse tragedy *Rājā o Rānī* in early 1889 while in Sholapur, Maharashtra, and published it in August the same year. The play underwent several transformations in succeeding editions. Thirteen scenes were omitted from the thoroughly revised second edition, published in June 1894. However, a third version of the play in Tagore's first volume of collected poetry (1896) restored all but three scenes of the original and, apart from minor changes, became the basis for the definitive text included in Tagore's collected works in 1939.[1] In early 1929 Tagore revised the play for a production in Calcutta, the new version being staged under the title *Bhairaver Bali*. This text has survived in three scripts prepared specifically for the production. Generally speaking, Tagore condensed the play for this performance, dropping nine scenes and three characters altogether.[2] Later in the year he completely rewrote the play in prose, first giving it the name *Sumitrā*, and then changing the title to *Tapatī* for publication in September 1929. A second edition, incorporating most of the changes made for the stage premiere,[3] appeared in May 1931; it became the standard edition of this play.

The plot of *Rājā o Rānī* and *Tapatī* is pseudo-historical: in other words, the characters are not historical figures, but the kingdoms of Kashmir and Jalandhar did exist in medieval India, and their kings did occasionally have differences which they periodically resolved on the battlefield. What should interest the reader most in the quest for source material is Tagore's intriguing change of the title to *Tapatī* for the final version. Tapatī, daughter of the sun god Sūrya, is a mythological figure whom we hear about in the *Mahābhārata* as well as in other storehouses of Hindu mythology. Given Tagore's wide reading and knowledge of Hindu legends, we can assume that he had read about Tapatī. I summarise here her story, taken from the Chaitraratha Parva in the Ādi Parva of the *Mahābhārata*.[4]

Tapatī was unequalled in beauty and religious devotion; the great king Saṁvaraṇa was renowned as an illustrious monarch and humble worshipper of Sūrya. One day while hunting in the hills Saṁvarana saw a beautiful girl:

For a moment he thought
    she was the goddess Lakṣmī.
Her beauty radiated from her
    like sunrays from the sun.

Her body shone
    like a straight flame,
her spotless beauty
    was like the moon's.

She stood, a black-
    eyed beauty on the hill-top,
statuesque,
    like a golden girl.

The hill, its creepers,
    its bushes, all flamed
with the golden beauty
    of the golden girl. [1:173:25–28][5]

She was more beautiful than any girl he had seen before, and he professed his love for her. The girl — Tapatī — told him she reciprocated his feelings, and asked him to request her father for her hand. The king's priest Vasiṣṭha acted as intermediary and succeeded in gaining Sūrya's approval for the marriage. After their wedding —

He delegated his minister
    to rule, in his absence,
his kingdom, his capital,
    his woods and forests.

*   *   *

For twelve years he
    and his wife delighted
in each other's company
    in the hill's woods.

*   *   *

For twelve years,
    not a single drop of dew
fell in Saṁvaraṇa's kingdom.
    No crops could grow.

*   *   *

> Crazed with hunger,
> the people left their homes,
> and driven by despair
> scattered in all directions.
>
> They moved about like
> skeletons; and the city
> became a land of the dead
> and the dying. [1:175:38, 40, 43, 45–46][6]

Vasiṣṭha witnessed these events and decided to bring the royal couple back to the capital. As soon as they returned, rain fell, crops flourished and the people smiled once again. The grateful king and queen offered oblations to the gods. They later had a son, Kuru, distant progenitor of Arjuna and his brothers, the heroes of the *Mahābhārata*.

Rājā o Rānī was first staged by members of the family at the Calcutta residence of Tagore's elder brother Satyendranath, some time during the Pūjā celebrations (usually observed in September-October) in 1889. Tagore acted as Bikram in this private performance. The play opened on the professional stage at the Emerald Theatre in Calcutta on 7 June 1890 with Mahendra Basu, the "tragedian of Bengal", distinguishing himself in the role of Kumarsen. Thereafter *Rājā o Rānī* proved to be one of Tagore's most successful plays in the Calcutta theatres; Mahendra Basu stole the show again as Kumarsen at the Classic Theatre on 24 July 1897. Amarendra Datta, who acted as Bikram, appeared in the same role at the Star Theatre on 18 May 1912, and in some later performances took the role of Kumarsen as well. Ahindra Chaudhuri, another famous leading man of the Bengali stage and later Head of the Drama Department at Rabindra Bharati University, starred as Kumarsen in a revival at the Star on 29 August 1923.[7] The 1929 production of the revised version, *Bhairaver Bali*, took place on 27 April at the Empire Theatre. The premiere of *Tapatī* occurred on 26 September 1929 at Jorasanko, with Tagore (aged 68) once again creating the much younger part of Bikram; the production ran for four nights. However, when the pioneering professional director Sisir Bhaduri staged the play at the Cornwallis Theatre on 25 December 1929, himself playing Bikram in a reportedly powerful performance highly recommended by the critics, the audience found the changed play too abstruse and the production flopped miserably.[8] At the final curtain the spectators remained seated, expecting the play to continue, until Bhaduri himself came on stage again to tell them the play was over. On later nights Bhaduri played to near-empty houses. Sushil Mukherjee has put it succinctly: "whatever popularity *Raja O Rani* had earned as a straightforward melodrama was lost when Rabindranath made *Tapati* out of it." [9]

PREFACE

Rājā o Rānī was a composition of my younger years, it was my first attempt at writing plays.

There is strife within the relationship between Sumitra and Bikram — that strife is terminated by Sumitra's death. Bikram's severe addiction, which was hindered from possessing Sumitra completely, came to a conclusion with Sumitra's death; only within that peace was it possible for Bikram to truly appreciate Sumitra; this indeed was the basic theme of *Rājā o Rānī*.

Due to faults in composition this idea was not obvious. The account of Kumar's and Ila's love has obstructed the play through irrelevance, and the unjustifiable prominence Kumar has gained in the play's final portion has burdened and divided the subject of the drama. At this play's end an amazing attempt at creation finds expression through Kumar's death — this death is not the inevitable finale to the story-line.

For a long time the flaws of *Rājā o Rānī* have distressed me. Some days ago when Sri Gaganendranath made preparations to stage this play,[10] I had tried to make it stageworthy by condensing and changing it as far as possible. I noticed that revision was not possible through such incomplete amendments. Right then I decided that unless this play was written anew from beginning to end it could not be disposed of. Having written it, I have paid my dues concerning this book to the best of my abilities.

Since an old play has been written anew, it is necessary to see it staged in order to cut attachments to the old and establish its new identity. I have been engaged in that attempt. On this occasion it is essential to explain in brief my views about arrangements on the stage.

Scenery has entered modern European stage-decoration in the form of a pestilence. It is childishness. An attempt to charm people's eyes. It is flung into the middle of literature and dramaturgy by physical force. Kalidasa had written *Meghadūta*,[11] a poem that is an art gallery in metrical language. If, with brush in hand, a sketcher were to apply his sketch-commentary along its margins, it would express as much disrespect to the reader as injustice to the poet. His own poetry is sufficient for the poet; outside help is not at all help for him, it is a hindrance, and in many cases, audacity.

An idea of the hermitage in *Śakuntalā*[12] exists even in its poetic aura. That itself is adequate. Only because it is not defined too much through painted pictures can it do its own work unopposed in the spectator's mind. A poetic drama stakes claim upon the spectator's imagination; painting belittles that claim; the harm from that occurs to the spectator himself. The business of staging is swift, lively, mobile; scenery is its opposite; having entered unrightfully it remains in the midst of movement mute, still, delusory; by motionlessly enclosing the spectator's mental vision it keeps him thoroughly constrained. The rule of bidding farewell to the mind by setting a scene in the place where the mind should take its position has become prevalent in the mechanised age, it was not there previously. In the *yātrā* narrative plays long prevalent in our country, the site indeed becomes constrained due to the crowds of people, but the mind is not constrained by the impertinence of scenes. For this very reason I do not indulge the childishness of raising and lowering scenery every now and then in those dramatic performances where I have any hand. Because it ridicules realistic truth as well as obstructs idealistic truth.

19 Bhādra, 1336
[4 September 1929]   Rabindranath Tagore
Santiniketan

THE CHARACTERS IN THE PLAY[13]

Sumitra (Sumitrā)	Rani of Jalandhaı (Jālandhar)[14]
Bikram (Vikramdev)	Raja of Jalandhar
Naresh (Nareś)	Bikram's step-brother
Bipasha (Vipāśā)	Sumitra's confidante
Debdatta (Devdatta)	The Raja's confidant
(Nārāyanī)[15]	Debdatta's wife
Gauri, Kalindi, Manjari	
(Gaurī, Kālindī, Mañjarī)	Maids of the royal palace
Kumarsen (Kumārsen)	Crown Prince of Kashmir (Kāśmīr)
Chandrasen (Chandrasen)	Kumar's paternal uncle
Shankar (Śaṅkar)	Kumar's experienced old servant
Tribedi (Trivedī)	Royal Priest of Jalandhar
Bhargab (Bhārgav)	Priest of the temple at Mārtanḍa in Kashmir

Ratneshwar (Ratneśvar), Shikharini (Śikharinī), Kunjalal (Kuñjalāl), crowds et al.

1

Courtyard of the temple to Bhairav[16]
Debdatta and a group of worshippers

Song[17]

All pettiness is scorched by the flames of your wrath,
O Bhairav, give us strength, and look upon your devotees.
Mahārudra,[18] banish
What is mean, enchanting;
Death will be disregarded by enthusiastic life.
Nectar[19] will rise from the swift churning of sorrow
And those afraid of death will be delivered from their dread.
Your blazing, fearful heat
Will make the mountains melt,
A stream of renunciation released from chains of stone.

Exit everyone except Debdatta

Enter Bikram

BIKRAM: What's the meaning of this? I have arranged for a *pūjā* to Mīnaketu[20] today. Why did you people introduce it with a hymn to Bhairav?

DEBDATTA: The common people just aren't able to accept this *pūjā* of the Raja's yet. In fact, they are afraid.

BIKRAM: Why, what do they fear?

DEBDATTA: They're stunned on seeing your boldness. A *pūjā* to Kandarpa in His *pūjā*-forest, in Whose own hermitage Pañ-chaśar was scorched?[21] Won't trouble follow as a consequence of this?

BIKRAM: That time Kandarpa came hidden like an offender — this time I'll call Him publicly, He'll come unhesitantly worthy of a god — head raised, banner flying. The fear of trouble calls forth trouble.

DEBDATTA: Maharaja, right since ancient times there's been hostility between those two gods.

BIKRAM: Only men have been harmed by it. One god deprives men of the favours of another god. Brahman, you people have forever made a business of worshipping gods by mixing the *śāstras*, that's why you don't know anything at all about gods.

DEBDATTA: That is correct, our acquaintance with gods is through books. We die pushing through crowds of verses; we get gifts, but don't even get the time to come close to Them.

BIKRAM: My Mīnaketu is not of the *śāstras*; He doesn't abide by the restraints of *anushṭubh* or *trishṭubh*.[22] He is the god of doomsday itself. His interior is indeed similar to Rudra-Bhairav's[23] — Siva's bow assumes the disguise of His bow of flowers.[24]

DEBDATTA: Maharaja, I've tried to continue avoiding that god to the best of my abilities. From the little acquaintance I've had of His presence, I haven't been able to see enough similarities with Bhairav, at least not in clothes and ornaments.

BIKRAM: That's because so far Rati[25] has dressed Kandarpa with some of her own clothes. She has dyed Him in the blackness of her own collyrium, the redness of saffron, the blueness of a blue blouse, — He is overwhelmed and absorbed by the beautiful woman's care and charm, that's why He makes a profession as a spy shamefully at the court of Indra the Thunderer.[26] That's why the fire of Rudra's manliness had scorched Him.

DEBDATTA: Well, that history is finished. Why this disturbance about that burnt god again? Does He have to be burnt once more or what?

BIKRAM: No, He'll be saved from the very midst of death — for that reason I need the strength of a hero. Your hymn to Bhairav will not be complete if our hymn to Mīnaketu is not added to it.

Leave the bed of ashes and insult, Pushpadhanu,[27]
Lift your smouldering body from the flames of Rudra.
  Let all that is mortal perish,
Wake up in a memorable meditative image.
  What's harsh, what's ignorant in you,
What's coarse, let these be scorched; emerge eternally anew.
  Awake from death Pushpadhanu,
O Atanu,[28] take body in a hero's body.

You people don't know, Maheśvar gave Madan a boon of fire,[29] He made him immortal through death itself. Ananga[30] Himself became the authority to give nectar.

Bring nectar from that death by which
Mrityuñjay[31] has caused destruction.

    Let that divine, radiant burning
  Release an endless stream of fiery fountains of passion.
    Let it make union keen, intense,
  Let separations be unendurably beautiful.
    Arise from death Pushpadhanu,
  O Atanu, take body in a hero's body.

Mīnaketu's path is not an easy path, it's not a flower-strewn path of pleasures, it doesn't give the gratification of comfort.

DEBDATTA: Hearing about it makes me afraid. But the trouble occurs because Ananga-dev doesn't allow any other god to enter the room which He marks off with the smear of the dust on His feet. That only gives birth to envy in the minds of those worthy of worship.

BIKRAM: Seems like the comment is aimed at me. Getting bolder?

DEBDATTA: Friendship with a raja is the ultimate overboldness. As bad luck would have it, the raja's friend is outspoken. Not according to his wishes.

BIKRAM: Then speak up. Say quite clearly, what are the citizens saying about me?

DEBDATTA: They are saying, the whole kingdom is in the gloom of evening now, under the veil of the inner chamber.[32] In the queen's shadow the state goddess[33] is pale.

BIKRAM: Outspoken man, do we need a Sītā exiled once more in an attempt to please the citizens?[34]

DEBDATTA: Well, you yourself want to exile her to the inner chamber; the citizens want her on the royal throne for all. Her heart is certainly not yours in entirety, one part is the citizens'. Is she merely the royal wife? She is the mother of the people too.

BIKRAM: Debdatta, parts lead to all strife. They led to Kurukshetra.[35] There she comes, in the part of the royal wife, or the mother of the people?

DEBDATTA: Then I must leave, Maharaja.

                              Exit

Enter Sumitra, the Queen

BIKRAM: *Devī*,[36] where are you going? Listen to me!

SUMITRA: What, Maharaja?

BIKRAM: There's a bit of good news.

SUMITRA: What, let me hear.

BIKRAM: I am fortunate to have the supreme honour of public censure.

SUMITRA: Censure for what?

BIKRAM: People are saying I've been able to ignore even duty for your love. Such big words.

SUMITRA: May the words of those who say it be false.

BIKRAM: May this truth be endless, be celebrated in history, be spoken by the poet's voice, be expounded in aesthetic theory, be beyond the blame or praise of mean people.

SUMITRA: Maharaja, the love that's above even royal duty should be received by the gods, could I possibly take it?

BIKRAM: The God will take whatever is His due through you. I've seen the Supreme Wonder in your face. Don't feel shy, listen to my words. Those who go around conquering countries in greed of fame are Lakshmī's clowns.[37] Their lifetime goes in vain, achievements too don't stay forever, Lakshmī sits smiling. I'm not in their group. I'd gone to Kashmir and fought only to attain you.

SUMITRA: Your military expedition was successful. Now what more do you want?

BIKRAM: I've got the vina. At what auspicious time will I have ownership, with music? I cannot tune the keys; even after getting it I'm losing at every step. The gift I've got from fate, that same gift puts me to shame.

SUMITRA: You've kept it pressed inside your fist and are imagining you haven't got it. But don't I too have something to ask from you?

BIKRAM: You can ask for everything; because you don't ask for anything my royal riches are useless.

SUMITRA: I want my raja.

BIKRAM: You haven't got him?

SUMITRA: No, I haven't. You've come down from the throne to this woman. Why don't you raise me up, take me near your throne?

BIKRAM: I've given you a place on the highest peak of the heart — no glory in that either?

SUMITRA: Maharaja, don't decorate me with words like that — it doesn't become you. It belittles me too. What's the point of

eulogising me? Fulfil my request. I've come to inform you of a
prayer on behalf of the citizens.

BIKRAM: In this garden? The king of seasons [38] has authority here
today. At least today, even if for one day, accept him completely.

SUMITRA: Well, I haven't made a mistake in following your orders
— in order that the festival is beautiful I've certainly made
those arrangements. But don't you have something to do as
well? You do that with your royal power, in order that the
festival turns out excellently.

BIKRAM: Tell me, what have I to do?

SUMITRA: The covetous bands who came to Jalandhar with you
from Kashmir, order those parasites to return to Kashmir
this very day.

BIKRAM: You have anger in your mind for these foreign courtiers
of mine.

SUMITRA: That I have.

BIKRAM: They had joined with me in the Kashmir conquest, that's
the reason for it.

SUMITRA: Yes Maharaja, I know, the enmity of traitors is good,
their friendship unclean.

BIKRAM: They'll follow their dharma but how can I be ungrateful?

SUMITRA: They have sinned in support of you, forgive them if you
have to; but they're acting unjustly against you, do you have
to forgive them that too? The shelter of your forgiveness brings
oppression to the citizens, even that won't prevent you?

BIKRAM: The citizens are creating baseless slander; they're envious
because those are foreigners.

SUMITRA: Well, that too needs a trial.

BIKRAM: When you intervene in all these matters, Maharani, wise
judgment becomes difficult. You yourself bring the accusation,
can I give any witness a place above it? Upon your request I had
to dismiss Yudhājit even without a trial. Do you want more
courtier-sacrifices?

SUMITRA: That's good then. Don't have trials. Just fulfil my prayer.
Even if the locusts from Kashmir haven't committed any
offence, they're still my embarrassment night and day. Save me
from that.

BIKRAM: They admitted their flaws and stood beside me facing danger ahead. Even at your word I won't be able to abandon them. Look, love, your claim is to the Raja's heart alone, not to the Raja's duties, keep this fact in mind.

SUMITRA: Maharaja, I don't get happiness from keeping in mind that I'm a companion for your dalliance, but I'm nobody in your royal office.

Exit

BIKRAM: Listen, Queen.

SUMITRA: (*Coming back*) What, tell me.

BIKRAM: Why don't you wake up? What's this subtle screen for? I haven't been able to remove it with all my Raja's strength. Reveal yourself — be seen, be held. Don't harass me with this excessive invisible deception.

SUMITRA: I'm telling you the very same thing too. You're the Raja, I can't see your complete appearance — you've kept your strength covered in darkness. You haven't woken up. You've come snatching me away from Kashmir — dispel that insult to me — you have to give me the position of a Rani.

BIKRAM: All right, all right, I throw my entire royal treasury at your feet — you want to give to the citizens, give as much as you please. Let this kingdom overflow with your flood of charity.

SUMITRA: Forgive me Maharaja, your treasury can stay your own. The ornaments on my body can stay for my citizens. If I don't have a queen's authority to defend citizens from the hands of injustice, then all these are only prisoner's clothes and trinkets — I won't be able to bear them. If you accept a queen you'll get an attendant too, otherwise only a slave! That I'm not.

Exit

Enter Minister

BIKRAM: Who made the accusation about Yudhājit to the Rani? You?

MINISTER: I do not confer outside the council-chamber, Maharaja!

BIKRAM: Then who brought all these words to her ears?

MINISTER: Those who have suffered themselves.

BIKRAM: How did they get to meet the Rani?

MINISTER: The compassionate one herself keeps track of those who deserve compassion.

BIKRAM: Let it be remembered that those who pass me over to take petitions to the Rani deserve punishment.

MINISTER: Punishment they've got. Everyone knows the story how their fields of ripe grain were burnt by those against whom the accusations were made.

BIKRAM: Minister, I have noticed that you search by various devices for an opportunity to discredit these courtiers.

MINISTER: I may discredit the discreditable but not through devising.

BIKRAM: These foreigners are protected by me, my royal duty is especially to defend them from the envy of you people.

MINISTER: I'll remain silent concerning them. But there's subject matter for more serious conference. Maharaja, for an instant —

BIKRAM: Now's not the time. Go, give word to Bipasha that tonight's her dance in the *bakul*-grove,[39] at midnight. Tell Tribedi that I will not tolerate any lapses in his recitation of mantras at the *pūjā* for Mīnaketu.

MINISTER:The Kashmiri courtiers have sent word that they'll all come to the festival.

BIKRAM: Be alert, on no account should they meet with the Maharani.

Exit both

Enter the Raja's brother Naresh, and Sumitra's companion Bipasha

BIPASHA: I won't accept that story. You people have conquered Kashmir! I won't accept it.

NARESH: Beautiful one, unappreciative history does not care for the consent of sweet voices.

BIPASHA: Prince, the boastful language of arrogant voices isn't its language either.

NARESH: But surely you'll have to accept the testimony of the sword. It speaks up with Yama-raja in front. Our Maharaja has conquered Kashmir.

BIPASHA: He has not. Our crown prince was absent. He'd gone to bring ceremonial water from Mānas-sarovar.[40] So it wasn't a war, it was robbery.

NARESH: His uncle[41] Chandrasen was the deputy. He fought.

BIPASHA: He made a pretence of war. In order to buy back the looted throne himself, at the cost of feigning acceptance of defeat. Your court-poet has written a poem in great detail about this. Your war's a fraud, your history's a fraud. So you're smiling quietly! No shame!

NARESH: Well, Maharani Sumitra isn't a fraud. She's certainly come down from the mountains as a follower of our goddess of victory.

BIPASHA: Shut up, shut up. Do not remind me of sorrowful things. The princess was then a girl, aged sixteen. The Regent came and said she'll have to surrender to the victors, otherwise a treaty's impossible. The princess went to die by jumping into a fire she had lit. The city elders came and said, "Mother, save us, claim with your hand the hand that is dispensing death — let there be peace."

NARESH: But the Maharani surely doesn't remember any disgrace from that day. She has taken her place on the throne with gracious dignity.

BIPASHA: She has great strength equal to forget great sorrow, for she's the perfect wife. Her wedding had as witness the fire that had burnt for her death. She has purified herself by fasting and sitting in meditation for three days at the temple to Kailāsnāth.[42] She came to your people's house only after having thoroughly scorched within herself the unbearable insult. If the forgiveness of a heroic woman hadn't been there your throne would have caught fire.

NARESH: You know Bipasha, that heroic woman has traced with her crystalline dignity a radiant Milky Way[43] to Kashmir for our hearts. She has distracted the minds of Jalandhar's youths toward Kashmir. She has awoken within their meditations an incomparable image of light. You don't know how many madmen have gone from Jalandhar to Kashmir, to find the treasure of their austerities.

BIPASHA: But alas, that isn't waging a war. There may still be a way there to use your weapons, but through your barbarity you've cut off the path to winning hearts over there.

NARESH: One has to practise austerities — for there's happiness in that too.

BIPASHA: Do that, but give up hope of salvation.

NARESH: Salvation will occur, I will prove that by myself — without even going to Kashmir!

BIPASHA: Your ambition is just as great as your pride.

NARESH: My ambition is itself my pride. My aspiration is the inaccessible peak of a mountain. There I see the unattainable stars of daybreak, in the dreams of dawn.

BIPASHA: I take it you came having memorised the lesson from your poet?

NARESH: That's not necessary. The one from whom I get harsh words outside, she herself gives me the boon of speech internal'y, secretly. I'll tell you her name if you give me courage.

BIPASHA: There's no need for such courage.

NARESH: Then let it be. But this lotus bud, what's wrong in taking it? For it too doesn't open its mouth to say anything.

BIPASHA: No, I won't take it.

NARESH: I brought its bulb from a lake in Kashmir. After many days, much hesitation, this bud has shown itself. I think my good luck has sent its first testimonial — someone's invisible signature is inside this. You won't take it? I'll keep it here near your feet.

Going out

BIPASHA: Listen, listen, I say again you people have not conquered Kashmir.

NARESH: Certainly we have. You can feel angry about it, you cannot ignore it. We have conquered.

BIPASHA: By deceit.

NARESH: No, by war.

BIPASHA: That's not called war.

NARESH: Yes, of course it's called war.

BIPASHA: It's not conquest.

NARESH: Of course it's conquest.

BIPASHA: Then take back your lotus bud.

NARESH: I don't have the ability to take it back.

BIPASHA: I will tear it into little shreds.

NARESH: Tear it up if you can — but I gave and you took, this fact remains in the Creator's mind — for all time.

Exit

Enter Sumitra

SUMITRA: What are you thinking, Bipasha, standing alone with a lotus bud in the hand?

BIPASHA: I'm quarrelling with the flower in my mind.

SUMITRA: Your quarrels in this world don't wish to be settled, on any account at all. Quarrel about what? Besides, what kind of quarrel could you have with a flower?

BIPASHA: I'm telling it, "You're a flower from Kashmir, why is your face still pleased here? You've forgotten insults so very easily?"

SUMITRA: If God's flowers kept man's crimes in mind then this earth would become a desert.

BIPASHA: You yourself are that flower of God, Maharani, but thorns too are God's own creation. Tell me truthfully, doesn't the injustice that has occurred over Kashmir ever come across your mind? Why do you stay silent? You won't answer me? In the name of your motherland, give me an answer to this.

SUMITRA: In the name of that motherland of mine, just let me keep this one and only fact in mind, that I'm Rani of Jalandhar.

BIPASHA: Forget all else that you can forget; I won't ever let you forget that you are Kashmir's daughter.

SUMITRA: I haven't forgotten. That's why in order to protect Kashmir's honour I have to keep the honour of duty. Otherwise would I smear body and mind with the stain of a slave here?

BIPASHA: I can understand that every day, Maharani. You've made Kashmir the victor in the hearts of these people. I'm no one at all; still in the light of your dignity they see me too in such a way, with a fascination that never even touched the eyes of anyone in Kashmir.

SUMITRA: I take it you're being modest?

BIPASHA: It's not modesty, Maharani. I'm amazed at myself. Don't laugh; these days they keep saying such words addressed to me, those words are not in the Kashmiri language, at least not to my knowledge.

SUMITRA: In the dawn when you came down here, the time still hadn't come for the Kashmiri language to awake completely in your ears. Nevertheless, some slight murmurs had begun; I suppose you don't remember those words today? Anyway, I see you still have not dressed for the festival.

BIPASHA: I'd started dressing, at that time somebody came and said they had conquered Kashmir. I've thrown away the garland from my braids, my blood-red silk rolls on the path in the *śirīṣ*-forest.[44] Why are you smiling, Rani?

SUMITRA: You call that place a path in the forest? Well, when I was coming here I saw your blood-red silk on someone's head.

BIPASHA: See there, Maharani, no shame, the young men here have bad habits, that's stealing!

SUMITRA: I suspect that your blood-red silk lies on the thief's road only to teach the art of stealing. I've heard his education is complete; now the final test of his stealing follows, with you as the subject.

BIPASHA: The Raja's orders or what?

SUMITRA: Come, decorate the altar of Him Who gave the orders. Let that lotus bud itself be your first offering.

BIPASHA: Don't go, let me ask you one question then, tell me truthfully. Are you enthusiastic about the festival that will occur tonight, in *pūjā* to Makarketan?[45]

SUMITRA: The Maharaja's command.

BIPASHA: Well that I know, but what does your own mind say? — Will you stay silent?

SUMITRA: Yes, I will indeed stay silent.

BIPASHA: All right, fine. But one question I haven't had the courage to ask you all these days — I'll certainly ask today — it won't do to stay silent.

SUMITRA: What's your question?

BIPASHA: Do you truly love the Maharaja? You must tell me.

SUMITRA: Yes I love him. Well, you are silent after hearing the answer!

BIPASHA: Then let me tell you the truth. This question wouldn't ever have come to my mind even a few days ago; I'd have accepted the answer too after hearing it.

SUMITRA: I see that you're comparing things with your mind today.

BIPASHA: I won't hide that from you, you know everything — of course I'm comparing, but I cannot compare correctly.

SUMITRA: How can they compare? That day I had consented to surrender to the Maharaja, having acknowledged the dishonour to Kashmir out of a feeling of defending the citizens; then for what did I practise *tapasyā*[46] at the temple to Kailās-nāth for three days?

BIPASHA: If I were you I'd practise *tapasyā* for the downfall of Jalandhar.

SUMITRA: I'd wanted this strength, that by Rudra's grace my marriage wouldn't be pleasurable. That I wouldn't feel greed any day for anything at all in Jalandhar's royal palace; then only would the insult not be able to touch me.

BIPASHA: Didn't your mind happen to waver any day, Maharani?

SUMITRA: Every day it happened — a thousand times it happened.

BIPASHA: Forgive me Maharani, I have a suspicion that you ignore him.

SUMITRA: Ignore! Don't say such words, Bipasha. There's nothing at all insignificant within him. His strength is tremendous — there's no filthiness of luxury in that strength, there's the recklessness of delight. If I came and stood at the edge of that bank-breaking flood, everything of mine would drift away, religious duties, education and upbringing. My mind has become like stone merely by trying incessantly to stop the invincibility of that strength. Such innumerable gifts no woman ever gets — I feel such unendurable conflict with myself for refusing to accept this invaluable good fortune. If I could ignore the Maharaja, well then everything would be easy. Only He to Whom I made a vow knows how unbearable my sorrow is, inside and outside.

BIPASHA: So you kept the vow, Maharani, but love!

SUMITRA: What are you saying, Bipasha? For this same vow has kept my love alive, otherwise it would have sunk amidst the curses. If love is the subject of shame, what could be better than that for its destruction? The ascetic Mrityuñjay has saved my love. I have received this love from the wedding's sacrificial fire[47] — there's no end to the oblations any more.

BIPASHA: Your god is cruel, I wouldn't have been able to obey Him.

SUMITRA: How do you know? You too would have to obey as soon as He calls. But Bipasha, it's a crime to reveal the words of a vow; today I did wrong, pardon me Master of my vows. —

BIPASHA: No, pardon me Maharani. But where are you going?

SUMITRA: I heard from Debdatta-*thākur*[48] that citizens have come from far for the purpose of the festival. Today they will be given an audience in the temple garden. I hear that the Raja, having got that news, has ordered the door to be shut.

BIPASHA: Will you be able to open that door?

SUMITRA: Perhaps I won't. Still I'll go to see if it has any gaps anywhere.

BIPASHA: These people are so skilful at the art of blocking doors that you won't find any flaw at all in it — I can tell you this.

Exit both

Enter Debdatta. Enter Ratneshwar quickly

RATNESHWAR: *Ṭhākur*, Debdatta-*thākur*.

DEBDATTA: I see that they'll get me in danger as well by shouting for me. Why, what's happened?

RATNESHWAR: An offender to the Raja. I've come here after beating his guard.

DEBDATTA: Beaten him? Hearing that makes my body thrill. Why did the wish for such a violent joke dawn suddenly in your mind?

RATNESHWAR: I came to the capital after much trouble, only in the hope that I'd gain an audience with the Raja at the festival. The doorkeeper said the festival door is closed. So I had to thrash him. If I don't get a meeting on coming to lodge a complaint, well at least I'll arrive in front of the Raja under that pretext, of committing an offence.

DEBDATTA: What kind of idiot are you? Do you think the Raja's guard will admit, even if he dies, the fact that he got a thrashing at the hands of a stubborn fool from Budhkot? His wife won't even let him enter the house if she hears.

RATNESHWAR: *Ṭhākur*, I've come from very far.

DEBDATTA: You're still very far off. Can one get an audience with the Raja easily? Even after calculating the *yojanas*[49] there's such a distance.

RATNESHWAR: I'm a village person, the Maharaja will have pity just by knowing that I don't understand the manners and customs of a royal audience.

DEBDATTA: The method for a royal audience that you have invented with your intelligence and physical strength, isn't prevalent in the capital or the court. Have you brought some payment for the courtier-class?[50]

RATNESHWAR: I haven't brought anything else besides my complaint, I don't have anything either.

DEBDATTA: I can understand that you're a village person.

RATNESHWAR: How did you understand, *thākur*?

DEBDATTA: You still haven't learnt the lesson that the Raja wants to hear from your mouths, that everything in the kingdom is going well, a *satya*-yuga, the realm of Rama.[51]

RATNESHWAR: If everything isn't going well?

DEBDATTA: Then if that isn't made secret it'll go even worse.

It's high treason to tell the Raja unpleasant things.

RATNESHWAR: If there's trouble for us?

DEBDATTA: If there is, then it occurs only for you. If you go to inform the Raja, it'll be trouble for the Raja.

RATNESHWAR: *Thākur*, I suspect that you're joking.

DEBDATTA: Fate does the joking. Let me explain the present situation. Today's the fourteenth day of the bright fortnight in Phālgun.[52] Here, at the moment of moonrise, a *pūjā* to the god Makarketan in the garden of saffron, the Raja's orders. There'll be a lot of song and dance, music; your tone of voice won't agree with them even a little.

RATNESHWAR: Let it not agree, but the Raja's feet I'll find.

DEBDATTA: Getting the Raja in the court alone is getting; in the improper place it's anarchy to him. Wait a bit, tomorrow I'll go and take you along myself.

RATNESHWAR: *Thākur*, you people can stand delay. But my whole body is burning, each moment is intolerable. Our greatest misfortune is this, that even when we feel the agony of death, when we're impaled upon the stake of insults, we still have to keep waiting for the Raja's sentence, our own hands crippled. Curse God.

DEBDATTA: Now stop a while, there comes the Maharani. Don't become impertinent by groaning to her.

RATNESHWAR: My good fortune, the Maharani herself has come; in fact I have come the entire way desiring an audience with her.

DEBDATTA: You people want to cause sorrow to the very person who feels sorrow? Don't you know, the weight of judgment isn't upon her, the Raja does the administration of the kingdom.

RATNESHWAR: Maharani, Mother!

Enter Sumitra

SUMITRA: What, my boy, who are you?

DEBDATTA: He's nobody, his name's Ratneshwar, come from Budhkoṭ; he has no introduction more than this. He'll go away just after taking the dust of your feet. Well, you've had the audience — now come home, you'll get my Brahman-wife's food-offerings.

SUMITRA: Budhkoṭ, now that's under Silāditya's control. Tell me what his behaviour's like.

DEBDATTA: Maharani, all these questions can't be heard well amidst the calls of the cuckoos[53] here. I will take him to the royal court tomorrow myself.

RATNESHWAR: Royal court! Maharani, it's because I haven't any hope there that I've brought the complaint to this festival courtyard.

SUMITRA: Why isn't there hope?

RATNESHWAR: Śilāditya himself is present in the capital, to cover up our weeping. He sits near the Raja's ears, we stay at a distance.

SUMITRA: You shouldn't have any fear, say to me what you want to say.

RATNESHWAR: There's a Satī-shrine[54] below Mount Bhṛigukūṭ. Maheśvarī, a queen of our own royal family, followed her husband to death there, that's now a five-hundred-year-old story.

SUMITRA: That tale of sati I heard on my wedding day from the mouths of bards.

RATNESHWAR: Her own container of vermilion is there, in her resting-place.

SUMITRA: I wore vermilion from that container at the time of my wedding too.

RATNESHWAR: Our girls go to the shrine, wear vermilion from that container on their heads, in holy prayer. So far there haven't been any obstacles.

SUMITRA: Has an obstacle occurred now?

RATNESHWAR: Yes, Maharani.

SUMITRA: What kind of obstacle?

RATNESHWAR: Śilāditya has set a tax at the door of the shrine. It's become difficult for poor girls. The tax is being collected by snatching bangles from their hands.

SUMITRA: What are you saying! Does the Maharaja consent to this?

RATNESHWAR: I don't know the mysteries of royal affairs, Mother, I don't have the courage to speak out.

SUMITRA: *Thākur*, tell me, does the Maharaja consent to this?

DEBDATTA: There's no necessity for consent, there's a flourishing income in this.

SUMITRA: Tell me truthfully, does the royal treasury receive this money?

DEBDATTA: That day the court-pandit had explained that whatever

Agni[55]receives has no dirtiness in it; the Raja's tax is that
fire.

SUMITRA: I don't want to hear the pandit's explanations — tell me,
does this money come to the royal treasury?

DEBDATTA: Of course some comes for the observance of laws,
but the gulp of lawlessness is much bigger than it; the greater
portion gets sunk in that cavity. Maharani, the leftovers of
many sinners accumulate in the royal treasury.

RATNESHWAR: Mother, don't feel miserable about such a little
thing — our food and supplies are short, our voices are tired
crying tears over them. We have stopped complaining about it
whenever someone makes those supplies even shorter. But
even we have a place in our hearts where there's no difference
between raja and subject; if the Raja puts his hand there we
won't stand for it.

SUMITRA: Tell me everything. Don't be afraid.

RATNESHWAR: We're extremely timid, Maharani, but even we get
freed from fear in extreme misery. For that very reason I've
been able to come away like this. I know the danger's tremendous, but where disgrace is more unbearable than danger even
the weak like us don't pay heed to danger. The misery of
dying without food isn't slight but some conditions exist
when no misery's greater than staying alive.

SUMITRA: I understand about that too. Say to me all that you have
to say.

RATNESHWAR: The Raja's attendants are employed to gather the
tax at the door of the shrine; every day beautiful girls fall into
danger.

SUMITRA: What disaster! Are you telling the truth?

RATNESHWAR: I've come only to speak out about those things
which people get ready to die for, Maharani, this is my shame.
My younger sister went to the shrine; the unfortunate girl
hasn't yet returned.

SUMITRA: You have tolerated this too?

RATNESHWAR: I set out making a vow that I will not tolerate it.
I'll have to raise the rod to my own hands, but before that I'll
make a last appeal to the sceptre. After that only Dharma[56]
knows, and I myself know.

SUMITRA: Is all this done through Śilāditya's knowledge?

RATNESHWAR: According to his own wishes.

SUMITRA: *Thākur*, tell me truthfully, has this story not reached the Raja's ears yet?

DEBDATTA: I haven't ever told lies to you, I will not today either. Ratneshwar, your petition's over; now go, you can see my house there.

Exit Ratneshwar

SUMITRA: *Thākur*, this complaint hasn't come to the Raja?

DEBDATTA: Yes it's come. The Minister had hesitated, I myself informed him.

SUMITRA: What was the result?

DEBDATTA: No use hearing. When rajas act unjustly they become truly formidable in supporting it.

SUMITRA: *Thākur*, formidability is the disguise of injustice; let's not give it respect out of fear. The unjust man has to be known as base, truly base, however big a rod he may have in his hand. If we're afraid of him then we'll be even baser than him. Śilāditya has come to the capital with an invitation to the festival?

DEBDATTA: Yes, he's come.

SUMITRA: Give orders to the Minister that I want to meet with him.

DEBDATTA: Maharani!

SUMITRA: I know all that you have to say, and knowing everything I say that I need to have a meeting with him today.

DEBDATTA: Let the festival conclude first.

SUMITRA: If this sin isn't put on trial the festival just can't be held today.

DEBDATTA: Maharani, there's a great necessity to be careful.

SUMITRA: Don't make me pause. I went to plunge into fire once; on the advice of better wisdom I paused. If I'd maintained my resolve right then such misfortune wouldn't have occurred in this world. If Śilāditya is not tried I won't bear the shame of being Rani of this kingdom. I can hear a roar outside the door over there.

DEBDATTA: Merciful one, how much after all did you hear? If all of it reached your ears you would become deaf. The helpless ones in front of whom every door's shut, their voices remain shut too, that's why we exist comfortably. I take it the barriers have moved somewhat today — so we could hear a little bit of sound from the sea of sorrow, suffering in suppressed grief.

SUMITRA: *Thākur*, so there may be barriers — but why stand and

groan in front of them, cowards all. Don't they even know that
God doesn't take pity on those whom He disregards? Let them
break down the doors. They don't get justice only because
they ask fearfully for justice. Their right is to ask for justice
with the same great strength with which the Raja demands
taxes from them. The precepts of dharma aren't gifts of man's
grace. Take me along *thākur*, to their midst.

DEBDATTA: Maharani, you can save them only by staying in your
own place; your strength is where your position is.

SUMITRA: My position! I haven't got my position. I cannot bear that
emptiness day and night; my mind just keeps saying my post
is near the feet of Rudra-Bhairav,— may He show the path,
may He break impediments, deliver His servant from the
insult of futility.

Exit both

Enter Naresh and Bipasha

NARESH: Listen, listen Bipasha, listen here.

BIPASHA: I'll listen only if there are words worth listening to.

NARESH: I've come to say that Jalandhar has not conquered Kashmir.

BIPASHA: When did your delusion break?

NARESH: Every day it breaks. Every day I get proof, Kashmir
herself has conquered Jalandhar. I admit defeat. Now be
pleased.

BIPASHA: The time for that hasn't come.

NARESH: When will it come?

BIPASHA: When with soldiers you people go to war once more in
Kashmir.

NARESH: We'll go to war, we'll try to return defeated too.

BIPASHA: You won't have to try, brave hero. Let me not die until I
see that war. I'll admit that Dharma exists only when it gets
crushed, that taking pride in calling deception your glory.

NARESH: I'm speaking the truth, I'd be relieved if I could throw
away that glory.

BIPASHA: Why so, tell me.

NARESH: Because I've seen a thing of much more value than that
glory.

BIPASHA: You've seen Rani Sumitra.

NARESH: About her it goes without saying. I was saying —

BIPASHA: You don't have to say any more. There isn't anything

greater in your country than her. Can your Raja come within
reach of her? Well, why do you keep quiet? I see you have
shame. Why don't you acknowledge it?

NARESH: I've acknowledged it for many days. The Maharaja went
to conquer Kashmir at a bad time. He lost his own country by
conquering it. He has welcomed and brought an inauspicious
star[57] into the country from Kashmir, even nourishing it with
offerings of sin. Bipasha, I won't keep it secret from you — the
net of danger is surrounding us on all sides, knot by knot, our
wilfully blind Maharaja keeps sitting unperturbed in its very
midst; we must be prepared, there isn't any time.

BIPASHA: Therefore?

NARESH: Therefore I want to hear a song from your lips while this
opportunity lasts.

BIPASHA: My song, a prologue to danger!

NARESH: The flute's note removes the snake's inactivity, my sword
will wake up to your song.

BIPASHA: You want a song of war?

NARESH: No, that song is in my bone-marrow, I'm a Kshatriya.

BIPASHA: Then?

NARESH: You know which song I love.

BIPASHA: I have to sing at the time of the festival anyway, hear it
then.

NARESH: I'll have only one mere part of what everybody gets. Give
me one complete gift, that's only mine alone.

BIPASHA:

Song

My mind tells me I know, I know
    The scent that drifts upon this breeze.
Who can call her a foreigner
    The Chaitra-nighttime[58] *chāmeli*?
Within my blood he left his speech
And in my dreams he'd come and go —
What age, what pathway of the wind,
    What forest or what ocean-shore?
In this remote and alien land
His flute enters my life today.
The bird from those days in my past
Calls out upon hearing his call,
Awakening inside my heart
    The *bhairavī*[59] of tearful eyes.

NARESH: Bipasha, I want to hear one word.

BIPASHA: Well there's your greedy nature. You said ' I want to hear a song", as soon as the song is finished the cry rises "I want to hear one word." From one word it'll be two words, after which my time for work will be over. I'm going.

NARESH: Listen, listen, answer one question, then go. That song there, was it true? Has a flute sounded in the foreign land?

BIPASHA: Insensitive man, it's best not to sing songs at all for some-one to whom a song has to be explained through words. For you've gone beyond even students of the art of rhetoric.

NARESH: Then let explanations be, the song itself is enough for me.

Exit both

Enter Kalindi, a woman of the royal palace. She recites a poem to herself. Enter Manjari, Gauri

GAURI: Whom are you talking to by yourself? To a forest-god?

KALINDI: Oh no, to the god of the mind. I'm committing to memory a hymn to Manmatha.[60] The Raja's orders.

GAURI: It's enough to keep that in the heart, what's the need for bringing it to the voice?

KALINDI: The footpath to the heart is in the voice.

GAURI: Oh my, woman of Jalandhar, I've been here so many days, I haven't yet been able to understand the manner of your people.

KALINDI: It isn't surprising, oh woman of Kashmir, one needs brains in order to understand. Why don't I hear which part seems incomprehensible?

GAURI: In the Vedas there are hymns to Agni, Sūrya, Indra, Varuṇa,[61] indeed many gods, but one doesn't hear even the name of this god of yours.

KALINDI: The sages and ascetics of *satya*-yuga who would so carefully avoid Him, would also fall in danger just as carelessly. They wouldn't utter His name from their mouths, so they got beaten and died inwardly. I take it you haven't read the Puranas?

GAURI: It's good I'm stupid, learned woman. What's the need for such learning, sister, in order to drag the tainted tales of *satya*-yuga along into *kali*-yuga?[62] The ship of sins in *kali*-yuga is loaded enough.

KALINDI: You really put me to shame—"I could not show arrogance because I'm stupid"—indeed Kashmir remains victorious there.

MANJARI: Sister, stop your Kalindi-cacophony[63] a little while. Tribedi-*thākur* says, Kalindi's tongue has learnt the art of biting from its neighbours, her set of teeth. You've raised an argument about the god whom you don't accept merely in order to assert that art. Before you become devoted to the new god, let the austerities to your desired god be complete.

KALINDI: After that there's the undesirable god. Be a little quiet, sister, let me repeat the hymn once more. A god can pardon our lapses, but our court-poet makes us cry if he finds the slightest fault in the recitation of his composition.

MANJARI: There comes Tribedi-*thākur*, let's settle our doubts with him today.

Enter Tribedi while reciting

TRIBEDI:

He's like camphor, whose strength when burnt is still perceived by every man,

Whose power no one can prevent—to Makarketu, *namaskār.*[64]

MANJARI: What are you prattling to yourself, *thākur?*

TRIBEDI: Do not disturb me, I'm memorising.

MANJARI: What are you memorising?

TRIBEDI: A hymn to Makarketu. The Raja's orders.

KALINDI: You're in this state too?

TRIBEDI: Don't you see, even the humming of bees can't be heard. Sanskrit, Śaurasenī, Māgadhī, Ardha-māgadhī, Mahārāshtrī, Persian, Greek,[65] it's being practised in various languages today. From this it can be understood that Makarketu has punditry in every language of every land.

KALINDI: But he understands unspoken languages best of all. *Thākur*, give us the answer to one question. In which Veda have you found precepts about *pūjā* to Makarketu?

TRIBEDI: Quiet, quiet. What a tone of voice you palace-women have got.

KALINDI: Unappreciative man, do you have to lose even your judgment and understanding of tones of voice because you've become aged? Your own poet has compared this voice to a cuckoo's.

TRIBEDI: He hasn't been unjust. That bird hasn't the habit of saying anything secretly.

KALINDI: *Ṭhākur*, I'm not in a state of mind to say secret things to you. I want a judgment on the *śāstras*. They were saying, Atanu isn't embodied[66] in the Puranas, while there isn't the slightest mention of him in the Vedas — what is left? To whom then will the *pūjā* occur?

TRIBEDI: Ah quiet, quiet — bring the tone down another octave.

MANJARI: Why, *ṭhākur*, whom do you fear?

TRIBEDI: Those who want to hold the *pūjā* to the new god use bodily strength more than devotional strength. I'm a simple man, I'm much more afraid of these devotees of the gods than of the gods.

GAURI: *Ṭhākur*, I was saying why have *pūjās* at all for all these sudden-gods?

TRIBEDI: Idiot, the traditional gods don't have such harshness. In earthly life the sudden-gods alone are tremendous. To have *pūjās* for them is futile, not to have *pūjās* is disastrous. Therefore leave the arguments, wear the anklets, bring the vinas, string the garlands — and now go sharpen the arrows of Pañchaśar.

KALINDI: But from where did you get your mantra, *ṭhākur*?

TRIBEDI: The composition of the *pūjā*-mantra is by him who has proclaimed the *pūjā*. I will receive it by means of the *śrutis* and reveal it by means of the *smṛitis*.[67] You'll see, the *śruti*-scholar in the royal court will say "Excellent"; the *smṛiti*-scholar will say, "Oh how marvellous!"[68]

MANJARI: Oh what's that, oh sisters, I heard the clatter of weapons outside.

KALINDI: Maybe that's not real. Maybe there's a practice going on for some play at the festival.

GAURI: Tribedi-*ṭhākur*, I suppose this too is a unique feat in your Jalandhar? A play of bloodshed at the festival for Mīnaketu?

TRIBEDI: Beautiful one, this play has been enacted in the world again and again. Once in the *tretā*-yuga *rākshasas* and *vānaras* together caused a conflagration with this play.[69] In the *kali*-yuga their family has increased rather than decreased. Whatever be the case, I do not like the sound — go now, go and take shelter in the temple.

Exit all

2

Enter Sumitra and Guard

SUMITRA: I want that citizen, Ratneshwar's his name.
GUARD: We cannot find him anywhere, Maharani.
SUMITRA: He was here only a little while ago.
GUARD: But we can't get his whereabouts from anyone.
SUMITRA: Isn't he in Debdatta-*thākur*'s home?
GUARD: The *thākur*'s wife said no one had come there. Well, there comes the *thākur* himself.

Exit

Enter Debdatta

SUMITRA: Where's Ratneshwar?
DEBDATTA: I've come to search for him too.
SUMITRA: But we need to find him immediately.
DEBDATTA: That's precisely the reason why finding him will be extremely difficult. I told the wretch to take shelter in my home.
SUMITRA: Do you then suspect that —
DEBDATTA: I suspect but I'm not naming.
SUMITRA: Will we have to bear this too?
DEBDATTA: Of course we will. Since there's no proof.
SUMITRA: Because of that you'd set the sinner free?
DEBDATTA: The sinner himself knows the honest means to freedom, we won't have to do anything at all.
SUMITRA: *Thākur*, you won't do anything at all then?
DEBDATTA: If it were possible I'd create a thunderbolt from my bones and crash down on his head.
SUMITRA: You want to say there isn't anything at all to be done? Why do you keep quiet, *thākur* — out of shame? Lest you have to do something — out of that fear? I certainly cannot stay patient. Bipasha, what are you doing here?

Enter Bipasha

BIPASHA: I've assembled and brought Maharani's offerings for the *pūjā* to the god Ananga.
SUMITRA: Throw them away, throw them away, throw them all far

away. I'll go to Rudra-Bhairav's temple, *ṭhākur*, have a *pūjā* prepared.

DEBDATTA: The Maharaja has employed the priest Tribedi in his work today.

SUMITRA: You'll be my priest.

DEBDATTA: Me the priest?

SUMITRA: Yes, you. But you're silent, what fear is on your mind?

DEBDATTA: I fear God. I can read mantras with my lips, but after all the Creator knows the story inside. But Maharani, what's the necessity for you to be at a *pūjā* to Bhairav?

SUMITRA: A weak mind, I want strength.

BIPASHA: The one who needs strength isn't you, it's the Maharaja. The state goddess has acknowledged defeat to the uncommon beauty which you've brought to the world — whom should I blame for that? If you forgive me, I'll say the blame's your own.

SUMITRA: Explain to me.

BIPASHA: Will you hear the reason why the Raja has seated those Kashmiri rascals in the heart of the state? You won't get angry?

SUMITRA: I want only to hear the reason.

BIPASHA: The Raja had wanted to express pride in his love very lavishly; he'd have been relieved to be able to give a very expensive gift with great fanfare. You haven't been able to understand this little thing?

SUMITRA: Well I didn't give him any trouble.

BIPASHA: Didn't give trouble? You kept standing somewhere remote with that world-enchanting beauty. You didn't want anything, you didn't take anything; what was this cruel detachment? You were like a swan, your feathers didn't want to get wet with water from the Raja's undulating sea of desires; the net of royal opulence could not hold you even slightly; the more you stayed free, the more the Raja himself became prisoner. Finally one day he cut his own country into pieces and scattered, threw them away into the hands of those Kashmiri kinsmen — he thought he'd given them to you.

SUMITRA: I never knew anything at all about that.

BIPASHA: That I know, the Raja thought he would astonish you by the insanity of his benevolence. He still hadn't known you. But what an unfortunate man — dying of restlessness as he sits upon the royal throne; wanting to give but not able to give, wanting to take but without the worthiness to take. Because of the jeers about his vain stupidity he gets angry now at everybody. You too are among them.

SUMITRA: *Ṭhākur*, until today I hadn't been able to understand well where my offence lies.

DEBDATTA: Maharani, I can't at all times think about when or where I might wake up Kali[70]with a nudge.

BIPASHA: *Ṭhākur*, you have thought, you don't want to speak. But I'll speak. I do not fear anyone. The Maharaja's relationship with the Maharani had begun with injustice; Kali entered through the opening made by that sin.

SUMITRA: Bipasha, shut up.

BIPASHA: Why should I shut up? Do we have to go spreading this lie, that these people have ownership of you by conquering Kashmir? I really get surprised by seeing your patience, Maharani. You have conquered sin through virtue. But has the Maharaja been able to realise the gift of that virtue?

SUMITRA: Shut up, shut up, Bipasha.

BIPASHA: Don't shut me up. It's good to hear from outside too the words that you know inside the heart. There comes the Raja. I'll go. I cannot stay; in the end I'd say something that I didn't mean to say. *Exit*

Enter Bikram

BIKRAM: Maharani, what surreptitious conference goes on with Debdatta?

SUMITRA: I'm having a *pūjā* today in the temple to Bhairav; I've made him the priest.

BIKRAM: *Pūjā* to Bhairav today? Can this possibly be?

SUMITRA: I felt fear seeing the image of sin; I'll invoke Him Whom all fears fear.

BIKRAM: What image of sin did you see?

SUMITRA: An insult to Satī's creed at Satī's shrine, yet there isn't any redress for it in this country; on hearing this report I didn't venture to join the festival.

BIKRAM: Who gave you this report? Debdatta?

SUMITRA: Only one of those who are heartbroken, afflicted by the oppression.

BIKRAM: Maharani, have you established a rival court of law in the inner chamber? You want to rob my authority?

SUMITRA: Maharaja, haven't I taken a solemn oath to become your wife? Doesn't the country's sin touch me too at the very same moment that it touches you?

BIKRAM: Debdatta, who has brought the accusation? Who has been accused?

DEBDATTA: A citizen has come from Budhkot, his name's Ratneshwar; the accusation's against Śilāditya.

BIKRAM: Why pass me over to take this accusation to the Rani?

DEBDATTA: Since you ask me I'll say the truth, the accusation was in fact brought to you previously.

BIKRAM: Did I not listen?

DEBDATTA: You did listen, you said you did not believe.

BIKRAM: Well, that's the judgment. If you give a courtier a bad name falsely, won't the Raja have to make a judgment on it too? You know, the burden that's on Śilāditya is extremely difficult. He alone has to defend the border with Pratyanta.[71]

DEBDATTA: As a representative of the Raja his work is also to defend the faith.[72]

BIKRAM: Who says he hasn't done that?

DEBDATTA: It's being said inside your own heart, that's why you're getting so angry at me. I myself have taken the accuser to you. The Minister did not dare. Didn't I see your frowns frequently that day, at the time of judgment? Won't you admit the fact that in your weak wavering you have desisted from punishing him even after being ready to do so many times?

BIKRAM: Careful! I weak! Weak from fear of what!

DEBDATTA: Today it's difficult even for yourself to oppose the strength that you've given Śilāditya—this is the only reason for your wavering. You have begun to fear them—therein lies our fear.

BIKRAM: Your audacity's intolerable! Your day for repentance is imminent.

SUMITRA: My husband, to punish us is an easy thing—your royal power won't be necessary for it. But Śilāditya's trial must be held this very day.

BIKRAM: Where's the man who made the accusation?

SUMITRA: It's me.

BIKRAM: You?

SUMITRA: The poor unfortunate who had come cannot be found.

BIKRAM: He escaped in fear of his lies.

SUMITRA: Maharaja, surely you know who has removed him?

BIKRAM: Maharani, judgment isn't made through blind pity and unclear conjecture.

Enter Naresh with Ratneshwar

NARESH: Silāditya's people were taking him along by force in front of the royal court. They didn't listen to my forbiddance. I had to draw my sword in order to remind them of the fact that there's a Raja.

BIKRAM: Why were they taking him along?

NARESH: They said, Śilāditya's orders. What are your orders above those orders, I'm waiting to hear them.

RATNESHWAR: Maharani, I know there's no saving me, but I want a trial—that trial should be held this very day, should be held in front of you too, I appeal to you.

SUMITRA: Fool, the Maharaja is over there, inform him of your accusation.

RATNESHWAR: Maharaja, our sorrow is heartrending—that sorrow won't heed obstacles, won't bear delays, it's intenser than the throes of death.

BIKRAM: Shut up! Debdatta, who is indulging them like this? Do they want to snatch judgment away from me by force? Where's the doorkeeper?

Enter Doorkeeper

DOORKEEPER: What, Maharaja?

BIKRAM: Take him and keep him in the guards' quarters. The trial will be tomorrow.

DOORKEEPER: As you command.

RATNESHWAR: Maharani, my today is over, I've no confidence in tomorrow. Live or die, whatever happens to me can happen, but I go having placed the complaint of a citizen at your feet, you'll have to pick it up. I take my leave.

SUMITRA: I'll remember, Ratneshwar.

Exit Doorkeeper and Ratneshwar

NARESH: Maharaja, the Minister has sent some news through me— an early conference is essential.

BIKRAM: You people bring one disturbance after another concocted by yourselves.

NARESH: Do we have such strength that we can create disturbances?

BIKRAM: There's no need to create. Even in *satya*-yuga there was no lack of disturbances in the country. But disturbances are spread over lands and ages. You people have accumulated and arrayed them within just one day today. All the evidence that remains dispersed when it concerns your friends, you people want to organise, blacken and present before me today when it concerns your enemies — today on this festival day you merely want to set up this image of Kālī[73] over the light and say these words, that you alone have had the victory. Know this fact for certain, I won't admit defeat to this dressed-up phantasm[74] of yours. There's news about a disturbance, why not let it be, quite certainly it can wait until tomorrow.

NARESH: Certainly it can wait, Maharaja, but what is news today stands to become a crisis tomorrow. I'll go then, inform the Minister.

BIKRAM: They are my favourites, I'm partial towards them, I cannot make judgments over them, I'm incapable of giving them punishment — all these statements of yours are lies, lies. When I give sentences to those who deserve sentencing you'll be stunned by fear. You yourselves are feeble, weak, what do you know of duty! Your sense of duty is turbid with forgiveness, kindness, tears — you dare to make judgments! The time will come, I'll make judgments, but not by hearing that weeping of yours. Maharani, where are you going? Don't leave, stop.

SUMITRA: Don't give me such orders. Come Prince, to that summer-house, I want to hear what news the Minister has sent.

BIKRAM: Maharani, this latent disrespect of yours is making my duty more impossible. Listen to me — I am ordering you. Come back.

SUMITRA: What, speak.

BIKRAM: You haven't been able to know me — you don't have a heart, woman! Can you treat Śankar's *tāṇḍav*[75] indifferently? It isn't exactly the dance of an *apsarā*.[76] My love is vast, it's fierce, in it is my prowess — it isn't smaller than my royal power. If you could accept its glory everything would be easy. You've read the holy texts, you're God-fearing — your guru's teaching is to consider as noble the loading of duty's burden upon the shoulders of the servant of work. Forget them, those mantras in your ears. The flood of the primal Shakti upon which the bubbles of creation continue to foam, the huge waves of that Shakti are in my love — look at it, make *praṇāms* to it, set afloat upon it all your deeds and misdeeds, doubts and disputes; this alone is called freedom, this alone is called destruction, this alone brings a new epoch to life.[77]

SUMITRA: I don't have the courage, Maharaja, I don't have the courage! Your love has gone far beyond the object of your love — before it I'm extremely small. This boat of mine isn't enough to cross over the tempestuous waves that rise in the ocean of your heart — if I set it afloat while impassioned it would sink instantaneously. My position is at the door of your citizens' wealth and welfare — if you gave me a place even in the dust there, my shame would disappear. Your ears are deaf with the roar of your own waves, how would you know what insurmountable sorrows are on all sides of you? I've lost hope of explaining to you what heartrending echoes of crying move about the cavity of my heart agitatedly, day and night. When everyone on all sides is deprived, then however large a fortune you give me, it won't be to my taste. Come Prince, come and tell me what appeal the Minister makes.

BIKRAM: Listen Naresh, tell me what news you've brought.

NARESH: Maharaja, you'd ordered Ýudhājit to resign; he just hasn't listened to it. I've a feeling that a mutual relationship has formed between them.

BIKRAM: What makes you have that feeling?

NARESH: The moment the Maharani sent a summons to Śilāditya, the very next moment he went away from the capital. He didn't even heed the Maharani's orders.

BIKRAM: Again you've created a crisis? Why did you attempt to handle royal affairs, Maharani?

SUMITRA: Not royal affairs, the duty of a relative. If I don't have authority over anything in Jalandhar, I do have a responsibility to Kashmir.

BIKRAM: Whom should you blame if you've received disrespect in return for wounding the self-esteem of a respectable man?

SUMITRA: I'm not complaining about it if a relative has treated a relative dishonourably. But I want judgment on behalf of your citizens for an offence against the Raja.

BIKRAM: If you want judgment you'll have to wage war first.

SUMITRA: Yes, indeed I'll have to wage war.

BIKRAM: War! But it's not an easy job for a woman.

SUMITRA: If you want the help of a woman's arms I'm certainly prepared.

BIKRAM: Look love, the only purpose of a war is victory, it's not for flaunting. It has to wait for time and opportunity.

SUMITRA: Prince Naresh, let me ask you, isn't there any way at all to save the citizens from the hands of the depraved?

BIKRAM: Maharani, keep in mind that there's injustice in the misjudgments of kindness too. It is as irreverent to believe that punishing wrongdoers is impossible for me, as it is an exaggeration that oppression continues upon the citizens. All this talk shouldn't occur either today, or with you. Debdatta, you haven't received priesthood from the Raja—Tribedi's the priest. Today he has no respite, the *pūjā* will be tomorrow. If you unrightfully lay hands on the Raja's work or the work of the *pūjā*, the Raja's laying hands on you won't be pleasant. Maharani, you still haven't worn the dress for the festival. Go, Raja's orders, have the dress changed at once. For this is the dress of a queen-consort—

SUMITRA: I'll do just that Maharaja, I'll do just that, have the dress changed. Curse this country! Curse me, Rani of this country!

Exit everyone except Debdatta and Bikram

DEBDATTA: Maharaja, I'm going too. But I'll say an unpleasant thing before going. The rebellion in the country had commenced the day you gave power indiscriminately to the hands of those Kashmiris. So many people got death sentences, so many exile. So many respectable people of aristocratic families took shelter in other countries. Only because you faced such obstacles did your decrees become so insufferable, under the pressure of self-conceit.

BIKRAM: Debdatta, what was the necessity for reciting this chronicle?

DEBDATTA: Maharaja, I'm not capable of anything else, I can only keep danger in front of me and tell you unpleasant things. Once you'd wanted to prove exclusively by the logic of weapons that everybody in this country was doing wrong except for yourself. By cutting many throats you had throttled the country. I know that to rectify the error of such a great public arrogance would ultimately be difficult for you. Consequently the Creator has to take that burden himself.

BIKRAM: The simple meaning of these words is, you people will rebel?

DEBDATTA: You know that's impossible for me — God's become the rebel, hard times have come to the country; this will conclude in tremendous sorrow.

BIKRAM: You're using the name of God to try to frighten me?

DEBDATTA: Maharaja, is it a game, to try to frighten you? For us fear of you is the most fearful of all. Raise your rod, let the first blow fall upon us who are your very own. Let those who have made your injustice into their shame, take your wrath upon their heads in the form of sorrow. Give me punishment.

BIKRAM: And if I don't give it?

DEBDATTA: I'll go ahead and take it. Today there's no rest for us, no respect. Go Maharaja, hold the festival. I'll have to make a *pūjā* to Rudra-Bhairav. What if you don't let us enter the temple — I can hear the summons to His *pūjā* everywhere today in the winds of this country.

BIKRAM: You want to insult me through the pretence of speaking plainly; one day my words too will become extremely plain — it won't be long.

Exit both

Enter Bipasha

BIPASHA: Listen, listen Prince, listen.

Enter Naresh

NARESH: What, speak.

BIPASHA: This garland is yours, worthy for a hero's neck.

NARESH: You've learnt about me?

BIPASHA: I have.

NARESH: So easily?

BIPASHA: I can see the future.

NARESH: What can you see?

BIPASHA: You will rescue the honour of Jalandhar's Rani. Why do you keep quiet, Prince?

NARESH: The time for speaking hasn't yet come.

BIPASHA: I say that the time for speaking has now gone.

Song

The thief of light has come concealed out there,
Where are you now, heroes who conquer gloom?
  Who will initiate us
    In conquering this mist?
The white hue has become unclean,
Stolen is the gold from the sun,
Silent is the radiant daybreak
    From feeling shame.
He arrives from the shores of the sea of slumber
    With face covered,
      Body blackened.
Oh rays of sunlight, where are you,
Where are the darkness-cleaving knives,
Shout from the mountain-top of dawn
    "Be not afraid!"

NARESH: Where did you find this song Bipasha?

BIPASHA: We sing this song in the temple of the Sun-god[78] in Kashmir when in late autumn anarchy comes to the realm of light on the mountain-peaks.

NARESH: But why let me hear this song?

BIPASHA: You alone are the messenger of light in the troubled skies here. Let Mīnaketu's altar break, your place is not there; I'll bring Rudra-Bhairav's flower-offerings for you. Here He's Bhairav, in Kashmir He's the Sun; that's the god you should please, hero. Give to me once the dagger that you drew this morning to relieve the oppressed. (*Touching the sword to her forehead*) You alone are the fire in Rudra's third eye,[79] you alone are the sunshine in the bright glance of the morning Sun, you the dagger in a hero's hand; I *namaskār* you.

    Awake, O Rudra, awake.
The sleep-entangled gloomy net
    I can endure no more, no more.
Come to the bolted doors
And liberate them all,
    Body-mind-life, wealth-men-respect,
      O great ascetic, pray for them.

Prince, look there!

NARESH: That lotus-bud of mine! You've still kept it?

BIPASHA: It has spoken today—Kashmir's heart has awakened within it.

NARESH: There comes the Raja with the Minister. Maybe there's need for me — you go wait in the temple-courtyard.

Exit Bipasha

Enter Bikram and the Minister

BIKRAM: The citizens are rebellious? Where?

MINISTER: In Budhkot, in Simhagar.

BIKRAM: Don't talk about forgiveness. The audacity of the power-less is unworthy of forgiveness most of all.

NARESH: Actually their rebellion is against the foreign vassals.

BIKRAM: Are they not my representatives?

NARESH: Not when they look for their own interests, instead of the citizens' or the Raja's. Give me the order and I will go pacify the citizens.

BIKRAM: You! You people have made my administration loose. You alone have united with the Maharani in indulging the citizens; no one has dared to express so clearly as you an envy of the foreigners. Guard, where's the Maharani? Go inform her of my summons at once. Let her hear that her citizens, flaming with kindness, have rebelled today — the cowards have dared to rebel with her support. But can she save them? She herself will have to receive judgment foremost. Right now, right here. Minister, you people have continued defaming me that my mind's weak, my love for the Rani is blind. Today I'll show you were wrong. Even your Maharani will be judged. You think I cannot send her into exile? Our dynasty is Rām-chandra's, the Sūrya dynasty.[80]

MINISTER: Maharaja.

BIKRAM: What, speak. Why do you keep still?

MINISTER: The army of the vassal rajas is nearby. Śilāditya is their general.

BIKRAM: Aiming for the throne?

MINISTER: Yes Maharaja.

BIKRAM: What arrangements have you made for defence?

MINISTER: The soldiers aren't prepared; to trust them all is difficult too.

NARESH: Give me the responsibility, Maharaja. There's no time for hesitation. I'll get the soldiers prepared.

BIKRAM: Guard, where's the Maharani?

GUARD: She isn't in the inner chambers.

BIKRAM: Where's she? In the Bhairav temple?

GUARD: I haven't caught sight of her there.

BIKRAM: Where then?

GUARD: The doorkeeper says, she went away riding a horse on the path to the north.

BIKRAM: What does it mean? Prince, surely you know where she's gone.

NARESH: I don't know anything at all, Maharaja.

BIKRAM: Went away? To excite the rebellious citizens? Bring her back, bring her captive, bring her tied with chains — profligate woman!

NARESH: Don't utter such words. We won't stand for it.

BIKRAM: I was spellbound! Curse me! Blind, I just couldn't see, Kashmir's daughter was sitting behind the throne conspiring. There's no trusting women, no trusting them. Who'd keep her in the inner chambers! She needs the prison!

NARESH: Do not consider such a sin, Maharaja!

BIKRAM: Every one of you is in this. You are too, surely you are. Went away! First I'll give you people punishment, then my other work. Where's Debdatta? Where's that traitor?

MINISTER: Don't get unnecessarily agitated, Maharaja. The Maharani has gone to calm her mind, surely she'll come back on her own. By insulting her out of impatience we'll lose her for all time.

BIKRAM: Do I not know that she'll come back? She left merely to show me her daring. She thinks I'll get her to return by cajoling and pleading. She thinks wrong. She knows me only as some such coward, it seems! She hasn't learnt my identity. I have tremendous power to be cruel. I must be feared — this time she'll understand that.

Enter Messenger

MESSENGER: This letter of the Maharani's, from the northern path.

BIKRAM: (*While reading the letter*) Prince Naresh, what's all this Sumitra has written? What's its meaning? — "Before marriage I went one day to offer myself to Rudra-Bhairav. I brought back

His own sacrifice and came to give it to you, to your country. It
was futile; you never received it, your country too was obstructed from receiving it."

NARESH: Maharaja, you know well, the Maharani went to leap in
the fire; the townspeople brought her back and gave her into
your hands.

BIKRAM: That fire which she brought with her has scorched me.
Take this Naresh, read; the letters are dancing in my eyes, I
cannot read!

NARESH: The Maharani writes, "I go to return the offering to Whom
it was dedicated. The Sun-god will accept me at the shrine to
Dhruva[81] in Kashmir. I have not been able to satisfy you with
my beauty; I was not able to banish your country's woes with
my good wishes. If my *tapasyā* is successful, if I can please God,
then I will be able to benefit you from afar. Do not desire me,
this is my final request to you. Cast me off, let there be peace
for yourselves."

BIKRAM: She didn't give, she didn't give anything at all; everything's a fraud! I, the sovereign, haven't received even an iota
of the nectar that the woman brought to the homes of even my
poorest citizens — my days and nights dried up in thirst,
sitting on the shore of the sea of nectar.[82] Naresh, tell me what I
have to do today, I cannot make up my mind.

NARESH: Maharaja, if you listen to my words you won't try to bring
her back.

BIKRAM: What did you say! I won't try! My masculinity will be
mocked in front of the world! First bring her back, after that
I'll cast her off in public. Tell the Governor to bring her as a
prisoner.

NARESH: That won't be, Maharaja, that won't be, while I have life
I won't let that happen.

BIKRAM: Rebellion?

NARESH: Yes, rebellion! You're distracted, I could not insult you by
doing your bidding. It'll still take her three or four days to cross
your border. I'll go myself to bring her back.

BIKRAM: Go, then go at once, go quickly.

Exit Naresh

Minister, you think that I'm forgiving her and bringing her
back. Absolutely not. She's a rebel against the state, I would

myself send her into exile. She's escaping, avoiding my punishment, this is my grief.

MINISTER: Maharaja, you're causing all of us sorrow by speaking about giving her punishment. As soon as she comes near you'll see that you don't have the ability to give her punishment.

BIKRAM: That may be, I'm spellbound. Let this snare of infatuation go away, let it be torn apart; I won't bring her near me. Guard, bring Prince Naresh back quickly. Let her go, let her go, let Kashmir's daughter go back to Kashmir.

MINISTER: Listen to a servant's entreaty, Maharaja. Let Prince Naresh bring her back, after that it won't take long to forget these wounds and agonies of today.

BIKRAM: I'll never bring her back by pleading, never, never on any account. I brought her once to Jalandhar by waging war, I'll bring her back to Jalandhar only by waging war again.

MINISTER: Waging war?

BIKRAM: Yes, only by waging war. She goes to Kashmir because of Kashmir's pride — she'll announce Jalandhar's disgrace! With Kashmir prostrate and fallen in the dust before her eyes I'll take her back as a prisoner, in the way slaves are taken back. She has neglected me all these days by nourishing secretly in her mind this Kashmiri audacity. Only after extracting its roots with my sword will I find peace this time. Minister, do not attempt futile arguments — go tell them this minute to prepare the soldiers.

MINISTER: Maharaja, will you then let the rebel vassal rajas occupy the country meanwhile without resistance?

BIKRAM: No.

MINISTER: So at present we finish the war with them, then other matters?

BIKRAM: Not a war.

MINISTER: Then?

BIKRAM: An alliance.

MINISTER: Did the Maharaja say an alliance?

BIKRAM: Yes, we'll make an alliance. They will be my companions on the Kashmir expedition.

MINISTER: Make an alliance! Maharaja, you're saying such things only as an outlet for grief.

BIKRAM: Your time for giving advice has passed. Now comply with my orders without discussion.

MINISTER: Still I must speak. All the citizens of the country will get furious with what you've resolved.

BIKRAM: If fury remains secret it becomes static — if fury is expressed it's easy to quell it. That's why I don't have any worries. Send for a messenger to come.

Exit both

Enter Bipasha and Young Women with Kandarpa's flower-image and pūjā *articles*

BIPASHA:

Song

On the stream of southerly winds comes the flood of *bakul* scent.
Pushpadhanu, launch the vessel from the shores of paradise.[83]

The Maharaja said the procession will begin from here. He'll go with us to the *mādhavī*-pavilion.[84] But where, I don't see him.

FIRST WOMAN: He'll show himself as soon as he hears our song.

Song. Continued

Palāś[85] buds on every side
Spell your name out everywhere,
They have awakened restlessness in mountains and in forests.

SECOND WOMAN: But the Maharaja hasn't come — the twilight hour's[86] passing away. There, on the horizon, the moon's outline shows itself.

BIPASHA: What if the hour comes or goes, what does it matter to us? Don't stop singing. The Maharaja said to keep the festival inspired, so that it doesn't become even slightly melancholy.

Song. Continued

Across the sky there exists a lonely place laid out for one, —
The word of hope awakes in him forever separated.[87]
In the leaves and in the grass
Letters of new life arrive,
In *palāś, jabā, kanak-chāṅpā, aśok* and *aśvattha.*[88]

Enter Bikram

BIPASHA: Maharaja, the time's come.

BIKRAM: Yes, the time's come — now throw all this away, trample and throw them away in the dust.

FIRST WOMAN: Maharaja, what have you done, this is the god's image after all.

BIKRAM: So powerless, so futile, so false, you call him a god! Mockery! Here, I trample him under my foot. Doorkeeper.

DOORKEEPER: What, Maharaja?

BIKRAM: Tell them to put out all these rows of lights. Beat the war-drums near the door.

Exit Raja and Young Women

Enter Naresh

NARESH: Bipasha, listen to me.

BIPASHA: What, speak.

NARESH: She went away.

BIPASHA: Who went away?

NARESH: Our Maharani.

BIPASHA: Where did she go?

NARESH: Don't you know?

BIPASHA: No.

NARESH: She's gone alone riding a horse on the path to Kashmir.

BIPASHA: Tell me, tell me everything.

NARESH: She's sent a letter that she won't return again. She'll take shelter in the Sun-temple at the shrine to Dhruva.

BIPASHA: Ah, what happiness. Freedom after so long!

NARESH: But Bipasha, no one tied her up.

BIPASHA: They could not put her in chains, they kept her in a cage. They had fastened her wings with gold. In trying to hold her they lost her. What unusual glory in this loss. The western journey of rays at sunset. But could these blind men see the splendour of this virtuous form?

NARESH: We'll go to bring her back. By this time she's come near the fields of Nandīgar.

BIPASHA: Don't go, don't go, she's not yours; you haven't found her, you'll never find her. From the midst of the disrupted festival today she found release like a heartbroken fountain from stone.

Song

When you forgot about yourself and danced the doomsday
dance
O Nataraj, your knots of matted hair had opened up.[89]
So Ganga[90] in a free cascade
Intoxicated, lost her way,
Her waves rose up and to the music swayed.
The sun's light answered from across the sky.
It pledged safety to one who had left home.
Entranced by her own current, she
Became companion to herself,
Lost all but regained all, along her banks.

We sing this song in the mountains in spring when the snow
begins to melt, and the waterfalls come out on the paths. This is
its time again — the touch of Phālgun has reached the summits
of the mountains, the Himalayas' reticence has been broken.

NARESH: Are you very happy, Bipasha?

BIPASHA: I'm very happy.

NARESH: Your mind doesn't hurt from any sorrows at all?

BIPASHA: Where will I find such happiness, Prince, that doesn't
have any sorrows at all?

NARESH: Well, the ties are cut, now what will you do?

BIPASHA: I'll take to the path with the same person with whom I
stayed at home.

NARESH: I won't be able to turn you back either?

BIPASHA: What's the point in turning me back, friend? You might
make a mistake by tying me down.

NARESH: All right, go. My mind says, we'll meet one day. I've no
place here either.

BIPASHA: Why not, Prince?

NARESH: The Maharaja has decided he'll go to war in Kashmir —
he'll bring the Maharani back only by winning her in a war.

BIPASHA: That's just fine. If the Raja's manliness awakens through
getting angry like this, well, that's just fine.

NARESH: You're making a mistake, Bipasha. This isn't manliness,
this is wantonness — this can't be called Kshatriya prowess.
This is just a transformation of that agitation, that frenzy in
which he was not ashamed to be oblivious of himself all these
days. He wants obsession or intoxication in any form, he just

has to forget himself, this is his nature. He's gone to smear
Mīnaketu's own flag with the colour of blood — not bene-
faction. I have to go to Kashmir too.

BIPASHA: To fight?

NARESH: To inform the Maharani of this fact, that those who've
come to Kashmir to wage war are Jalandhar's undesirables,
so that she doesn't call all of us the offenders for their sins.

BIPASHA: You'll go? Really go?

NARESH: Yes, really go.

BIPASHA: Then I too am your fellow-traveller.

NARESH: If that's so, may this path never come to an end.

BIPASHA: You won't ever return?

NARESH: The door to return is closed. The Raja has started to suspect
me. The place for the Raja's friends is far away from that spot
where the royal sceptre is in the hands of blind distrust.

Exit both

3

Kashmir

FIRST MAN: Disastrous! What are you saying!

SECOND MAN: Come, no more delay.

FIRST MAN: You know for certain?

SECOND MAN: I'd gone to the *tarāi*[91] to sell bearskins — I saw Jalandhar's soldiers with my own eyes. And I saw Dhandatta, Chandrasen's messenger. Negotiations are continuing between both sides.

FIRST MAN: Won't their path be blocked?

SECOND MAN: Who'll block it? The Regent's leaving his own path open. Now, just when we citizens have stood together to make the crown prince the Raja, such is destiny, that very same day foreign bandits come and arrive. The Regent is now trying to establish his own right to the throne by mounting Jalandhar's umbrella on top of Kashmir's royal umbrella.[92]

FIRST MAN: But look Balabhadra, don't break up the coronation by disclosing this news now. Let the ceremony here continue, it'll surely be completed by the end of today. Meanwhile let's go and do what we can. Send Ranajit to the inauguration. And send word to the woodcutters' locality in Jathiyā — I'm going to Rangīpur. We need to round up as many horses from as many people as possible. We'll have to appropriate the wheat granary of the merchants at Pānchmuri — war rations for at least two months are required.

SECOND MAN: This time, whether we live or die, we won't on any account let that vampire's intentions be fulfilled. Kumar's coronation must be performed today. As soon as that's over, we'll consider Chandrasen as a traitor to the state. Hey you, hang up the wreaths of deodar-branches[93] on the portals quickly. Why not tell the drummer to beat the drum?

FIRST MAN: Let everyone gather round. Well, here's Mahīpāl — you're needed urgently.

MAHIPAL: Why, what's happened?

SECOND MAN: It won't do to speak about that here. Come that way. Do not delay.

FIRST MAN: Got some news just now, Chandrasen's coming this way. I suppose to break up the coronation.

SECOND MAN: No, I believe to warn the crown prince tactfully.

Chandrasen may do everything else, but he won't ever tolerate them taking Kumar away as prisoner. But come, no more delay.

Exit all

Another Group

FIRST MAN: What's the matter, brother?

SECOND MAN: Did you drop from the skies or what?

FIRST MAN: Well, it's almost like that. Let me tell you the sad story. You know of course that I joined the Regent's band of guards one day impelled by hunger. A very fat salary, otherwise men wouldn't want to do his work. My wife's body was covered with ornaments — but in shame she stopped going to the well to draw water. Kundan lives in our locality; he fits verses to everybody's name. He gave me the name "Uncle Ganeśa's nephew the rat".[94] Hearing that, people across the land laugh loudly, except for me.

THIRD MAN: Aha, your Kundan's dug up the right name. The excesses of the nephew-rats are increasing in the land. Oh, they've even made holes in the foundations of houses, setting their teeth into just about everything; this time I'll set fire to their holes. After that, fool, I suppose you couldn't tolerate Lord Ganeśa's trunk patting your back?

FIRST MAN: I endured a lot for many days. Finally, the day the pleased Regent made me sardar of the guards' quarters — that day I met my youngest sister-in-law in the middle of the street. You know that she—

SECOND MAN: Sure I know. She's your beautiful one, oh, a fine girl! In fact your versifier calls her "The Weapon of Death".

FIRST MAN: On seeing me she gave the ground a kick with her left foot, made the dust fly, and her anklet jingled — she made a face and went away. Couldn't stand it any more.

THIRD MAN: Ha ha! Nephew Rat's tail got cut by one blow from her fair foot!

FIRST MAN: I threw down my turban at the door of the guards' quarters, went away to Mālkhaṇḍa in the north. All through summer I graze goats; in the winter I bring them to the capital, and sell blankets. I've resolved that when I get some money in my hands, I'll place a gold band on my turban — go to my sister-in-law's house, she'll take back that kick of the left foot;

only then other matters. I was thinking about this matter
while coming with my herd of goats, going toward the capital.
In the middle of my path a group of people making a loud
uproar drove me along here together with my goats, saying
this is our capital here — in this Udaypur.

SECOND MAN: Idiot, keep in mind, from today its name isn't
Udaypur, it's Kumārpur.

FIRST MAN: It'll be difficult to keep in mind, brother, my grandfather-in-law's house is here, I've always known —

THIRD MAN: Why worry, in the new kingdom we'll give your
grandfather-in-law a new name.

FIRST MAN: So do that, but my goat-merchant lives in that place
which I knew as the capital. I have debts as well as fees to settle
with that man. Otherwise I'd be happy if you changed his name
too.

SECOND MAN: All right, fine, the debt from the Regent's reign will
be considered paid in Raja Kumar's reign.

FIRST MAN: And the fees?

SECOND MAN: That we'll see about later — in due time.

FIRST MAN: The stomach's reminders won't heed time, brother.
Well, whatever happens, a capital is surely not created by
words from your mouths, brothers; I don't see such evidence.

THIRD MAN: Does everything have to be seen by the eyes? See with
the imagination.

FIRST MAN: But it won't do for me to get the price of the goats in
the imagination. Explain the matter to me a little, brother.

THIRD MAN: Then listen, Kumar came from a pilgrimage, but the
Regent still held on to the throne tightly. We saw there'd be
bloodshed if we used force. We've decided we'll establish the
crown prince's capital right here and make him the Raja.
Today's the coronation.

FIRST MAN: In this walnut-forest?[95]

SECOND MAN: Where did this stubborn man come from? The
throne will be wherever the Raja sits. And even if I place you
on Indra's seat, goats will bleat from under it.

FIRST MAN: If they didn't bleat I wouldn't be happy either, brother,
my mind would feel uneasy. But one thing I cannot understand. There was one raja, that became two rajas; can they
bear the responsibility? One horse with two riders; one will
pull the reins at the front end, the other one at the tail end;

which road will the animal take?

SECOND MAN: Hey, the riders will have more trouble than the animal — the one who stays at the tail end will fall off all by himself. Have you understood?

FIRST MAN: There's a lot left to understand. Whom will I pay taxes to, before the man on the tail falls off?

THIRD MAN: Taxes have to be paid to Maharaja Kumarsen.

FIRST MAN: After that?

THIRD MAN: After that there isn't anything else.

FIRST MAN: Well, the Regent hasn't taken a vow to fast while sitting on the throne. When his hunger starts increasing, then?

SECOND MAN: The Regent will worry about that. We have all resolved to pay taxes to Maharaja Kumarsen, no one else.

FIRST MAN: You're telling the truth, brother, all have resolved?

SECOND MAN: Yes, all.

FIRST MAN: All along I've seen you foremen shouting out from the back, "Wonderful!" and in front the house falls on our own heads. You're telling the truth, all will pay taxes to Maharaja Kumar, no one will withdraw?

THIRD MAN: No one, no one. Today we'll touch the Maharaja's feet and swear an oath.

FIRST MAN: This business is good. For beatings are written in my forehead anyway. It's just sad that I alone get them. If the entire land sits down to a feast of beatings, I'm not afraid to enjoy the hospitality.

SECOND MAN: This matter's settled?

FIRST MAN: Yes, settled.

THIRD MAN: You won't withdraw?

FIRST MAN: Only you people keep the road to withdraw open; we can never even find that road.

THIRD MAN: Hey stupid man, it's not that we cannot die, but if we die what will your condition be?

FIRST MAN: Our cremation rites would stop.

Enter a Group of Women

FIRST WOMAN: Is it time for the Raja's coronation?

SECOND MAN: No, it'll be later. But you are prepared?

FIRST WOMAN: Oh don't think about us, don't. Among you men alone we see some are ahead while some are behind. Some say work according to time, some say time according to work. Meanwhile time goes by.

SECOND WOMAN: I came from watching your law scholar, still sitting and arguing whether the raja's the one who sits on the throne, or the one who sits on the throne is the raja. The two sides are breaking their heads over this in our locality. The women spent the whole of last night preparing trays of propitious objects.

THIRD WOMAN: Since dawn they've all set out from their respective villages.

FIRST MAN: Don't put us to shame any more. We admit it that one can't find men like women. You do have a group of singers?

SECOND WOMAN: Yes, they've almost arrived.

SECOND MAN: The daughter of your Umichānd?

THIRD WOMAN: She's the one who's bringing the whole group along.

SECOND MAN: Indeed, a worthy girl from Nandapallī. The other day our Karamchānd went to the ghat on the Vitastā[96] to tell her a couple of sweet things. After getting just one blow from her bangle his mouth's shut.

FIRST WOMAN: So you don't know, she said she'll take the name of Vetravatī[97]—she'll stand behind Maharaja Kumar's throne as his serving-woman.

FIRST MAN: Brother, if that happens I'll leave the trade of goat-grazing and become the Raja's umbrella-bearer.

SECOND MAN: Hey fool, just a little while ago I saw you in two minds, what made you fill up with loyalty in an instant?

FIRST MAN: From one fire burns another fire.

THIRD MAN: Well, you'd gone to graze goats, have you brought any news from Uttarkhand?

FIRST MAN: I'll speak only if you don't tell anyone.

THIRD MAN: What're you afraid of? Why not speak up?

FIRST MAN: Didn't you say my credibility's gone? I've seen Rani Sumitra herself, in *bhairavī*'s[98] clothes, going to the Dhruva-shrine.

SECOND MAN: He's mad!

FIRST WOMAN: Oh no, he isn't telling lies. Indeed, I've heard it too. I haven't had the courage to tell anyone.

THIRD MAN: From whom did you hear it?

FIRST WOMAN: Over there, my niece[99] Mandākinī. She was returning from the shrine. They met on the path. The princess is going to be initiated as a devotee of the Sun-god.

SECOND MAN: How can I believe this? Fool, did she say anything to you?

FIRST MAN: I made a *pranam* and said, "You're our Princess Sumitra." She said, "My name's Tapatī."[100] Well, you know that incomparable beauty. That grace seemed to have come bathed in fire. I said, "*Devi*, I'll go along as a servant at your feet." She raised her forefinger silently and made a sign for me to go back.

THIRD MAN: The princess going alone to an inaccessible shrine, didn't you inform the royal residence on coming here?

FIRST MAN: I went to inform one or two people—they were ready to beat me. They said I'd been drinking!

Enter Another Man

FOURTH MAN: He wouldn't agree on any account.

SECOND MAN: Who are you talking about?

FOURTH MAN: Our court-poet Dardur. Didn't have the courage to leave the Regent's protection. Surely we need some kind of a court-poet for the coronation today.

THIRD MAN: Of course we do. It'll do if we observe the custom for today and just dismiss him summarily afterwards.

FOURTH MAN: I've located one. Mannu is bringing him. A foreigner, going to the Dhruva-shrine, there's a woman with him.

THIRD MAN: Just from this you determined he's a poet?

FOURTH MAN: I saw the girl sitting under a tree singing, and he was playing an *ektārā*.[101] I suspected just from seeing his face that the man could compose songs, even if he couldn't do anything else. I went straight to him and said, "You're a poet, come to the Raja's coronation." He wasn't by any means ready to admit the first bit. Thought I'd said he was a madman, or a fool. The girl with him said, "Yes, of course he's a poet, certainly a poet, so we must go to the coronation." Instantly the man melted—there wasn't a chance of saying "no" any more.

THIRD MAN: I've a feeling the girl isn't the sort to whom one can say "no".

FOURTH MAN: Most definitely not. I saw he's quite accepted her

control. If the girl said, "Come, you'll fight", then he'd run
immediately to fight, so writing poems is a trifling matter.
SECOND MAN: I understand, hearing you, the man's a poet. Surely
you remember our Dharanīdās. Gaurī-tarāi's Nathani wove
shawls; Dharanī would come quietly and stand in the corner
of her courtyard. And she'd toss her head, making her eardrops
jingle, by virtue of which Dharanī wrote seven books full of
rhymes. Khetulāl, you've caught it right, the man's a poet.
FOURTH MAN: Whether he is or not, his appearance is suitable.
There he comes.

Enter Naresh and Bipasha, with Mannu

BIPASHA: (*To Naresh*) Poet Narottam,[102] do not deprive them. I
can't find the courage to tell you to sing. But after all I'm your
own disciple; give me the command in due time, I'll sing.
NARESH: I'm pleased by your devotion. Good, I command you,
sing.
BIPASHA: What's that, master, right now? But the time hasn't come
yet.
NARESH: Even after so many days with me you haven't learnt this
lesson, that no time's unsuitable for songs?
FIRST MAN: The poet hasn't spoken unjustly. Don't you see there,
people have gathered. The time's come.
BIPASHA:

Song

Day after day passes in this dark room,
I worry looking at your empty place.
  O friend, the flower-tray
  Is full of buds today,
To string in a necklace of pain placed at your feet.
Counting the sound of every step, the stars of night awake.
The wind from a scarf[103] comes to touch the forest full
          of flowers.
  In Phālgun's breast cry out
  Songs of expectation,
The words of life lose their speech and are shed as tears.

FIRST MAN: Ah, ah, a genuine poet indeed. We cannot let him go.
I'll give him a place in one corner of my grandfather-in-law's

thatch pavilion.[104]

SECOND MAN: Poet, sure the composition's your own? Why isn't
there a signature-line?[105] Our Vaṁśīlāl adds a very elaborate
signature-line to his work.

NARESH: I don't observe the formality of a signature-line. I know
the song's his who sings it. Whether the song's mine or yours —
if you do not forget about this extremely unnecessary question
then that song's not a song at all.

THIRD MAN: But look, poet, somehow I have a feeling I've heard
this song previously, here in Kashmir too.

NARESH: I'm very happy to hear about this. You're a witty man.
As soon as one hears a good song one has the feeling "I've
heard this song before."

THIRD MAN: I've a feeling our poet Śaśāṅka had one like that —

NARESH: Nothing ever is impossible; there are some poets whose
compositions become just like other people's compositions.

THIRD MAN: Poet, I'd like to give you a garland.

NARESH: I don't accept garlands. Whoever has my songs on her
voice, my garlands fall round her voice too.

FOURTH MAN: Well, that's a good speech. She's certainly worthy of
wearing garlands. You there, there are so many garlands on
your trays, why not give me one to put on her.

FIRST WOMAN: Yes, sure I'll give you!

FOURTH MAN: Simpleton's daughter, what's the fault in giving?

SECOND WOMAN: Why would you people see any faults? For your
nature's to go everywhere putting garlands on everyone.

THIRD MAN: Aunty, why are you getting angry?

SECOND WOMAN: You don't have to "Aunty" me any more.

THIRD MAN: All right, I'll stop saying "Aunty", I'll say whatever
makes you happy. Why not give me a garland for the time
being, to put on her.

THIRD WOMAN: Have you people swallowed all shame? No
certainty about where she's from, the Raja's coronation garland has to be given to her! It's not that cheap, you know.

FIRST MAN: Don't say such things grandmother-in-law, if the Raja
was here he'd give her the garland himself.

SECOND WOMAN: Man from Bharat-tali,[106] what sort of customs
do you people have? By what relationship do you call her
grandmother-in-law? She's my niece.[107]

FIRST MAN: I didn't have the courage to call her "Aunty". I thought, she lives in my grandfather-in-law's village, the name for that relationship won't be unbecoming.

FIRST WOMAN: The Raja's coming over there, from the camp. But it isn't time yet. All these people have brought him out by creating a disturbance with their singing.

ALL: Victory, victory to Maharaja Kumarsen!

Enter Kumarsen

KUMARSEN: Quickly, get my horse ready.

THIRD MAN: Poet, start, start a song quick.

BIPASHA:

Song

Your place is empty now, O hero make it full,
For over there I see the trembling mother earth.
  The war-horns ring on pathways in the sky,
  The sun arrives on a chariot of fire,
This morning hold in your right hand the sword of victory.
Dharma is your ally, your ally the word of the world.
Immortal valour is your ally, Vajrapāni[108] too.
  The inaccessible path will accept
  Your footprints with all due honour and pride,
Wear on your chest the fearless armour that is in your heart.

KUMARSEN: (*Calling Bipasha aside with a gesture*) You've come here all of a sudden?

BIPASHA: I've found freedom, Crown Prince.

KUMARSEN: Sumitra?

BIPASHA: That prisoner too has found freedom.

KUMARSEN: Death?

BIPASHA: No, new life.

KUMARSEN: What do you mean, explain to me.

BIPASHA: She's left Jalandhar. She's gone to the Dhruva-shrine, to be initiated as a devotee.

KUMARSEN: My mind still cannot quite accept your words.

BIPASHA: Well Crown Prince, you know Sumitra. Who besides that radiant one could adopt *tapasyā* for the sun these days? Rudra-dev cannot tolerate the confinement, in a storehouse of pleasures, of those who are the messengers of light.

KUMARSEN: And I suppose the Raja of Jalandhar follows her with shackles in hand.

BIPASHA: In order to collect in the royal storehouse the stream of a river by damming it with an earthen dam; ask about him from my fellow-traveller over there.

KUMARSEN: Your fellow-traveller?

BIPASHA: Yes Crown Prince, my fellow-traveller. You're keeping silent! From this I understand you've understood. I don't have to tell you my secret.

KUMARSEN: After so long you've accepted confinement, Bipasha?

BIPASHA: The Bipasha meets the Sindhu river,[109] it's a meeting of free currents.

KUMARSEN: Tell me his name.

BIPASHA: His name's Naresh. Raja Bikram's step-brother. I'll call him.

KUMARSEN: *Namaskār*, Prince.

NARESH: *Namaskār*.

KUMARSEN: Having a guest like you makes this a gratifying day for me.

NARESH: I'm my Maharani's follower — I'm a pilgrim, a guest of the path. Have you had news of the guest who comes uninvited to your door today? Surely you're prepared?

KUMARSEN: I got the news just now. I haven't made arrangements, but I have to invite him. Especially since I haven't even been able to understand till now what the reason was for his war against me.

NARESH: There's no necessity for a reason. Blind malice, blind envy don't search for a path from outside; their shelter is inside the character itself. He cannot tolerate your reputation; the unjustifiable agitation about it is at the centre of his affliction. Well, this is the Creator's curse. On top of that he secretly suspects that Maharani Sumitra has received your indulgence or has come to pray for your indulgence.

KUMARSEN: Has he not learnt even after so long that's impossible for Sumitra?

NARESH: If he had the strength to learn, the misfortune of losing her wouldn't have occurred to him.

Enter Brahmans

PRIEST: Maharaja, our duty's to begin the business of the coronation right now. I've a feeling delay might create hindrances. Rumours of various kinds can be heard.

KUMARSEN: Make the business of the coronation brief. It won't brook delay.

PRIEST: Then come Maharaja, to that dais under the pipal. Everyone, be joyful!

Sound of horns, drums, conches

ALL: Victory to the Maharaja of maharajas, Lord of Kashmir, victory!

KUMARSEN: What's that tumult outside?

Enter Attendants

ATTENDANT: The Regent's arrived suddenly. The guards are saying while they have life they won't allow him to enter here. They're prepared to die fighting. Give the order, Maharaja.

KUMARSEN: Calm the guards. Welcome the Regent and bring him here.

Exit Attendants

BIPASHA: We'll stay concealed, then.

Exit Naresh and Bipasha

Enter Chandrasen

ONE GROUP: Where are you going, Chandrasen? Sinner, hypocrite! Where do you go to, traitor? Take him prisoner!

KUMARSEN: Stop, you people. What sort of mentality is this of yours? He's come to me with trust.

CHANDRASEN: Don't have any fears, child, I didn't come by relying upon trust alone. If they have a desire for accidental death I won't disappoint them.

KUMARSEN: My *pranām*, respected uncle. The moment of my coronation is made propitious by your arrival. Give me your blessings.

CHANDRASEN: That can wait. There's no time at all. Hear why I've come. The Raja of Jalandhar's arrived unexpectedly in Kashmir with his army.

KUMARSEN: I've heard that news. I'll conclude the business of the coronation swiftly.

CHANDRASEN: Let the coronation be for now. Come to him without delay and surrender.

KUMARSEN: Surrender! Not battle?

CHANDRASEN: Where are your soldiers?

KUMARSEN: Why? There's no shortage of soldiers in the capital.

CHANDRASEN: Well, it's not yours yet.

KUMARSEN: But it's Kashmir's, surely!

CHANDRASEN: Well, Bikram doesn't want Kashmir, he wants just you.

KUMARSEN: Are my honour or dishonour not Kashmir's?

CHANDRASEN: What are you saying! This is but a slight family dispute. Give up to him, ask for his affection and forgiveness; everything will be resolved happily.

KUMARSEN: Regent, I don't have time to argue, I'll ask you for the last time — I won't get soldiers from the capital?

CHANDRASEN: Capital! Are you taunting me? I've heard Kashmir's capital is in that same walnut-forest. Make the announcements of your orders right from here. For you don't have any need of me. I am leaving.

Exit

ALL: Curse you, curse you! Be damned! May you be condemned to hell for ten million births! Worm of the throne, after digesting the throne may you become extinct in its dust!

KUMARSEN: Be silent! Listen! Jalandhar has come to attack Kashmir, I'll have to fight him alone.

ALL: Maharaja, justice is on your side, dharma is on your side, the whole heart of Kashmir is on your side. Victory to Maharaja Kumarsen, victory! Curse, curse Chandrasen, curse him hundreds of times!

KUMARSEN: Shut up, don't lose your strength in futile agitation. Go at once and gather the soldiers.

ALL: And the coronation?

KUMARSEN: So the coronation won't be held.

ALL: That won't do, Maharaja, that won't do. Chandrasen's conspiracy will be successful in the end! We could not bear this, on any account. We're here, we'll go at once to arrange for the gathering of soldiers. But the festival must continue, let the ceremony be finished.

KUMARSEN: Have no fear, my coronation will be over in an instant under the water of the shrine, by having God as witness in the temple. If I come back I'll complete the festival. But you people, go. No more delay.

ALL: Victory to Maharaja Kumarsen! Curse Chandrasen! Curse him, curse him, curse him.

Exit All

Enter Another Group

FIRST MAN: Maharaja, no more time. You have to escape.

KUMARSEN: Why?

FIRST MAN: Jalandhar's soldiers have come up to the Andhamuni field, there's no other way now except to escape. Come, I know a path through the Śambhuprastha forest.

Exit both

SECOND MAN: But the Regent had come just now.

FIRST MAN: Cunning, cunning. He's pointed out directions to the enemy himself.

SECOND MAN: People have gone to all the villages to collect soldiers, but we just cannot find time. Oh, they didn't even let us fight a battle.

THIRD MAN: This is like an encircling fire, we won't be able to do anything at all, we'll just die. Unbearable!

FIRST MAN: Jalandhar's sinners call this fighting a battle. But this is murdering of people!

Another Group

FIRST MAN: Oh, they've burnt Nāgpattan, burnt it.

SECOND MAN: What did you say?

THIRD MAN: Yes, the people there screamed themselves hoarse, till the end—"Victory to Maharaja Kumarsen, victory."

SECOND MAN: The Regent is behind this. Since Nāgpattan never did acknowledge him, this time he took revenge just for that through the foreigners.

THIRD MAN: If that's so the activities of many towns indeed will end.

Enter Debdatta

DEBDATTA: Listen, listen, is there any one from Kuntīpur among you?

FIRST MAN: But why, tell us.

DEBDATTA: Maharaja Bikram had a conference with Chandrasen, he'll send soldiers there to create a disturbance.

SECOND MAN: Who are you, sir? You seem like a foreigner.

DEBDATTA: Yes, a foreigner.

THIRD MAN: One from Jalandhar?

DEBDATTA: You've guessed right.

FIRST MAN: How did you get such a good conscience?

DEBDATTA: Occasionally such things happen through the Creator's astonishing powers. I've seen gentlemen born into the same family in which Chandrasen was born, in your Kashmir.

SECOND MAN: Well spoken, *thākur*, well spoken. You're a Brahman, surely?

DEBDATTA: Yes, a Brahman.

ALL: We *praṇām* you.

SECOND MAN: Against your own Raja you—

DEBDATTA: By what logic do you say this is against the Raja? The more I prevent my Raja from sinning, the more my loyalty should be realised.

THIRD MAN: But surely there's danger, *thākur*, if the Raja—

DEBDATTA: Well, apprehensions of danger are not any fewer for those who commit injustices today on behalf of the Raja. If anti-dharma can give courage, should dharma be cowardly?

SECOND MAN: You've said very important words, *thākur*. Give me, once again give me the dust of your feet.

DEBDATTA: Has Crown Prince Kumarsen been able to escape from here?

FIRST MAN: *Thākur*, forgive us, we can't do that, it won't do to speak about the crown prince even with you.

DEBDATTA: You don't have to say anything; I want to know is he out of danger?

FIRST MAN: Who can say about dangers and difficulties? However, there won't be lapses in our efforts.

THIRD MAN: Look, look, at that mountain in the west. It seems they've started a fire near Achaleśvar. The whole forest is burning. Why did they come to create unnecessary destruction! Tigers eat when they feel hungry, when they feel frightened snakes come charging out; but this sin of theirs is motiveless, unjustifiable malice.[110] What race of men are they, *thākur*?

DEBDATTA: Demons, demons. They feel pure animosity toward the gods. O insane, depraved, blind one, your deadly sin takes you away to a great downfall; who can save you today? Curse your friends!

Exit

Enter Bikram and a Spy

BIKRAM: What did you say? No trace could be found?

SPY: No, Maharaja.

BIKRAM: But then Chandrasen said his coronation's being held right here. That wasn't too long ago either.

SPY: I saw them just now bringing his horse back. He has entered the Śambhuprastha forest. It doesn't take longer than a moment to become invisible on the path to the caves there.

BIKRAM: Go seize those who know the path.

SPY: Maharaja, they won't tell even if they die. Besides, no one even has the courage to go there to search. For that's a jungle possessed by ghosts.

BIKRAM: Go call Chandrasen.

Enter Chandrasen

Where's Kumarsen?

CHANDRASEN: The citizens have united to conceal him somewhere, finding him's impossible.

BIKRAM: Set fire on all sides, he'll come out by himself.

CHANDRASEN: Without knowing where he is, setting fires would be malicious childishness.

BIKRAM: You've found trace of him, you're concealing it.

CHANDRASEN: I've engaged in sin, but I'm not so great an ignoramus as to add stupidity to it. Why should I cause danger to myself by concealing it from you?

BIKRAM: I do not trust you.

CHANDRASEN: All the people of Kashmir are cursing me; I did not expect that I'd ultimately hear such words from your mouth too.

BIKRAM: Is it not true that you'd come here to Kumar a little while ago?

CHANDRASEN: I came to give him advice to surrender to you.

BIKRAM: You let him know by that same strategy that I'd come. You've made him cautious by feigning dependence upon me.

CHANDRASEN: Do not distrust me by making a mistake, Maharaja.

BIKRAM: That would be just fine, but there's no time for making mistakes by trusting you. I'm giving orders to the general, you'll be held captive under watch; if I don't find Kumar and Sumitra in the end then I'll take you to Jalandhar, put in a cage like an animal; even giving you the death sentence would be an honour for you.

Enter Second Spy

SPY: News of the queen has been received.

BIKRAM: Speak, speak, where is she?

SPY: She's gone to the temple of the Sun-god, at the shrine to Dhruva.

BIKRAM: Come, let's go there right now. This instant.

CHANDRASEN: Maharaja, do not express defiance of Kashmir's god. The abduction of the Sun-god's devotee from the house of god won't be tolerated.

BIKRAM: Well, it's your Sun-god himself who's abducted my queen. I will not accept a god's thievery.

CHANDRASEN: What's this you're saying? Don't you have fear?

BIKRAM: No, I've no fear.

CHANDRASEN: Then sentence me to death. I won't be able to carry the responsibility for this sin.

BIKRAM: The death sentence is at the very end. Not as long as I have hope of extracting work out of you. General—

Enter General

GENERAL: What, Maharaja?

BIKRAM: Come, on the path to the Sun-god's temple.

GENERAL: It's impossible to go with soldiers on the inaccessible path to that temple.

BIKRAM: The impossible has to be made possible. Whether the temple's inaccessibility is earthly or unearthly, ghostly or godly, I won't ever yield to it. I've taken a vow that I'll destroy all shelters in Kashmir for Sumitra.

CHANDRASEN: God's temple isn't within the limits of this world, Maharaja, it's quite outside earthly Kashmir.

BIKRAM: That may hold good concerning gods, but not concerning Sumitra; as long as she is within the limits of this world she's mine, she's not a god's. During that time there's no releasing her from me, nor even release for me from her.

CHANDRASEN: Maharaja, I'm your elder, I place my head at your feet; go ahead and behead me, do not insult the god of Kashmir.

BIKRAM: Does your head have value, that the insult to me will decrease in exchange for it? You won't get deliverance by deceiving me. General, besiege Udaypur. Surely Kumar is hiding right here, and Chandrasen is concealing that fact. After that we'll go on the path to the shrine. I've already been introduced to the god Kandarpa in the past, now I'll ask for an introduction to the Sun-god. That festival which I'd begun in Jalandhar's temple of god will be concluded in Kashmir's temple of god.

4

The shrine to Dhruva. The Sun-temple[111]
Bipasha, Priests, and Worshippers at the temple
The hymning of a Vedic mantra at sunrise

So that He may see the world, rays hold aloft Sūrya,
The radiant one aware of all creatures.
Seeing Sūrya arrive, the witness of the world, those stars
Escape like thieves, together with the night.[112]

Enter Sumitra with a lotus-offering in her hands

BIPASHA:

Song

Awake, awake,
   Lethargic one asleep.
Awake, awake,
   Submerged in deepest dark.
Let the sun's compassion rain down and wash
Away all turbid visions wrapped in sleep;
   Awake, awake,
Dejected and bent low with sorrow's load.
Let the treasure of light fill up your heart
With richness that destroys the lure of wealth,
   Awake, awake,
Wear holy clothes upon your naked shame.

Enter Bhargab, the priest

BHARGAB: Mother.
SUMITRA: What, my child Bhargab?
BHARGAB: I've been noticing for some days the comings and goings
   of people of various descriptions on the path to this inaccessible
   shrine. They aren't of pious intent.
SUMITRA: No fault in that, no fear either.
BHARGAB: I've a feeling, though, they're foreigners.
SUMITRA: The horizon of the god Sūrya's dawn covers all lands.
   Who is a foreigner in His land?
BHARGAB: Don't take offence, *devī*, but for some days we've been

blocking the foreigners' way here.

SUMITRA: Then my way here is blocked too.

BHARGAB: Forgive us, *devī*. It's our ignorance, our audacity to think that we will defend you from danger. Don't take offence at a weak judgment, there won't be any obstacles for the travellers.

Enter Shikharini

SHIKHARINI: Mother Tapatī.

SUMITRA: What, Shikharini, why are you here?

SHIKHARINI: They have killed my husband.

SUMITRA: What is it you're saying? But he was a saintly man, why kill him?

SHIKHARINI: They were trying to get information out of him about where the crown prince was. Everyone in the land knew him as truthful, that's precisely why this disaster happened to him. *Devī*, I just can't find consolation at all; explain it to me, why does Dharma kill and cause such sorrow only to those who spend their earthly lives obeying Dharma?

SUMITRA: Only those who have died know the principle behind this fact. Do not grieve for those who find truth through death.

SHIKHARINI: I will not grieve, Mother; he has removed my fear of death and gone, this is his last gift to me. People in the village call me an unfortunate woman; what'll they understand! It was my supreme good fortune that he was my husband.

SUMITRA: He has conquered through death those who killed him, they won't ever understand this fact; this above everything else is cause for grief. But child, why have you come here?

SHIKHARINI: If I could take shelter here at your feet, I'd survive then. But Mother, if the light of a family dies the family still exists. I have my girl — she's lost the embrace of a father like that, for her welfare alone I have to stay in that darkness. For her alone I've come to you.

SUMITRA: Speak, what must I do?

SHIKHARINI: I've brought these ornaments for safekeeping in the temple of god. I got them from my mother, I'll keep them for my daughter. Chandrasen is having Jalandhar's soldiers loot all the possessions of those for whose families he holds a grudge. Here Mother, take, let these gain your touch — my girl's body will be purified.

Enter Kunjalal

KUNJALAL: There's no deliverance today from our sorrow anywhere outside, *devī*, but I feel as if you can destroy that sorrow
on the inside, so I've come.

SUMITRA: Speak, my child, what you have to say.

KUNJALAL: Udaypur, that city which is your grandmother's[113]
birthplace, had remained independent all these days by rejecting Chandrasen. Whenever he came with soldiers to create
disturbances the citizens would leave by evacuating the entire
city. This time the crown prince's capital was established
right there and arrangements made for his coronation, but an
obstacle arose. Raja Bikram's soldiers have surrounded
Udaypur. The citizens' way to get out is blocked.

BHARGAB: Kunjalal, what's this idea of yours? Just look what
great sorrow you've given her. Why all these reports at this
peaceful shrine?

KUNJALAL: Mother, why do you remain still like this, gazing at the
sky? There isn't even anything to worry about, the way to
death is open, no insults at all reach there. Give me the *pūjā*
flowers today with your own hands, to take away to them, and
give me a piece of writing in your hand, a blessing—all their
sorrows will be brightened.

Exit all

Enter Naresh

NARESH: Bipasha, shall I tell you what I think?

BIPASHA: Well, tell me.

NARESH: Our love is fulfilled after coming here. Want to hear the
surprising part?

BIPASHA: What, tell me.

NARESH: My mind today does not even wait to hear your songs—
all sounds here have become light, the sensations enter within
me. Don't you perceive it?

BIPASHA: My love, your happiness today makes me happy, I can't
say anything more than that.

NARESH: In today's light I see you in the form of light, and with it
myself as well. I don't feel distressed any more.

Enter Sumitra

SUMITRA: Kumar has come, call him here quickly, Bipasha.

Exit Naresh and Bipasha

Enter Kumarsen

KUMARSEN: After traversing the paths of the kingdom I finally had to come to this very shrine, sister.

SUMITRA: There's much need for you in another place. If it hasn't come to an end, why come here?

KUMARSEN: In order to protect you.

SUMITRA: From whose hands?

KUMARSEN: Maharaja Bikram has promised, taking a vow to the goddess at Jvālāmukhī,[114] he'll remove you from here by whatever means. It's impossible for the army to come on the path to the shrine, so he's filling up all sides with his people gradually, one by one.

SUMITRA: He wants me?

KUMARSEN: Yes.

SUMITRA: What else does he want?

KUMARSEN: And he wants me.

SUMITRA: Why, what's his dispute with you?

KUMARSEN: If there was clear reason for a dispute with me then the danger would pass by just dispelling that reason. The reason's in his blind nature, that's why it's so uncontrollable, so terri-fying.

SUMITRA: If I go, will he give you freedom?

KUMARSEN: But how will you go to him? For you belong to a god. I don't think about the state any more, but I cannot let an insult occur to the god of Kashmir.

SUMITRA: What will you do?

KUMARSEN: If nothing else, at least I'll die. After all it's a sin not to do anything to prevent sin.

VOICE OFFSTAGE: Maharani!

SUMITRA: What's this, it's Debdatta-*ṭhākur*!

Enter Debdatta

DEBDATTA: For some days I've been trying for an audience; the apprehension in the minds of your attendants on seeing my

appearance doesn't cease. Their condition's just the same as
the *rākshasas* becoming suspicious on seeing Hanumān in the
aśok-forest.[115] Don't know why they suddenly became satisfied
today, just now. I came to see you as soon as I was released.
I have a petition — you just have to hear my words.

SUMITRA: Speak.

DEBDATTA: I can't bear it any more, Maharani. Village to village,
town to town, conflagration, scarcity, bloodshed, rape. The
intoxication of sin has possessed absolutely all of Jalandhar's
soldiers—they cannot stop, the degree just continues increasing.
I went and cursed the Maharaja, saying, "I pray to Lord Yama
daily that he may take you away." The Raja had me imprisoned,
the guard took pity and released me. No one else, only you'll
be able to forbid the Maharaja today.

KUMARSEN: *Thākur*, how can you say such a thing, Sumitra will
go to him? There isn't any way for her to return to this temple.
It'll certainly raise an uproar in heaven and earth.

DEBDATTA: I know the business is very difficult indeed, I also know
that the Raja's not in his right senses now. Still I say, *devī*
Sumitra, today you're beyond all honour and dishonour,
happiness and sorrow, — you're pure, sin will recoil from you,
you can descend into this repulsiveness with an unperturbed
mind.

KUMARSEN: There isn't time today to think about what can or cannot happen to Sumitra — but I won't let it happen that Sumitra
insults the god of Kashmir and goes away from here. A daughter
of our dynasty will rob a god's treasure and take it away to the
coffers of man's pleasures!

SUMITRA: Brother Kumar, I'll invite him to come here.

KUMARSEN: Here? In this house of god?

SUMITRA: Let him come right here, otherwise he won't ever find
freedom. This is my last task, I have to save him — I'll go away
after tearing up his knot of obsession.

DEBDATTA: But this is a very critical matter, Maharani. He's
committed many sins; if the depraved man ultimately comes
to the house of god and dishonours the god, if he brings
defilement to a holy place?

SUMITRA: Don't fear, *thākur*, don't have any fear. My master, my
golden splendour, will scorch all sins, thoroughly reduce them
to ashes. That Rudra has accepted me; no one at all has such

strength that can tear me away from His side. Kumar, is Shankar with you?

KUMARSEN: He's over there, standing in the courtyard.

SUMITRA: Shankar!

SHANKAR: What, sister? What, *devī*? Here, I've come. The day they snatched you away, that day I felt sorrow greater than death; my life was finally fulfilled on seeing that the god of Kashmir himself had rescued the daughter of Kashmir.

SUMITRA: Go as my messenger to Raja Bikram.

SHANKAR: I'll go right now. Tell me what to inform him.

NARESH: *Devī*, not Shankar, send me instead; if the Raja insults him the old man won't be able to bear it.

SUMITRA: No Prince, this is my last invitation — in whose hands should I send it if not my dearest friend's? Shankar, in my childhood you had once accepted me in your lap. At the time of death Father gave his last regards to you as well. Today you alone have to go with a message from that Sumitra of yours, perhaps into the face of insult. Tell the Maharaja calmly and patiently, Sumitra will wait in the temple at the feet of the god, for the final stage of the relationship with him. And the treasure of your greatest affection, Kumar, don't worry about that Kumar; he does not fear death. That friend, that judge of the world Dharma-raja[116] remains his support.

SHANKAR: Sister, hear one word from the old man; I know Kumar doesn't have armed forces, I know Chandrasen's against him; still he'll have to go to the battlefield itself with those few among us who are his followers. His motherland will accept him there in her holy lap.

DEBDATTA: That will churn up the country's sorrows even more, Shankar. Don't feed more fuel to the fire of madmen's frenzy.

KUMARSEN: Shankar, go, bring the Maharaja with you. He's a guest, I'll receive him like a guest.

SHANKAR: O Rudra, O golden-handed one, why's your light veiled today? Ward off the shame of your attendants. Come out with sparkling glory — uncover your fiery banner. *Namaskār* to you, *namaskār* to you, again and again *namaskār* to you.

Enter Bhargab

BHARGAB: Maharaja Bikram's not very far off, that's the rumour

I hear. Give the command, I will bolt all the doors.

SUMITRA: Open them, open them, open up all the doors, the doors
for coming and the doors for going. Go, go Bhargab, invite
him in.

BHARGAB: He's promised he will snatch you away from the god.
I'm priest of this temple, surely I have to do my duty.

SUMITRA: Do your duty then. Do not block the god's path — my
god will come to rescue me by that same path down which the
Raja's soldiers will come. Go right now, open up the main
gate of the temple.

Exit Bhargab

DEBDATTA: Then Shankar, you stay, as the Maharani's messenger
I myself will ask him to come in.

Exit

SHANKAR: Sister, they had snatched you away that time from the
royal palace, will you let them snatch you away this time from
the house of god? Will we put up with this, too, in silence?

SUMITRA: Don't fear, Shankar. Who has the ability to take me
today?

SHANKAR: Then tell me, what have you resolved?[117]

SUMITRA: Many days ago I'd offered myself to Rudra. An inter-
ruption occurred, earthly life made me impure. I've undertaken *tapasyā*, my mind and body are purified. That long-
standing resolve of mine will be completed today. I'll merge my
energy with His supreme energy.

SHANKAR: May my ignorance[118] be removed, Sumitra, my ignorance removed. So that I don't dissuade you.

Exit Shankar

SUMITRA: Bipasha!

Enter Bipasha

BIPASHA: Speak, *devī*.

SUMITRA: My bed of fire's been prepared for many days now, you've
seen those arrangements of much sorrow. Today the time's
come, be joyful, light the flame, do not delay.

BIPASHA: As you command, *devī*.

Lies down with her head at Sumitra's feet

SUMITRA: Get up, Bipasha, let me make my final *pūjā* now. Are
   the offerings prepared?
BIPASHA: They are, *devī*.

Sumitra with lotus-offerings in her hands

BIPASHA:

Song

The new white conches resound all over your skies,
   Auspicious songs of waking ring.
Your feet grace their place in the lustre of the sun,
   My lotus-heart[119] is blossoming.
      Receive and welcome it
      On the dark other shore,[120]
With the most pure touch, sanctifying and gladdening.

SUMITRA:
   May Sūrya's rising, radiant rays today
   Rescue and guard us from sins, blameful deeds.[121]
      May earth bring peace, the skies
      Bring peace, heaven bring peace.
      Śāntih, śāntih, śāntih.[122]

FINAL SCENE

*A glow can be seen from the flames of the funeral pyre offstage
Everyone circles the altar to the chant of the Vedic mantra*[123]

May my life-breath and this body merge ashes with the air.
Om, reflect upon one's duties, and upon successful deeds.
Reflect upon one's duties, and upon successful deeds.
   O Agni, take us on the virtuous path.
   O God, you know about our every deed,
   Destroy all our dissimulating sins.
   We *namaskār* you, again and again.[124]

Music plays offstage. Enter Bikram, Debdatta, Shankar.

FORMLESS JEWEL

(ARŪP RATAN)

NOTE ON THE PLAY

Tagore wrote and published the play *Rājā* in late 1910. Ten years later, in early 1920, he published a rewritten "stageworthy" version titled *Arūp Ratan* in which he deleted the character of the invisible Raja altogether. In the following year he prepared the second edition of *Rājā*, restoring many passages from his original manuscript which he had excised from the first edition (1910); the text of this longer second edition is the one currently in circulation. In December 1931 Tagore published a musical drama, *Śāpmochan*, based on the story of *Rājā*, which he revised again for performances in March 1933. The current text of *Śāpmochan* dates from 1933. Then in 1935, Tagore completely reworked the text of *Arūp Ratan* for a production in Calcutta; this version appeared as the second edition of *Arūp Ratan* and formed the basis for the definitive text of the play published in the collected works.[1] In actuality, much of this play corresponds to the equivalent sequences in *Rājā* — of which, for all practical purposes, it is only a more compact edition. As such, the final recension of *Arūp Ratan* — which I have translated here — assumes a certain degree of importance because of its status as the last published dramatic work on the *Rājā* theme, a theme that obviously preoccupied Tagore for the last three decades of his life.

The legend of Sudarshana and her royal husband goes back to ancient Buddhist lore. Since Tagore admitted having read and borrowed tales for some plays from Rajendralala Mitra's *The Sanskrit Buddhist Literature of Nepal* (1882), in which Sudarshana's story appears twice, we can safely surmise that he came across the legend in this book.[2] Although the relation between Tagore's plays and Mitra's anthology is as distant as that between, say, Shakespeare's plays and Holinshed's chronicles, it may nevertheless be of interest to extract some relevant passages from Mitra for comparison. The story of the beautiful Sudarśanā and the hideous King Kuśa appears in the "Kuśa Jātaka" and the "Mahāvastu-Avadāna", both in Mitra's collection. The latter gives a lengthier rendition of the tale, from which I quote extracts:[3]

> Mahendraka, the tribal king of Bhadrakasat in Kānyakubja, had a
> very beautiful daughter. Alindā immediately after Kuśa's accession, set

a negotiation on foot for her son's marriage to that princess. The match was soon settled. . . . But Alindā was apprehensive lest her fair daughter-in-law would commit suicide at the sight of so deformed a husband. She, therefore, prepared rooms underground where, under the plea of family customs, she placed the young couple. No light was admitted into the room. The couple enjoyed their honey-moon in the dark. But Sudarśanā, the princess, grew impatient to see her beloved husband . . . Alindā, to avoid Sudarśanā's seeing the ugly husband, made one of her step-sons personate Kuśa on the throne, while the real Kuśa with his thick lips, corpulent belly, deformed head, held the royal umbrella. Sudarśanā was pleased with her supposed husband, but she expressed her indignation at so black and ugly a person being allowed to hold the parasol. On one occasion when walking in the royal park she fled from him as from a monster.

But in a short time, her mistake was corrected. At a great conflagration of the city the elephant park was saved, simply by the activity of the king. . . . Sudarśanā then found out her error. She learned, to her great surprise and grief, that the monster at the park was her real husband. She instantly begged the permission of her mother-in-law to proceed to Kānyakubja. The permission was granted, and she set out for Kānyakubja to hide her shame.

The king, unable to bear the separation, appointed one of his half-brothers as regent, and proceeded himself to the north . . . in private he tried to persuade his refractory wife, but to no purpose. . . .

In the meanwhile, the scandal of Sudarśanā's leaving, and in a way divorcing, her husband spread far and wide. Seven feudatories of the king of Kānyakubja offered to marry her. But their offers were indignantly rejected by the king. They made a common cause with one another, and advanced to seize the capital. The king, in wrath scolded his refractory daughter, and threatened to cut her into seven pieces for these seven rebels, if he got worsted in the coming conflict. Sudarśanā, trembling with fear at so terrible a threat, had now recourse to her almost divorced husband. . . . He promised to save her, and to fight her father's cause. . . . The hero advanced on an elephant and towards his enemies, and by a shout at the onset so quailed their spirit that they surrendered themselves his captives. . . . Kuśa set out in the company of his humbled wife for his own kingdom. On his way, he looked at his own image reflected in a glassy brook, and was so much disgusted at his deformity that he wanted to drown himself. But just at that time Indra manifested himself before him, and presented him a garland set with the rare jewel called Jyotirasa. "Put this on, and it will make you," said Indra, "the most beautiful man on earth. When you wish to assume your own form, cover this with your clothes and your beauty will be hidden." Kuśa put on the jewel, and Sudarśanā was transported with delight, when she found her husband blessed with a celestial form.

Explicating this story to his disciples, the Buddha told them that he was Kuśa and Yaśodharā, his wife, was Sudarśanā.

The title of the play requires special attention. It is truly untranslatable, *Formless Jewel* being a literal and rather vague rendering of an essentially theological concept. At the crux of the problem lies the word *rūp*, which means all of the following: form, body, shape, beauty, grace. Thus *arūp*, its negative, means "formless", "bodiless", and so on, even "ugly"—adjectives that certainly fit the Raja in the play. But these English words have pejorative connotations, whereas the Indian word carries positive associations of something that transcends the narrow circumscriptions of form or body or mere physical beauty. Consequently, in the monistic philosophy of the Vedanta school *Arūp* is an epithet of Brahman or Brahma, the supreme universal spirit or absolute godhead that cannot be described in human terms because it would be futile to try to do so. Tagore was fond of the phrase *arūp ratan*, using it often in his writing; one of his songs begins with a line that roughly goes, "I have dived in the ocean of *rūp*, in the hope of locating the *arūp ratan*".[4] Our mortal world is the ocean of forms and beauty, in which one tries—or at least should try—to find the elusive formless jewel. This quest underlies the present play from start to finish, as it does much of Tagore's creative work.

The first performance of *Rājā* took place at Santiniketan on 15 March 1911 with Tagore in the role of Thakurda.[5] It was repeated at the same venue as part of the author's fiftieth birthday celebrations on 7 May, with Tagore speaking the part of the Raja in addition to acting as Thakurda.[6] After an abortive attempt at staging *Arūp Ratan* in 1920, a tableaux production of this play was staged on 15 September 1924 at the Alfred Theatre in Calcutta, with Tagore as the narrator while the cast mimed the play. During the week-long festivities in Calcutta marking Tagore's seventieth birthday, the students of Santiniketan performed *Śāpmochan* for the first time, on a double bill with *Natīr Pūjā*, at Jorasanko on 31 December 1931. Tagore recited and a chorus sang, accompanying the mime and dance sequences onstage.[7] He revised the musical drama slightly for performances in Lucknow on 6–7 March 1933—the first time a

production by Tagore was staged outside Bengal—and extensively
for repeat performances on 29–30 March 1933 at the Empire Theatre.
The production subsequently toured to ecstatic reviews, notably in
Bombay (November 1933) and Srilanka (May 1934).[8] In October
1934, Tagore added a few more songs to it for a performance in
Madras, during the course of a tour of south India by the Santiniketan
troupe. Tagore staged the revised version of *Arūp Ratan* on 8
December 1935 in Santiniketan and then on 11–12 December at
the New Empire in Calcutta, once again playing Thakurda and the
invisible Raja, at the age of 74. These were his final acting roles,
and according to his biographer the production "proved to be a
success".[9] Finally, in December 1940, *Śāpmochan* was enacted in
Santiniketan; despite his failing health, Tagore selected the songs
for the performance and set some dialogue to music.

PREFACE

Sudarshana sought the Raja externally. She sent the bridal garland[10] to the place where things can be seen by the eyes, touched by
the hands, amassed in the storehouse, where there's men and money
and fame. With the vanity of intelligence she must have determined
that she could attain success in life externally by the strength of
intelligence alone. Her companion Surangama told her that it
would not be wrong to know the Lord in all respects through ex-
ternals, but only after He is known in the interior secret chamber
where He comes Himself and summons; however it would be
wrong to call "rajas" those who delude the eyes through maya.
Sudarshana did not heed these words. She surrendered herself in
her mind to Subarna on seeing his beauty. Then — how a fire started
on all sides of her; how a battle over her ensued among a group of
many false external rajas as soon as she left the Raja internal; how
her introduction to her own Raja occurred in the midst of that conflagration; how her vanity was destroyed by the shock of sorrow;
and eventually how after accepting defeat, leaving the palace,
standing in the street, she gained the company of that Lord of hers,
the Lord Who can be perceived in all lands, in all times, in all
forms, in the blissful *rasa* of one's own interior; — all that has been
narrated in this play.

This allegorical drama is the condensed stageworthy edition of
the play *Rājā* — newly rewritten.

Māgh 1326   Sri Rabindranath Tagore
[January 1920]

CAST OF CHARACTERS

CAST OF CHARACTERS [11]

The Raja
Sudarshana (Sudarśanā)
Surangama (Surangamā)
Thakurda (Ṭhākurdā)
Subarna (Suvarṇa)
Rajas Basusen (Vasusen), Bijaybarma (Vijayvarmā), and Bikrambahu (Vikrambāhu)
A Group of Foreign Travellers:
Birajdatta (Virājdatta), Bhadrasen (Bhadrasen), Madhab (Mādhav)
A Group of Local Travellers:
Kaundilya (Kauṇḍilya), Janardan (Janārdan), Kumbha (Kumbha)

Thakurda's Followers	A Guard
A Group of Women	A Bāul
A Group of Foot-soldiers	A Sentry
Boys	A Messenger
A Group of Singers	A Soldier
Two Groups of Citizens	

PROLOGUE

Song[12]

Oh, their sight rushes forward
On the road to wealth and pride, to plenty[13] —
    Oh, in droves.
They have made a vow to see,
    But the mind does not know whom to see,
When they look into love's gaze
    Oh, their eyes must overflow with tears.
    Do not call upon me,
I go to the ferry-ghat, the formless-*rasa*-ocean.
Winds unfettered strike the sail,
    At the time of going toward the coast
I will drown both of these eyes
    Oh, within the shoreless nectar-sea.[14]

1

The palace-garden

SURANGAMA: Lord, I have a word to say.

VOICE FROM BEHIND THE SCENE: What, tell me.

SURANGAMA: It seems Princess Sudarshana wants to receive[15] only you, won't you be kind to her?

VOICE: Does she know me?

SURANGAMA: No lord, she wants to know you. You'll surely make yourself known to her, otherwise how would she be able to?

VOICE: There are many obstacles.

SURANGAMA: But that's why you have to be merciful to her.

VOICE: The screen, however, is removed through much sorrow.

SURANGAMA: Give her, give her that same sorrow.

VOICE: With my name she'll become greater than everybody, this self-conceit makes her want me.

SURANGAMA: Take this opportunity to break her self-conceit. Bring her down near your feet, lowered beneath everybody.

VOICE: Tell Sudarshana, I will accept her in darkness.

SURANGAMA: Flutes won't play, lights won't shine, there won't be festivities?

VOICE: No.

SURANGAMA: Won't she give you a garland of flowers on the welcome-tray?

VOICE: Those flowers haven't blossomed as yet.

SURANGAMA: That indeed is best, Maharaja. The seed stays in darkness alone; after sprouting it comes to light by itself.

CALL FROM OUTSIDE: Surangama.

SURANGAMA: There comes Princess Sudarshana.

Enter Sudarshana

SUDARSHANA: It seems like your skies here are decorated with offerings,[16] it seems like the touch of a morning washed in dew. Tell me what you have scattered in the winds of this place.

SURANGAMA: I've scattered song.

SUDARSHANA: Speak to me about that raja of rajas, Surangama, I'll listen.

SURANGAMA: I can't begin to speak, it's not a very easy job.

SUDARSHANA: Speak, is he very beautiful?

SURANGAMA: Beautiful? One day I went to play with beauty, the day that play ended my heart burst, that day I understood what's called beauty. One day I felt frightened in calling him terrifying, today I rejoice in calling him terrifying—I tell him "You are the storm", I tell him "You are sorrow", I tell him "You are death", at the very end I say—"You are bliss".

Song

When I was blind,
Time passed in happy games but bliss I could not find.
I built the walls of a dollhouse[17]
I was absorbed in my day-dreams,
You broke the wall and came inside
            My bonds were then destroyed,
The happy games appeal no more
            I have found bliss.
            O terror mine, destruction mine,
            My sleep has now become short-lived,
In violent agony, anew
            You tuned all my desires.[18]
            The day you came disguised as fire
            And took away all that was mine,
That day did I become complete
            My conflicts were destroyed,
Beyond the banks of grief and joy
            I found you, bliss.

SUDARSHANA: At first you weren't able to know him?

SURANGAMA: No.

SUDARSHANA: But see, I won't be delayed at all in knowing him. To me he'll show himself in beauty.

SURANGAMA: Before that you'll have to abide by one thing.

SUDARSHANA: I will, I've no hesitation about anything.

SURANGAMA: He said the meeting with you will occur only in darkness.

SUDARSHANA: Always?

SURANGAMA: About that I can't say.

SUDARSHANA: All right, I abide by everything. But he won't be able to stay hidden from me. If the day has been decided surely everybody must be informed.

SURANGAMA: What's the point of informing? For everyone doesn't have place in that darkness.

SUDARSHANA: I cannot inform anyone that I have gained the raja of rajas?

SURANGAMA: You can inform, but nobody will believe.

SUDARSHANA: Can it be they will not believe such a great event?

SURANGAMA: But you won't be able to call people to give proof.

SUDARSHANA: Of course I will, certainly I will.

SURANGAMA: All right, try and see.

SUDARSHANA: Surangama, I'm not so very meek as you, I am strong. He will accept me in front of everyone — this he won't be able to avoid.

SURANGAMA: No need to think about that today, Princess; you should accept him completely yourself, only then will all be easy.

SUDARSHANA: Why say those words? For I have been prepared just for that purpose. But don't delay any more.

SURANGAMA: On his side everything has already been prepared. Today, then, we should part.

SUDARSHANA: Where are you going?

SURANGAMA: The spring-festival[19] comes near, arrangements for it have to be made.

SUDARSHANA: Of what kind does the arrangement need to be?

SURANGAMA: Well, the *mādhavī*-grove doesn't have to be rushed. In the mango forest, too, buds blossom by themselves. What's in the power of every man among us to give doesn't want to be revealed easily. But on that day it won't do if it's concealed. Some will give songs, some will give dances.

SUDARSHANA: What will I give that day, Surangama?

SURANGAMA: About that only you can say.

SUDARSHANA: I'll string a garland with my own hands to send as offering to beauty.

SURANGAMA: That indeed is best.

SUDARSHANA: How will I see him?

SURANGAMA: That he alone knows.

SUDARSHANA: Where will I have to go?

SURANGAMA: Nowhere, right here.

SUDARSHANA: What do you say, Surangama, the meeting in dark-

ness right here? Where I've always been, right here? Won't
I have to dress up?

SURANGAMA: What if you don't dress up? One day he himself will
dress you up in the dress that suits you.

Song

Lord, tell me, tell me when
The colours of the dust upon your path
Will make my *āñchal* colourful.
The scarlet dust of your forest
Causes the *pūjā* flowers to bloom,
Alas, when will that dust
Accept me as its own?
All those poor pilgrims of the dust
Who go to place *praṇāms* upon
Your feet, will recognise
Me as one of their own.

SUDARSHANA: But I do not wish to delay even a little longer.

SURANGAMA: Don't delay—call him, he'll be kind right here.

SUDARSHANA: But Surangama, I do think that I'm calling; I don't
get an answer. Perhaps I don't know how to call. Why don't
you call on my behalf—he knows your voice.

Surangama sings

Open, open the door,
Don't keep me standing outside any more.
Give me, give me an answer, look this way
Come out with arms outstretched.
The work is over now,
The evening star has risen,
The ferrying of the light is done
Across the sunset sea.
I've brought an urn filled up with water
I've dressed in white silk-cloth,
I've tied my hair, I've plucked some flowers
I've strung with buds a garland.
The cows return from pasture
The birds come back to nest,
And all the paths that crossed the world
In darkness have been lost.

Gradually the light diminishes and it becomes dark

SUDARSHANA: Well, I cannot see anything at all in the darkness. Are you in here?

VOICE: Here I am.

SUDARSHANA: I will receive you, but will it be without seeing you?

VOICE: By seeing with the eyes you'll see wrong -- purify the mind and look within.

SUDARSHANA: But inside my heart is trembling in fear.

VOICE: If there's no fear within love the feeling[20] doesn't become intense.

SUDARSHANA: You can see me in this darkness?

VOICE: Yes I can.

SUDARSHANA: What do you see?

VOICE: I can see that in you is embodied the meditation of countless yugas, the light of this world and the next, the flower and fruit of many hundreds of autumns and springs. You're the new form of the very ancient.

SUDARSHANA: Go on, speak this way. I feel as if I've been hearing the song of time immemorial through all my lives.[21] But lord, this darkness is like solid black iron; it is pressing upon me like sleep, like a swoon, like death. How will the union between you and me occur in this place? No no, the union won't happen, won't happen. Not here, I'll see you only in the world of eyesight — for I stay there myself.

VOICE: All right, see me. You yourself will have to identify me.

SUDARSHANA: I'll identify you, I'll identify you among lakhs of people; there won't be a mistake.

VOICE: Try to see me among all the people on the full-moon night of the spring-festival. Surangama.

SURANGAMA: What, lord?

VOICE: The full-moon night of the spring-festival has arrived.

SURANGAMA: What work will I have to do?

VOICE: Today's not your day for work, it's the day for decoration. Bring together the joy of life with the joy of the flowering forests.

SURANGAMA: That will be done, lord.

VOICE: Sudarshana wants to see me with her eyes.

SURANGAMA: Where will she see you?

VOICE: In that southern grove where flutes will play to the cuckoo's

note,[22] red powder will fly from flower stamens,[23] embraces
will take place between light and shadow.

SURANGAMA: Won't her eyes be dazzled?

VOICE: Sudarshana's curiosity is aroused.

SURANGAMA: Well, things of curiosity are scattered profusely
everywhere. But you're beyond curiosity.

Song

Alas, where do they fly, outside and far away,
Your restless eyes like forest birds escape into the forest.
Oh, when the flute plays charming sounds within your heart,
Then of your own accord you'll return crying, to yield,
Your haste, and dying to wander here and there, will end—
Ah, now those eyes like forest birds escape into the forest.
Why don't you see who comes and goes at the heart's door,
Do your ears hear the message brought by the south wind?
Now with flower-fragrance, happy laughter, ardent song,
Eternal Spring has entered life in search of you,
Returned from seeking him outside, you're almost mad,
Ah, now those eyes like forest birds escape into the forest.

Exit both

2

BIRAJDATTA: Oh, mister.

GUARD: What's the matter?

BHADRASEN: Where's the road? I see neither the Raja here, nor do I see the road. We're foreigners, show us the road.

GUARD: Which road?

MADHAB: Well, we've heard that there'll be a festival today in the country of the Elusive Raja. Down which way can we go?

GUARD: Here all roads are the road. Whichever way you go you'll get there fine. Go straight ahead.

BIRAJDATTA: Listen, just listen to the words. He says everything is one road. If that's so then what was the need for so many?

MADHAB: Well brother, why get angry? To every country its own system. In our country we may as well say there aren't roads at all—crooked lanes, those too a maze. Our Raja says, better not to have open roads anyway — as soon as they find a road the citizens will walk out. It's the opposite in this country, no one ever prevents going, no one ever prohibits coming — but still I see enough people too — our kingdom would've become desolate if it was as open.

BIRAJDATTA: Hey Madhab, that's one of your big faults.

MADHAB: What fault did you notice?

BIRAJDATTA: You criticise your own country heavily. So the open road alone is nice? Tell us, brother Bhadrasen, whether the open road is considered nice.

BHADRASEN: But brother Birajdatta, you've seen in Madhab all along that same kind of cockeyed reasoning. Some day he'll fall into trouble — if it reaches the Raja's ears he won't find a person to even throw him into the filth at a crematorium.

BIRAJDATTA: Well brother, since coming to this country of open roads we've had no happiness in eating or sleeping — day and night the body fills with loathing. We don't have any knowledge whatsoever about who comes, who goes. —Rama, Rama.[25]

BHADRASEN: And then too we came only on hearing that Madhab's advice. Such a thing hasn't ever happened in our family. You must know my father — what a great mahatma he was — according to *śāstra* he drew a circle measuring precisely forty-nine cubits and spent his entire life well within it — didn't place a foot outside it for a single day. After his death talk arose that the cremation should indeed be well within those forty-nine cubits — that was one complicated problem — finally the *śāstrī*[26] ruled there's no way to get out of those two digits in forty-nine; therefore reverse that four-nine, forty-nine, and make it nine-four, ninety-four — for only then could we burn him outside the house, otherwise we'd have to cremate at home itself. My, such rigidity! Is this any ordinary country you've got!

BIRAJDATTA: Exactly so, even while dying we have to think; is this a small task?

BHADRASEN: His body's from the soil of that country, yet Madhab says after all, open roads alone are nice.

Exit all

Enter Thakurda with his Followers

THAKURDA: Oh, we'll have to keep equal pace with the southerly wind — it won't do to accept defeat — today we'll go flooding all the roads with songs.

Enter a Group of Women

FIRST WOMAN: Thakurda, let me ask one question, where's the festival taking place?

THAKURDA: Whichever direction you look, in that direction.

FIRST WOMAN: So this is called the festival of your raja of rajas!

THAKURDA: Well, we call it that.

SECOND WOMAN: Even the smallest of feudal princes in our country appears on the streets with more pomp and grandeur than this.

THAKURDA: Because, if not able to make themselves known, they're deprived.

THIRD WOMAN: And that unseen raja about whom you people speak?

THAKURDA: If not able to know him, we ourselves are deprived.

FIRST WOMAN: What way of knowing have you created?

THAKURDA: We're tuning voices with him. This south wind that blows, the mango buds that blossom, if we can answer in the same key, understanding takes place inside.

SECOND WOMAN: So your bosses haven't provided deposits for the drums? All the authority is entirely upon you people?

THAKURDA: If not that, what else? Festivities by rental? What are you, we, here for? Oh, why don't you begin a song, brothers.

Song

The southern gate is open now —
    Oh come, oh come, oh come, my spring.
In my heart's cradle you will swing,
    Oh come, oh come, oh come, my spring.
On a new chariot, green and beautiful,
Come on the path strewn with *bakul*,
Come playing the eager flute,
Wearing the pollen of *piyāl* flowers,[27]
    Oh come, oh come, oh come, my spring.
Come to the dense clusters of leaves
    Oh come, oh come, oh come.
Come to the wild *mallikā* groves
    Oh come, oh come, oh come.
With a soft, sweet, intoxicating smile
Come to the land of maddened winds,
Free your impatient scarf
Letting it fly into the sky,
    Oh come, oh come, oh come, my spring.

Exit Women

The east gate is done. Now come toward the west gate.

Enter Group of Local Travellers

KAUNDILYA: Thakurda, at this antique age you're revelling about with a group of boys?

THAKURDA: I've come out to call to the young.

JANARDAN: Does that become you?

THAKURDA: Oh, but at the time of falling mature leaves themselves awake new leaves before going.

Song[28]

At parting time my withered leaves repeatedly
Call on the doors of the new leaves.

KAUNDILYA: Indeed, I can see that you've called them, you have excited the locality.

THAKURDA: I'm finding in them my own young years—the old man's got covered up.

Song

> So in this shaded forest of my life
> Phālgun comes returning on the south breeze,
> Songs fly upon new tunes across the sky,
> Flowers bloom in new colours abundantly.

KAUNDILYA: Well, that you have remained quite new is true, you didn't find time to get old.

THAKURDA: Because if I'm not new myself I don't find that newness.

Song

> Oh stop, my always new, and smile: I will
> Go to your banquet in a young disguise.
> When light on the path fades at close of day,
> As soon as my voyage ends on the sea-shore,
> Within the evening darkness your flute plays
> And in my void the rows of stars arise.

KAUNDILYA: Save it, grandfather, save your songs. One thing keeps striking me this day.

THAKURDA: What, tell me.

KAUNDILYA: This time people have come from all over the world; all are saying "Everything we've seen is fine but why haven't we seen the Raja?" —I cannot give anyone an answer. That has remained one big gap here.

THAKURDA: Gap! Well, the entire kingdom has become absolutely stuffed with the Raja only because the Raja doesn't show up in one place in this country of ours—you call that a gap! But he has even made all of us into rajas.

Song

> We are all rajas in this kingdom of our Raja.
> > For otherwise by what right could we meet our Raja?
> > We do whatever pleases us
> > Yet we roam within his pleasure,

We're neither bound nor in the dreadful power of a slave-
    king.
    For otherwise by what right could we meet our Raja?
    The Raja gives us all respect
    Respect that he gets back himself,
No one has kept us down, belittled by any untruths.
    For otherwise by what right could we meet our Raja?
    We'll go according to our views
    But finally will meet his path,
None of us will die in the deadly whirl of fruitlessness.
    For otherwise by what right could we meet our Raja?

KUMBHA: But whatever you say, grandfather, people spontaneously
say what they please about him because they don't get to see
him; that is intolerable.

JANARDAN: Don't you see, here there's punishment if someone
abuses me but if someone abuses the Raja there's nobody to
shut his mouth.

THAKURDA: There's sense in that; the blow touches only the body
of that part of the Raja that is mingled within the citizens,
nothing at all strikes the body of Him Who transcends it.
The light of the sun that is in a lamp can't stand the weakest
puff, but if a thousand people together puff at the sun, the sun
still continues to remain bright.

Exit all

Enter the Group of Foreigners again

BIRAJDATTA: Look brother Bhadrasen, the actual truth is, basically
they have no Raja at all. All of them together have kept a
rumour in circulation.

BHADRASEN: Well, I too have had that thought. For in every
country the souls of people country-wide begin shivering in
fright like bamboo leaves on seeing a raja, and here the Raja
can't be found even after searching! If nothing else, if from
time to time in some cases he rolls his eyes and says without
reason, "Bring me the fellow's head", at least then we'd understand there's a Raja like a raja indeed.

MADHAB: But the kind of order we've seen all along in this kingdom,
surely this doesn't happen if no raja exists.

BIRAJDATTA: After living so long in a raja's country your wisdom comes to this? If order itself exists then what's the need for a raja to exist?

MADHAB: Here, don't you see, so many people rejoicing together today — if the Raja didn't exist they wouldn't even be able to meet like this.

BIRAJDATTA: Hey Madhab, you are of course avoiding the actual issue itself. There's an order — sure I see it; the festival's taking place, that too can be seen clearly, sure, no complications created there at all — but where's the Raja, where did you see him, tell us that.

MADHAB: My opinion is this, that you people only know such a kingdom where the Raja can be seen with the eyes alone, but there aren't any signs of him within the kingdom, merely ghost-*kīrtans* there — but look here —

BHADRASEN: Coming around again to that very same story! Why don't you reply to Birajdatta's actual question, hm — yes or no? Have you seen the Raja, or haven't you?

BIRAJDATTA: Save it brother Bhadrasen, even his logic is becoming of this country's nature. Since he has begun to look without eyes, there isn't any hope. If he's allowed to eat without food for some days his reasoning may become clear like a normal person's again.

Exit all

Enter Bāul
Song[29]

The person for my life is in my life
        That's why I see him everywhere.
He's in the stream of light within my eyes,[30]
            That's why I don't lose him,
Oh yes, that's why I see him here and there
        Whichever way I look.
    To hear his words
    I went so far,
        But could not hear, I could not hear,
Today, returning to my land
            I hear them now,
    I hear his speech in my own songs.
        Who are you who search for him
        Dressed as beggars, door to door,

> You never see him, never see—
> Oh you, come running, take a look
> Within my heart—
> Oh look within these eyes of mine.

Exit

Enter a Group of Foot-soldiers and the Local Travellers

FIRST FOOT-SOLDIER: Move away, you all, move away. Keep a distance.

KAUNDILYA: Eh, is that so? An important person indeed. Walks with long strides. Why, my boy, why should we move? Are we all street-dogs or what?

SECOND FOOT-SOLDIER: Our Raja's coming.

JANARDAN: Raja? Raja of what?

FIRST FOOT-SOLDIER: Our Raja of this country.

KUMBHA: Has the man got mad or what? Since when does our Raja of this strange country appear on the roads with foot-soldiers announcing him?

SECOND FOOT-SOLDIER: The Maharaja won't stay concealed any more today, he'll hold today's festival himself.

JANARDAN: Is it true, brother?

SECOND FOOT-SOLDIER: Why don't you look there, the flag's flying.

KAUNDILYA: Hey that's right, it's the flag all right, no doubt.

SECOND FOOT-SOLDIER: There's a flame-of-the-forest[31] flower painted on the flag, don't you see?

KUMBHA: Oh, hey, a flame-of-the-forest flower all right, no doubt, he hasn't lied—it's glistening all over.

FIRST FOOT-SOLDIER: So! My word was not believed much, eh!

JANARDAN: No brother, I certainly did not disbelieve. That Kumbha alone created the disturbance. I didn't even speak one word.

FIRST FOOT-SOLDIER: That one's probably an empty vessel,[32] so the noise is greater.

SECOND FOOT-SOLDIER: Who's the man, hm? Who is he to you people?

KAUNDILYA: Nobody, nobody. He's the uncle-in-law[33] of the headman of our village—his house is in another locality.

SECOND FOOT-SOLDIER: Yes, yes, the appearance is indeed the type of an uncle-in-law; the intelligence too is necessarily of the uncle-in-law mould.

KUMBHA: The intelligence became like this after much sorrow.

Just the other day a raja appeared from somewhere, stuck
three hundred and forty-five titles in front of his name and
went around the city beating his drum — did I follow behind
him any less? How much food I offered, how much service
I performed, the time came I almost had to sell the ancestral
home. Where did his kingliness finally reach? When people
want land from him, he opens almanac and scripture and
cannot ever find an auspicious day. But at the time of collecting
taxes from us — Maghā, Aśleshā, triple-lunar-day conjunc-
tions[34] — nothing at all blocked him, it seems.

SECOND FOOT-SOLDIER: Yes Kumbha, you want to say our Raja's
a fake raja like that, hm?

KUMBHA: No, please, don't get angry. I rub my nose on the ground[35]
— I'll stand apart just as far away as you say.

SECOND FOOT-SOLDIER: All right, keep standing here nicely in a
row. Since the Raja's coming — we'll go ahead to set the road
properly.

Exit Foot-soldiers

JANARDAN: Kumbha, you'll die only by fault of that mouth of
yours!

KUMBHA: No brother Janardan, it's not the mouth's fault, it's the
fault of fate. When the false raja appeared I didn't even say a
word — like an utter simpleton I caused my own destruction—
and this time maybe the true Raja has appeared, so the im-
prudent word came out of my mouth. That's fate.

JANARDAN: This I understand, whether the Raja's true or false, he
always has to be obeyed. Do we know rajas that we may judge
them? Like pitching brickbats in the dark — the more you
pitch, one or the other will strike. So I go on kowtowing from
one side — if he's true I gain, if false what do I lose after all?

KUMBHA: If the brickbats were merely brickbats there wouldn't
be worries — they're costly things — by spending on incidental
expenses you get broke.

KAUNDILYA: Well, there comes the Raja. Ah, a Raja like a raja
indeed. What an appearance. Like a doll made of cream.[36] So
Kumbha, what do you think now, hm?

KUMBHA: Looks good — what do I know brother, he may be.

KAUNDILYA: Exactly as if moulded into a raja. I fear, should he
melt away touched by the sun.

Enter Figure Wearing Royal Attire

ALL: Victory, victory to the Maharaja.

JANARDAN: We're waiting since morning for an audience. Please have kindness.

KUMBHA: I feel very confused, I'll go call Thakurda.

Exit all

Enter Group of Foreign Travellers

MADHAB: Hey, it's the Raja, hey, the Raja. Come and see.

BIRAJDATTA: Raja, keep me in mind, I'm the grandson of Udaydatta of Kuśalīvastu. My name's Birajdatta. I came running as soon as I heard the Raja's appeared, I haven't paid heed to any person's words — I've obeyed you before all others.

BHADRASEN: Listen once, for I've stood here since dawn — even the crows hadn't called then — where were you so long? Raja, I'm Bhadrasen of Vikramsthalī — keep your devotee in remembrance.

ROYAL FIGURE: I'm most pleased at your devotion.

BIRAJDATTA: Maharaja, our wants are plenty — we hadn't received audience for so many days, whom could we inform?

ROYAL FIGURE: I'll fulfil all your wants.

Exit Royal Figure

Enter Local Travellers

KAUNDILYA: Hey, it won't do to fall behind — mixed up in the crowd we won't catch the Raja's eye.

BIRAJDATTA: Look, look, look once at Narottam's doings! There are so many of us, he has pushed everyone aside and begun fanning the Raja with a palm-leaf fan from somewhere.

KAUNDILYA: Hm, that's true, the man's audacity isn't slight, indeed.

MADHAB: We'll have to hold and remove him by force — is he worthy to stand beside the Raja?

KAUNDILYA: Oh, can't the Raja understand even this much, hm? For this is excessive devotion.

BIRAJDATTA: No, oh no — if rajas really had brains what's their need of having crowns? He'll be deluded, just fed by the breeze of that palm-fan.

Exit all

Enter Kumbha, with Thakurda

KUMBHA: But he went down this very road just now.

THAKURDA: Hey, just by going down a road one becomes a raja or what?

KUMBHA: Grandfather, we saw absolutely clearly with our eyes — not one person, not two people, but the people on both sides of the road have seen him.

THAKURDA: But for that reason alone it's suspicious. When does my Raja go dazzling the eyes of people on the roads?

KUMBHA: Well, if he has willed it today, could we tell?

THAKURDA: Hey, we could, we could — my Raja's will is always fixed — it doesn't change every moment!

KUMBHA: But grandfather, what shall I say — a downright doll of cream. I feel like keeping him protected with my whole body.

THAKURDA: When did you get such intelligence? My Raja a doll of cream, and you will keep him protected!

KUMBHA: Whatever you say grandfather, he's very beautiful to see — so many people have gathered today, I haven't seen anybody like him.

THAKURDA: My Raja wouldn't even have caught your eye.

KUMBHA: But I got to see the banner too. People also say the Raja's appeared for this festival.

THAKURDA: Has appeared, sure. But no foot-soldiers with him, no heralds.

KUMBHA: I take it nobody can even identify him?

THAKURDA: Perhaps some people can.

KUMBHA: Whoever can probably gets exactly what he wants.

THAKURDA: He doesn't want anything. It's not the petitioner's karma to know the Raja. The lesser petitioner is only set up to call a greater petitioner a raja.

Exit all

Enter Rajas Bijaybarma, Bikrambahu and Basusen

BASUSEN: Will the Raja of this festival not show himself even to us?

BIKRAM: What kind of procedure is this to run his kingdom? A festival in the Raja's forest, there too no restrictions at all on any of the common people?

BIJAY: It would've been proper to keep a completely separate place made for us.

BIKRAM: We will insist on having one made.

BIJAY: Just by seeing all this I have suspicions, there's no Raja here, a hoax is afoot.

BIKRAM: But Princess Sudarshana of Kāntik is certainly visible.

BIJAY: We must see her. I'm not inquisitive about one who doesn't show himself, but if we return without seeing one who's worthy to be seen we'd be cheated.

BIKRAM: Why not try an intrigue then.

BASUSEN: Intrigue's a very good thing, if one is able not to entangle oneself in it.

BIKRAM: Who are these coming this way? Clowns or what? One's dressed as a raja.

BIJAY: The Raja here can tolerate this burlesque but we certainly won't tolerate it.

BASUSEN: It could be a rustic raja from somewhere, though.

Enter Foot-soldiers

BIKRAM: Where's your raja from?

FIRST FOOT-SOLDIER: This country. He's appeared today to hold the festival.

Exit Foot-soldiers

BIJAY: What words are these? The Raja here has appeared!

BASUSEN: That's right. If that's so we'll have to return after seeing only him! The other vision?

BIKRAM: Why do you listen? Just because there's no Raja here, who-ever wants to introduces himself without scruple as the Raja. Don't you see, he's come as if dressed for a part — extremely over-dressed.

BASUSEN: But the man looks handsome, he has an appearance to charm the eyes.

BIKRAM: Eyes may be charmed but if you just look properly there's no mistake. I will reveal his deception right in front of you.

Enter the Royal Figure, Subarna

SUBARNA: Rajas, welcome. I trust there haven't been any deficien-cies in your reception here?

RAJAS: (*Making* namaskārs *in feigned deference*) None at all.

BIKRAM: The dearth that was there has been filled by the Maharaja's visitation itself.

SUBARNA: I'm not visible to the commoners but you're my depen-
dents; for this reason I've come to show myself once.

BIKRAM: It's difficult to bear such abundance of favours.

SUBARNA: I won't stay excessively long.

BIKRAM: I've perceived that already—I don't see a nature that
remains fixed too long.

SUBARNA: Meanwhile if you have any supplications—

BIKRAM: Of course we do. But we feel hesitant to inform you in
front of attendants.

SUBARNA: (*To followers*) You, go away for a moment—(*To the
Rajas*) now you can inform me unhesitantly of your supplications.

BIKRAM: We'll inform you unhesitantly all right—as long as you
too don't have the least bit of hesitation.

SUBARNA: No, don't have such apprehensions.

BIKRAM: Come then—make a *praṇām* to each of us by touching
the ground with your head.

SUBARNA: It seems my servants have distributed the *vāruṇī*[37] wine
rather liberally, indeed, in the royal camp.

BIKRAM: Impostor-raja, what's known as wine has fallen on your
own portion beyond measure, for that very reason you're
now in a position to sprawl in the dust.

SUBARNA: Rajas, the jest doesn't befit royalty.

BIKRAM: Those who have the authority to jest are quite nearby and
prepared. General!

SUBARNA: That's no longer necessary. I can see quite clearly I owe
you all obeisance. The head bows down just by itself, there
won't be need to drag it in the dust by some sharp method.
Since you have recognised me, I too will recognise you. Therefore please accept these, my *praṇāms*. If you kindly give me
permission to escape then I won't delay.

BIKRAM: Why escape? We are making you, yourself, Raja here.
Let's finish off the jest, after all. You have any followers?

SUBARNA: I do. At the outset when my following was not great,
then everybody was suspicious—the more the people kept
increasing, the further suspicion went away. Now the people
in the crowd are thrilled just by seeing their own crowd,
I don't have to get into any difficulties.

BIKRAM: Good for you. From now on we will help you. But you'll
have to do one job for us too.

SUBARNA: I'll keep and honour the commands and the crown you've given.

BIKRAM: We don't want anything else, we want to see Princess Sudarshana — you'll have to do that.

SUBARNA: To the best of my abilities, there won't be deficiencies in the attempt.

BIKRAM: We don't have faith in your abilities, you'll have to go according to our judgment. Listen to my advice, don't make mistakes.

SUBARNA: There won't be mistakes.

BIKRAM: Princess Sudarshana's palace is right inside the Park of Young Elephants.

SUBARNA: Yes, Maharaja.

BIKRAM: Set fire to that park. Afterwards, in the confusion of the conflagration we'll accomplish our work.

SUBARNA: Won't it be an offence?

BIKRAM: Look here impostor-raja, we're being unnecessarily careful, there's no Raja in this country.

SUBARNA: I've come to remove that anarchy; for the commoners it's necessary to present a raja, whether true or false, otherwise mischief occurs. One thing I cannot understand, Maharaja.

BIKRAM: In fact, you won't be able to understand many of my words. Still, tell me.

SUBARNA: Why don't you send a messenger to the Maharaja, the Princess' father, to beg for his daughter, as is customary?

BIKRAM: But virtually everyone has done that. I'm not in the category of everyone, though. Fire will do my matchmaking, I'll cross over trouble by creating trouble.

SUBARNA: You'll undoubtedly cross over, Maharaja; I'm an ordinary person, I may not even reach the shore.

BIKRAM: That's not impossible. But what does that matter? An ordinary person, it's enough that you're put to work, after which whether you live or not isn't even matter for thought. — Come, don't procrastinate any more.

BIJAY: Look, look, that man's coming again with a group of people.

BASUSEN: It seems he is operating a ferry to the festival; he's escorting new groups up to the door.

Enter Thakurda with his Followers

BIJAY: Well then, when and from where do you keep coming round, there's not even an opportunity to get some clues.

THAKURDA: We're disciples of Naṭarāj, he spins and makes spin. Is there time to stand still anywhere — for the horn keeps sounding.

Dance and Song [38]

Who dances in my heart the dance eternal?
What mridanga beats with it incessantly?
Smiles and tears, emeralds and diamonds, swing in fate,
Good and bad tremble to the rhythm, keeping time,
Birth and death dance at one another's heels.
What happiness, what happiness, what happiness,
For freedom and confinement dance all day and night,
I flow with those waves, joyful, at their heels.

Exit

BASUSEN: There's some fun in the man.
BIKRAM: But there's no point in joining the fun of all these men — it would indulge them — come let's move away.

Exit Rajas

3

At a window in the garden-house
Surangama sings

When from outside wrongs attack
   Will delusions break within?
Burning with the poison-grief
   Will she beg your grace at last?
When the flaming sun is done
Will her shower of rain descend?
     After blushing, full of shame,
     Will the heart blush with love's hue?
However far away she goes
     Will not the bonds get stronger still
     And pull her with their painful pull?
On the black clouds of vanity
The monsoon winds will swiftly strike,
     Then will the passion of her tears
     Obey any restraints at all?

Enter Sudarshana

SUDARSHANA: Surangama, you people might make mistakes, but I cannot ever be mistaken. I'll be the Rani. So that, of course, is my Raja.

SURANGAMA: Whom are you calling Raja?

SUDARSHANA: There, the one over whose head the umbrella of flowers is held.

SURANGAMA: There, the one whose flag has a painted flame-of-the-forest?

SUDARSHANA: Well, I knew him as soon as I saw him, why's your mind having doubts?

SURANGAMA: He's not your Raja. Because I know him.

SUDARSHANA: Who is he?

SURANGAMA: He's Subarna. He goes around gambling.

SUDARSHANA: Don't speak lies. Everyone's calling him Raja. Apparently you know more than everybody?

SURANGAMA: But he's offering everyone false temptations, for that reason he has influenced everyone. When they get disillusioned they'll die of remorse.

SUDARSHANA: You've become very arrogant. You know better than I?

SURANGAMA: If I had arrogance, then I wouldn't have known.

SUDARSHANA: I have sent the garland to him, though.

SURANGAMA: That garland will become a snake to come and bite you.

SUDARSHANA: Curse me? Your audacity certainly isn't slight. Go away from here, I won't see your face.

Exit Surangama

My mind's really become so restless today. It hasn't been like this ever before. Surangama.

Enter Surangama

SUDARSHANA: Has my garland really gone the wrong way?

SURANGAMA: Yes.

SUDARSHANA: Again that very same story? All right, fine, I've made a mistake, that's fine. Why does he not show himself and disillusion me? But I won't accept your words. Go away from me — do not confuse my mind for nothing.

Exit Surangama

Moon-god, you just continue to look askance upon my restlessness today. For the entire sky has filled with bemused curiosity. Sentry.

Enter Sentry

SENTRY: What, Princess?

SUDARSHANA: The festival boys over there, singing as they go along the path in the mango forest, call, call them, bring them along. Let's hear some songs.

Exit Sentry

Enter Boys

Come, come, all you embodiments of young spring, begin your song. My whole body and mind sing songs, not reaching my voice. You sing for me.

The Boys sing

In whose hands did you send this garland
This morning of a Phālgun day?
    Its colour bears your name in traces,
        Its scent is written with your ways,
    I've tied that garland round my forehead
        This morning of a Phālgun day.
Your song has come across the sky
Upon the winds this Phālgun day.
    But oh, how did you put together
        My name upon your melody,
    Behind that song you remain hidden,
        This morning of a Phālgun day.

SUDARSHANA: Enough, enough, no more. Hearing this song of
  yours makes my eyes fill with tears — makes me think that
  there's no way to get hold of things which are wanted — there's
  no need to get hold of them.

Exit Boys after making pranām

At a door in the garden-house
Enter Thakurda and Local Travellers

THAKURDA: Well brothers, are you done?
KAUNDILYA: Very much done, Thakurda. Don't you see here,
  they've made us absolutely red. No one's left.
THAKURDA: What're you saying? They reddened the rajas as well
  or what?
JANARDAN: Oh! Hey, enough! Who'll approach them! They all
  remained standing upright inside the enclosure.
THAKURDA: Ah, what a pity, that's a big omission. You couldn't
  make even a little colour stick to them? You should have
  entered by force.
KUMBHA: Oh grandfather, their redness, it's of another colour.
  Their eyes are red, the turbans of their foot-soldiers are red,
  on top of that the kind of stance I saw of drawn swords, they'd
  have reddened us absolutely in the ultimate red if we'd ap-
  proached even a little closer.
THAKURDA: You've done well not to approach. They're exiles on

earth—we just have to go about keeping our distance from
them.

The Bāul enters and sings[39]

All that was black and white
Has reddened with your hues.
Like the red colour of your feet
        Which is no longer different.
Red are my clothes and ornaments,
Red are my sleep and dreams,
See how my mind's become
        Restless like a red lotus!

THAKURDA: Good, brother, good—were the games very exciting?[40]
BAUL: Very, very. Everything was red. Only the moon in the sky
     gave us the slip—he just remained white.
THAKURDA: From outside it looks like he's quite innocent. If you
     removed his white sheet and saw him, then you'd catch on to
     his intelligence. He has quietly scattered so much colour
     tonight, I've seen it all standing here. Yet will he continue to
     stay white himself just like this?

Song

Ah, with you is my game of life,
        O love, O love of mine.
My soul's too excited tonight,
        Will it admit defeat?
Will you alone just redden me
        Like this and run away?
Lord, let yourself be caught and take
        My colour on your chest —
Red pollen from this lotus-heart[41]
        Will redden that fine robe.[42]

                                                    Exit all

Enter Subarna and Raja Bikrambahu

SUBARNA: What deed is this you've done, Raja Bikrambahu?
BIKRAM: I merely wanted to set a fire somewhere near this palace;

I did not even think that the fire would spread so quickly in every direction like this. Tell me quickly, where's the way to get out of this garden?

SUBARNA: Where's the way? But I don't know anything at all. I can't see even a single one of those who brought us here.

BIKRAM: But you're a man of this very country—certainly you know the way.

SUBARNA: I've not ever entered the garden of the inner chamber before.

BIKRAM: That I couldn't care about; you just have to tell me the way, otherwise I'll cut you into two pieces.

SUBARNA: That'll extract my life, it won't be any means of extracting the way.

BIKRAM: Then why did you go around saying you yourself were the Raja here?

SUBARNA: I'm not the Raja, not the Raja. (*Falling to the ground, with folded hands*) Where's my Raja, save me. I'm a sinner, please save me. I'm a rebel, give me punishment, but save me.

BIKRAM: What's the use of yelling at emptiness like that? Let's make an attempt to find the way instead.

SUBARNA: I will lie right here—what'll happen to me will happen.

BIKRAM: That won't do. If I die burning, I certainly won't die alone—I'll take you as accomplice.

FROM OFFSTAGE: Save us, save us. The fire's on all sides.

BIKRAM: Idiot, get up, don't delay any more.

Enter Sudarshana

SUDARSHANA: Raja, save me. Fire surrounds me.

SUBARNA: Where's the Raja? I'm not the Raja.

SUDARSHANA: You're not the Raja?

SUBARNA: I'm an impostor, I'm a scoundrel! (*Throwing his crown to the ground*) Let my deception become dust.

Exit with Raja Bikram

SUDARSHANA: Not the Raja? He's not the Raja? Then god of the sacrificial fire,[43] scorch me; I will surrender myself only into your hands.

VOICE: Where are you going that way? Your inner chamber has caught fire on all sides, do not enter inside it.

Enter Surangama

SURANGAMA: Come.

SUDARSHANA: Where'll we go?

SURANGAMA: Right through the heart of that fire, come.

SUDARSHANA: What is it you're saying?

SURANGAMA: Have faith in the fire, it's better than the one whom
   you had faith in.

SUDARSHANA: Where's the Raja?

SURANGAMA: The Raja himself is inside that fire. He will burn the
   gold.

SUDARSHANA: You're speaking the truth?

SURANGAMA: I'm taking you with me, I know the road within the
   fire.

Exit both

Enter a Group of Singers
Song

> All is fiery, caused by fire.
>   Victory to fire.
> All the lies that gird the heart
> Why not let them burn this time,
> In the midst of death may your life be revealed.
> Now the fire goes searching for
> Stains that hide inside your soul.
>   Let your barriers be destroyed,
>   Let your shame be wiped away,
> Let your fears turn into ashes for all time.

Exit Group of Singers

Enter Sudarshana and Surangama again

SURANGAMA: Shouldn't fear, you shouldn't fear.

SUDARSHANA: I don't have fear—but shame! Shame that has come
   along with me like fire. It has kept my face, eyes, my whole
   heart reddened.

SURANGAMA: Those flames will take time to extinguish.

SUDARSHANA: They won't ever be extinguished, they won't ever be
   extinguished.

SURANGAMA: Don't get dejected. At least your desire's been fulfilled, for you did see him today right inside the fire.

SUDARSHANA: Did I want to see him in the midst of such destruction? I don't know what I saw, but my heart still trembles inside.

SURANGAMA: What did you see?

SUDARSHANA: Terrible, it's terrible. I am afraid to even remember it. Black, black. I thought of the sky that's climbed by a comet, black like that sky—black like storm clouds—black like a shoreless ocean.

Exit

SURANGAMA: The blackness you saw tonight that made your heart tremble, that same blackness will one day make your heart tender. What else is love for?

Song

I won't enchant you with appearances,
    I will enchant you with my love.
Oh, I won't open with my hands the door,
    I'll have it opened with my songs.
I won't burden you down with ornaments,
I won't dress you with necklaces of flowers,
I'll make a garland of my love
    And place it round your neck.
No one will ever know which tempest caused
The rows of waves to dance within the soul,
By unseen forces like the moon's
    My tides will churn the waves.

Enter Sudarshana again

SUDARSHANA: But why doesn't he block my path by force? Why doesn't he hold my locks of hair and keep pulling me back? He isn't telling me anything, for that reason alone it seems even more unbearable.

SURANGAMA: Who told you the Raja isn't saying anything?

SUDARSHANA: Not like that, but shouting with the roar of thunder—by drowning all other words in my ears. Raja, don't let me off so easily, don't let me go.

SURANGAMA: He'll let you off, but why should he let you go?

SUDARSHANA: He won't let me go? Of course I'll go.

SURANGAMA: All right, go.

SUDARSHANA: I'm not at fault. He could have held me back by force but did not. He didn't restrain me — I'm leaving. Now let him give orders to his guards, let them prevent me.

SURANGAMA: No one will prevent you. You can move unrestricted just as the torn cloud moves unrestricted in the face of the storm.

SUDARSHANA: The speed is gradually increasing too — now the anchor's torn. Perhaps I'll sink but I won't return again.[44]

Quick exit

4

The main road[45]
Enter a Group of Citizens

FIRST: Our Princess Sudarshana caused this.

SECOND: Woman is truly at the root of every calamity. Indeed, it's in the Vedas too — isn't it, why not tell us, eh Batukeśvar? You're the son of a Brahman.

THIRD: It's there, it's there, of course. Whatever you search for you'll find in the Vedas — Ashṭāvakra has said, "Women and those with claws and those with horns are always up in arms" — which means —[46]

SECOND: Hey, I understand, I understand — I stay in Tarkaratna-pārā, — I don't get a chance to avoid a single syllable of ums and uhs.[47]

FIRST: This is like a *Rāmāyaṇa* of the *kali*-yuga for us. The ten-headed Rāvaṇa gets into the room from somewhere, unexpectedly bringing about the affair in Laṅkā.[48]

THIRD: So the winds of war are blowing, meanwhile no one has discovered where the Princess has disappeared. So the Maharaja is a prisoner, meanwhile there's not even any clue as to who's running the battle.

SECOND: But I'm wondering, what's our solution now? We had one Raja, now we're about to have seven; surely there isn't a parallel corresponding to this anywhere in the Vedas or Puranas.

FIRST: Of course it corresponds — think about the story of the five Pāṇḍavas.[49]

THIRD: Hey, that was five husbands —

FIRST: Same old thing. They were husbands, these are kings. Indeed, the excesses of neither are commendable.

THIRD: Our five-pennyworth has virtually become Vyāsa,[50] eh — he doesn't talk of anything except the *Rāmāyaṇa* and *Mahābhārata*.

SECOND: Well, you people have warmed to a party in the middle of the street about the *Rāmāyaṇa* and *Mahābhārata*, meanwhile no one has news of what's occurring on our own Kurukshetra.

FIRST: Oh my god — who'll go there? When the news comes, it'll come and fall upon our shoulders by itself—there'll be nothing left to know.

SECOND: Hey, what're you afraid of?

FIRST: Sure, that's right. Why don't you go?

THIRD: All right, why not come to Dhanañjay's there. He knows all the news.

SECOND: Even if he doesn't know he knows how to concoct.

Exit all

Enter Sudarshana and Surangama

SUDARSHANA: Once everybody called me fortunate, wherever I went the light of wealth would burn. What is this woe I've brought with me today? That's why I left home and came to the street.

SURANGAMA: *Mā*,[51] so long as you don't reach the home of the Raja, the street itself will surely be a friend.

SUDARSHANA: Shut up, shut up, don't speak any more about him.

SURANGAMA: But you're only going back to him.

SUDARSHANA: No, never.

SURANGAMA: Whom are you getting angry at, *mā*!

SUDARSHANA: I don't want to even mention his name.

SURANGAMA: All right, don't mention names, he'll bear it patiently.

SUDARSHANA: I entered the streets, he didn't come along?

SURANGAMA: He straddles over the entire street.

SUDARSHANA: He didn't even forbid me once? Why do you keep quiet, hm? Why not tell me, what kind of behaviour is this of your Raja?

SURANGAMA: But that everyone knows, my Raja's cruel. Can anyone ever make him otherwise?

SUDARSHANA: Then why do you call him like this day and night?

SURANGAMA: Let him stay firm like this forever just like a mountain. My sorrows can stay mine, let that firmness alone be victorious.

Exit Sudarshana

Surangama sings

O master of my life,
So many ways has your love made you cruel.

> For you won't even let me sit,
> That's why all day and night there ring
> In my soul such harsh tunes.
> O master of my life,
> Because of you my sorrows seem so sweet.
> Your searching compels me to search,
> Your agony, oh, makes me weep,
> All rest is banished too.

Exit Surangama

Enter Raja Bikram and Subarna

BIKRAM: Someone said that Sudarshana escaped down this street. To make her father a prisoner of war would be useless if she gives us the slip and escapes.

SUBARNA: If she's already escaped, then surely the danger has passed. Now please desist.

BIKRAM: Why so, tell me.

SUBARNA: It's overboldness.

BIKRAM: If there's not even that, then what's the pleasure in being engaged in work?

SUBARNA: It'll do, not even feeling afraid of the Raja of Kāntik, but —

BIKRAM: If you start feeling afraid of that "but", surviving on earth becomes risky.

SUBARNA: Maharaja, what if you blow away that "but" from the mind, but then it shows itself suddenly by just flying in from outside. Why not think about the business that occurred in the garden. You'd indeed arranged safeguards very well, yet from somewhere a "but" got into their midst displaying a fiery image.[52]

Enter Basusen and Bijaybarma

BASUSEN: I came round the inner chamber, but she can't be found anywhere. The diviner said that our journey was auspicious, so was that a lie?

BIJAY: Perhaps not finding is actually more auspicious than finding, who can tell?

BIKRAM: What's this, you're talking like a stoic.

BASUSEN: What's this? An earthquake or what?

BIKRAM: Sure, the earth itself is quaking, but we will not allow feet to quake because of that.

BASUSEN: This is an ill omen.

BIKRAM: No omen at all is an ill omen, if there's no accompanying fear.

BASUSEN: I don't feel afraid of anything visible, but one can't continue a battle with an invisible spirit.[53]

BIKRAM: The invisible One comes along quite visibly, then the battle with Him continues very well.

Enter Messenger

MESSENGER: Maharaja. Nearly all the soldiers have escaped.

BIKRAM: Why?

MESSENGER: A kind of panic went and got inside them, without cause — we cannot keep blocking them any longer.

BIKRAM: All right, I'll bring them back. One may lose after a war but I cannot accept defeat before a war.

Exit Bikrambahu and Messenger

BIJAY: The one whom the war's over herself escapes, those who fight the war escape too, now is it a fault if we escape as well?

BASUSEN: My mind is baffled, I still cannot make a decision.

Exit both

Enter Surangama
Song

Spring, finish off your fun,[54]
The frenzied blossoming of flowers,
     Its waves undisciplined.
Now stop your revelry
Of scattering and blowing away,
Let them return to nest,
     Your birds that lost their way.
So many cherished buds were shed,
They turned to dust, and filled the dust.
Oppressed by severe heat
Take up the order of fruition,
Your spell of carelessness
     This time will be broken.

Enter Sudarshana

SUDARSHANA: What is this? I move about and keep coming to that very same place. I can hear the commotion over there, it seems the war continues on all four sides of me. Over there the sky's dark with dust. Will I just move around eternally in the company of the dust in this whirlwind? How do I get out of this?

SURANGAMA: But you only want to go away always, you don't want to return, that's the reason you cannot reach anywhere.

SUDARSHANA: You're talking about returning, where?

SURANGAMA: To our Raja. I keep saying, you won't find an end anywhere to the path that doesn't take you near him.

Enter Soldier

SUDARSHANA: Who are you?

SOLDIER: I'm doorkeeper of the royal palace in the city.

SUDARSHANA: Tell me quickly, what's the news there?

SOLDIER: The Maharaja's become a prisoner.

SUDARSHANA: Who's become a prisoner?

SOLDIER: Your father.

SUDARSHANA: My father! Become whose prisoner?

SOLDIER: Raja Bikrambahu's.

Exit Soldier

SUDARSHANA: Raja, Raja, I'd gone out indeed quite prepared to bear sorrow, but why did you spread my sorrow in all directions? Am I taking along with me the fire that set my garden ablaze? What fault has my father done to you?

SURANGAMA: Well, none of us is alone. Good and bad has to be shared by everybody, after all. Surely that's the only reason for fear; what's fear to someone alone?

SUDARSHANA: Surangama.

SURANGAMA: What, Princess?

SUDARSHANA: If your Raja had the power to save, what then, could he have stayed unmoved today?

SURANGAMA: Why ask me? Do I have the power to answer for my Raja? If he does answer then he'll do so himself in such a way that nobody will have anything left to understand.

SUDARSHANA: Raja, if you came so as to save my father, then your fame would increase, definitely not decrease.

Departing

SURANGAMA: Where are you going?

SUDARSHANA: To Raja Bikram's camp. Let him make me prisoner,
and let my father go. I will humble myself as far as I can; let's
see what it takes to stir your Raja's throne.

Exit both

Enter Basusen and Bijaybarma

BASUSEN: The war is virtually over as soon as it began; can a battle
ever continue by gathering broken soldiers together?

BIJAY: I couldn't make Bikrambahu return by any means at all.

BASUSEN: He's addicted to the intoxication of self-destruction.

BIJAY: But someone told me, as soon as he had reached the battlefield he was wounded in the chest. No one can say anything at
all about what's happened to him by now.

BASUSEN: To me the most strange thing seems to be just this, that
we'd made arrangements many days ahead, the festivities were
lavish, but whatever took place in a mere instant at the time of
finishing off—we could not understand it well.

BIJAY: As all the stars of night go out at just one glance of the
dawning sun.

BASUSEN: Now come.

BIJAY: Where?

BASUSEN: To give up.

BIJAY: To give up, or escape?

BASUSEN: It'll be easier to give up than escape.

Exit both

Enter Surangama
Song

The darkness still hasn't gone,
The barrier still remains.
The vow to die hasn't yet
In her life been attained.
When will the pangs of grief
Become garlands of joy,
The weeping of late night
Dazzle in the sun's love?[55]
Still her own shadow
Creates so much maya.

> Why does she still in vain
> At all times look behind,
> A sudden lightning flash
> Strikes and dazes the eyes.

Enter Sudarshana

SURANGAMA: This shame will pass.

SUDARSHANA: Of course it'll pass, Surangama — the day's come for me to be humbled before the entire world. But where, why hasn't the Raja yet come to take me? What else is he waiting for?

SURANGAMA: I keep telling you, my Raja's cruel — very cruel.

SUDARSHANA: Surangama, please go once and bring back news of him.

SURANGAMA: But I don't know anything at all about where to find news of him. I've sent for Thakurda to be called — perhaps when he comes we'll get information out of him.

SUDARSHANA: Ah fate, such is my condition, I have to find news of him by calling other people! — No, no, I won't have regrets — what has happened was indeed proper — it's all for the best — nothing unjust has happened.

Enter Thakurda

SUDARSHANA: I've heard you're my Raja's friend — please accept my *pranām*,[56] please bless me.

THAKURDA: What're you doing, what're you doing? I do not accept anybody's *pranām*. Everybody's on smiling terms with me.

SUDARSHANA: Show me that smile of yours — please give me good news. Tell me, when will my Raja come to take me?

THAKURDA: Well, there you've asked a very difficult question. I don't understand anything at all of my friend's attitudes and activities, what more can I say about it? The war has certainly come to an end, but there isn't any clue about where he is.

SUDARSHANA: He's gone away?

THAKURDA: Well, I can't find any signs of existence at all.

SUDARSHANA: He's gone away? Your friend's such a friend?

THAKURDA: For that reason people malign him as well as doubt him. But my Raja doesn't even pay attention to it.

SUDARSHANA: He went away? Oh, oh, how harsh, how harsh.

Absolute stone, absolutely adamant.[57] I pushed with all my heart — my heart burst asunder — but he didn't stir. Thakurda, how do you manage with such a friend?

THAKURDA: Because I've understood — I've understood him through happiness and sorrow — now he can't make me weep any more.

SUDARSHANA: Won't he let me understand too?

THAKURDA: Of course he will. Why else give you such sorrow? He'll release you after making you understand well, for he's no easy person.

SUDARSHANA: All right, all right, I'll see how great is his cruelty. I will lie down quietly by the side of the street — I won't even move a foot — let's see if he doesn't come.

THAKURDA: Sister, you are young — you can lie down stubbornly for many days — but I stand to lose even if just one moment passes. Whether or not I find him, I'll go once to search.

Exit

SUDARSHANA: I don't want, I don't want him. Surangama, I don't want your Raja. For what reason did he come to make war? Not in the least for me? Was it merely to show bravery?

SURANGAMA: If he had the desire to show it then he'd show it in such a way no one at all would have any doubts. Has he shown any?

SUDARSHANA: Go, go, go away — I think your words are intolerable. He humbled me so, yet his wishes weren't satisfied? He went away after leaving me lying here in front of all the people in the world?

Exit both

Enter Group of Citizens[58]

FIRST: Oh yes, so many rajas got together to start the battle, I thought there'd be great fun — but I just could not understand whatever took place all of a sudden.

SECOND: Didn't you see, they began having problems among themselves; not one has faith in the others.

THIRD: Well, the strategy was not right. Some want to advance, some want to retreat — some go this way, some go that way; can this ever be called a war? But Raja Bikrambahu battled, that fact must be admitted.

FIRST: Because he doesn't want to lose even after losing.

SECOND: The weapon finally came and struck him in the chest.

THIRD: Well, he was losing at every single step, didn't even seem to be aware of it.

FIRST: The other rajas just left him, there's no certainty about who escaped where.

Exit all

Enter Another Group

FIRST: I heard Bikrambahu isn't dead.

THIRD: No, but what kind of judgment did Bikrambahu get?

SECOND: I heard the justice has placed the royal crown on him with his own hands.

THIRD: But this I just cannot understand at all.

SECOND: The judgment sounds like quite an inappropriate one.

FIRST: That's certainly so. For whatever offences committed were by that Bikrambahu himself.

SECOND: If I were the judge, would I have ever kept him whole? No signs of him would ever be seen again.

THIRD: What do we know, I haven't seen the justice, perhaps we can't see his intelligence either.

FIRST: Do they have anything called intelligence! Everything in all this is arbitrary. For there aren't any people to issue orders.

SECOND: Whatever you say, brother, if the responsibility of administration had fallen into our hands, then we'd have run it in a much better way than this.

THIRD: You can say that again.

Exit all

Enter Thakurda and Bikrambahu

THAKURDA: What's this, Raja Bikram, why are you on the streets?

BIKRAM: Your Raja has expelled me to the streets himself.

THAKURDA: Well, that's his nature.

BIKRAM: After that there isn't any sight of him.

THAKURDA: That too is one of his jests.

BIKRAM: But how many more days will he evade me in this way? When I didn't want to even acknowledge him as the Raja on any account, he came like a northwester[59] from somewhere, in an instant blowing my flags and pennants away, causing my downfall; and today I move about on the streets in order to acknowledge defeat by him, there just isn't any sight of him.

THAKURDA: Let that be; however great a Raja he may be, he'll surely have to acknowledge defeat to the acknowledger of defeat. But Highness, why appear at night?

BIKRAM: I'm not yet able to discard that bit of shame. Raja Bikram searching about for the temple of your Raja with crown laid on a platter, if people see this in the light of day then they'll certainly laugh.

THAKURDA: True, that's the plight of people. The rascals[60] laugh on seeing precisely that which should make tears come out of the eyes.

BIKRAM: But Thakurda, why are you too on the streets?

THAKURDA: I too am looking down the street to destruction.

Song

I sit here with all that I own,
Destruction as my hope.
I look toward the path for him
Who sets people adrift.

BIKRAM: But Thakurda, tell me what's the point in giving up to one who doesn't give up?

THAKURDA: By giving up to him, at one and the same time you can give up and find release as well.

The one who does not show himself
But looks and loves concealed,
My mind's drowned in the secret love
Of that intense, dark depth.

Exit both

Enter Surangama
Song

Companion of the path, I bow repeatedly.
Accept the *namaskār* of travellers.
  O danger, O farewell,
  O master at the close of day,
    Accept the *namaskār* of broken nests.
  O light of newborn dawn,
  O refuge for eternity,
    Accept the *namaskār* of newborn hope.

O charioteer of life,
I'll always travel down this path,
Accept the *namaskār* of travelling.

Enter Sudarshana

SUDARSHANA: I've survived, I've survived, Surangama. I've survived
after acknowledging defeat. Oh my, enough! What tremendous
vanity! Doesn't want to soften under any circumstances. Why
should my Raja have to come to me — I myself should go to
him, I could not make my mind say these words by any means
at all. The entire night I lay in the street, rolling in the dust,
weeping — the southerly wind blowing with moans like the
grief in my breast, and in the darkness of the dark fortnight
the cuckoo[61] calling repeatedly through the twelve hours of
the night — it seemed like the weeping of darkness.
SURANGAMA: Ah, I felt last night seemed not to ever want to end
at all.
SUDARSHANA: But you won't believe it if I tell you, again and again
I kept feeling as if his vina played somewhere within it all. Can
the harsh hand of one who is cruel play a melody so earnest?
People outside have only seen my disrespect — but with the
sole exception of my heart surely no one else heard that
melody in the secret night. Did you hear that vina, Surangama?
Or was it my dreams?
SURANGAMA: Well, I've kept close to you just so as to hear that
vina. I lay listening closely, knowing for sure the vanity-melting
melody would play.

Exit both

Enter Group of Singers[62]
Song

Your garland I will take today
    In exchange for my vanity.
And when tonight comes to an end
    My spell of weeping I must end.
My hardened heart I throw
Away by the wayside,
Your feet will give the tender touch
    To it that can melt stone.

The darkness that I had,
You made it disappear,
Your love came in the form of fire
    Illuminating it.
The "me" that to myself
Was dearer than all else
I now extract to decorate
    Your ceremonial tray.[63]

Exit

Enter Sudarshana and Surangama again

SUDARSHANA: His promise remained after all — he turned me out
on the streets, then released me. If we meet I'll tell him just this
much, "I've come myself, I did not wait for your coming."
I'll say I've come shedding tears — I've come treading a hard
path. I won't discard this pride.
SURANGAMA: But even that pride of yours won't last. For he came
even before you; who else has the capacity to turn you out?
SUDARSHANA: Well, perhaps he came — I felt a presence but could
not believe it. As long as I sat down feeling offended I thought
he too had left me — as soon as I went out on the road setting
my vanity adrift I thought he had come out too; I've begun
finding him along the road itself. Now there aren't any more
worries on my mind. So much sorrow because of him, this
sorrow itself gives me his company — a road of such hardship
that it hurts under my feet as if in tune — as if this were my
vina, the vina of my sorrow — to this same song of pain he's
come out himself on this hard stone, on this dry dust — he's
held my hand — as he used to hold my hand in the midst of
that darkness of mine — suddenly starting up, a shiver would
run down my body — this too is like that. Who said he isn't
here — Surangama, can't you understand that he's come
hidden?

Surangama sings[64]

I will delay no more,
For I have heard the beating out there of your drums.
    Lord, are you standing there
        On the path I will take,

> I think from time to time
> From my window
> I can see you.
> My dreams became complete,
> The morning star now plays the vina in my life.
> Of all I had to give
> Nothing's left in my hands,
> Your garland of blessings
> I will put on
> Round my forehead.

SUDARSHANA: Oh, who's that? Take a look, Surangama, for yet another traveller's appeared on this dark path so late at night.

SURANGAMA: But *mā*, this is Raja Bikram I see.

SUDARSHANA: Raja Bikram?

SURANGAMA: Don't be afraid.

SUDARSHANA: Afraid! Why should I be afraid? My days of fear are over.

Enter Raja Bikrambahu

BIKRAM: So you too are going. I'm a traveller on this very same path too. Don't be afraid of me at all.

SUDARSHANA: It's good, indeed, Raja Bikram — this is right, the two of us going to him side by side. My contact with you occurred at the very outset of departing from home — who could have supposed earlier that that same contact would become such an auspicious one today on the path back home.

BIKRAM: But that you should go walking, well, this does not become you. If you grant permission then I can have a chariot brought right now.

SUDARSHANA: No, no, don't speak such words — my coming away will be fruitful only if I return treading on foot all the dust of that path down which I came far away from him. If taken by chariot I would be cheated.

SURANGAMA: Well Maharaja, today you too are in the dust. I haven't ever seen anybody's elephant, horse or chariot on this path.

SUDARSHANA: When I was in the palace, I trod right in the midst of only gold and silver — today I'll undo that ill fate of mine by going through his dust. Who'd have known this happy news,

I am united today with that Raja of dust and earth at every
step in this dust and earth.

SURANGAMA: Look there, take a look toward the east, the dawn is
approaching. Not much longer—the top of the golden pin-
nacles of his palace can be seen.

Enter Thakurda

THAKURDA: The dawn's breaking, sister, the dawn's breaking.

SUDARSHANA: I've reached through blessings from all of you.

THAKURDA: But have you seen the likes of our Raja? No chariot,
no music, no festivities.

SUDARSHANA: What are you saying, no festivities? The sky's absolutely red over there, the air's absolutely teeming with
greetings from the fragrance of flowers.

THAKURDA: That may be, but however cruel our Raja may be we
cannot be as harsh—for we feel hurt. You're going to the
royal residence in these wretched clothes, can we tolerate this
sight? Wait a bit, I'll go run and bring back a Rani's clothes for
you.

SUDARSHANA: No, no, no. He has removed those clothes from me
for all time—has dressed me in servant's clothes in front of
everyone—I've survived, I've survived—I'm his servant
today—whoever he has, I'm beneath all of them today.

THAKURDA: Your opponents will mock you seeing this condition
of yours, that becomes intolerable for us.

SUDARSHANA: Let my opponents' mockery be unending—let them
throw dust on my body.[65] That dust itself is my make-up for
today's rendezvous.[66]

THAKURDA: There's nothing more to add to this. Now let the very
last game of our spring festival begin—let the pollen of flowers
be for now, this time let the dust blow about on the southerly
wind. Today everybody will go together, in grey, to the Lord.
We'll go and see, dust smears his body too. For do you suppose
anybody spares him? After all, whoever can throws fistfuls of
dust on his body.

BIKRAM: Thakurda, don't forget me too in this dust-game of yours.
I will have to get this royal attire so soiled that it can't be recognised again.

THAKURDA: That won't take too long, brother. Whatever false honour you had, all's been destroyed here, where you've come down—now the colour will return in an instant. And see this Rani of ours, she got very angry at herself—she thought she could stain her world-famous beauty by throwing her ornaments away, but that beauty has blossomed even more from the shock of the insult—as if it didn't have anything more concealed anywhere. It's said our Raja has no relation with beauty[67] himself, that's why he loves varied beauty so much, but this beauty indeed is the decoration on his chest. That beauty has removed the veil of its pride—but what melodies has the vina played by this time today in my Raja's home, the spirit becomes restless to hear them.

SURANGAMA: The sun rises over there.

Exit all

Song

The night becomes the dawn, the path comes to an end.
Listen to every region raise the song of light.
    O traveller you're fortunate,
    Fatigued by sleepless nights,
Your dusty ashen life indeed is fortunate.
    Close to the forest's lap
    The winds have woken up;
    Honey-beggars[68] in rows
        Come to the garden-doors.
    So the journey's complete,
    Wipe off the flow of tears,
    Shed are the shame and fears,
        Vanity is destroyed.

A dark room

SUDARSHANA: Lord, do not ever return the affection which you've
   snatched away; I'm a servant at your feet, give me the right to
   serve.

RAJA: Will you be able to bear me?

SUDARSHANA: I will, Raja, I will. I wanted to see you in my pleasure-
   grove, in my Rani's chamber—there even the lowest among
   your servants seems more beautiful to the eyes than you. The
   desire to see you in that way is absolutely destroyed in me—
   you're not beautiful, lord, not beautiful, you're unequalled.

RAJA: My equal is within yourself.

SUDARSHANA: If so then it's unequalled too.

RAJA: I'll open wide the door of this dark room today—the game[69]
   here is over. Come, now come with me, come move outside—
   into the light.

SUDARSHANA: Before going, I must *pranām* my lord of darkness,
   my cruel one, my terrible one.

                                                              Exit

Song[70]

The formless vina plays concealed behind beauty,
That vina began playing within the heart today.
      My world fills up with melody,
      Dissensions end both near and far,
That raga I have put to use in all my work.
All the bonds of getting and seeing are cut,
All the weeping came to fruition today.
      Being lost in the divine *rasa*,
      That is seeing and that is getting,
Estrangement, union in one garb unite today.

Notes

Introduction to Tagore's Plays

PREAMBLE

[1] Tagore, *Letters to a Friend* (London: George Allen and Unwin, 1928), p. 48.

[2] Tagore, *The Cycle of Spring* (London: Macmillan, 1917), p. 33.

[3] Stanley Hochman, ed., *McGraw-Hill Encyclopedia of World Drama*, 2nd ed., 5 vols. (New York: McGraw-Hill, 1984), 5:1–3.

[4] Phyllis Hartnoll, ed., *The Oxford Companion to the Theatre*, 4th ed. (Oxford: University Press, 1983), p. 808.

[5] Oscar G. Brockett, *History of the Theatre*, 4th ed. (Boston: Allyn and Bacon, 1982), p. 313.

[6] Tagore, *My Reminiscences* (London: Macmillan, 1917), pp. 181–82.

[7] Tagore, *Creative Unity* (London: Macmillan, 1922), p. 50.

[8] In *Personality* (London: Macmillan, 1917), pp. 143–44, Tagore recalls reading Browning's *Luria* to the children in his school, translating the play into Bengali as he went along. An American writer reported that Tagore had told him Browning's plays were "wonderful"; see Bailey Millard, "Rabindranath Tagore Discovers America", *Bookman* 44 (November 1916): 249.

[9] Sati Ghosh, *Rabindranath* (Calcutta: Bookland, 1966), p. 103.

[10] Niharranjan Ray, "Symbolist Plays of Tagore", in *Homage to Rabindranath Tagore*, ed. B.M. Chaudhuri (Kharagpur: Indian Institute of Technology, 1961), pp. 55–56.

[11] Satyendranath Ghoshal, "Rabindranath Tagore and His Dramatic Genius", *Patna University Journal* 22 (January 1967):43–44.

[12] Kalidas Nag recorded this conversation with Tagore on the subject of Maeterlinck's drama, in his diary for 17 January 1915; see *Viśva-pathik Kālidās Nāg* (Calcutta: Writers Workshop, 1986), pp. 172–73. The translation from the original Bengali is mine.

[13] M.U. Malkani, "Tagore the Playwright", *Indian Literature*, April 1958, p. 62.

[14] D.V.K. Raghavacharyulu, "The Plays of Rabindranath Tagore: III", *Aryan Path* 32 (June 1961):253; Krishna Kripalani, *Rabindranath Tagore: A Biography* (Calcutta: Visva-bharati, 1980), p. 341.

[15] K.R. Srinivasa Iyengar, *Rabindranath Tagore* (Bombay: Popular Prakashan, 1965), p. 66. See also B.C. Chakravorty, *Rabindranath Tagore: His Mind and Art* (New Delhi: Young India, 1971), p. 141.

[16] S.C. Sen Gupta, *The Great Sentinel: A Study of Rabindranath Tagore* (Calcutta: A. Mukherjee, [1948]), p. 179.

[17] Shiv S. Kapur, "Rakat [sic] Karabi—Notes on a Play", *Quest*, April–May 1956, p. 38.

[18] Mohan Lal Sharma, "Rabindranath Tagore as a Playwright", *Modern Drama* 13 (May 1970):92.

[19] H.H. Anniah Gowda, *Anjali: The Tagore Lectures* (Annamalainagar: Annamalai University, 1976), p. 40.

[20] Nirmal Mukerji, "The Plays of Rabindranath Tagore", in *Perspectives on Indian Drama in English*, ed. M.K. Naik and S. Mokashi-Punekar (Madras: Oxford University Press, 1977), pp. 72 and 75.

[21] Hirankumar Sanyal, "The Plays of Rabindranath Tagore", in *A Centenary Volume: Rabindranath Tagore 1861–1941* (New Delhi: Sahitya Akademi, 1961), p. 240.

[22] Ray, p. 50; Ghoshal, p. 45.

[23] L.M.T. [L.M. Thapalyal], "Looking Back and Ahead", *Natya: Theatre Arts Journal*, Tagore Centenary Number (1961), p. 3.

[24] Mary M. Lago, *Rabindranath Tagore* (Boston: Twayne, 1976).

[25] Ibid., p. 119.

[26] J.C. Ghosh, *Bengali Literature* (London: Oxford University Press, 1948), p. 175.

[27] Sukumar Sen, *History of Bengali Literature*, 3rd ed. (New Delhi: Sahitya Akademi, 1979), p. 280.

[28] Ray, p. 51.

[29] Pramathanath Bisi, *Rabīndra-nātya-pravāha*, 2 vols. (Calcutta: Orient Book, 1958–60), 1:173.

[30] Som Benegal, *A Panorama of Theatre in India* (New Delhi: Indian Council for Cultural Relations, 1967), p. 83.

[31] J.C. Ghosh, p. 176.

[32] E.J. Thompson, *Rabindranath Tagore: His Life and Work* (Calcutta: Association Press, 1921; London: Oxford University Press, 1921); and Edward Thompson, *Rabindranath Tagore: Poet and Dramatist* (London: Oxford University Press, 1926). A second, revised, edition of the latter book appeared from the same publisher in 1948.

[33] C. Paul Verghese touches upon the subject of Tagore's bilingualism in *Problems of the Indian Creative Writer in English* (Bombay: Somaiya, 1971), pp. 157–58.

[34] K.S. Ramaswami Sastri, *Sir Rabindranath Tagore: His Life, Personality and Genius* (Madras: Ganesh, [1916]); *Rabindranath Tagore: A Study of His Later Works* (Madras: S. Ganesan, 1920); *Rabindranath Tagore: Poet, Patriot, Philosopher* (Srirangam: Sri Vani Vilas, 1924).

TAGORE AS DRAMATIST

[1] Tagore, *Rabīndra-Rachanāvalī*, 26 vols. (Calcutta: Visvabharati, 1939–48), 12:98. The translation is mine.

[2] Amar Mukerji, "The Dramas of Rabindranath Tagore", *Modern Review* 85 (June 1949):483.

[3] For historical accounts of Bengali drama and theatre see Kironmoy Raha, *Bengali Theatre* (New Delhi: National Book Trust, 1978) and P. Guha-Thakurta, *The Bengali Drama: Its Origin and Development* (London: Kegan Paul, Trench, Trubner, 1930). The latter contains a number of inaccuracies but was the first book in English in its field. For the different styles of Bengali folk drama see the first volume of Hemendranath Das Gupta, *The Indian Stage*, 4 vols. (Calcutta: Metropolitan and M.K. Das Gupta, 1934–44). In spite of its title, this work deals mainly with the Bengali stage, and still remains an essential reference work for studies undertaken on Bengali theatre.

[4] Sushil Kumar Mukherjee, *The Story of the Calcutta Theatres: 1753–1980* (Calcutta: K.P. Bagchi, 1982), p. 2. This book is an invaluable compendium of information about the professional theatre in Calcutta.

[5] *India Gazette*, quoted by Das Gupta, 1:277.

[6] *Calcutta Star*, quoted by Raha, p. 10.

[7] Advertisement in *Calcutta Gazette*, 5 November 1795; reprinted in Mukherjee, p. 9.

[8] Das Gupta (1:286–87) says the production premiered in 1833; it lasted from 12:30 a.m. to 6:30 a.m., and thunder and lightning apparatus had been specially imported from England for it.

[9] Das Gupta gives the date as 1856 or earlier.

[10] Quoted by Rustom Bharucha, *Rehearsals of Revolution: The Political Theater of Bengal* (Calcutta: Seagull, 1983), p. 22. Readers interested in Bengal's theatre of rebellion should refer to this book, a fine analysis of the strong tradition of political theatre in Bengal, which still exists today.

[11] Reprinted in Mukherjee, p. 793.

[12] Reprinted in Mukherjee, p. 794.

[13] Reprinted in Mukherjee, pp. 794–95. This advertisement considerately offered an alternative performance "For the Convenience of gentlemen of weak and delicate health".

[14] Reprinted in Mukherjee, p. 44.

[15] Das Gupta devotes virtually all of his third volume to Girish Chandra Ghosh, whom he calls the "Father of the Bengali Stage".

[16] Reprinted in Mukherjee, p. 84.

[17] Reprinted in Mukherjee, p. 86.

[18] Reprinted in Sylvain Lévi, *The Theatre of India*, 2 vols., trans. Narayan Mukherji (Calcutta: Writers Workshop, 1978), 2:107.

[19] In the interests of maintaining a continuous focus on Tagore's plays, I shall not detail his prodigious output in other literary genres. Several books, such as Kripalani's biography already cited, provide general accounts of his works helpful to the interested reader.

[20] Although the entire translation has not survived, a fragment consisting of the Witches' Scene was published in 1880 and reprinted in Tagore's *Rabīndra Rachanāvalī*, 15 vols. (Calcutta: Government of West Bengal, 1961–67), 15:103–5. It shows Tagore's dexterity in the handling of Bengali metre, and understanding of Shakespeare's craft.

[21] "The Genius of Valmiki". I have translated the titles of the plays in subsequent notes, except when the title is a proper name. My literal translations differ on occasion from the titles of existing English versions.

[22] "Broken Heart".

[23] Probhat Kumar Mukherji narrates how Tagore, reading its proofs for a reprint edition much later on, became so exasperated with the play that he scribbled "Rubbish!" on the proofs and halted its publication. See Mukherji's *Life of Tagore*, trans. Sisirkumar Ghosh (New Delhi: Indian Book Company, 1975), p. 37.

[24] "The Fateful Hunt".

[25] Tagore, *My Reminiscences*, p. 196.

[26] "Nature's Revenge".

[27] Tagore, *My Reminiscences*, p. 238.

[28] "The Game of Maya".

[29] Tagore, *My Reminiscences*, p. 196.

[30] "Comedies".

[31] "Raja and Rani" and "Sacrifice".

[32] Tagore, *My Reminiscences*, p. 183.

[33] "Error at the Outset".

[34] "Satires".

[35] "Vaikuntha's Notebook".

[36] Thompson, *Life and Work*, p. 25.

[37] "The Farewell Curse".

[38] "Tales".

[39] "Autumn Festival".

[40] "The Crown".

[41] "Penance".

[42] "The Immovable Institution".

[43] "The Post Office".

[44] An incident related by Tagore's son Rathindranath testifies to the wide dissemination of this play. A friend of theirs travelling in the Italian Riviera came across a fisherman on a beach reading a book; when asked what he was reading the testy reply came: "Don't think I am reading a trashy romance. Don't you see it is Tagore's *Post Office*?" See Rathindranath Tagore, *On the Edges of Time* (Bombay: Orient Longmans, 1958), p. 126.

[45] "Full Moon in Phalgun".

[46] "The Guru", "Formless Jewel" and "Repayment".

[47] "Heaven and Earth".

[48] "Red Oleander"

[49] "Spring".

[50] "The Chariot Procession".

[51] "Housewarming" and "Settling of Accounts".

[52] "The Celibates' Club".

[53] "The Dancer's Puja".

[54] "Last Rainfall" and "The Beautiful", published in the anthology *Ritu-Utsav* ("Festival of the Seasons"). The former first appeared in 1925.

[55] "Play of the Seasons".

[56] "Saved in the End".

[57] "Deliverance".

[58] "Siva's Request".

[59] "The New".

[60] "Freed of the Curse".

[61] "Nataraj: Theatre of the Seasons".

[62] "The March of Time". The plays in it were *Rather Raśi* ("The Chariot Rope") and *Kavir Dīkshā* ("The Poet's Initiation").

[63] "Land of Cards".

[64] "Flower Garden".

[65] "Song of Sravan".

[66] Tagore's use of Manipuri, till then a neglected dance form outside the state of Manipur, led to a revival of interest in this lyrical dance style

[67] "Requital".

[68] "The Way to Freedom".

[69] "Roundtable Conference in Heaven".

[70] Ramaswami Sastri, *Rabindranath Tagore: Poet, Patriot, Philosopher*, p. 203.

TAGORE AS THEATRICIAN

[1] Tagore, *Rabīndra-Rachanāvalī* (Visvabharati), 25:425. The translation is mine.

[2] Tagore, *My Reminiscences*, p. 194.

[3] Rathindranath Tagore, p. 103.

[4] A detailed comparison of the different versions has appeared in Bengali, written by Asrukumar Sikdar, *Rabīndra-nātye-Rūpāntar o Aikya* (Calcutta: Granthanilay, 1967).

[5] See G.D. Khanolkar, *The Lute and the Plough: A Life of Rabindranath Tagore*, trans. Thomas Gay (Bombay: Book Centre, 1963), p. 47.

[6] *Sādhāraṇī*, 27 February 1881; translated by Kironmoy Raha in "Tagore on Theatre", *Natya: Theatre Arts Journal*, Tagore Centenary Number (1961), p. 7.

[7] Related by Indira Devi Chaudhurani, "Reminiscences of Mayar Khela", *Visva-Bharati Quarterly*, New Series, 14 (November 1948):162.

[8] Abanindranath Tagore, *Abanīndra Rachanāvalī*, 5 vols. (Calcutta: Prakas Bhavan, 1973–83), 1:156.

[9] Indira Devi Chaudhurani, *Rabīndra-smṛiti* (Calcutta: Visvabharati, 1962), p. 34.

[10] Abanindranath Tagore, 1:133, 149 and 151. With characteristic humour, Abanindranath confesses it was impossible to tell whether the "boar" was indeed a boar or just a goat. He also recounts that the banyan tree from which they periodically lopped off branches for their productions was soon reduced to half its original size due to the persistent demands for foliage.

[11] Tagore, "The Stage", trans. Surendranath Tagore, *Modern Review* 14 (December 1913):543–45.

[12] W.W. Pearson, *Shantiniketan: The Bolpur School of Rabindranath Tagore* (New York: Macmillan, 1916), pp. 61–62.

[13] Rathindranath Tagore, p. 99.

[14] Ibid., pp. 98–99.

[15] Sahana Devi quoted by Asok Sen, *Rabīndra-nātya-Parikramā* (Calcutta: A. Mukherjee, 1975), p. 59.

[16] Rathindranath Tagore, p. 99.

[17] Ibid., p. 100.

[18] *Ānanda Bājār Patrikā*, 8 May 1961; translated by Raha, "Tagore on Theatre", p. 9.

[19] Ramananda Chatterjee, *The Golden Book of Tagore* (Calcutta: Golden Book Committee, 1931), p. v.

[20] Asit Haldar and Sahana Devi, translated by Raha, "Tagore on Theatre", p. 9.

[21] Ibid., p. 9.

[22] Thompson, *Poet and Dramatist*, p. 99.

[23] The following passage occurs in an essay in the collection titled *Pather Sañchay*, written in 1912 on his way to England. The extract is translated by Raha, "Tagore on Theatre", p. 7.

[24] Rathindranath Tagore, p. 102.

[25] Prabhatkumar Mukhopadhyay, *Rabīndra-jīvanī o Rabīndra-sāhitya-Praveśak*, vol. 2, 4th ed. (Calcutta: Visvabharati, 1977), p. 506.

[26] Sukumar Sen, p. 279.

[27] Thompson, *Life and Work*, p. 53.

[28] Ajit Kumar Chakravarty, "*The Cycle of Spring*", *Modern Review* 22 (October 1917):424. Chakravarty alludes to the English translation of the play, where the Poet says a play must be staged "without any special preparations. Truth looks tawdry when she is overdressed." (Tagore, *The Cycle of Spring*, p. 34)

[29] *Bhāratī*, Phālgun 1916; translated by Raha, "Tagore on Theatre", p. 8.

[30] Thompson, *Poet and Dramatist*, p. 254. For some reason Thompson dropped these lines from the revised edition of his book.

[31] Ibid., p. 255.

[32] Rathindranath Tagore, p. 105.

[33] Indira Devi Chaudhurani, *Rabindra-smṛiti*, p. 37.

[34] Tagore to William Rothenstein, ?4 November 1912, in *Imperfect Encounter: Letters of William Rothenstein and Rabindranath Tagore 1911–1941*, ed. Mary M. Lago (Cambridge: Harvard University Press, 1972), p. 58.

[35] Khanolkar, p. 269.

[36] Tagore, "The Art of Movement in Education", in *Rabindranath Tagore: Pioneer in Education*, ed. L.K. Elmhirst (London: John Murray, 1961), pp. 105–6.

[37] *Nāchghar*, 3 June 1927; translated by Raha, "Tagore on Theatre", p. 7.

[38] See my translation of the Preface later in this volume.

[39] For the material in this paragraph I have relied on information provided by Santidev Ghosh, *Gurudev Rabīndranāth o Ādhunik Bhāratīya Nṛitya* (Calcutta: Ananda, 1983), pp. 205–6.

[40] Pabitra Sarkar, *Nāṭmañcha Nāṭyarūp* (Calcutta: Prama, 1981), p. 91.

[41] Amita Tagore, interviewed by Shyamasree Lal, Calcutta, 15 March 1985.

[42] Ibid. In contrast, for his earliest plays, Tagore often rented or bought period costumes from professional dressmakers.

[43] Niharranjan Ray, *An Artist in Life: A Commentary on the Life and Works of Rabindranath Tagore* (Trivandrum: University of Kerala, 1967), p. 179.

[44] Marjorie Sykes, *Rabindranath Tagore* (Madras: Longmans, Green, 1947), p. 108.

[45] Press reviews of productions were often reprinted in issues of the *Visva-Bharati News*, and can be found in volumes 1 (1932–33) to 7 (1938–39), passim.

[46] Guha-Thakurta, p. 178.

[47] Balwant Gargi, "The Plays of Tagore", in *The Genius of Tagore*, ed. Mahendra Kulasrestha (Hoshiarpur: Vishveshvaranand V.R. Institute, 1961), p. 106. Gargi is among the handful of writers advocating the performance of Tagore's plays above treating them merely as literature: "His plays must be judged in terms of production and not by their written texts which are like dead butterflies pinned to a blank sheet of paper."

[48] Raha, *Bengali Theatre*, p. 138. For a sensitive Bengali review, see Sankha Ghosh, *Kāler Mātrā o Rabīndra-nāṭak* (Calcutta: De's, 1978), pp. 93–102. Ghosh terms the production a "milestone" in Bengali stage history.

[49] L.M. Thapalyal, "Tagore on Delhi Stage", *Natya: Theatre Arts Journal*, Tagore Centenary Number (1961), p. 80.

[50] Adya Rangacharya, *The Indian Theatre* (New Delhi: National Book Trust, 1971), p. 146.

[51] Shiv S. Kapur, "Two Plays, Two Productions and a View", *Natya: Theatre Arts Journal*, Tagore Centenary Number (1961), pp. 18–19.

[52] Ibid., p. 19. But Sankha Ghosh (p. 97) deemed this sequence totally appropriate.

[53] Kapur, "Rakat Karabi — Notes on a Play", p. 40.

[54] Thapalyal, "Tagore on Delhi Stage", p. 80.

[55] Raha, *Bengali Theatre*, p. 138. Sankha Ghosh, in his lengthy review in Bengali (pp. 83–92), contends that the production was not completely successful. He suggests that some of the flaws may be intrinsic to the play itself, which Tagore rectified by rewriting it as *Arūp Ratan*.

[56] Shiv S. Kapur, "Delhi Scene", *Natya: Theatre Arts Journal*, Autumn 1966, p. 43.

[57] Thapalyal, "Tagore on Delhi Stage", p. 80.

[58] Sombhu Mitra, "Reflections on Tagore's Plays", *Illustrated Weekly of India*, 7 May 1961, p. 41.

[59] Sombhu Mitra, "Building from Tagore", *The Drama Review*, Spring 1971, p. 204.

[60] Ibid., p. 201.

[61] Ibid., pp. 204 and 202.

TAGORE'S THEMES

[1] Tagore, *The Religion of Man* (London: George Allen and Unwin, 1931), p. 139.

[2] Sujit Mukherjee, *Passage to America* (Calcutta: Bookland, 1964), p. 154; S.K. Desai, "Symbolism in Tagore's Plays", in *Critical Essays on Indian Writing in English*, ed. M.K. Naik, S.K. Desai, G.S. Amur (Dharwar: Karnatak University, 1972), p. 153.

[3] K.P.K. Menon, *Tagore Lectures, 1973* (Annamalainagar: Annamalai University, 1976), pp. 37–38.

[4] Nirmal Mukerji, p. 73.

[5] Tagore, *Personality*, p. 47.

[6] Ibid., p. 51.

[7] Ibid., p. 56. Tagore also quotes, finding support from, Kabir and Walt Whitman.

[8] Tagore to Lokendranath Palit, ? July 1892; translated by Visvanath Chatterjee in "Tagore as a Shakespearean Critic", *Tagore Studies*, 1972–73, p. 20.

[9] Tagore, "Letters from Java", *Visva-Bharati Quarterly*, Old Series, 6 (April 1928):3.

[10] Tagore, *Letters to a Friend*, p. 49.

[11] Sanyal, p. 240.

[12] Vishwanath S. Naravane, *An Introduction to Rabindranath Tagore* (Madras: Macmillan, 1977), p. 96.

[13] Guha-Thakurta, p. 214.

[14] Ray, "Symbolist Plays of Tagore", p. 53.

[15] Ibid., p. 58.

[16] Srinivasa Iyengar, p. 48.

[17] Amar Mukerji, "Rabindranath Tagore's Theories of Tragedy and Comedy", *University of Allahabad Studies (English Section)*, 1950, pp. 67–68.

[18] Tagore, "My Religion", in *A Tagore Testament*, trans. Indu Dutt (London: Meridian Books, 1953), p. 61.

[19] Ibid., p. 59.

[20] Tagore, *Personality*, p. 178.

[21] Ibid., p. 183.

[22] Ibid., p. 184.

[23] See his essay on "Woman" in *Personality*, pp. 169–84.

[24] Tagore, *The Diary of a Westward Voyage*, trans. Indu Dutt (London: Asia, 1962), p. 30.

[25] Tagore, *Creative Unity*, p. 51.

[26] Ibid., p. 59.

[27] Niharranjan Ray, *Rabīndra-Sāhityer Bhūmikā* (Calcutta: New Age, 1962), p. 332; and *Artist in Life*, p. 224.

[28] Sujit Mukherjee, p. 155.

[29] Desai, p. 152.

[30] S.K. Desai, "Tagore's 'Red Oleanders': A Revaluation", in *Aspects of Indian Writing in English*, ed. M.K. Naik (Madras: Macmillan, 1979), p. 246.

[31] Ibid., p. 242. My italics.

[32] *Red Oleanders* is the title of the authorised translation of *Rakta-karavī*. This and subsequent quotations are from Tagore, "*Red Oleanders*: An Interpretation", transcribed by Leonard K. Elmhirst, *Visva-Bharati Quarterly*, New Series, 17 (November 1951):208–17. Tagore delivered this talk in Argentina, in late 1924.

[33] Tagore, "*Red Oleanders*: Author's Interpretation", *Visva-Bharati Quarterly*, Old Series, 3 (October 1925):283–85. For more detailed exposition of Tagore's views on the materialism of the West, see the essay "East and West" in *Creative Unity*, pp. 93–112. "The Modern Age" in the same book (pp. 115–30) provides insights into his attitudes on the exploitation of natural resources.

[34] Jaygopal Banerjee, "*Red Oleanders*: An Appreciation, III", *Calcutta Review*, Third Series, 18 (February 1926):234.

[35] Dusan Zbavitel, "Rabindranath Tagore in 1913–1930", *Archiv Orientálni* 26 (1958):383.

[36] Sombhu Mitra, "*Rakta Karabi*: producer's interpretation", *Natya: Theatre Arts Journal*, Tagore Centenary Number (1961), p. 61.

[37] Tagore, *Towards Universal Man* (Bombay: Asia, 1961), p. 305. Tagore delivered this address, City and Village" (pp. 302–22), at his Institute of Rural Reconstruction in Sriniketan, February 1928.

[38] See Rajendra Verma, *Rabindranath Tagore: Prophet Against Totalitarianism* (Bombay: Asia, 1964), p. 39; and Basavaraj S. Naikar, "Drama as Satire: *Red Oleanders*", *Journal of the Karnatak University — Humanities* 24–25 (1980–81):55–68. Naikar's essay is the most comprehensive recent analysis of the play.

[39] Thapalyal, "Tagore on Delhi Stage", p. 80.

[40] Kanak Bandyopadhyay, *Rabindranāther Tattva-nātak* (Calcutta: S. Banerjee, 1965), pp. 212–21.

[41] See Tagore's Preface to the play, later in this volume.

[42] Santikumar Dasgupta, *Rabindra-Nātya Parichay* (Calcutta: Bookland, 1963), p. 48; see also Somendranath Basu, *Rabindra-nāṭake Ṭrājidī* (Calcutta: Tagore Research Institute, 1974), p. 43. Both authors make detailed comparisons of the two plays.

[43] Srikumar Bandyopadhyay, *Rabindra-Sṛishṭi-Samīkshā*, 2 vols. (Calcutta: Satabdi, 1965; Orient Book, 1969), 1:165.

[44] Upendranath Bhattacharya, *Rabindra-Nātya-Parikramā* (Calcutta: Orient Book, 1960), p. 157.

[45] Kanak Bandyopadhyay, *Rabindra Nāṭya Samīkshā* (Calcutta: A. Mukherjee, 1967), pp. 205–6.

[46] Tagore to Nirmalkumari Mahalanabis, 8 August 1929, in Tagore, *Rabindra Rachanāvalī* (Govt. of West Bengal), 10:839 (my translation); and 1 September 1929, in *Deś*, 6 May 1961, p. 22.

[47] Tagore, "*Sakuntala*: Its Inner Meaning", trans. Jadunath Sarkar, *Modern Review* 9 (February 1911):175.

[48] Ibid., p. 172.

[49] Tagore, "Kalidas, the Moralist", trans. Jadunath Sarkar, *Modern Review* 14 (October 1913):348. The next quotation also comes from this page.

[50] Ibid., p. 349.

[51] Tagore, *Creative Unity*, p. 56.

[52] Tagore, "*Sakuntala*", p. 172.

[53] Tagore, *Gitanjali (Song Offerings)* (London: Macmillan, 1913), p. 68.

[54] Tagore, "*Sakuntala*", p. 175. Tagore's italics.

[55] Tagore to William Rothenstein, 17 June 1913; in Lago, *Imperfect Encounter*, p. 113.

[56] Ramaswami Sastri, *Sir Rabindranath Tagore*, p. 324.

[57] Heinz Mode, "Tagore's King of the Dark Chamber' and Its Folkloristic Background", *Folk-Lore* 1 (November 1960):361–68.

[58] Quoted by Kapur, "Delhi Scene", p. 43.

[59] Tagore, "My Religion", p. 60.

[60] Tagore, *Rabīndra-Rachanāvalī* (Visvabharati), 11:233. My translation.

[61] Sen Gupta, p. 172.

[62] Desai, "Symbolism in Tagore's Plays", p. 147; Menon, p. 28.

[63] *The Isa Upanisad*, trans. P. Lal (Calcutta: Writers Workshop, 1968), p. 3.

[64] My translation. See p. 281 in this volume.

[65] My translation. See p. 318 in this volume.

[66] Tagore, *"Sādhanā": The Realisation of Life* (London: Macmillan, 1913), p. 85.

[67] Tagore, *Gitanjali*, p. 45.

[68] Tagore, *Three Plays*, trans. Marjorie Sykes (Bombay: Oxford University Press, 1950), pp. 49–50.

[69] *Isa Upanisad*, p. 3.

[70] Abu Sayeed Ayyub, *Tagore's Quest* (Calcutta: Papyrus, 1980), pp. 23–24.

TAGORE'S RECEPTION IN ENGLAND AND AMERICA

[1] In Lago, *Imperfect Encounter*, p. 166.

[2] See Alex Aronson, *Rabindranath through Western Eyes*, 2nd ed. (Calcutta: Rddhi-India, 1978), pp. 22–23.

[3] "Drama", *Athenaeum*, 17 January 1914, p. 99. I also quote from the following reviews of *Chitra*: "From the Unreal to the Real", *Nation* (London), 24 January 1914, pp. 716–17; Walter de la Mare, "Poets from Afar", *Westminster Gazette*, 7 February 1914, p. 6; "Tagore's Ideal Woman", *New York Times Review of Books*, 22 March 1914, p. 129; "Plays and Books about the Drama", *American Review of Reviews* 49 (April 1914):503; Arthur Davison Ficke, "A New-Old Tagore Play", *Little Review* 1 (April 1914):33–35; "East and West", *Times Literary Supplement*, 14 May 1914, p. 236; "Drama", *Nation* (New York), 21 May 1914, pp. 611–12; "Rabindranath Tagore, as a Playwright, Issues a Message to Women", *Current Opinion* 56 (May 1914): 358; "Plays by Tagore", *Boston Evening Transcript*, 29 July 1914, p. 21; Abraham E. Sinberg, "Rabindranath Tagore", *Colonnade* 8 (September 1914):88; Henry Baerlein, "The Works of Tagore", *Bookman* 47 (December 1914):100; and E.M. Forster, *Abinger Harvest* (New York: Harcourt, Brace, 1936), pp. 327–29. In instances where an article deals with more than one book (as in *American Review of Reviews* above), I cite only those page numbers that refer specifically to Tagore.

[4] In announcing the award in its issue of 14 November 1913, the *New York Times* commented, "It is the first time that this prize has been given to anybody but a white person" (p. 4). The next day the paper editorialised: "some of us feel a surprise more than faintly tinged with resentment at an award of the Nobel Prize for Literature that passes over all Occidental writers of prose and poetry and falls on a Hindu bard with a name hard to pronounce and harder to remember." The writer argued that the award went against the principle that money and glory should be kept in the family, but derived consolation from the fact that "Babindranath [*sic*] Tagore, if not exactly one of us, is, as an Aryan, a distant relation of all white folk. Moreover, though of Eastern birth, he is of Western education, and though he is said to write his verses first in Sanskrit—which seems queer, that being a language now spoken by nobody — he translates them into good, sound English before submitting them to the large public" ("Topics of the Times: Our Case Isn't Desperate", *New York Times*, 15 November 1913, p. 10). The paper had misspelt Tagore's first name in the item on the previous day as well.

[5] I quote from the following reviews: "A Child Drama", *New York Times Review of Books*, 5 July 1914, p. 301; "Plays by Tagore", *Boston Evening Transcript*, 29 July 1914, p. 21; "'The Post Office'", *Times Literary Supplement*, 15 October 1914, p. 455; "Drama", *Athenaeum*, 7 November 1914, p. 486.

[6] "Mr. Tagore's New Play", *Times Literary Supplement*, 18 June 1914, p. 294; "Drama", *Athenaeum*, 25 July 1914, p. 128; "Rabindranath Tagore as Dramatist", *Guardian*, 17 September 1914, p. 1087; G.C., "'The King of the Dark Chamber'", *Manchester Guardian*, 6 October 1914, p. 4; "Notes", *Nation*, 12 November 1914, p. 585; "Books of the Autumn", *Independent*, 16 November 1914, p. 244; Henry Baerlein, "The Works of Tagore", *Bookman* 47 (December 1914):100; A.C.H., "Two Kings", *Poetry* 5 (December 1914): 133–34; Homer E. Woodbridge, "Plays of To-day and Yesterday", *Dial*, 16 January 1915, pp. 48–49; Helen Bullis, "Tagore and a Mystic", *New York Times Review of Books*, 14 February 1915, pp. 49 + 51; "'The King of the Dark Chamber'", *Dramatist* 6 (April 1915): 568–69.

[7] "Tagore's Poems and Stories in English", *New York Times Review of Books*, 10 December 1916, p. 541.

[8] "'The Cycle of Spring'", *New York Times Review of Books*, 11 March 1917, pp. 87–88; "Dramatists and the Drama", *American Review of Reviews* 55 (June 1917):663; Reginald R. Buckley, "Tagore's New Books", *Bookman* 52 (July 1917):120–21; O.W. Firkins, "Verhaeren, Claudel, Cammaerts", *Nation*, 16 August 1917, p. 176; "A Hindoo Drama", *Independent*, 29 September 1917, p. 512; "New Books", *Catholic World* 106 (November 1917):247; "The Newly Published Plays", *Theatre Arts Magazine* 2 (December 1917):62.

[9] The volume contained the following plays: *Sanyasi, or the Ascetic*

(*Prakritir Pratiśodh*), *Malini* (*Mālinī*), *Sacrifice* (*Visarjan*), and *The King and the Queen* (*Rājā o Rānī*).

[10] "Recent Literature", *London Quarterly Review* 129 (January 1918): 136; "The Play at Home and Abroad", *American Review of Reviews* 57 (January 1918):109; "The Newly Published Plays", *Theatre Arts Magazine* 2 (February 1918):116; Padraic Colum, "New Plays and a New Theory", *Dial*, 28 March 1918, p. 296; O.W. Firkins, "Traditions and Modernities", *Nation*, 25 April 1918, p. 506.

[11] The volume contained the following plays: "Kacha and Devayani" (*Vidāy-Abhiśāp*), "The Mother's Prayer" (*Gāndhārīr Āvedan*), "Ama and Vinayaka" (*Satī*), "Somaka and Ritvik" (*Narakvās*), and "Karna and Kunti" (*Karṇa-Kuntī-Saṁvād*).

[12] B.S., review article, *Manchester Guardian*, 15 November 1921, p. 5; "Moonshine from the East", *Saturday Review*, 19 November 1921, pp. 588–89; E.S., "Two Eastern Singers", *Sunday Times*, 4 December 1921, p. 9; Fillmore Hyde, "Poetry in Prose", *Literary Review*, 10 December 1921, p. 255; Richard Le Gallienne, "Two Wise Men from the East", *New York Times Book Review and Magazine*, 11 December 1921, p. 3; "Briefer Mention", *Dial* 72 (March 1922):325.

[13] "Drama", *Times Literary Supplement*, 9 July 1925, p. 465; "The Bookman's Table", *Bookman* 69 (November 1925):136; Gilbert Norwood, "Plays", *London Mercury* 14 (July 1926):324–25; "Drama", *Saturday Review of Literature*, 18 September 1926, p. 122.

[14] Hugh I'A. Fausset, "Tagore's Poems and Plays", *London Mercury* 35 (December 1936):206–7; Vincent Engels, "A Hindu Poet", *Commonweal*, 29 January 1937, pp. 391–92; Barrett Parker, "Rabindranath Tagore and His Poetry", *Boston Evening Transcript*, 30 January 1937, part 6, p. 3; Robert E. Keighton, "Book Reviews", *Crozer Quarterly* 14 (April 1937):184–85; "Theatre Arts Bookshelf", *Theatre Arts Monthly* 21 (April 1937):331–32.

[15] George Cloyne, "Passages from India", *Times*, 23 February 1961, p. 15.

[16] "The Irish Players", *Times*, 11 July 1913, p. 8; J.W., "Royal Court Theatre", *Westminster Gazette*, 11 July 1913, p. 3; "'The Post Office'", *Era*, 16 July 1913, p. 14; "The Court", *Stage*, 17 July 1913, p. 20. I have also used extracts from reviews quoted by Mary Lago (*Tagore*, pp. 118–19): "An Indian Allegory", *Evening Standard*, 11 July 1913, p. 6; "An Indian Play at the Court", *Globe*, 11 July 1913, p. 4; and "Indian Poet's Dream Play", *Standard*, 11 July 1913, p. 5.

[17] Quoted by Olivia Howard Dunbar, *A House in Chicago* (Chicago: University of Chicago, 1947), p. 99.

[18] Ernest Rhys, *Rabindranath Tagore: A Biographical Study* (London: Macmillan, 1915), p. 80.

[19] Lennox Robinson, *Ireland's Abbey Theatre: A History 1899–1951*

(London: Sidgwick and Jackson, 1951), p. 109.

[20] Among the few reports of such readings, see "Mr. Tagore's Poetry", *Times*, 10 May 1913, p. 8 (on a reading of *Chitra* at the Cromwell Road Centre in London, 9 May 1913); Bailey Millard, p. 250 (on a reading of *The King and the Queen* at the Columbia Theater in San Francisco, 5 October 1916); and Literatus, "Rabindranath Tagore in America", *Modern Review* 21 (May 1917):553 (the same play read at the Trinity Auditorium in Los Angeles, 14 October 1916). A "tremendous" crowd showed up for this last reading, the organisers being compelled "to seat about 75 on the stage."

[21] *Times*, 8 June 1915, p. 11. The *Times* noticed this performance in its early edition the next day (9 June 1915, p. 11), but I have not been able to locate a copy of this issue of the early edition, which even the *Times* office in London does not have on file.

[22] William Chislett, *Moderns and Near-Moderns* (New York: Grafton, 1928), p. 216. *The Post Office* probably premiered on 18 November 1916: Pal (1997).

[23] Allardyce Nicoll, *English Drama 1900–1930: The Beginnings of the Modern Period* (Cambridge: University Press, 1973), p. 980. Later references to Nicoll in this section all denote this page, where he lists several performances of Tagore's plays. The absence of reviews for some productions is confirmed in J.P. Wearing, *The London Stage 1910–1919: A Calendar of Plays and Players*, 2 vols., and *The London Stage 1920–1929: A Calendar of Plays and Players*, 3 vols. (Metuchen, New Jersey: Scarecrow, 1982–84).

[24] "The Union of East and West", *Era*, 19 February 1919, p. 12; "The Comedy", *Stage*, 20 February 1919, p. 16.

[25] "Prince of Wales Theatre", *Daily Telegraph*, 5 May 1920, p. 11; "The Prince of Wales's", *Stage*, 6 May 1920, p. 16; "Indian Art and Dramatic Society", *Observer*, 9 May 1920, p. 10.

[26] Rathindranath Tagore, pp. 136–37.

[27] Alexander Woollcott, "The Trials of Tagore", *New York Times*, 11 December 1920, p. 11; O.W. Firkins, "Drama: St. John Ervine and Rabindranath Tagore", *Weekly Review*, 29 December 1920, p. 659.

[28] "Rabindranath Tagore's Plays in London", *Graphic*, 2 August 1924, p. 177.

[29] "Irving Theatre", *Times*, 15 May 1952, p. 8.

[30] These productions are listed by Prafulla C. Mukherji, "Rabindranath Tagore in America", *Modern Review* 110 (November 1961):387. Three earlier university productions from 1959–61 are mentioned by Robin Noel Widgery, "Survey of Asian Plays Produced in the United States from 1929 to 1966", *Afro-Asian Theatre Bulletin*, February 1967, p. 7.

[31] Howard Taubman, "Tagore's King of Dark Chamber' Opens", *New York Times*, 10 February 1961, p. 21; Whitney Balliett, "Off Broadway", *New Yorker*, 18 February 1961, p. 93; Robert Brustein, "Off Broadway's

Trials and Triumph", *New Republic*, 6 March 1961, pp. 21–22; Theophilus
Lewis, "Theatre", *America*, 11 March 1961, p. 768; Howard Taubman,
Innocence of Spirit", *New York Times*, 9 April 1961, part 2, p. 1; Tom F.
Driver, "Revolutionless Worlds", *Christian Century*, 26 April 1961, pp. 535–
37; Alan Pryce-Jones, "Alan Pryce-Jones at the Theatre", *Theatre Arts*
45 (April 1961):68; "An Offbeat Stage Hit on a Poet's Birthday", *Life*,
9 June 1961, p. 125.

[32] See J.L. Dees, *Tagore and America* (Calcutta: United States Information
Service, 1961), p. 36.

[33] See Prafulla Mukherji, p. 390.

[34] Krishna Shah, "The Director and the Play", in *Rabindranath Tagore
Centenary*, ed. Rose Mukerji (brochure published on the occasion of the
production of *The King of the Dark Chamber*, New York, 1961), p. 23.

[35] *Bulletin* (Sydney), 17 December 1925; quoted by Aronson, p. 100.

[36] Mary Carolyn Davies, "Rabindranath Tagore: India's Shakespeare
and Tasso in One", *Forum* 51 (January 1914):140–44; and Alice Corbin
Henderson, "Rabindranath Tagore", *The Drama* 4 (May 1914):161–76.

[37] Rhys, p. 89.

[38] Thompson, *Rabindranath Tagore: Poet and Dramatist* (London: Oxford
University Press, 1926). All page references are to this, the first, edition.
Thompson had previously authored a shorter volume published by the
Y.M.C.A. in Calcutta, which had not received very wide distribution, titled
Rabindranath Tagore: His Life and Work (Calcutta: Association Press, 1921).

[39] Tagore to William Rothenstein, 20 April 1927; in Lago, *Imperfect
Encounter*, p. 321.

[40] Ramananda Chatterjee, "Mr. Thompson's Book on Rabindranath
Tagore", *Modern Review* 42 (July 1927):99–102.

[41] William Radice, "Tagore's Poetry in English Translation", *Visvabharati
Quarterly*, New Series, 42 (May 1976):12. Radice has since revised his opinion,
now considering Thompson's book "distressingly unsuccessful." See Rabindranath Tagore, *Selected Poems*, trans. William Radice (Harmondsworth,
Middlesex: Penguin, 1985), p. 8.

[42] P. Guha-Thakurta, *The Bengali Drama* (London: Kegan Paul, Trench,
Trubner, 1930). See specially Chapter 29, "His Dramatic Art".

[43] V. Lesný, *Rabindranath Tagore: His Personality and Work*, trans. Guy
McKeever Phillips (London: George Allen and Unwin, 1939).

PREVIOUS ENGLISH TRANSLATIONS

Translated by Shyamal Kumar Sarkar in "Tagore on Translation",
Visvabharati Quarterly, New Series, 43 (May 1977):69.

[2] Tagore to Ajit Kumar Chakravarty, 4 January 1913 and 13 March 1913;

translated by Shyamal Kumar Sarkar, ibid., pp. 74 and 76.

[3] Tagore to Amiya Chakravarty, 6 January 1935 and 7 March 1935; translated by Shyamal Kumar Sarkar, ibid., pp. 70 and 69.

[4] Tagore to William Rothenstein, ? February 1914; in Lago, *Imperfect Encounter*, p. 148.

[5] Shyamal Kumar Sarkar, pp. 74–75.

[6] Amiya Chakravarty interviewed by Mary Lago, *Imperfect Encounter*, p. 150.

[7] Shyamal Kumar Sarkar, pp. 72 and 75.

[8] Tagore to Ajit Kumar Chakravarty, 12 May 1913, and to Ramananda Chatterjee, 28 October 1917; translated by Shyamal Kumar Sarkar, ibid., p. 79.

[9] Ibid., pp. 75–77.

[10] Tagore to Amiya Chakravarty, 23 October 1934; translated by Shyamal Kumar Sarkar, ibid., p. 81.

[11] For full bibliographical details about all the English translations mentioned in this section, see "Appendix E: List of Tagore's Plays and Their English Translations", later in this volume.

[12] K.V. Suryanarayana Murti, "Tagore's 'Chitra': A Grammatical Clue to Character", *Aryan Path* 37 (July 1966):311–16.

[13] Tagore to Ajit Kumar Chakravarty, ? August 1912; translated by Shyamal Kumar Sarkar in "The King of the Dark Chamber: Text and Publication", *Visvabharati Quarterly*, New Series, 38 (November 1972):28.

[14] Tagore, *The Post Office*, trans. Devabrata Mukerjea (London: Macmillan, 1914), pp. 44, 69, 38 and 6 respectively.

[15] Charles Whibley to Macmillan, November 1912; quoted by Lago, *Imperfect Encounter*, p. 22.

[16] John Masefield to William Rothenstein, 7 October 1912; quoted by Lago, ibid., p. 23.

[17] William Rothenstein to Tagore, 2 December 1912; ibid., p. 71.

[18] T. Sturge Moore to Marie Sturge Moore, 30 July 1913; quoted by Lago, ibid., p. 47.

[19] William Rothenstein to Tagore, 17 November 1912, 17 June 1913, 16 June 1914, and 29 June 1914; ibid., pp. 63, 115, 167 and 168 respectively.

[20] Interested readers may also refer to the comparison of original and translation made by William Radice, "Visarjan and Sacrifice", *Visvabharati Quarterly*, New Series, 45 (May 1979):10–32. Radice finds the translation inadequate.

[21] One reviewer had pointed out twenty errors in the thirty-page-long translation, to support his conviction that Thompson lacked a proper knowledge of Bengali. See Priyaranjan Sen, "Mr. Edward Thompson and Rabindranath Tagore", *Modern Review* 43 (January 1928):13–16.

²² Edward Thompson, Introduction to *The Curse at Farewell* by Tagore, trans. Thompson (London: George G. Harrap, 1924), p. 15.

²³ Thompson, *Poet and Dramatist*, p. 95.

²⁴ Thompson's comparisons appear on the following pages of his book; ibid., pp. 52–55 (*Sanyasi*), 93–97 (*The King and the Queen*), 98–99 (*Sacrifice*), 126–31 (*Chitra*), 138–39 (*Malini*), 170–71, 174 and 178 (*The Fugitive*), and 218 (*The King of the Dark Chamber*). More sensible comparisons are made by Sujit Mukherjee, chapter 7 passim, though Mukherjee is not too sympathetic toward Tagore's symbolic plays.

²⁵ Sykes, Notes to *Three Plays* by Tagore, p. 177.

²⁶ Ibid., p. 180.

²⁷ Lago, *Imperfect Encounter*, p. 48.

²⁸ Ibid., p. 221.

²⁹ William Rothenstein to Tagore, 4 August 1914; ibid., p. 171.

³⁰ Shyamal Kumar Sarkar, "The King of the Dark Chamber", pp. 25–40.

³¹ Tagore to Jagadananda Ray, 18 October 1912; in *Pravāsī*, Chaitra 1341, p. 752.

³² Shyamal Kumar Sarkar, "The King of the Dark Chamber", p. 31.

³³ William Rothenstein to Tagore, 16 June 1914 and 29 June 1914; in Lago, *Imperfect Encounter*, pp. 167–68.

³⁴ Tagore to William Rothenstein, 8 July 1914; ibid., p. 170.

³⁵ William Rothenstein to Tagore, 4 August 1914; ibid., p. 171.

³⁶ That it was a poor translation had been noticed quite early in India, in a review article by Surendranath Das Gupta, "*The King of the Dark Chamber*", *Modern Review* 20 (July 1916):30–34.

³⁷ Shyamal Kumar Sarkar, "At Unison with Him", *Tagore Studies*, 1972–73, p. 46.

³⁸ Quoted by Shyamal Kumar Sarkar, ibid., p. 47.

³⁹ See p. 294 in this volume.

⁴⁰ Quoted by Radice, "Tagore's Poetry in English Translation", p. 21.

⁴¹ See p. 283 in this volume.

⁴² Tagore to Amiya Chakravarty, 11 October 1923; in Tagore, *Chithipatra*, 12 vols. (Calcutta: Visvabharati, 1942–86), 11:36–37.

⁴³ All subsequent page references in this section are to Tagore, *Red Oleanders* (London: Macmillan, 1925). In order not to confuse the reader, I have not indicated the page numbers of the corresponding passages from my translation which I have extracted here.

THE PRESENT TRANSLATION

¹ John Alan Haughton, "Study India's Music, Tagore's Word to Western World", *Musical America*, 27 November 1920, p. 5.

NOTES

²Eric Bentley, Introduction to *The Caucasian Chalk Circle*, by Bertolt Brecht (New York: Grove Press, 1966), p. 11.

³Dhurjati Prasad Mukerji, *Tagore—A Study* (Bombay: Padma, 1944), p. 122.

⁴Marjorie Sykes, Preface to *Three Plays* by Tagore, p. v.

⁵Peter Arnott, "Greek Drama and the Modern Stage", in *The Craft and Context of Translation*, ed. William Arrowsmith and Roger Shattuck (Austin: University of Texas, 1961), p. 84.

⁶Sujit Mukherjee, p. 157; Lago, *Tagore*, p. 118.

⁷Mervyn D. Coles, "The Plays of Tagore", *Contemporary Review* 183 (May 1953):293.

⁸K.R. Srinivasa Iyengar, *Indian Writing in English*, 5th ed. (New Delhi: Sterling, 1985), p. 123.

⁹Tagore, *My Reminiscences*, pp. 194–95.

¹⁰Ibid., pp. 205–6.

¹¹Beerendra Bandyopadhyaya, *Rabindra-sangit: The Songs of Tagore* (Calcutta: Granthalaya, [1981]), p. 60.

¹²Nirmal Mukerji, p. 60.

¹³Tagore, *Creative Unity*, p. 78. He expressed his feelings about this sect in "An Indian Folk Religion", pp. 69–90 of the same book.

¹⁴Tagore, *My Reminiscences*, p. 208.

¹⁵Shah, p. 25.

¹⁶Dhurjati Mukerji, p. 125.

The Plays

RED OLEANDER

[1] The publication history — as well as Tagore's lengthy preface to the Bengali first edition, in which he suggests thematic links between his play and the *Rāmāyaṇa* — can be found in the notes to the definitive edition, in Tagore's *Rabīndra-Rachanāvalī* (Visvabharati), 15:545–49. The first draft of the play was recently printed in *Rabīndra-vīkshā*, Paush 1393, pp. 1–66. Another draft, with the title *Nandinī*, has also appeared in print recently: see the magazine *Bahurūpī*, 1 May 1986, pp. 9–62.

[2] Bisi, 2:157–58. The translation is mine.

[3] Elmhirst to Krishna Kripalani, in Kripalani, p. 321.

[4] Ibid., p. 323. "Gagen" was Gaganendranath Tagore, Tagore's nephew.

[5] The relevant extracts are quoted by Amal Mitra in *Kaviguru Rabīndranath o Naṭarāj Śiśirkumār* (Calcutta: Tagore Research Institute, 1977), p. 10. The translation is mine.

[6] Ibid., p. 55.

[7] See Tagore's letters to Reba Ray, cited by Gaurchandra Saha in *Rabīndra-Patrāvalī: Tathyapañjī* (Calcutta: De's, 1984), pp. 264–65. Tagore asked Reba Ray to take the part of Nandini, but she fell ill and the production fell through.

[8] See Tagore's letter to Nirmalkumari Mahalanabis, 21 March 1934, in *Deś*, 23 September 1961, p. 695; and letter to Hemantabala Devi, 7 April 1934, in Tagore's *Chithipatra*, 9:227.

[9] Of the innumerable reviews that appeared in Bengali, the one by Sankha Ghosh which I have cited earlier in my section on "Tagore as Theatrician" (pp. 327–28) is perhaps the most sensible, sensitive and substantive.

[10] Early editions of the play did not have this Introduction, which was taken from Tagore's manuscript and first incorporated into his collected works in 1943, in the volume containing the definitive text, published after his death.

[11] Yakshapurī or Yakshapur, literally "City of Yakshas". In Hindu mythology, the Yakshas form a class of demigods serving Kubera, appointed to guard the underground treasures of the earth. Although usually depicted as benign (for instance by Kalidasa in *Meghadūta*), sometimes they are portrayed as malevolent spirits, capable of causing demonic possession. Yakshapurī is another name for Alakā, Kubera's capital and the wealthiest city in the world, supposedly located in the Himalayas. In early mythology Kubera was the leader of dark or evil spirits; he later became identified as the god of riches.

¹² The *makar* or *makara* is a mythical sea-monster, often incorrectly equated with crocodiles, sharks or dolphins, but probably possessing some of the attributes of each, as well as the head and forelegs of a deer. The Hindu god of love, Kāma, has the *makar* as his emblem and displays it on his banner; the *makar* recurs as a common motif in Hindu architecture. Significantly, the *makar* is also one of the nine legendary treasures of Kubera. Tagore's Raja clearly embodies both the strong sensual attractiveness of Kāma and the greedy, repulsive rapacity of Kubera.

¹³ The word *pārshad* indicates an attendant, particularly of a god. However, it also has associations of a courtier who flatters and fawns.

¹⁴ *Gosāiṁ* is a title commonly applied to Vaishnava religious gurus. The suffix *ji* is an honorific form appended to any Indian name or title to express the speaker's respect for the person addressed. Its function resembles that of "sir" in English. The Gosain's given name, we learn later, is Kenārām: there is a pun on *kenā*, which means "to buy". The Gosain has clearly been bought off by the sardars.

¹⁵ Tagore did not compile a dramatis personae for this play. I have given first the characters' names as spelt in my translation, followed by their English transliteration in parentheses. The etymology of a few of their names is significant.

Nandinī means "daughter". But the *Matsya Purāṇa* also gives it as one of the names of Durgā, wife of Siva, personification of the Shakti principle, and most important of Hindu goddesses, who comes to earth to slay demons and presides over the good fortune of all humanity. The parallel between Tagore's Nandini and the goddess Durgā as deliverers of men from various "demons" cannot be underestimated. In its root form, *nandinī* denotes "delightful", "charming", and "pleasing".

Viśu, a commonly abbreviated form of Viśvanāth, "lord of the universe", is one of the appellations of Siva. One may also associate with Bishu's name the connotations of the adjective *viśuddha*: pure, cleansed, free from vice.

While the name of Ranjan cannot figure in the cast list, his is one of the central functions in the play. Literally, *rañjan* signifies the act of colouring, but like the root form of *nandinī*, it has the additional meanings of "entertaining", "rejoicing", "charming" and "delighting".

¹⁶ The title of the play and its dominant motif is *Rakta-karavī*, the Red Oleander, or more precisely the red-blossomed variety of the plant *Nerium odorum*. The word *rakta*, however, primarily means "blood", and a more accurate translation would perhaps be "blood-red oleander", which would also express the grimmer aspects of the theme.

¹⁷ A gloss for "Tāl-Vetāl", the names of a pair of Siva's attendants, also variously represented as necrophagous creatures or spirits occupying a corpse. The term "occult communion" is also a gloss, for *śava-sādhanā*, signifying

a cultic rite performed by meditating while sitting upon a corpse in a crematorium, usually on a new-moon night.

[18] In Hindu mythology Rāhu, "the Seizer", is a demon who swallows the sun and moon, thereby causing eclipses. In astronomy he is depicted as a dragon's head. Vishnu decapitated Rāhu, whose head became fixed in the skies and has ever since sought revenge on the sun and moon (who had revealed him to Vishnu) by periodically swallowing them. Hence the Professor's next line, "It isn't whole itself. . .".

[19] The border or end of a sari draped over the left shoulder of an Indian woman. In the absence of a more accurate English equivalent, translators usually gloss this word as "veil", which of course is misleading.

[20] Three different species of very fragrant white flowers. The *mallikā* is popularly known as the Arabian Jasmine, *Jasminum sambac*; the *chāmeli* as the Spanish Jasmine, *Jasminum grandiflorum*. The *mālatī* generally refers also to *J. grandiflorum*, but in this case it probably denotes the climbing shrub *Aganosma caryophyllata*, also called *mālatī* by Bengalis.

[21] While apparently an abbreviation of Nandini's name, this term carries several other layers of association. As a noun, it means "delight" or "felicity". As a proper noun, it is a name given to Durgā. On the other hand, it is also the name of a river flowing near Alakā, the capital of the Yakshas.

[22] Specifically the *kunda* flower, *Jasminum pubescens*, with large clusters of fragrant white blossoms. Since it recurs frequently, the word "jasmine" in the text always refers to this particular flower which, again significantly, is considered one of Kubera's nine treasures. Some lexicons also equate *kunda* with the Oleander—possibly the variety with white blossoms.

[23] The ninth month of the Bengali calendar, corresponding to the second half of December and the first half of January.

[24] The word *digvadhū* refers, strictly speaking, to any one of the young female deities who preside over the "ten quarters" of the globe.

[25] A category of evil demons, usually regarded as grotesque nocturnal creatures prowling around funeral pyres, upsetting sacrifices, and feeding on mortals. Mythologically their home was Laṅkā — supposedly the present Srilanka — and their king was Rāvaṇa, killed by Rama in the *Rāmāyaṇa*. In any case, the usage of the word has degenerated now to suggest demons in general. Therefore a Western production may not lose much by substituting "demon" instead.

[26] Again, an abbreviation that reflects an attempt to be more intimate and also reveals further verbal meaning. The adjective *nandin* denotes "gladdening", "rejoicing", or "delighting".

[27] The actual term used, *āgamanī*, while referring generally to a song of welcome, specifically alludes to the songs heralding the arrival of Durgā at her father's home. The term *lagna* indicates the auspicious time that Indian

astrologers define in advance as fortunate for the undertaking of an activity. See p. 181 for another example of *lagna*, "auspicious moment".

[28] Chandī is the name of a fierce manifestation of Durgā who battles demons. Once again Tagore uses the imagery of the Durgā myth.

[29] In Hinduism, *pūjā* signifies the act of worshipping a god or goddess. "Worship" is the closest English replacement.

[30] The word *pāgal* literally means "mad" or "madman", but depending on the circumstances of its usage (as for instance between lovers) it can be merely an affectionate endearment. Nandini and Bishu constantly use this word when addressing each other, and it reflects their deep bond of friendship. Of course, like all proverbial lovers and poets, both of them are in a sense mad. Here Phagulal also uses the word in an affectionate way, but perhaps not as intimately as do Nandini and Bishu with each other.

[31] In India people often address one another with various familial titles as a mark of respect or closeness, though they are not necessarily relatives. Here Chandra calls Bishu her *beyāi*, which actually means the father-in-law or uncle-in-law of one's son or daughter. Later in this conversation Phagulal addresses Bishu as *dādā*, "elder brother", while Gokul calls Bishu *bhāi*, "brother". Generally speaking, *dādā* is used to address men older than oneself and carries associations of respect; *bhāi* is used for close peers or contemporaries, or people slightly younger than oneself.

[32] The word *ghomṭā* defines the *āñchal* of a sari when used to cover a woman's head. Often, especially when drawn forward to partially hide the face, it reflects the wearer's modesty. The Professor mentions this "veil" in his talk with the Puranic Scholar (p. 165).

[33] *Beyān*, the feminine of *beyāi*, thus strictly speaking the mother-in-law or aunt-in-law of one's son or daughter. At the beginning of this sentence Phagulal addresses Bishu as *bhāi*, "brother". Readers may assume that Gokul has left after his last speech, since the standard edition does not offer any stage direction indicating his exit later on.

[34] The Bengali *ras* (Sanskrit *rasa*), an untranslatable concept because of its many levels of meaning. *Rasa* suggests all of the following: any liquid; the sap of plants; the marrow; the quintessence of the human body; the essence of something; enjoyment or pleasure; taste or flavour; and of course in Indian poetics, the aesthetic flavour of a work or the mood prevalent in it.

[35] Indians have traditionally used the broad leaves of the banana tree as platters from which to eat. The comparison, therefore, lies between natural and man-made receptacles.

[36] The *vorā* snake, *Vipera russelli*, or Russell's Viper.

[37] In Bengali, *daś-pañchis*, literally "10–25", an indoor game similar to dice, usually played with cowrie shells. The phrase "a game of dice" could replace "the game of 10–25" for the benefit of an English-speaking audience.

[38] By using this term, Bishu makes a direct connection between the Raja and the god of wealth, Kubera. Yaksha-raja, "king of the Yakshas", is the name of Kubera. A couple of speeches earlier Bishu had hinted at the connection by calling their town "Yakshapur", another name for Kubera's capital city. The Professor frequently does the same (see pp. 136, 165).

[39] The word *navānna*, "new rice" or "new grain", refers to the ceremony of eating the first fruits of a new crop. Specifically, it denotes the festival of eating newly-grown autumnal rice in the month of Agrahāyan (November–December).

[40] The word *dādā* also means "grandfather" in Bengali and, like other familial suffixes, is appended to names or titles to express veneration or affection. A person might respectfully address with this word a stranger clearly much older than himself; here the Sardar, though no stranger, reciprocates the gesture by calling Chandra *nātnī*, "grand-daughter".

[41] The *sāras* or Sarus Crane, *Grus antigone*, come to teach a group of *bak*, herons or egrets in general, to dance. The Sarus Crane, a large bird, is known for its spectacular if not altogether graceful breeding dances. The *bak* is popularly considered a deceitful bird of great cunning and circumspection; hence figuratively used the word implies a hypocrite, scoundrel or cheat. Curiously enough, *bak* is also a name given to Kubera, though the Sardar probably does not know of this unconscious allusion.

[42] In India, *praṇām* defines the act of making obeisance to a god by lying prostrate, or the act of bending and touching another person's feet in reverence. The accompanying physical gesture on stage ought to clarify the meaning of the word to audiences in the West.

[43] The *kūrma* or tortoise, Vishnu's second incarnation, descended to earth at the mythical churning of the oceans, which was made necessary in order to recover *amrita*, the nectar of the gods, lost during a deluge that had covered the world. Mount Mandara was used as the churning stick, and Vishnu played a literally pivotal role by supporting the mountain on his rounded back.

[44] The term *kīrtan* literally means "repeating, saying, or glorifying" God. Specifically it signifies a class of Vaishnava devotional songs in praise of and about Krishna and his love Rādhā. "Hymn" may be used as a substitute in Western performances.

[45] The word *nāmāvali* refers to a piece of cloth with names of gods and deities printed on it, wrapped around a devotee's shoulders. The Vaishnava Gosain would have the "Hare Krishna, Hare Rama" chant on his *nāmāvali*.

[46] One of the names of Vishnu. As an exclamation (later used by the Gosain), it expresses various emotions ranging from amazement to disgust.

[47] As a Hindu priest, the Gosain should know Sanskrit; but in this sentence he lapses into incorrect Sanskrit while attempting to quote a maxim of un-

certain origin. It is quite impossible to convey his difficulty with Sanskrit in an English translation.

[48] Correct Sanskrit this time, literally meaning "No enemy is greater than pride." Scholars sometimes attribute this well-known dictum to Chānakya, the shrewd and pragmatic advisor to Chandragupta Maurya, emperor of India (c. 321 B.C.–c. 297 B.C.).

[49] Lakshmī, Vishnu's consort, is the Hindu goddess of good fortune, grace and beauty, wealth and prosperity. The Gosain's phrase, mā-lakshmī, is frequently used in Bengal to address a woman affectionately.

[50] The word śāstra refers to any Hindu religious treatise or sacred book, or even — as in this case — the whole body of teaching on religion and mythology. "Scripture" might work as a performance substitute in the West. Bishu alludes to Vishnu's third incarnation, the varāha, when in the form of a giant boar he used his tusks first to kill a demon who had pulled the earth underwater, and then to lift the submerged earth to the surface once again.

[51] A common Indian interjection of contempt, reproach or disapproval.

[52] In Bengali, pāgal-bhāi, literally "mad brother". Bishu's response, pāglī, is a feminine diminutive of pāgal and reflects the closeness of their relationship. It is difficult to suggest alternatives for a performance in which a director feels this kind of exchange in English may sound too awkward. Perhaps proper names could suffice instead, but the repetition of Nandini's and Bishu's pet names for each other at the end of the play evokes strong emotional reactions in the spectator that may be lost if they are omitted.

[53] The word sudhā is a synonym for amrita, the nectar of the gods. It also means "moonlight" in Bengali, which links this song to the first line of Bishu's next song.

[54] The compound varan-mālā, "welcome garland", connotes particularly the garland that a woman places round the neck of a suitor chosen by her, most commonly her husband at their wedding.

[55] The planet Śani, equivalent to the Western Saturn. In Indian astrology Saturn's influence on human beings is usually malign, therefore references to it forebode evil or ill fortune.

[56] The most popular dramatic form in rural Bengal, the yātrā represents a folk-theatre tradition characterised by open-air, often all-night performances of plays based usually on mythological legend, and occasionally on historical fact. In a Western production, the phrase "the yātrā" could be replaced with an easily comprehensible substitute such as "our plays".

[57] Another untranslatable word, līlā, which suggests a multiplicity of meaning. Literally signifying play, sport, dalliance, amusement or diversion, it also evokes associations of grace, charm, beauty and elegance. However, on the other hand, the word brings with it the awareness that all līlā is mere pretence, appearance, a sham. Sarcastically used, it connotes undesirable

activities (as of politicians). And philosophically, it denotes God's "play", the universe, which in the Hindu world-view constitutes maya, a vast illusion unintelligible to mortals. See p. 174 for another use of *līlā* as "game".

⁵⁸ The *nīlkaṇṭha* or Indian Roller, *Coracias benghalensis*, commonly called the Blue Jay, traditionally released at the end of Durgā Puja. The name literally means "blue-throated", and is one of the appellations of Siva, perhaps significant since "Nandini" applies to Durgā.

⁵⁹ The *dhruva-tārā*, which in Indian culture possesses the same attributes as it does in the West: constant, eternal, immutable, a fixed goal or guide.

⁶⁰ The word *ṭip* indicates the round mark usually of vermilion or saffron worn on the forehead by Indian women either for purely decorative effect, or to distinguish the wearer as belonging to a particular sect or having performed a religious observance. In this case Nandini has obviously worn it for the former reason. It is of consequence to note that the word *rañjan* also refers to saffron.

⁶¹ The *sārengi*, or *sāraṅgī*, is an Indian stringed instrument played with a bow while placed in an upright position.

⁶² "Fortress of Kubera" — one of the most direct references in the play to the fact that Yakshapuri resembles the mythological city of Kubera.

⁶³ In the Bengali, Deputy Sardar literally translates as "Second Sardar", while Assistant Sardar translates as "Little Sardar".

⁶⁴ The word *sevādāsī* means a young, usually Vaishnava, woman dedicated to the service of a temple or deity. Used as an innuendo, however, the word denotes a concubine.

⁶⁵ In Bengali the word *purāṇ* literally means "old" or "ancient", but also refers to the class of Hindu sacred works known as the Puranas, the subject of the Scholar's specialisation.

⁶⁶ The phrase *māyā-mṛigī*, "magic doe" or "doe of illusion", alludes to the *Rāmāyaṇa*, where a deer apparently of gold succeeded in diverting Rama and his brother so that Rāvaṇa could abduct the heroine, Sītā. Thus it came to have the meaning of a dangerous illusion or temptation. Tagore changes the gender of the deer for obvious reasons.

⁶⁷ The word *pretpurī*, "city of spirits", refers specifically to the underworld, the abode of the god Yama.

⁶⁸ The *tāl* or Palmyra Palm, *Borassus flabellifer*, is one of the most common and important of Indian trees; among other things, Indians regard this tall and erect palm species as a measure of height. The evergreen *tamāl* ("dark-barked") tree, *Garcinia xanthochymus*, has a straight trunk and strong, hard wood.

⁶⁹ The third month of the Bengali calendar, corresponding to the second half of June and the first half of July. The term *chaturdaśī* specifies the fourteenth day in a lunar fortnight.

[70] "Locality of Īśānī", the latter being another name for Durgā. This statement provides one more clue to the parallel between Nandini and Durgā.

[71] The word *pralay*, glossed here as "doomsday", defines the Hindu belief in the annihilation of the universe at the end of a *kalpa* (an eon that measures 4,320,000,000 human years and marks the temporal duration of our world). Apocalyptic events accompany *pralay*: a drought continues for a century; seven suns glow in the sky, causing all water to evaporate; firestorms and howling winds ravage the earth; elephant-shaped clouds laced with lightning accumulate and a downpour lasting twelve years floods the planet. Brahma re-creates the world again after a hiatus. A *kalpa* is considered as just one day in the life of Brahma.

[72] Vedic god of the atmosphere and sky, lord of rain. He destroyed with his thunderbolt the demons of darkness, and symbolised altruistic heroism. More than any other god, he became the object of songs and prayers from early Hindus, probably because of his role as bringer of rain and his reputation for providing generous help to mankind. Later he became subordinate to the triad of Brahma, Vishnu and Siva, but still remained the greatest of all other deities in the popular imagination.

[73] The closely-knit society of rural life makes the inhabitants of a village consider themselves virtually members of one family, so that often people within the same rural community address one another as relatives although they are not related.

[74] At this point the Headman probably does prostrate himself fully at the feet of the Sardar. This provides a humorous touch to his own sentence later on decrying flatterers for making *pranāms* obsequiously, and his statements in his next speech about his son's attempts to *pranām* the Sardar.

[75] *Sindur*, vermilion or minium, which a Hindu woman wears in the parting of her hair to signify that her husband is alive.

[76] The semi-mythical *ajagar* ("goat-swallower"), a common Indian name for the Indian Python, *Python molurus*.

[77] Feminine of *rākshas* (see Note 25). "Demoness" might suffice.

[78] The Hindu god who originally ruled over the spirits of deceased forefathers and the dead, in their blissful heavenly abode. He also sentenced the wicked to annihilation or to a dark netherworld. In later mythology he came to be depicted as a terrible deity who presided over hell (heaven having become a reward for virtuous living) and punished sinners with elaborate methods of torture.

[79] From the root *rakshā*, to "protect" or "guard", the word *rākhī* denotes a bracelet or amulet worn as a charm. It specially signifies a piece of thread or silk tied around the wrist, usually by a sister on her brother at a particular annual festival, as a safeguard against all evils, a mark of love and respect, and a symbol of mutual dependence. No English word can adequately convey all its connotations.

TAPATI

[1] I have relied here on information documented by Pulinbihari Sen, *Rabīndra-grantha-pañjī*, vol. 1 (Calcutta: Visvabharati, 1973), pp. 259–60.

[2] Somendranath Basu, pp. 111–26, provides a minute description (in Bengali) of one of the scripts of *Bhairaver Bali*.

[3] Santidev Ghosh, who took part in the production, lists these changes in *Rabīndra-saṅgīt Vichitrā* (Calcutta: Ananda, 1972), pp. 138–57.

[4] Vyāsa, *The Mahābhārata*, trans. P. Lal, vol. 21 (Calcutta: Writers Workshop, 1970), pp. 25–41.

[5] Ibid., p. 28.

[6] Ibid., pp. 39–40.

[7] For the history of the play on the professional stage, I have consulted Harindranath Datta, *Rabīndranāth o Sādhāraṇ Nātyaśālā* (Calcutta: Tagore Research Institute, 1983), passim.

[8] Extracts from reviews have been collected by Amal Mitra, pp. 26–31.

[9] Sushil Mukherjee, p. 545.

[10] Gaganendranath Tagore was primarily responsible for the performance of *Bhairaver Bali*, the revised version Tagore refers to, staged on 27 April.

[11] A long romantic lyric, Kalidasa's *Meghadūta* was one of Tagore's favourite poems. He often referred to it in his literary criticism, and wrote an essay on it in 1891.

[12] Kalidasa's play, regarded unanimously as the zenith of classical Sanskrit literature, influenced Tagore considerably. See his essays on "*Sakuntala*: Its Inner Meaning" and "Kalidas, the Moralist", from which I have quoted in my analysis of *Tapatī* in the section titled "Tagore's Themes" (pp. 53–55).

[13] The spelling used in my text for the names is followed by their standard English transcription in parentheses. The etymologies of the more important names may be worth mentioning. *Sumitrā* literally means "having good friends". On the other hand, *Vikram* means "valour", "power", "force", "heroism". *Nareś* translates as "best amongst men", while *Vipāśā* (literally "untied, unfettered") is the ancient name of the Beas river, one of the five rivers of the Punjab.

[14] The kingdom of Jālandhar, with its capital city of the same name (corresponding to the present town in the state of Punjab), was at its height in the post-Gupta period of Indian history, c. 550–700 A.D. Its location directly south of the Kashmir valley made it one of the more powerful neighbours of the kingdom of Kāśmīr (roughly the present state of Jammu and Kashmir) at that time. As a kingdom, of course, Kashmir outlasted most of its rivals, remaining a strong independent power over many centuries.

[15] The character of Nārāyaṇī existed in the first edition of *Tapatī*, carried over from the dramatis personae of *Rājā o Rānī*. During the course of re-hearsals, however, her role was cut, no doubt to unify the play further by dispensing with the domestic subplot of Debdatta and his wife. Although she does not appear in later editions, her name has remained on the list of characters for the definitive text, probably through some editorial oversight.

[16] "The Terrible", "The Formidable", "The Frightening", Bhairav is the name of Siva in his fearsome aspect as the Destroyer. Siva's violent traits are said to be emphasised in this manifestation.

[17] Tagore added this song to the script nine days before opening night. Santiniketan had just received confirmation that Jatin Das, the revolu-tionary, had died after fasting for nearly two months in the Lahore Jail in Punjab, to protest ill-treatment at the hands of British authorities. The news upset Tagore no end: he could not concentrate on the rehearsal in the evening and eventually had to cancel it. He composed this song the same night. See Santidev Ghosh, *Rabīndra-saṅgīt* (Calcutta: Visvabharati, 1962), pp. 204–5.

[18] "The Great Rudra", name of an awesome manifestation of Siva. Rudra, "The Roarer", was originally the Vedic god of storms, closely associated with Indra and Agni, and later identified with Kāla (Time). He was depicted as a terrible destroyer but also had the epithet *śiva*, "benevolent", which in course of time became another name for him, as he gradually lost his link with storms. By the time of the later mythology Rudra had turned into one of Siva's eight commonly recognised forms. Rudra was also associated with fire, and the mention of flames in this song clearly presages the end of the play.

[19] The word *amṛita*, literally "not dead", alludes specifically to the gods' nectar of immortality produced at the mythical churning of the oceans.

[20] "Fish-bannered", a name of the god of love, Kāma, whose flag bears the emblem of the *makar* fish.

[21] Pañchaśar ("Five-arrowed", because Kāma wields five arrows tipped with flowers) and Kandarpa are both names of Kāma. The story goes that Kāma was vapourised by a fiery flash from Siva's eye, for interrupting Siva's absorption in austerity and celibacy by trying to arouse in him sensual desire for his consort-to-be, Pārvatī. Kalidasa based his long poem *Kumāra-sambhava* on this myth; Tagore refers to it in his essay "Kalidas, the Mora-list".

[22] The *anuṣṭubh* is a Sanskrit metre originally containing four quarter-verses of eight syllables each; later it denoted a class of metres consisting of 4 times 8 syllables. The *triṣṭubh* was a metre of 4 times 11 syllables and later applied to all metres of that length. Bikram suggests that his god is a living god, not confined to the pages of religious scripture. The names of the metres may be replaced by a phrase such as "Sanskrit versification".

[23] A compound of the names Rudra and Bhairav. The use of several

different names for the same god may confuse non-Hindu spectators. A Western director may thus find it practical to convert all occurrences of recondite nomenclature to either Siva or Kāma, whichever is appropriate.

[24] The word in the text, *pināk*, is the name of Siva's mythical bow or trident, which some say symbolises lightning. The "bow of flowers" is a literal translation of *pushpa-dhanu*, alluding to the weapon Kāma carries.

[25] Wife of Kāma and goddess of sexual passion.

[26] The appellation *Vajrapāni*, "thunderbolt in hand", refers to the god Indra, whose sceptre and chief weapon was *Vajra*, the thunderbolt.

[27] Another name for Kāma: see Note 24.

[28] Literally "without body", another name for Kāma, derived from the myth that Siva burnt him to ashes. There is a triple play on "body" in this line.

[29] Maheśvar, "the great god", is a name given to various gods, but most commonly to Siva. Madan is the name of Kāma.

[30] Literally "bodiless", another name for Kāma.

[31] "Conqueror of death", a name of Siva, the "immortal one".

[32] The *antahpur* or "inner chamber" signifies that portion of a palace where the women reside, forbidden to strangers. Debdatta implies that Bikram fritters away most of his time there.

[33] The term *rājlakshmī* refers to the good fortune of a king, personified as a female deity who safeguards the kingdom and makes it prosper.

[34] Bikram alludes to the episode in the *Rāmāyana* when Rama reluctantly exiled his wife Sītā because his subjects doubted her chastity.

[35] Kurukshetra, in the present state of Haryana, was the site of the epic internecine battle that forms the core of the *Mahābhārata*. As a result, the word has come to indicate any terrible battle or fight, or even a rowdy brawl.

[36] Literally "goddess", this form of respectful address is directed to any venerable woman. The closest English equivalent, "lady", has connotations of social class absent in the Indian word, but it may be employed here.

[37] The word *vidūshak* specifically indicates the stock character of clown in classical Sanskrit drama. Lakshmī is the goddess of fortune and beauty.

[38] The "king of seasons", *riturāj*, is a metaphor for the spring.

[39] The *bakul*, often known as the Indian Medlar, is the evergreen tree *Mimusops elengi*. It usually blooms in the spring and summer, producing dull-white, star-shaped, scented flowers used in making garlands.

[40] The Mānas lake, now in Tibet, is a sacred lake and place of pilgrimage for Hindus, situated at the foot of Mount Kailās, the mythical home of Siva.

[41] The word *pitrivya* strictly means "paternal uncle". Others, later in the play, call Chandrasen *khuro-mahārāj*, literally "paternal uncle-maharaja"; I have converted this latter term to "Regent" wherever it occurs.

[42] "Lord of Kailās", another of Siva's names. Mount Kailās, in the outer range of the Himalayas in Tibet, is the mythical location of Siva's heaven.

⁴³ The word *chhāyā-path*, "shadow-path", is the name given to the Milky Way galaxy in Bengali.

⁴⁴ One of the best known of Indian trees, the Siris, *Albizzia lebbek*, is large, with spreading branches and sweet-scented pink or greenish-white flowers.

⁴⁵ Makar-ketan, or Makar-ketu, "*makar*-bannered", are names of Kāma, derived from the emblem of the aquatic creature, the *makar*, on his flag.

⁴⁶ Literally "produced by heat", *tapasyā* is an important concept in Hinduism, representing devout and severe austerities, asceticism and self-discipline. This activity, if practised correctly, is supposed to engender tremendous *tapas*, "heat", approximating the power of creative cosmic energy. Siva is its prototypical practitioner. To suggest performance alternatives is difficult, "asceticism" being perhaps the best of many weak possibilities.

⁴⁷ The sacrificial fire into which symbolic offerings are made is the most important component of Hindu wedding ceremonies. Sumitra's remark that "there's no end to the oblations" strikes an ominous note.

⁴⁸ Literally "deity" or "lord", the respectful term *ṭhākur* is commonly used to address Brahmans. "Priest" may serve as an English substitute, though the Brahman thus addressed may or may not be a priest.

⁴⁹ A *yojana* is a measure of distance equivalent to four *krośas*, or roughly nine miles. The word "miles" is a sufficient alternative.

⁵⁰ The Bengali compound is *pārishad-varga*, "courtier-group", but the word *pārishad* implies a courtier who fawns and flatters, a toady.

⁵¹ The *satya*-yuga is the first of the four ages in the history of the world according to Hindu myth, during which period everything was supposedly perfect. "Golden Age" would be a fairly accurate rendition in English. The term *Rām-rājatva*, "kingdom of Rama" (more often *Rām-rājya*, "reign of Rama"), alludes to the rule of Rama as depicted in the *Rāmāyaṇa*—a rule so unblemished that these terms came to bear the meaning of an ideal realm. So as to retain a figurative association, one could use an English word such as "Utopia".

⁵² The eleventh month of the Bengali calendar, corresponding to the second half of February and the first half of March.

⁵³ The bird here is the *kokil*, the onomatopoeic name for the Indian Koel, *Eudynamys scolopacea*. One of the commonest of Indian birds, the Koel belongs to the cuckoo family, and is a ubiquitous presence in Indian art. Because its distinctive musical cry rising to a crescendo supposedly arouses tender emotions, it frequently finds a place in love poetry. But sceptics would say it calls ad nauseam, especially since in the spring it is often at its most vociferous during the night and before the dawn.

⁵⁴ Satī is the name of an incarnation of Durgā, Siva's consort. She put an end to herself by undergoing austerities because of an insult to Siva, her husband (later tradition has it that she immolated herself). Siva's grief at

her death reached such a dangerous frenzy that Vishnu finally had to cut her corpse into fifty-two pieces and scatter them all over India for Siva to come to his senses. The phrase *Satī-tīrtha*, "shrine to Satī", thus denotes any of the fifty-two places of pilgrimage where these pieces are said to have fallen. Satī's name became synonymous with the model of an ideal wife; in Sanskrit it sometimes refers to a female ascetic, but in common later usage (anglicised to "suttee") it identifies the faithful widow who burns herself on her husband's funeral pyre. Ratneshwar alludes to such an incident in his next sentence. The mentions of Satī gradually accumulate dramatic irony in this play, with forebodings of the conclusion. The first such instance was in the dialogue between Naresh and Bipasha (p. 204), where the latter calls Sumitra "the perfect wife". The original phrase there was *Satī-lakshmī*, meaning a wife devoted to her husband who also brings him good fortune.

⁵⁵ Literally "fire", Agni is the name of the god of fire. A very important Vedic god, he assumed the role of divine intermediary between gods and mortals since all sacrificial fires symbolised him. Debdatta alludes to one of Agni's attributes, that he remained pure whatever he consumed, and also purified impure offerings in the process of "eating" them. In later Hinduism this purifying aspect of Agni became most important, and he is honoured during all serious Hindu ceremonies, for instance those marking marriage or death.

⁵⁶ Literally "religion", "morality", "virtue", "justice", Dharma is Law or Justice personified. A relatively new god, his rise parallels the emphasis placed by later Hinduism on duty and virtue as the paths to salvation.

⁵⁷ The term *pāp-graha* refers to any inauspicious star or planet in Indian astrology, such as Śani (Saturn) or Rāhu (the cause of eclipses).

⁵⁸ The twelfth month of the Bengali calendar, corresponding to the second half of March and the first half of April.

⁵⁹ One of the ten seminal ragas of north Indian music, *bhairavī* is among the most popular modes in both folk and classical styles. A heptatonic scale, it uses flats for the second, third, sixth and seventh notes (D,E,A and B). It is an early morning raga, though tradition requires that musicians conclude any performance with a composition set to *bhairavī*. It evokes a tranquil, pensive mood often devotional in nature.

⁶⁰ Another of Kāma's names. Kalindi is punning on the word *man*, "mind".

⁶¹ The major Vedic deities. Sūrya ("sun") was the name of the sun-god, brother of Indra and Agni, forming with them the original Vedic triad: he reigned in the heavens, Indra in the atmosphere, and Agni on earth. He lost his prominence in later mythology, but retained some honour as a benefactor of man. Varuṇa was in earliest times considered the supreme deity, the Prime Mover; he created the universe and preserved it, possessed omnipotence and omniscience, judged and punished sinners. From this preeminent

position he gradually fell as divine spheres of influence were delegated to other gods; he gained suzerainty over the oceans, becoming a Hindu counterpart of Neptune.

[62] The last and worst of Hinduism's four ages, the *kali*-yuga is the age of vice, said to have begun on 18 February 3102 B.C. At the end of this yuga the world is destroyed. Physical and moral deterioration of man characterises each successive yuga in the Hindu time-cycle. Thus, in the *kali*-yuga, men suffer from natural calamities, military conflicts and oppressive rulers; they themselves are wicked and degenerate, and inhabit towns populated by thieves; their women are gossipy and promiscuous, and bear too many children. "The present age" is perhaps an appropriate English equivalent, if juxtaposed with the term "the golden age".

[63] Manjari makes an alliterative pun here at the expense of Kalindi's name, which is also a name for the river Yamuna. She speaks of Kalindi's *kala-kallol*, an onomatopoeic compound meaning "murmur-roar", particularly of water or waves.

[64] The *namaskār* is the traditional Hindu method of greeting, with the palms of the hand joined together in front of the chest. Tagore took this couplet from the *Subhāshita-ratna-bhāndāgāra*, perhaps the most widely known anthology of Sanskrit epigrams.

[65] Śaurasenī was a Prakrit dialect spoken in Mathura, in the present state of Uttar Pradesh; in Sanskrit plays it was occasionally used for the speech of upper-class women. Māgadhī and Ardha-māgadhī were also regional Prakrit dialects, peculiar to Magadha, an area in the present state of Bihar. The former was the language of the Magadha people, the latter the language of Jain sacred literature. Mahārāshtrī was the language of Maharashtra, the state in western India, and survives as the modern language Marathi. The word Yāvanik, "Ionian", refers to the variety of Greek spoken in the Indo-Greek kingdoms bordering northwest India at this time in history.

[66] There is an obvious play here on *tanu*, "body", and the name Atanu, "The Bodiless". The crux of the conversation is that Kāma is a much newer god than the Vedic divinities mentioned. However it is not true that he is absent from the Vedas — he exists in them as a creative force, usually in conjunction with another god like Agni.

[67] The terms *śruti* and *smriti* can be easily translated as their literal meanings, "hearing" and "memory" respectively. Indeed, a Western director may find it necessary to insert these simplified renderings. But the words have specific definitions as well: *śruti* indicates the revealed knowledge of Hinduism orally transmitted by generations of Brahmans, thus incorporating the Vedas and Upanishads; and *smriti* represents sacred tradition handed down in writing, thereby including such works as the Puranas, the two epic poems, the Sutras and the laws of Manu.

[68] Tribedi exclaims "Oh how marvellous!" in Sanskrit. The gloss "scholar"

does not convey the original adequately. Tribedi uses the words *śruti-bhūshaṇ* and *smriti-ratnākar*, the second halves of which mean "ornament" and "jewel-mine" respectively. It was customary in royal durbars to decorate scholars of the court with such titles as a mark of honour and respect.

69 The *tretā*-yuga was the second of the four ages of the world, a "silver age" as it were. Tribedi alludes to events in the *Rāmāyaṇa*, which is supposed to have taken place during this yuga: the *rākshasas* in Laṅkā (enemies of Rama) had set fire to the tail of Hanumān, general of the *vānaras* (a tribe of semi-divine creatures resembling monkeys, allies of Rama). But he escaped and with his tail still ablaze, leapt from building to building, eventually torching the whole city. On another occasion, in the course of the war between these two camps, the *vānaras* undertook a nighttime foray into Laṅkā and once again set the city on fire.

70 The presiding deity of *kali*-yuga, Kali is the personification of strife, discord and conflict. He is supposedly the son of Anger and Malice, and has two children, Fear and Death.

71 Pratyanta-deś, literally "neighbouring land", is sometimes identified as an old name for Tibet

72 The word *dharma-rakshā*, literally "defence of religion", also connotes in certain contexts (as here) the protection of women's chastity.

73 Kālī (not to be confused with Kali) is the most terrifying manifestation of the goddess Durgā. Associated with dark rituals and blood sacrifices, she is portrayed as having black skin and a tongue dripping with the blood of demons; she carries on her person their severed hands and heads. Her victorious dance was so destructive that it endangered the stability of the world and Siva, her husband, finally stopped her by letting himself be trampled by her: she realised what she had done and ceased her deadly dance. The root meaning of *kālī* is "black", and the word also suggests "disgrace" or "defamation".

74 The word *vibhīshikā* literally means an act of terrifying, or a means of terror. In common usage it applies to a hallucination or fearful sight, but can also suggest a threat or intimidation. Bikram uses the word in all its senses, with specific reference to his own allusion to Kālī.

75 Śaṅkar is another name for Siva. The *tāṇḍava* is Siva's wild dance of annihilation which signals the end of the temporal world. Because destruction forms the necessary prelude to the creation of the next cycle of yugas in the Hindu scheme of time, Siva's dance is considered as much creative as it is destructive. It is ironic that Bikram, who has so far denigrated Siva, alludes to Siva's mythologically powerful role in this line. Although the concept may remain unclear, a possible translation is "Siva's wild dance".

76 The *apsarās* form a class of female divinities who inhabited Indra's heaven. Originally conceived of as water nymphs, they were promoted to their celestial position in later mythology. They are very beautiful, excep-

tionally talented in singing and dancing, and can change their shape at will. Bikram contrasts their pleasurable dances with Siva's frenzied dance of annihilation. The word *apsarā* is usually Englished as "nymph".

[77] Bikram mentions three Hindu theological concepts here: *mukti*, "freedom", signifies release from worldly attachments; *pralay*, "destruction", indicates the dissolution of the world at the end of a *kalpa*; and *yugāntar*, "a new epoch", refers to the subsequent re-creation of the universe by Brahma the Creator as the next cycle of yugas commences.

[78] The name here, Mārtanda, specifically identifies the rising sun (the sun has different phases, each originally personified as a deity). But in general use nowadays the name has become synonymous with the sun.

[79] Actually Siva has the third eye, in the centre of his forehead. One of his most potent weapons, it can emanate flames with which Siva carries out his role as Destroyer. He also turns it on those who annoy him, such as Kāma.

[80] Rāmchandra is the full name of Rama, hero of the *Rāmāyaṇa* and seventh avatar of Vishnu. Rama belonged to the solar race of kings, as opposed to the other great line of kings, the lunar dynasty, which included Krishna, the eighth avatar. The solar dynasty traced its genealogy to Sūrya, the sun-god; many Rajput royal families still claim descent from this line, as does the dynastic line of Kashmir, whose emblem is the sun — a fact which becomes more significant later in the play, when the link between Sumitra and the sun grows deeper. Even here, irony surfaces in the fact that Sumitra is the greater devotee of the sun. Bikram argues that he can exile her just as Rama exiled his queen, Sītā.

[81] The prince Dhruva represents the model of single-minded steadfastness in Hindu mythology on account of his incomparable devotion to Vishnu. He became immortalised as the pole star because of his constancy. A shrine to Dhruva adjoins the temple to the sun at Mārtanda, where Sumitra is headed.

[82] The word *sudhā-samudra*, "sea of nectar", alludes to the myth of the nectar of immortality produced by the churning of the oceans.

[83] The name Nandan is often used as a generic term for any divine garden, but it specifically denotes the most important among them, Indra's heaven.

[84] Literally "spring-flower", the *mādhavī* (*Hiptage madablota*) is a common Indian climbing shrub bearing fragrant white blossoms tinged with yellow.

[85] The tree *Butea monosperma*, a familiar sight on the Indian plains. Its brilliant orange and scarlet flowers cover the leafless branches in spring.

[86] The compound *godhūli-lagna* literally means "cow-dust moment", indicating the time when herds return from pasture, raising clouds of dust in their wake.

[87] The idea of *viraha* is important in Indian poetry. While the word literally means "absence" or "desertion", it is used almost exclusively to suggest separation from a lover and the melancholy accompanying such a state.

[88] The *jabā* is the Common Hibiscus or China Rose, *Hibiscus rosa-sinensis*, a garden shrub with large, vivid, usually crimson flowers. The *kanak-chāṁpā* is a tall evergreen tree, *Pterospermum acerifolium*, with large fragrant white flowers. The *aśok* is the Asoka tree, *Saraca indica*, bearing clusters of small delicately scented reddish-orange flowers. An important sacred tree, it is a symbol of love for Hindus (its name means "sorrowless"), dedicated to Kāma who uses its flower as one of the blossoms for his five arrows. A common conceit in Sanskrit poetry describes the sensitivity of the tree which, when touched by a beautiful woman, blushes and bursts into flower. Buddhists revere the tree too because the Buddha was supposedly born under its shade. The *aśvattha* is the Pipal, *Ficus religiosa*, a large spreading tree sacred to both Hindus and Buddhists, the latter because the *bo* tree at Buddh Gaya beneath which the Buddha received enlightenment was a pipal. Its destruction is considered a sin. All these trees bloom in spring and their flowers are used in religious ceremonies, except for the pipal which bears figs.

[89] Naṭarāj ("king of dance") is a name for Siva derived from his dance of destruction at the time of *pralay* (here translated as "doomsday"). Siva's dances — whether joyous or destructive — symbolise cosmic rhythm and the never-ending cyclical movement of the universe. He is depicted as having matted locks because of his identity as the supreme ascetic.

[90] The song alludes to the mythical descent of the river Gaṅgā to earth. When she was forced to descend, Siva broke her fall by collecting the water in his hair. The thick matted locks separated her into seven different streams, confusing and weakening Gaṅgā, but creating India's main rivers. On her way to the ocean she was swallowed by the sage Jahnu for flooding his garden; but he later relented and released her from his ear, thereby giving her the name Jāhnavī ("daughter of Jahnu"), the appellation used in the song.

[91] The *tarāī* region of the Himalayas is a belt of marshes and jungles in the foothills spanning the southern slopes of the entire mountain range. The word "foothills" could be substituted by a Western director.

[92] As part of their regalia, Indian kings traditionally had an open decorated ceremonial umbrella positioned over their thrones. This royal umbrella, like the western crown, developed into a metonym of kingly power.

[93] The Deodar or Himalayan Cedar, *Cedrus deodara*, is a very common tree of the western Himalayas. But in using the word *devdāru* Tagore probably had in mind the tree that Bengalis call by that name, popularly known as the Mast tree, *Polyalthia longifolia*, the leaves of which Hindus use to adorn pillars and doorways on festive occasions such as weddings.

[94] Gaṇeśa, Siva's son, is among the most popular of Hindu gods. Patron of wisdom, learning and success, he creates obstacles but also removes them; for this reason he is invoked at the start of any endeavour. Hindu iconography portrays him as having an elephant's head (some say to represent sagacity) and riding on, or being accompanied by, a rat — hence the joke here.

[95] The *ākhroṭ* is the Common Walnut tree, *Juglans regia*, widely found in Himalayan forests.

[96] Another name for the Jhelum river, which rises in Kashmir.

[97] Literally, the name means "cane-wielder", and signifies a female guard or doorkeeper. A director could consider adding after the name its literal meaning, as in "Vetravatī, the cane-wielder. . . ".

[98] A female Saiva ascetic, derived from Bhairavī, the name of Siva's consort when he takes on the aspect of Bhairav. "Ascetic" should suffice

[99] The term here, *bhāsur-jhi*, specifically refers to the daughter of an elder brother of one's husband.

[100] For the myth of Tapatī, see my introductory Note on the play (pp. 189–92). The name is derived from *tapas* (see Note 46), thus connoting purification by means of ascetic austerities: suffering pain, practising penance, undergoing self-mortification. The root Sanskrit word *tapa* means "to emit heat", "to shine", or "to destroy by heat" — which becomes significant at the play's end.

[101] Literally "one-stringed", the name given to any instrument consisting of a single string stretched over a sound box; Bengalis associate it chiefly with Vaishnava singers and folk singers such as the Bāuls. An appropriate descriptive gesture accompanying the word could convey its sense to a Western audience.

[102] Literally "best amongst men", thereby retaining in this pseudonym the root meaning of Naresh's real name.

[103] The Bengali word is *uttarīya*, which refers to a light outer garment draped across the shoulders and covering the upper torso, similar to a stole.

[104] The *āṭchālā*, "eight-roofed", defines an open structure with eight levels of thatch ceiling but no walls.

[105] A *bhaṇitā* is the conventional way of indicating authorship of a poem: the opening or (usually) closing line incorporates the composer's name.

[106] A village by this name exists in Doda district, to the south of the Mārtaṇḍa ruins. In lexicons, one meaning of the word *bharata* is a barbarian, specifically a mountaineer; the First Man, of course, works in the mountains.

[107] The word here is *bon-jhi*, specifically the daughter of one's sister.

[108] "Thunderbolt in hand", an epithet of the god Indra: see Note 26.

[109] Bipasha observes that her namesake, the present river Beas, flows into the Sindhu, the Indian name for the river Indus, perhaps the only major river regarded by Hindus as masculine. Geographically, however, she is wrong: the Beas is a tributary of the river Sutlej, which eventually meets the Indus.

[110] The word here is *hiṁsā* which, apart from its meanings of "malice" and "spite", also carries its original connotations of "killing" or "slaughter". In addition, loosely used nowadays, it expresses "envy" or "jealousy".

[111] The Mārtaṇḍa temple, sixty kilometres southeast of Srinagar in Kashmir, is a well-known place of pilgrimage. The temple to the sun here,

usually dated to the 8th century, counts among the oldest Hindu temples still standing, and remained a very important shrine up to the 12th century. Tagore visited it on a vacation in October 1915; presumably it impressed him enough to warrant his inclusion of it as the locale for this scene. Other observers too, such as the *Gazetteer of Kashmir and Ladak* (Delhi: Vivek, 1974), p. 592, speak of its stately architecture: "Occupying undoubtedly the finest position in Kashmir, this noble ruin is the most striking in size and situation of all the existing remains of Kashmir grandeur. The temple itself is not now more than 40 feet in height, but its solid walls and bold outlines, towering over the fluted pillars of the surrounding colonnade, give it a most imposing appearance." This book calls the temple "the wonder of Kashmir".

[112] A Sanskrit hymn to the sun, from the *Rig-Veda* (I:50:1–2).

[113] The word *mātā-mahī* specifically refers to a maternal grandmother.

[114] Literally "flame-mouthed", a celebrated shrine in the hills northeast of Jalandhar where a perpetual fire exists, fed by subterranean gas. The spot is revered as one of the fifty-two places in India where parts of Satī fell (see Note 54). According to other lore, Satī set herself on fire there. The dramatic irony here is two-fold, because the place of pilgrimage is sacred to Siva, whom Bikram earlier had rejected; and because the legend of Satī's self-immolation there foreshadows the conclusion of the play.

[115] Debdatta alludes to the episode in the *Rāmāyaṇa* when Hanumān, chief of the *vānaras* (see Note 69), infiltrated the city of *rākshasas*, Laṅkā, with the aim of locating Sītā, held captive by them. He found her in a grove of *aśok* trees, but was himself captured there after a brave fight. Hanumān is a popular mythological figure in India because of his loyalty to Rama.

[116] "King of justice", a name of the god of death, Yama, derived from his role as judge of the dead. This name should not be confused with that of the comparatively new god Dharma, whose nomenclature it predates.

[117] The word *saṅkalpa*, while usually meaning "resolution" or "determination", suggests in the context of religious worship, a vow to undertake something, solemnised particularly on the eve of a ritual.

[118] Ordinarily meaning "ignorance" or "delusion", the concept of *moha* in Hindu philosophy implies ignorance about the true nature of things, a state of mind which prevents the perception of truth and deludes men into believing in the reality of worldly life and material objects. In addition, *moha* commonly suggests both dotage and deep attachment, aptly fitting Shankar's character.

[119] The term *hriday-kamal*, "heart-lotus", refers to a poetic and artistic conceit which conventionally depicts the heart in the form of a lotus.

[120] The word *para-pār*, literally "other shore", also carries connotations of the "next world", the world beyond death.

[121] A Sanskrit couplet to the sun, from the *Rig-Veda* (I:115:6).

[122] A Sanskrit couplet from the *Atharva-Veda* (XIX:9:14). It mentions the

three worlds of Vedic cosmology — the earth, the "intermediary" region or the skies, and the heavens — and concludes with the traditional coda to a Hindu mantra or religious work, the word *śāntiḥ* ("peace") repeated three times.

[123] In the context of religious ritual, the word *pradakshin* defines a clockwise circumambulation round an altar or an object of worship. Amita Tagore, who created the role of Sumitra, recalls that the stage was darkened for this scene while lights in the wings simulated flames, some of the effect projecting on to the backdrop. The "music" was mostly of drums, which stopped as soon as Bikram entered. Apparently his expression as he realised what had happened "cannot be described in words" (Amita Tagore, interview).

[124] A Sanskrit verse from the *Īśā Upanishad* (18), one of the works of the Vedic period that exerted a profound influence upon Tagore.

FORMLESS JEWEL

[1] For publication history, I have relied on the notes to the definitive texts of these plays, in Tagore's *Rabīndra-Rachanāvalī* (Visvabharati), 10:648. 13:537–38, and 22:506. An incomplete manuscript and press copy of the 1935 *Arūp Ratan* have been printed in *Rabīndra-vīkshā*, Paush 1383, pp. 47–97.

[2] Rajendralala Mitra, *The Sanskrit Buddhist Literature of Nepal* (Calcutta: Sanskrit Pustak Bhandar, 1971). My references are to this reprint edition.

[3] Ibid., pp. 139–41.

[4] Tagore, *Rabīndra Rachanāvalī* (Govt. of West Bengal), 4:185.

[5] Mukhopadhyay, 2:315. Chakrabarti (1995) has pinpointed the date.

[6] For an enthusiastic eyewitness account, see Sita Devi, *Puṇya-smṛiti* (Calcutta: Maitri, 1964), p. 19.

[7] For the stage history of *Śāpmochan* I have relied on Santidev Ghosh, *Gurudev*, pp. 102–55. All of my subsequent notes which mention Santidev Ghosh refer to the chapter on *Arūp Ratan* (pp. 174–76) in this book.

[8] For extracts from press notices, see Pranaykumar Kundu, *Rabīndranāther Gītināṭya o Nṛityanāṭya* (Calcutta: Orient Book, 1965), pp. 372–75.

[9] Probhat Kumar Mukherji, p. 184. The statement is confirmed by newspaper reviews of the play; for samples from reviews, see *Visva-Bharati News* 4 (January 1936):55.

[10] The word *var-mālya* refers specifically to the garland of flowers which an Indian bride places round the groom's neck during their marriage ceremony, symbolising her acceptance of him as husband. The phrase also suggests a garland of high honour.

[11] Tagore did not compile a dramatis personae for this play. I have given first the names of the characters as spelt in my translation, followed by their English transliterations in parentheses. As with most of Tagore's plays, the etymology of some names is of interest. Sudarshana's name means "beauti-

ful", or more precisely, "lovely to look at"; it also has the generic meaning of "woman"—she represents, after all, the character of everyman. The name of Subarna, the impostor, literally means "bright in colour" but is now used almost exclusively as a synonym for gold, bringing to mind the adage about all that glitters. The names of the three rajas, all compound words, provide clues to their physical attributes: Basusen's name means "excellent commander (of an army)"; Bijaybarma's, "wearing a victorious coat of armour"; and Bikrambahu's, "having strong arms". The word *vikram*, of course, indicates all of the following: strength, power, valour, heroism. The word *thākurdā*—like so many of the familial terms used as forms of address in Indian social custom—defines a paternal grandfather but is also employed, as in this case, to address respectfully any elderly man.

[12] In his account of the 1935 production Santidev Ghosh writes that Tagore replaced this song with another one more suited to dancing, for he wished to start the play with a dance. The other song, about nature, begins with the line "I will not leave out anything"; but the song in the text is perhaps more apposite to the theme of the play. It emphasises the appeal to man of visual stimuli: the noun *chokh*, "eyes", occurs four times (the word "sight" in the first line is actually *chokh*) while forms of the verb *dekhā*, "to see", "to look", occur an equal number of times as well.

[13] The phrase here is *rūper hāte*, literally "in a market of *rūp*": see my Note on the play, p. 267, for the significance of this word. But figuratively the phrase signifies "abundance" or "plenty". The related word *arūp* surfaces again in line 9 of the song; I have again rendered it as "formless".

[14] The phrase *sudhā-sāgar*, "nectar-sea", alludes to the nectar of the gods created by the mythical churning of the oceans.

[15] The word *varan* suggests a ceremonial welcome or reception, as in the invocation of a god or the acceptance of a partner in marriage. It carries the association of humility on the part of the one who receives — a concept that soon becomes significant in this play. Surangama's phrase "welcome-tray" a few speeches later is a translation of *varan-dālā*, usually a wicker tray containing articles used ceremonially to welcome the honoured person.

[16] Here the word is *arghya*, specifically the gifts or offerings (originally also sacrifices) with which a god or honoured person is received.

[17] The phrase *khelā ghar*, literally "play room", applies to a dollhouse or similar structure built by children for play; but metaphorically it implies mankind's playroom: our earthly life. Tagore stresses the word *khelā*, "game", by employing it in lines 2 and 7 as well.

[18] The word here is *chhanda*, really "rhythm" or "metre", but also "desire", "inclination", "propensity", "manner" or "behaviour".

[19] The *vasanta-utsav*, "spring-festival", refers to the Hindu festival of *holi* or *dol* observed on the full-moon day in Phālgun (February-March), marking the advent of the vernal equinox and commonly associated with

Krishna. Tagore initiated an annual tradition in Santiniketan of performing a play at this time, and he prepared the first edition of this play expressly for the 1920 festivities. In this context it must be remembered that, unlike the two other plays I have translated, the present play is suffused with a spirit of optimism and celebration, perhaps characteristic of this season.

[20] The noun here is *ras*, which of course means everything from "flavour" to "essence", and in literary usage often suggests a deep love or attachment.

[21] In accordance with the Hindu belief in reincarnation, the compound *janma-janmāntar* denotes one's present life as well as the lives that preceded it and will succeed it.

[22] In this sense the word *pañcham*, "fifth", signifies the fifth note (G) of a C-major scale: as a mnemonic device, Indian musicology identifies this note with the pitch of a Koel's call; consequently *pañcham* also means "the Koel's note". The Koel becomes especially vociferous when spring approaches. The periodic references to the flute in this play might suggest to Hindu viewers the presence of Krishna, whom iconography depicts as playing this instrument; the image would not be inappropriate because *holi* is dedicated to Krishna.

[23] The "red powder" here is known as *phāg*, which revellers during *holi* smear on and throw at one another. Most lexicographers trace the etymology of both this word and the month Phālgun to the Sanskrit *phalgu*, "reddish". Red, however, is not the only colour in evidence at this popular festival — powder and coloured water of all hues are used, symbolising the return of spring in all its glory. Scholars generally ascribe the origins of *holi* to ancient fertility rituals, but most important in its observance now is the aspect of joyous merrymaking which sometimes reaches saturnalian levels, since on this day social inhibitions are suspended.

[24] Santidev Ghosh recalls that Tagore used one of his own songs about the arrival of spring to open this scene in the 1935 performance. The song, which begins "Oh bring whatever you may have,/ The breeze of giving blows on every side," was accompanied by dancing.

[25] This exclamation addressing the popular deity Rama often conveys disgust or abhorrence; in this case it expresses Birajdatta's revulsion at having to meet so many strangers whose social background is unknown to him. Tagore thus has a dig at the rigidities of the Hindu caste system.

[26] "One who knows the *śāstras*", a title given to someone — usually a Brahman — well-versed in the Hindu sacred texts. Again, Tagore debunks some of the narrow stipulations of orthodox Hinduism, which he considered meaningless. Words such as "Brahman" or "priest" could be used as a performance substitute.

[27] The tree *Buchanania latifolia*, characterised by dark grey, almost black, bark. Its small, profuse flowers are greenish-white in colour, and like the other plants mentioned in this song, it blooms in spring.

[28] According to Santidev Ghosh, Tagore was concerned that his voice would not carry while singing Thakurda's songs in the 1935 production. He therefore enlisted the services of Santidev Ghosh as one of his Followers, and asked him to lend his voice to the songs. Both this song and the next ("We are all rajas") owed a great deal in their delivery to Santidev Ghosh.

[29] Santidev Ghosh took the role of the Bāul in the 1935 performance. He remembers that he danced in the typical whirling style of the Bāuls while singing this song, with *ektārā* in hand. The song is based on a common Bāul melody, and its metaphysical lyrics too resemble those of the Bāuls.

[30] The word *nayantārā*, "star of the eye", refers specifically to the pupil, but figuratively also denotes somebody or something specially dear. The Bengali personal pronouns in this song provide no clue as to the gender of the "person" in question; hence my use of "he" and "him" may be misleading.

[31] "Flame of the Forest" is the popular English name for the *kiṁśuk* tree (*Butea monosperma*). In February-March its leafless branches become inundated with showy clusters of orange and scarlet flowers; according to botanists it looks from a distance "like fire on the horizon", hence its English name. The flowers yield a yellow dye used in making powder for *holi*, and the tree is associated with spring. Sacred to Brahma, its trifoliate leaves are considered an emblem of the Hindu triad, and poets love to allude to it.

[32] The term here is *śūnya-kumbha*, literally "empty pitcher", which used in a derogatory vein implies a worthless person, without any depth. Of course the obvious pun on Kumbha's name is impossible to duplicate in English.

[33] The phrase *khur-śvaśur* specifically identifies the younger brother of one's father-in-law, thus an uncle-in-law.

[34] In Hindu astrology, Maghā and Aśleshā are two of the twenty-seven *nakshatras* or lunar "mansions", asterisms through which the moon passes. Both are regarded as inauspicious. The third item, *tryaha-sparśa*, defines the conjunction of three lunar days in one solar (calendar) day. A phrase such as "inauspicious stars" could replace this list for the sake of clarity on stage.

[35] A mark of contrition or undergoing punishment.

[36] The phrase *nanir putul*, literally "doll of cream", is also applied ironically sometimes to a fragile person unable to endure hard work. But here it emphasises the person's good looks and the delicacy of his features.

[37] A kind of wine prepared from rice or jackfruit, mixed with the juice of dates or palms, and distilled.

[38] The refrain *tā-tā thai-thai* is repeated thrice after each of the following lines in this song: 1, 2, 5 and 8. This rhythmical chant of sounds symbolises and accompanies (in myth) Siva's *tāṇḍava* dance. Both song and refrain suggest the continuity inherent in the cyclical rhythm of life.

[39] As in the case of the Bāul's earlier song in the previous scene, Santidev

Ghosh (who played the role) recalls that he danced in the distinctive Bāul style while singing this song.

⁴⁰ In the 1935 production, Tagore cut this exchange between Thakurda and the Bāul, as well as the song immediately succeeding it.

⁴¹ The phrase here is *hṛit-kamal*, referring to the common poetic conceit that conventionally represents the heart in the shape of a lotus.

⁴² Here "fine robe" is a gloss for *uttarīya*, which indicates a light outer garment draped across the shoulders and covering the upper torso, like a stole. The word had occurred previously in line 16 of the song "The southern gate is open now" (p. 283), where I translated it as "scarf".

⁴³ The word *hutāśan*, meaning "oblation-eater", is also used to address the god of fire, Agni, but in modern usage can mean just a fire in general.

⁴⁴ Santidev Ghosh recounts that in the 1935 performance this scene had ended with a song, "I won't return, I won't return again" (with which Tagore had concluded his earlier play *Prāyaśchitta*). Sudarshana made her exit in the style of dance-drama, employing mudras, to the accompaniment of this song.

⁴⁵ In the time frame of *Rājā*, the subsequent episodes occur about a fortnight after the full-moon festivities of the play's first half. During the intervening period Sudarshana leaves, arrives at her father's capital in Kānyakubja, and war ensues between him and the contending kings who seek her hand—scenes eliminated by Tagore for *Arūp Ratan*, in his continuing quest to pare the original play down to its essentials.

⁴⁶ Ashṭāvakra was a Brahman renowned for his scintillating wit: his story is related in the third book of the *Mahābhārata*. The Third Citizen quotes in Sanskrit here and is about to translate when the Second Citizen interrupts.

⁴⁷ *Tarkaratna* is a title commonly given to Sanskrit pandits well-versed in philosophy, and *pārā* means "locality". The Second Citizen takes offence here because he knows Sanskrit: he claims he is constantly exposed to the *anusvar* and *visarga*, two characters in Indian alphabets that are most frequently used in Sanskrit, and which I have translated as "um" and "uh" respectively, approximating their sounds. The word "syllable" is my gloss for the Bengali word for "dot" (the written symbols of *anusvar* and *visarga* feature one and two dots respectively).

⁴⁸ The First Citizen alludes to events in the epic poem. Rāvaṇa was king of the *rākshasas*, ruler of Laṅkā, and traditionally depicted as having ten heads and twenty arms. A personification of evil in Hindu mythology, his wickedness had no limits. He abducted Rama's wife Sītā, which eventually led to war between his forces and those of Rama. The term *Laṅkā-kāṇḍa*, "affair in Laṅkā", is also a title given to Book Six of the *Rāmāyaṇa*, which narrates the war, while in figurative use it denotes an unruly melee or brawl.

⁴⁹ The five Pāndava brothers, heroes of the *Mahābhārata*, had one wife,

Draupadī. Arjuna alone had won her hand in marriage, but because their mother enjoined him on his return to share whatever he had won with his brothers, Draupadī became their common wife. In his next speech, the First Citizen puns on *pati*, "husband", and *nṛipati*, "king".

[50] Vyāsa is the name given to the mythical sage regarded as the original composer of the *Mahābhārata* and compiler of other works, such as the Vedas (he is also known as Veda-Vyāsa, the appellation used in the text). The term "five-pennyworth" is a rendering of *pāñch-kari*, literally "five cowries", the cowrie shell being at one time legal tender of the smallest denomination. It indicates pejoratively someone ineffectual, or of insignificant worth.

[51] The word for "mother", often used to address a girl or woman dear to the speaker, but also regularly applied to one of higher rank; Surangama's new tone of address should reflect a certain change in Sudarshana.

[52] The phrase *agni-mūrti*, "fiery image", is generally used metaphorically to connote a furious mood or appearance characterised by anger or wrath.

[53] The word here is *purush*, which literally means "man", but in philosophy refers to the life-principle in man (roughly equivalent to the soul or spirit), which in theology is identical with the soul of the universe (God). Basusen hints at the last meaning, and Bikram catches on, because he uses the honorific form for the pronouns in his reply.

[54] The word *raṅga* usually means "colour", but can also mean "fun", "game", "diversion", "entertainment". It can even suggest "play" in the theatrical sense, and thus is another word for "stage".

[55] The word *rāg* has several meanings of which the most important in this context are "colour" (especially red) and "love". It is also the Bengali counterpart of "raga", the term for the modes in Indian music.

[56] She does prostrate herself, as evidenced by Thakurda's response.

[57] The word here is *vajra*, which in this context means "diamond". In order to convey the sense of "hard as a diamond", I have used the adjective "adamant", which of course has the same etymological root as "diamond".

[58] Santidev Ghosh recalls that for the 1935 production, Tagore dropped these two short episodes, involving the Group of Citizens here and the other group that follows them a few lines further on.

[59] The *kāl-baiśākhī* is the typical thunderstorm of early summer (April–May) in Bengal, popularly known in English as a "northwester" because of the direction from which it generally strikes. It develops relatively suddenly, usually in the afternoons; although short-lived, it can be very destructive.

[60] The Bengali word *bāṅdar* refers to the monkey. Used in a derogatory way, however, it means "rascal" or "mischief-maker".

[61] The term *krishna-chaturdaśī*, "dark fourteenth day", specifies the fourteenth day of the dark fortnight of a month. The cuckoo mentioned here is

not the Koel but a "true" cuckoo, the *bau-kathā-kao*, an onomatopoeic
Bengali name for the Indian Cuckoo, *Cuculus micropterus*. Like its more
common cousin, the Koel, this bird becomes very vocal during breeding
season (March–August), particularly in the early hours before dawn and on
moonlit nights.

[62] Santidev Ghosh states that Tagore kept Sudarshana on stage for this
song: she performed in mime while the chorus sang the song.

[63] The word here, *varan-ḍālā*, is the same word used by Surangama at the
start of the play, where I translated it as "welcome-tray" (see Note 15).

[64] As with the previous song, in the 1935 production Tagore made his
heroine the subject of this song too. Santidev Ghosh recalls Sudarshana's
mime performance accompanying the song.

[65] The Bengali expression *dhulo deoyā*, "to throw dust (at)", is generally
employed figuratively, in the sense of "to scoff" or "to mock". Here it must
also be considered literally because, instead of *holi* powder, everyone will
wear the dust of humility. Thakurda ends his next speech too with this idiom,
subtly implying the metaphorical sense.

[66] Sudarshana's word "rendezvous" is *abhisār* in Bengali, which actually
means "love tryst". As in much of Hindu thought, sacred and profane love
coexist in this play.

[67] Thakurda returns us to the concept in the title of the play, the word *rūp*.
I have translated this word as "beauty" in this passage, since Thakurda
begins with an obvious reference to Sudarshana's physical appearance. But
in speaking of the Raja he also suggests the alternative meaning of "shape"
or "form". See my Note on the play, p. 267, for a closer analysis of this idea.

[68] The phrase is *madhu-bhikshu*, literally "honey-beggars", a poetic image
for bees, because they seek honey.

[69] The word is *līlā*, carrying associations of play, sport, amusement, dalliance, and diversion; the accompanying awareness that such pastimes are a
sham, because they are merely superficial; and philosophical overtones of
the divine "play", God's universe, which constitutes the vast illusion of maya.

[70] From Santidev Ghosh's account of the 1935 production, we learn that
Tagore interpolated the previous song, "The night becomes the dawn", at
this point, and followed it immediately with this final song, which was accompanied by ensemble dancing. The song revives several crucial themes of
the play. In the first line, "formless" (*arūp*) and "beauty" (*rūp*) hark back to
the title. The mention of "seeing"—twice—echoes the Prologue, as does
the phrase "divine *rasa*" (*surer ras*) recall the "formless-*rasa*-ocean" of the
Prologue. The word *sur* of course means "tune" or "melody", as in line 3,
but it also has a second meaning of "god", which needs emphasis here.
Finally, in the last line, "estrangement" is a translation of *viraha*, the separation of two lovers.

Appendices

Appendices

APPENDIX A

LIST OF TAGORE'S PLAYS AND THEIR ENGLISH TRANSLATIONS

The following list· is arranged chronologically according to date of first publication of the original texts, not according to date of composition. The dates indicate year of publication, regardless of whether the play appeared first in a periodical or in the form of a book. Dates of revision, if mentioned, reflect major changes made in later editions of the play. Subsequently, many of the texts were revised for the definitive edition of Tagore's collected works: *Rabīndra-Rachanāvalī*, 26 volumes and 2 supplements (Calcutta: Visvabharati, 1939–48).

The classification of the plays borrows for the most part Tagore's own labels with which he categorised them. Thus, *nātya* or *nātak* = drama; *gītinātya* = musical drama; *nritya-nātya* = dance drama; *kautuk-nātya* comic drama; *prahasan* = farce; *samlāp* = dialogue. I have not distinguished between the theoretically shorter *nātikā* and the full-length *nātak* or *nātya*, because many of Tagore's plays under the former rubric actually take as much time as some of his full-length dramas; therefore *nātikā* has also been rendered as ·'drama". I have converted Tagore's term *nātya-kāvya* (literally ·'dramatic poem") into ·'poetic drama", which seems more appropriate to the plays concerned.

If reference to translations does not accompany a particular entry, that play has not yet been translated into English. Unless specified otherwise, translations cited are by Tagore himself or must be accredited to him, in the absence of the translator's name. All the books in English mentioned here — whether anthologies or single plays — have Tagore's name as author, except for *Blue Magic and Other Poems* (item 58), authored by P. K. Saha.

1. *Vālmīki-pratibhā*. Musical drama. 1881. Revised 1886. See also *Kāl-mrigayā* (1882).

2. *Bhagna-hriday*. [Poetic drama.] 1881.

3. *Rudra-chanda*. [Poetic] drama. 1881.

4. *Kāl-mrigayā*. Musical drama. 1882. Incorporated into *Vālmīki-pratibhā*, 1886. See *Vālmīki-pratibhā* (1881).

5. *Prakritir Pratiśodh*. Poetic drama. 1884. Revised 1896.

   Translated as ·'Sanyasi, or the Ascetic" in *"Sacrifice" and Other Plays* (London: Macmillan, 1917).

6. *Nalinī*. Drama. 1884. See also *Māyār Khelā* (1888).

7. *Hāsya-kautuk*. Comic dramas. 1885–87. Fifteen short sketches collected in 1907 under the title mentioned above. One more added in 1961.

Three of these transcreated by Prithvindra Chakravarti as *Three Riddle Plays* (Calcutta: Writers Workshop, 1983). The volume contains "The Test" (*Chhātrer Parīkshā*), "The Reception" (*Abhyarthanā*), and "The Patron" (*Khyātir Virambanā*).

8. *Māyār Khelā*. Musical drama. 1888. Based on *Nalinī* (1884). See also *Māyār Khelā* (1950).

9. *Rājā o Rānī*. [Poetic] drama. 1889. Revised 1894, 1896. See also *Tapatī* (1929).

Translated as "The King and the Queen" in *"Sacrifice" and Other Plays* (London: Macmillan, 1917).
Translated by Shakuntala Rao Sastri as *Devouring Love* (New York: East West Institute, 1961).

10. *Visarjan*. [Poetic] drama. 1890. Revised 1896, 1899, 1926. Based on the novel *Rājarshi*. See also *Visarjan* (1961).

Translated as "Sacrifice" in *"Sacrifice" and Other Plays* (London: Macmillan, 1917).

11. *Chitrāṅgadā*. Poetic drama. 1892. Revised 1894, 1896. See also *Chitrāṅgadā* (1936).

Translated as *Chitra* (London: India Society, 1913). Reissued by Macmillan in 1914.
Translated by Birendra Nath Roy as *Chitrangada* (Calcutta: Sribhumi, 1957).

12. *Goṛāy Galad*. Farce. 1892. See also *Śesh Rakshā* (1927).

13. *Vyaṅga-kautuk*. Comic dramas. 1893–1901. Five satirical skits (one each published in 1893 and 1901, three in 1894) collected in 1907 under the title mentioned above.

14. *Vidāy-Abhiśāp*. Poetic drama. 1894.

Translated as "Kacha and Devayani" in *The Fugitive* (London: Macmillan, 1921). Virtually the same version, with minor differences, published as "The Farewell Curse" in *New Orient* 2 (May-June 1924): 1–5.

Translated by Edward Thompson as *The Curse at Farewell* (London: George Harrap, 1924).

Translated by Krishna Kripalani as "Kach and Debjani" in *Viśva-Bharati Quarterly*, New Series, 2 (February 1937):42–47.

15. *Mālinī*. [Poetic] drama. 1896.

Translated as "Malini" in *"Sacrifice" and Other Plays* (London: Macmillan, 1917).

16. *Vaikunṭher Khātā*. Farce. 1897.

17. *Kāhinī*. Poetic dramas and a farce. 1900.

  (a) *Gāndhārīr Āvedan*

     Translated as "Mother's Prayer" in *Modern Review* 25 (June 1919):563–67. This version published, with slight alterations, as "The Mother's Prayer" in *The Fugitive* (London: Macmillan, 1921).

  (b) *Satī*

     Translated as "Ama and Vinayaka" in *The Fugitive* (London: Macmillan, 1921).

  (c) *Narakvās*

     Translated as "Somaka and Ritvik" in *The Fugitive* (London: Macmillan, 1921).

     Translated by Bhabani Bhattacharya as "A Sojourn in Hell" in *The Golden Boat*, revised edition (Bombay: Jaico, 1955).

  (d) *Lakshmīr Parīkshā* (farce)

     Translated as "The Trial" in *Modern Review* 28 (July 1920):1–9.

  (e) *Karṇa-Kuntī-Saṁvād*

     Translated as "Karna and Kunti" in *Modern Review* 27 (April 1920):365–67. This version published, with slight alterations, as "Karna and Kunti" in *The Fugitive* (London: Macmillan, 1921).

     Translated by T. Sturge Moore as "The Foundling Hero" in *The Golden Hind* 1 (January 1923):9–12.

     Translated by Humayun Kabir as "Karna and Kunti" in *Indian Literature*, October 1959, pp. 1–9. This version recast in prose, under the same title, in *One Hundred and One* (Bombay: Asia, 1966).

18. *Śāradotsav*. Drama. 1908. See also *Riṅśodh* (1921).

Translated as "Autumn Festival" in *Modern Review* 26 (November 1919): 469–82. Reprinted as *Autumn-Festival* (Calcutta: Brahmo Mission Press, 1919).

19. *Mukuṭ*. Drama. 1908. Dramatisation of the novel *Mukuṭ*.

Incomplete translation in manuscript, "The Crown", printed in *Rabīndra-vīkshā*, Śrāvaṇ 1390, pp. 15–36.

20. *Prāyaśchitta*. Drama. 1909. Dramatisation of the novel *Bau-ṭhākurānīr Hāṭ*. See also *Paritrāṇ* (1927).

21. *Rājā*. Drama. 1910. Revised 1921. See also *Arūp Ratan* (1920) and *Śāpmochan* (1931).

Translated as "The King of the Dark Chamber" in *The Drama* 4 (May 1914):177–237. Slightly different version published soon after, as *The King of the Dark Chamber* (London: Macmillan, 1914).

22. *Achalāyatan*. Drama. 1911. See also *Guru* (1918).

23. *Ḍākghar*. Drama. 1912.

Translated as "The Post Office" in *The Forum* 51 (March 1914): 455–71. Same version published almost simultaneously in book-form, with the translation credited to Devabrata Mukerjea, as *The Post Office* (London: Macmillan, 1914). A limited edition issued by the Cuala Press, Churchtown (Ireland), on Saint John's Eve (23 June) the same year.

24. *Phālgunī*. Drama. 1915. Revised 1916.

Translated as *The Cycle of Spring* (London: Macmillan, 1917).

25. *Guru*. Drama. 1918. "Stageworthy" version of *Achalāyatan* (1911).

26. *Svarga-marta*. [Comic drama.] 1919. See also *Svarge Chakraṭebil Baiṭhak* (1938).

Translated by Bhabani Bhattacharya as "Heaven and Earth" in *The Golden Boat* (London: George Allen and Unwin, 1932).
Translated by Indu Dutt as "Heaven and Earth" in *Lipika* (Bombay: Jaico, 1969).
Translated by Aurobindo Bose as "Heaven and Earth" and "Indra's Heaven" in *Lipika: Prose Poems* (Delhi: Clarion, 1978).

27. *Arūp Ratan*. Drama. 1920. Revised 1935. "Stageworthy" version of *Rājā* (1910). See also *Śāpmochan* (1931).

28. *Rinsodh*. Drama. 1921. "Stageworthy" version of *Śāradotsav* (1908).

29. *Muktadhārā*. Drama. 1922.

> Translated as "The Waterfall" in *Modern Review* 31 (May 1922): 535–558g.
> Translated by Marjorie Sykes as "Mukta-dhārā" in *Visva-Bharati Quarterly*, New Series, 6 (February 1941):351–72; and 7 (February 1942):105–42. A revision of this version published as "Mukta-dhara" in *Three Plays* (Bombay: Oxford University Press, 1950).

30. *Vasanta*. Musical drama. 1923.

31. *Rath-yātrā*. Drama. 1923. See also *Kāler Yātrā* (1932).

> Translated as "The Car of Time" in *Visva-Bharati Quarterly*, Old Series, 1 (January 1924):321–42.

32. *Rakta-karavī*. Drama. 1924.

> Translated as "Red Oleanders" in *Visva-Bharati Quarterly*, September 1924 (Special Autumn Number), pp. 1–87. Same version published in book-form as *Red Oleanders* (London: Macmillan, 1925).

33. *Grihapraves*. Drama. 1925. Dramatisation of the short story *Sesher Rātri*.

> Translated by Mary Lago, Tarun Gupta and Amiya Chakravarty as "The Housewarming" in *"The Housewarming" and Other Selected Writings*, edited by Amiya Chakravarty (New York: New American Library/Signet, 1965).

34. *Sodhbodh*. Drama. 1925. Dramatisation of the short story *Karmaphal*.

> The story *Karmaphal* (1903) is almost entirely in the form of dialogue, and may easily be considered a play. A translation of the story, by Mary Lago, Tarun Gupta and Amiya Chakravarty, appears under the title "Consequences" in *"The Housewarming" and Other Selected Writings*, edited by Amiya Chakravarty (New York: New American Library/Signet, 1965).

35. *Sesh Varshan*. Musical drama. 1925.

36. *Chirakumār-Sabhā*. Drama. 1926. Dramatisation of the novel *Prajāpatir Nirbandha*.

37. *Naṭīr Pūjā*. Drama. 1926. Revised 1927.

Translated as ¨The Dancing Girl's Worship¨ in *Visva-Bharati Quarterly*, Old Series, 5 (April 1927):1–39.

Translated by Marjorie Sykes as ¨Natir Puja¨ in *Visva-Bharati Quarterly*, New Series, 10 (February 1945): 188–202; 11 (May 1945): 14–26; and 11 (August 1945):120–30. A revision of this version published under the same title in *Three Plays* (Bombay: Oxford University Press, 1950).

Transcreated by Shyamasree Devi as *The Court Dancer* (Calcutta: Writers Workshop, 1961; 2nd ed., 1979).

38. *Sundar*. Musical drama. 1926.

39. *Naṭarāj*. Musical drama. 1927. See also *Rituraṅga* (1927) and *Naṭarāj Rituraṅgaśālā* (1931).

40. *Śesh Rakshā*. Farce. 1927. ¨Stageworthy¨ version of *Goṛāy Galad* (1892).

41. *Paritrāṇ*. Drama. 1927. Revised version of *Prāyaśchitta* (1909).

42. *Rituraṅga*. Musical drama. 1927. Revised version of *Naṭarāj* (1927). See also *Naṭarāj Rituraṅgaśālā* (1931).

Prologue translated as ¨*Rituranga* (The Dance of the Seasons)¨ in *Visva-Bharati Quarterly*, Old Series, 5 (October 1927):273–74.

43. *Śiver Bhikshā*. Dialogue. 1928. See also *Kāler Yātrā* (1932).

44. *Tapatī*. Drama. 1929. Revised 1931. Based on *Rājā o Rānī* (1889).

45. *Navīn*. Musical drama. 1931. Revised 1931.

46. *Naṭarāj Rituraṅgaśālā*. Musical drama. 1931. Incorporates *Naṭarāj* (1927) and *Rituraṅga* (1927).

47. *Śāpmochan*. [Musical drama.] 1931. Revised 1933. Based on *Rājā* (1910).

48. *Kāler Yātrā*. Drama and Dialogue. 1932. Includes *Rather Raśi* and *Kavir Dīkshā*: revised versions of *Rath-yātrā* (1923) and *Śiver Bhikshā* (1928) respectively.

49. *Chaṇḍālikā*. Drama. 1933. See also *Chaṇḍālikā* (1938).

Translated by Krishna Kripalani as "Chandalika" in *Visva-Bharati Quarterly*, New Series, 3 (February 1938):317–26.

Translated by Marjorie Sykes as "Chandalika" in *Three Plays* (Bombay: Oxford University Press, 1950).

A version based on the earlier translations, with changes by Robert Steele and Donald Junkins, in *A Tagore Reader*, edited by Amiya Chakravarty (New York: Macmillan, 1961).

50. *Tāser Deś*. Drama. 1933. Revised 1939. Dramatisation of the short story *Ekṭā Āshārhe Galpa*.

Translated by Krishna Kripalani as "Kingdom of Cards" in *Visva-Bharati Quarterly*, New Series, 4 (February 1939):264–89. Reprinted as "*Tasher Desh* or *Kingdom of Cards*", with photographs of the 1939 revival, in *Modern Review* 65 (June 1939):658–68.

51. *Bāṅśari*. Drama. 1933.

52. *Śrāvaṇ-gāthā*. Musical drama. 1934.

53. *Chitrāṅgadā*. Dance drama. 1936. Revised 1936. Based on *Chitrāṅgadā* (1892).

54. *Pariśodh*. [Dance drama.] 1936. See also *Śyāmā* (1939).

55. *Chaṇḍālikā*. Dance drama. 1938. Revised 1939. Based on *Chaṇḍālikā* (1933).

Translated by Shyamasree Devi as "Chandalika" in *Orient Review and Literary Digest*, January–February 1956, pp. 53–60. Reprinted with "The Court Dancer" in *Two Buddhist Plays* (Calcutta: Writers Workshop, 1993).

56. *Muktir Upāy*. Drama. 1938. Dramatisation of the short story *Muktir Upāy*.

57. *Svarge Chakraṭebil Baithak*. Comic drama. 1938. Revised version of *Svarga-marta* (1919).

58. *Śyāmā*. Dance drama. 1939. Based on *Pariśodh* (1936).

Translated by P. K. Saha as "Shyama" in *Thought*, 31 July 1971, pp. 13–15. With minor changes, included in P. K. Saha, *Blue Magic and Other Poems* (Calcutta: Writers Workshop, 1974).

59. *Māyār Khelā*. Dance drama. 1950 (written 1938). Based on *Māyār Khelā* (1888).

Songs partially translated in "The Story and the Songs of Mayar Khela", *Visva-Bharati Quarterly*, New Series, 14 (November 1948). 165–73.

60. *Visarjan*. Children's drama. 1961 (written 1936). Abridged from *Visarjan* (1890).

61. *Mālañcha*. Drama. 1968 (written 1933). Dramatisation of the novel *Mālañcha*.

Manuscripts

In 1976 Rabindra Bhavan (the archives at Visvabharati University) initiated a programme of printing hitherto unpublished — and mostly unfinished — Tagore manuscripts in its collection. These began appearing in its biannual journal, *Rabīndra-vīkshā*. Several dramatic works figure in this series, as listed below:

1. *Arūpratan*. Manuscript and press copy. 1976 (written 1935).
2. *King and Rebel*. Original English play. 1977 (written 1912–13).
3. *Tāser Deś*. First draft. 1977–78 (written 1933).
4. *Ẏogāẏog*. Dramatisation of the novel of the same name. 1978 (written 1936).
5. *Sundar*. Musical drama, not to be confused with the 1926 play of the same name. 1984 (written 1929).
6. *Rakta-karavī*. First draft. 1986 (written 1923). Second draft. 1988. Third draft. 1989.
7. *Grihapraveś*. First draft. 1989.
8. *The King of the Dark Chamber*. Eighth manuscript. 1990.
9. *The Autumn-Festival*. Manuscript. 1994.
10. *Rinśodh*. Stage copy. 1995.

In addition, the following manuscript has been published in the magazine *Bahurūpī*, organ of the theatre group Bohurupee:

11. *Nandinī*. Early version of *Rakta-karavī*. 1986 (written 1923).

APPENDIX B

LIST OF FIRST PERFORMANCES OF TAGORE'S MAJOR PLAYS

Records of the stage history of Tagore's plays are quite deficient. Few detailed eyewitness accounts exist and, apart from Santidev Ghosh, none of the people involved in his productions has taken the trouble to put down recollections systematically or at any great length. This observation is particularly true of the early, pre-Santiniketan productions, about which we find only stray pieces of information usually of an anecdotal nature, as in the memoirs of Abanindranath Tagore. Consequently, we do not even know the month in which some of these plays were first performed within the family. In Santiniketan, too, nobody seems to have given much thought to the historical value of preserving theatre facts for posterity; and so we often cannot assign exact dates to first productions that occurred during the opening years of the school, though we can at least pinpoint the month.

It becomes additionally difficult to ascertain dates when different sources give conflicting evidence. Even the most respected and generally reliable theatre historians are at fault occasionally; Asutosh Bhattacharya's *Rabindra-Nāṭyadhārā*, for instance, contains several chronological inaccuracies concerning Tagore's plays. In preparing my own list I found the following sources to be the most useful: the works of Prabhat Kumar Mukhopadhyay, prime biographer of Tagore in Bengali; Kalidas Nag's published and unpublished diaries; Santidev Ghosh's books on Tagore (especially for productions after 1920); Harindranath Datta's *Rabīndranath o Sādhāran Nāṭyaśālā* (for productions on the professional stage); the newsletter of Visvabharati University, *Visva-Bharati News* (for productions in the 1930s); Tagore's letters in Bengali, in the series titled *Chiṭhipatra*; and the notes to his 26-volume collected works.

For each entry, the name of the play is followed by date of premiere, place of production, and role that Tagore took, if any. Except for the performances in Santiniketan, all productions took place in Calcutta: either in the Tagore ancestral home (Jorasanko) or in various other theatres. The plays that opened on the professional stage are marked with an asterisk. Names of institutions within parentheses identify amateur performances with which Tagore had no connection.

1881
Vālmīki-pratibhā. 26 February. Jorasanko. Tagore as Vālmīki.

1882
Kāl-mṛgayā. 23 December. Jorasanko. Tagore as Andha Rishi.

1888
Māyār Khelā. 29 December. Bethune College.

1889
Rājā o Rānī. Precise date uncertain; some time during the Puja holidays (September-October). Birjitalao. Tagore as Vikram.

1890
Visarjan. Precise date uncertain; some time between March–July. Jorasanko ? Tagore as Raghupati.

1892
Gorāy Galad. August. Jorasanko. Tagore sang.
Chitrāṅgadā. 17 December. Emerald Theatre.*

1897
Vaikuṇṭher Khātā. June. Jorasanko Baithakkhana. Tagore as Kedār.

1908
Śāradotsav. 24 September. Santiniketan.
Mukuṭ. December. Santiniketan.

1910
Prāyaśchitta. 8 May. Santiniketan.

1911
Rājā. 15 March. Santiniketan. Tagore as Ṭhākurdā.

1914
Achalāyatan. 26 April. Santiniketan. Tagore as Āchārya.

1915
Phālgunī. 25 April. Santiniketan. Tagore as Bāul.

1917
Ḍākghar. 3 May. Mary Carpenter Hall. (Brahmo Balya Samaj.)

1918
Guru. March. Santiniketan.

1921
Riṇśodh. 2 October. Santiniketan. Tagore as Śekhar.

1923
Vasanta. 25 February. Madan Theatre. Tagore as Kavi.

1924
Arūp Ratan. 15 September. Alfred Theatre. Tagore as narrator.

1925
Sundar. 13 April. Santiniketan.
Chirakumār-Sabhā. 18 July. Star Theatre.*
Śesh Varshan. 15 September. Jorasanko. Tagore sang.
Muktadhārā. 15 September. Calcutta University Institute. (Presidency College.)
G̥rihapraveś. 5 December. Star Theatre.*

1926
Naṭīr Pūjā. 8 May. Santiniketan.
Śodhbodh. 23 July. Star Theatre.*

1927
Naṭarāj. 19 March. Santiniketan. Tagore recited, sang.
Śesh Rakshā. 7 September. Cornwallis Theatre.*
Paritrān. 10 September. Star Theatre.*
Rituranga. 8 December. Jorasanko. Tagore recited.

1929
Tapatī. 26 September. Jorasanko. Tagore as Vikram.

1931
Navīn. 4 March. Santiniketan. Tagore recited, sang.
Śāpmochan. 31 December. Jorasanko. Tagore narrated.

1932
Kāler Ẏātrā. 30 September. Santiniketan.

1933
Tāser Deś. 12 September. Madan Theatre.

1934
Rakta-karavī. 6 April. Natya Niketan. (Tagore Dramatic Group.)
Śrāvaṇ-gāthā. 12 August. Santiniketan. Tagore as Naṭarāj.

1935
Chandālikā. 16 March. Santiniketan.

1936
Chitrāṅgadā. 11 March. New Empire Theatre. Tagore recited.
Pariśodh. 10 October. Asutosh College. Tagore recited, sang.

1938
Chaṇḍālikā. Before 5 March. Santiniketan.

1939
Śyāmā. 7 February. Sri Cinema.

Bibliography

The following bibliography represents an attempt to compile a comprehensive guide to material published in English on Tagore's plays. It includes all the secondary works I have quoted or referred to in this edition; in addition, the first two sections contain—to the best of my knowledge—all books, essays and theses in English that deal with Tagore's plays in some detail. Although I have consulted all these items, I have not discriminated in selecting the pieces for inclusion in these two sections. Consequently, the standard of criticism presented by these entries varies widely, from the very poor to the merely pedestrian to the highly illuminating.

In the sections succeeding the first two, I list only those works which I have myself cited. It does not make much sense to include here every book review or play review of Tagore's dramas; nor does it appear worthwhile to list the plethora of history and interpretation available in Bengali, since this volume is aimed at an audience that, I must presume, knows little or no Bengali.

I have not repeated here the bibliography of Tagore's plays and their English translations, which readers can find separately in Appendix A.

I. BOOKS AND ARTICLES

Anniah Gowda, H.H. *Anjali: The Tagore Lectures*. Annamalainagar: Annamalai University, 1976.

Appaswami Ayyar, K.S. *A Critical Study of Rabindranath's "Chitra"*. Madras: Chandra, 1952.

Aronson, Alex. *Rabindranath through Western Eyes*. 2nd ed. Calcutta: Ṛddhi-India, 1978.

Ayyub, Abu Sayeed. *Tagore's Quest*. Calcutta: Papyrus, 1980.

Bandyopadhyay, Asit Kumar. *History of Modern Bengali Literature: Nineteenth and Twentieth Centuries*. Calcutta: Modern Book Agency, 1986.

Bandyopadhyaya, Beerendra [Beerendra C. Banerjee]. "Dance and Song in Tagore's Plays". *Rhythm*, April 1961, pp. 64–68.

———. *Rabindra-sangit: The Songs of Tagore*. Calcutta: Granthalaya, [1981].

Banerjee, Jaygopal. "*Red Oleanders*: An Appreciation". *Calcutta Review*, Third Series, 17 (October 1925): 139–56; 17 (November 1925): 326–32; 18 (February 1926): 231–39; and 19 (April 1926): 37–49.

Basak, Radhagovinda. "The Kuśa-Jātaka of the Mahāvastu Avadāna and Tagore's Rājā and Śāp-mocan". *Indo-Asian Culture* 10 (July 1961): 19–29.

Bayapa Reddy, P. "Tagore's *The Post Office*: A Thematic Study". *Triveni*, April-June 1985, pp. 87–91.

Benegal, Som. *A Panorama of Theatre in India*. New Delhi: Indian Council for Cultural Relations, 1967.

Bhattacherje, M.M. *Rabindranath Tagore: Poet and Thinker*. Delhi: Kitab Mahal, 1961.

Bose, Arabinda Mohan. "*The Post Office*". *Modern Review* 31 (February 1922): 159–60.

Bose, Buddhadeva. *Tagore: Portrait of a Poet*. Bombay: University of Bombay, 1962.

Bose, Joges C. "Rift in the Lute—Tagore's Drama". *Modern Review* 111 (March 1962):216–19.

Bose, Somendranath. "Avadānas as Recreated in Tagore's Dramas". *Tagore Studies*, 1970, pp. 84–99.

Buck, Philo M., Jr. *Directions in Contemporary Literature*. New York: Oxford University Press, 1942.

Chakravarty, Ajit Kumar. "*The Cycle of Spring*". *Modern Review* 22 (October 1917): 421–28.

Chakravarty, Bikash. "Rabindranath's *Raja*: A Note on Ayyub". *Visva-bharati Quarterly*, New Series, 42 (November 1976): 223–37.

Chakravorty, B.C. *Rabindranath Tagore: His Mind and Art*. New Delhi: Young India, 1971.

Chandrasekharan, K. *Tagore: A Master Spirit*. Madras: Triveni, 1961.

Chatterjee, Ramananda. "Mr. Thompson's Book on Rabindranath Tagore". *Modern Review* 42 (July 1927): 99–102.

————, ed. *The Golden Book of Tagore: A Homage to Rabindranath Tagore from India and the World in Celebration of His Seventieth Birthday*. Calcutta: Golden Book Committee, 1931.

Chatterjee, Visvanath. "Tagore as a Shakespearean Critic". *Tagore Studies*, 1972–73, pp. 15–31.

Chattopadhyaya, Shyamal. *Art and the Abyss: Six Essays in Interpretation of Tagore*. Calcutta: Jijnasa, 1977.

Chaudhurani, Indira Devi. 'Memories". In *Centenary Number: Rabindranath Tagore 1861–1961*. New Delhi: Sangeet Natak Akademi, 1961.

————. "Reminiscences of Mayar Khela". *Visva-Bharati Quarterly*, New Series, 14 (November 1948): 161–64.

Choudhury, Ahindra. "Development of Tagore's Dramatic Art". *Natya: Theatre Arts Journal*, Tagore Centenary Number (1961), pp. 52–53.

Coles, Mervyn D. "The Plays of Tagore". *Contemporary Review* 183 (May 1953): 293–95.

Das Gupta, Hemendranath. *The Indian Stage*. 4 vols. Calcutta: Metropolitan and M.K. Das Gupta, 1934–44.

Das Gupta, Surendranath. "*The King of the Dark Chamber*". *Modern Review* 20 (July 1916): 30–34.

Dasgupta, Pranabendu. "One or Two Aspects of the 'Subjective Tradition' in the Plays of W.B. Yeats and Rabindranath Tagore". *Jadavpur Journal of Comparative Literature* 4 (1964): 46–67.

Datta, Bhabatosh. "Rabindranath Tagore on Shakespeare". In *Calcutta Essays on Shakespeare*. Edited by Amalendu Bose. Calcutta: University of Calcutta, 1966.

Davies, Mary Carolyn. "Rabindranath Tagore: India's Shakespeare and Tasso in One". *Forum* 51 (January 1914): 140–44.

Dees, J.L. *Tagore and America*. Calcutta: United States Information Service, 1961.

Desai, S.K. "The Post Office". In *Perspectives on Indian Drama in English*. Edited by M.K. Naik and S. Mokashi-Punekar. Madras: Oxford University Press, 1977.

———. "Symbolism in Tagore's Plays". In *Critical Essays on Indian Writing in English: Presented to Armando Menezes*. Edited by M.K. Naik, S.K. Desai and G.S. Amur. 2nd ed. Dharwar: Karnatak University, 1972.

———. "Tagore's 'Red Oleanders': A Revaluation". In *Aspects of Indian Writing in English: Essays in Honour of Professor K.R. Srinivasa Iyengar*. Edited by M.K. Naik. Madras: Macmillan, 1979.

Deshpande, P.L. "Rabindranath's Theatre" (abstract). *National Centre for the Performing Arts — Quarterly Journal*, September 1981, pp. 11–12.

Dev, Amiya. "*Raja* as a Play in Two Acts". *Visvabharati Quarterly*, New Series, 41 (May 1975): 103–13.

Dev Sen, Nabaneeta. "The Lotus with the Thunderbolt: A March from the Spring Festival to the Harvest Dance: some notes towards a fresh reading of *Raja* and *Raktakarabi*". *Visvabharati Quarterly*, New Series, 41 (May 1975): 139–63.

Doromal, Gaudelia V. "Tagore's Religious Humanism in 'Sanyasi, or the Ascetic'". *Danyag*, June 1976, pp. 48–53.

"East and West". *Visva-Bharati Quarterly*, Old Series, 3 (October 1925): 286–87.

Fabri, Charles. "Dance Dramas of Tagore". *Natya: Theatre Arts Journal*, Tagore Centenary Number (1961), pp. 10–15.

Gargi, Balwant. "The Plays of Tagore". In *The Genius of Tagore*. Edited by Mahendra Kulasrestha. Hoshiarpur: Vishveshvaranand V.R. Institute, 1961.

Ghose, Santidev. *Music and Dance in Rabindranath Tagore's Education Philosophy*. New Delhi: Sangeet Natak Akademi, 1978.

Ghose, Sisirkumar. *Rabindranath Tagore*. New Delhi: Sahitya Akademi, 1986.

Ghosh, J.C. *Bengali Literature*. London: Oxford University Press, 1948.

Ghosh, Sati. *Rabindranath*. Calcutta: Bookland, 1966.

Ghoshal, Satyendranath. "Rabindranath Tagore and His Dramatic Genius". *Patna University Journal* 22 (January 1967): 42–51.

Guha-Thakurta, P. *The Bengali Drama: Its Origin and Development*. London: Kegan Paul, Trench, Trubner, 1930.

———. "Rabindranath — The Dramatist". *Visva-Bharati Quarterly*, New Series, 7 (May 1941): 110–14.

———. "Tagore's Phalguni: An Interpretation". *Visva-Bharati Quarterly*, Old Series, 7 (October 1929): 272–78.

Haldar, Rangin. "The Working of an Unconscious Wish in the Creation of
    Poetry and Drama". *International Journal of Psycho-Analysis* 12 (April
    1931): 188–205.
Henderson, Alice Corbin. "Rabindranath Tagore". *The Drama* 4 (May 1914):
    161–76.
Kapur, Shiv S. "Delhi Scene". *Natya: Theatre Arts Journal*, Autumn 1966,
    pp. 41–44.
———. "Rakat [sic] Karabi—Notes on a Play". *Quest*, April–May 1956,
    pp. 37–40.
———. "Two Plays, Two Productions and a View". *Natya: Theatre Arts
    Journal*, Tagore Centenary Number (1961), pp. 16–19.
Khanolkar, G.D. *The Lute and the Plough: A Life of Rabindranath Tagore.*
    Translated by Thomas Gay. Bombay: Book Centre, 1963.
Kripalani, Krishna. Introduction to *Chandalika. Visva-Bharati Quarterly*,
    New Series, 3 (February 1938): 315–16.
———. Introduction to *Tasher Desh* or *Kingdom of Cards. Visva-Bharati
    Quarterly*, New Series, 4 (February 1939): 261–63.
———. "*Mukta-dhārā*: An Appreciation". *Visva-Bharati Quarterly*, New
    Series, 6 (February 1941): 347–50.
———. "*Natir Puja*: An Appreciation". *Visva-Bharati Quarterly*, New
    Series, 8 (February 1943): 175–80.
———. *Rabindranath Tagore: A Biography.* 2nd ed. Calcutta: Visva-bharati,
    1980.
Lago, Mary M. *Rabindranath Tagore.* Boston: Twayne, 1976.
———, ed. *Imperfect Encounter: Letters of William Rothenstein and Rabindra-
    nath Tagore 1911–1941.* Cambridge: Harvard University Press, 1972.
Lesný, V. *Rabindranath Tagore: His Personality and Work.* Translated by Guy
    McKeever Phillips. London: George Allen and Unwin, 1939.
Majumdar, Bimanbehari. *Heroines of Tagore: A Study in the Transformation
    of Indian Society 1875–1941.* Calcutta: Firma K.L. Mukhopadhyay,
    1968.
Malkani, M.U. "Tagore the Playwright". *Indian Literature*, April 1958, pp.
    62–66.
Mathur, O.P. "'Love's Lotus'—A Study of the Protagonist in Tagore's
    Major Plays". In *Indo-English Literature: A Collection of Critical Essays.*
    Edited by K.K. Sharma. Ghaziabad: Vimal Prakashan, 1977.
Menon, K.P.K. *Tagore Lectures, 1973.* Annamalainagar: Annamalai Uni-
    versity, 1976.
Mitra, Sombhu. "Building from Tagore". *Drama Review*, Spring 1971, pp.
    201–4.
———. "*Rakta Karabi*: producer's interpretation". *Natya: Theatre Arts
    Journal*, Tagore Centenary Number (1961), pp. 60–64.
———. "Reflections on Tagore's Plays". *Illustrated Weekly of India*, 7 May
    1961, p. 41.

Mode, Heinz. "Tagore's 'King of the Dark Chamber' and Its Folkloristic Background". *Folk-Lore* 1 (November 1960): 361–68.

Mukerji, Amar. "The Comedies of Rabindranath Tagore." *Saugar University Journal*, 1952–53, pp. 17–32.

———. "The Dramas of Rabindranath Tagore". *Modern Review* 85 (June 1949): 477–83.

———. "Rabindranath Tagore (1864 [*sic*]–1941)". *World Theatre* 5 (Spring 1956): 123–30.

———. "Rabindranath Tagore's Dramatic Beginnings—The Conflict and the Emergence: Early Playlets". *Journal of the Ganganatha Jha Research Institute* 8 (May 1951):269–307.

———. "Rabindranath Tagore's Theories of Tragedy and Comedy". *University of Allahabad Studies (English Section)*, 1950, pp. 53–102.

———. "The Season-Plays of Rabindranath Tagore". *Saugar University Journal*, 1951–52, pp. 35–44.

———. "Two Machine Dramas of Rabindranath Tagore". *Saugar University Journal*, 1954–55, Part I, pp. 45–64.

Mukerji, Dhurjati Prasad. *Tagore—A Study*. Bombay: Padma, 1944.

Mukerji, Nirmal. "The Plays of Rabindranath Tagore". In *Perspectives on Indian Drama in English*. Edited by M.K. Naik and S. Mokashi-Punekar. Madras: Oxford University Press, 1977.

Mukerji, Rose. "'King of the Dark Chamber' and Indian Classical Theatre". In *Rabindranath Tagore Centenary*. Edited by Rose Mukerji. Brochure published on the occasion of the production of *The King of the Dark Chamber*, New York, 1961.

Mukherjee, Sujit. *Passage to America: The Reception of Rabindranath Tagore in the United States, 1912–1941*. Calcutta: Bookland, 1964.

Mukherjee, Sushil Kumar. *The Story of the Calcutta Theatres: 1753–1980*. Calcutta: K.P. Bagchi, 1982.

Mukherji, Haridhan. "On Rabindranath's Raja (The King)". *Modern Review*, January 1978, pp. 42–45.

Mukherji, Prafulla C. "Rabindranath Tagore in America". *Modern Review* 110 (November 1961): 383–92.

Mukherji, Probhat Kumar. *Life of Tagore*. Translated by Sisirkumar Ghosh. New Delhi: Indian Book Company, 1975.

Murty, D.V.S.R. "The Message of Tagore's Post Office". *Modern Review* 128 (January 1971): 19–21.

———. "Nature in 'Chitra'". *Modern Review* 120 (July 1966): 13–16.

———. "Symbolism in 'The King of the Dark Chamber'". *Modern Review* 119 (February 1966): 158–60.

Naikar, Basavaraj S. "Drama as Satire: *Red Oleanders*". *Journal of the Karnatak University—Humanities* 24–25 (1980–81): 55–68.

Naravane, Vishwanath S. *An Introduction to Rabindranath Tagore*. Madras: Macmillan, 1977.

Narayanam, K.R. "Tagore's 'Chitra': A Critical Study". *Visva-Bharati Quarterly*, New Series, 10 (May 1944): 35–37.

Padma, T. "The Role of the Feminine Psyche in Tagore's *Sanyasi*". *Journal of Indian Writing in English*, January 1978, pp. 51–56.

Paul, K.T. "*Phalguni*: A Musical Play by Sir Rabindranath Tagore". *Modern Review* 19 (March 1916): 342–45.

Pearson, W.W. *Shantiniketan: The Bolpur School of Rabindranath Tagore*. New York: Macmillan, 1916.

Radhakrishnan, S. *The Philosophy of Rabindranath Tagore*. Baroda: Good Companions, 1961.

Radice, William. "Tagore's Poetry in English Translation". *Visvabharati Quarterly*, New Series, 42 (May 1976): 8–25.

———. "Visarjan and Sacrifice". *Visvabharati Quarterly*, New Series, 45 (May 1979): 10–32.

Raghavacharyulu, D.V.K. "The Plays of Rabindranath Tagore". *Aryan Path* 32 (April 1961, May 1961, June 1961): 148–51, 197–202, 252–55.

Raha, Kironmoy. *Bengali Theatre*. New Delhi: National Book Trust, 1978.

———. "Tagore on Theatre". *Natya: Theatre Arts Journal*, Tagore Centenary Number (1961), pp. 5–9.

Raju, Anand Kumar. "Characterization through Imagery: Tagore's 'Chandalika'". *Indian Literature*, September–October 1980, pp. 86–95.

Ramachandra Rao, K. "Tagore's *Chitra*—An Appreciation". *Triveni: Journal of Indian Renaissance*, January 1980, pp. 45–48.

Ramaswami Sastri, K.S. *Rabindranath Tagore: A Study of His Later Works*. Madras: S. Ganesan, 1920.

———. *Rabindranath Tagore: Poet, Patriot, Philosopher*. Srirangam: Sri Vani Vilas, 1924.

———. *Sir Rabindranath Tagore: His Life, Personality and Genius*. Madras: Ganesh, [1916].

Rangacharya, Adya. *The Indian Theatre*. New Delhi: National Book Trust, 1971.

Ranganathan, Sudha. "Rabindranath Tagore's *Malini* and W.B. Yeats's *The Countess Cathleen*: A Study in 'Hominisation'". *Osmania Journal of English Studies* 9 (1972): 51–54.

Rao, Ila. "Shakespeare's *Love's Labour's Lost* and Tagore's *Chirakumar Sabha*: A Comparison". *Triveni: Journal of Indian Renaissance*, January 1972, pp. 26–31.

Ray, Lila. "The Plays of Tagore". *Indo-Asian Culture* 6 (July 1957): 79–90.

Ray, Niharranjan. *An Artist in Life: A Commentary on the Life and Works of Rabindranath Tagore*. Trivandrum: University of Kerala, 1967.

———. "Symbolist Plays of Tagore". In *Homage to Rabindranath Tagore*. Edited by B.M. Chaudhuri. Kharagpur: Indian Institute of Technology, 1961.

Rhys, Ernest. *Rabindranath Tagore: A Biographical Study*. London: Macmillan, 1915.

Rollo, J.C. "Rabindra Nath's Chitra". *Indian Review* 15 (August 1914): 609–10.

Sanyal, Hirankumar. "The Plays of Rabindranath Tagore". In *A Centenary Volume: Rabindranath Tagore 1861–1941*. New Delhi: Sahitya Akademi, 1961.

Sarkar, Shyamal Kumar. "At Unison with Him". *Tagore Studies*, 1972–73, pp. 40–48.

————. "The King of the Dark Chamber: Text and Publication". *Visvabharati Quarterly*, New Series, 38 (November 1972): 25–40.

————. "Tagore on Translation". *Visvabharati Quarterly*, New Series, 43 (May 1977): 66–85.

Sathiraju, K. "The Cosmic Relevance of Tagore's Symbolic Plays". *Triveni: Journal of Indian Renaissance*, July 1965, pp. 47–56.

Sen, Priyaranjan. "Mr. Edward Thompson and Rabindranath Tagore". *Modern Review* 43 (January 1928): 13–16.

Sen, Sukumar. *History of Bengali Literature*. Revised 3rd ed. New Delhi: Sahitya Akademi, 1979.

Sen Gupta, S.C. *The Great Sentinel: A Study of Rabindranath Tagore*. Calcutta: A. Mukherjee, [1948].

Shah, Krishna. "The Director and the Play". In *Rabindranath Tagore Centenary*. Edited by Rose Mukerji. Brochure published on the occasion of the production of *The King of the Dark Chamber*, New York, 1961.

Sharma, Mohan Lal. "Rabindranath Tagore as a Playwright". *Modern Drama* 13 (May 1970): 83–92.

Srinivasa Iyengar, K.R. *Indian Writing in English*. 5th ed. New Delhi: Sterling, 1985.

————. *Rabindranath Tagore*. Bombay: Popular Prakashan, 1965.

Suryanarayana Murti, K.V. "Tagore's 'Chitra': A Grammatical Clue to Character". *Aryan Path* 37 (July 1966): 311–16.

Sykes, Marjorie. *Rabindranath Tagore*. Madras: Longmans, Green, 1947.

Tagore, Pratima. "Two Dance-Dramas of Gurudeva". In *Centenary Number: Rabindranath Tagore 1861–1961*. New Delhi: Sangeet Natak Akademi, 1961.

Tagore, Rabindranath. "The Art of Movement in Education". In *Rabindranath Tagore: Pioneer in Education*. Edited by L.K. Elmhirst. London: John Murray, 1961.

————. *Creative Unity*. London: Macmillan, 1922.

————. "The Cycle of Spring." *Modern Review* 19 (February 1916): 204–7.

————. *The Diary of a Westward Voyage*. Translated by Indu Dutt. London: Asia, 1962.

————. "Kalidas, the Moralist". Translated by Jadunath Sarkar. *Modern Review* 14 (October 1913): 347–49.

————. "Letters from Java". *Visva-Bharati Quarterly*, Old Series, 6 (April 1928): 1–13.

————. *Letters to a Friend*. Edited by C.F. Andrews. London: George Allen and Unwin, 1928.

————. "My Religion". In *A Tagore Testament*. Translated by Indu Dutt. London: Meridian Books, 1953.

————. *My Reminiscences*. London: Macmillan, 1917.

————. *Nationalism*. London: Macmillan, 1917.

————. *Personality: Lectures Delivered in America*. London: Macmillan, 1917.

————. *"Red Oleanders*: An Interpretation". Transcribed by Leonard K. Elmhirst. *Visva-Bharati Quarterly*, New Series, 17 (November 1951): 208–17.

————. *"Red Oleanders*: Author's Interpretation". *Visva-Bharati Quarterly*, Old Series, 3 (October 1925): 283–85.

————. *The Religion of Man: being the Hibbert Lectures for 1930*. London: George Allen and Unwin, 1931.

————. *"Sādhanā": The Realisation of Life*. London: Macmillan, 1913.

————. *"Sakuntala*: Its Inner Meaning". Translated by Jadunath Sarkar. *Modern Review* 9 (February 1911): 171–75.

————. "The Stage". Translated by Surendranath Tagore. *Modern Review* 14 (December 1913): 543–45. A later version in *The Drama* 5 (November 1915): 664–68. A different translation published as "The Message of Hindu Stage". Translated by Basanta Koomar Roy. *Open Court* 39 (March 1925): 129–30.

————. *Towards Universal Man*. Bombay: Asia, 1961.

Tagore, Rathindranath. *On the Edges of Time*. Bombay: Orient Longmans, 1958.

Thapalyal, L.M. [L.M.T.]. "Looking Back and Ahead". *Natya: Theatre Arts Journal*, Tagore Centenary Number (1961), pp. 2–4.

————. "Tagore on Delhi Stage". *Natya: Theatre Arts Journal*, Tagore Centenary Number (1961), pp. 79–82.

Thompson, Edward J. *Rabindranath Tagore: His Life and Work*. Calcutta: Association Press. 1921.

————. *Rabindranath Tagore: Poet and Dramatist*. London: Oxford University Press, 1926; 2nd ed., 1948.

Tuck, Donald R. "Tagore's Critique of Living Religious Traditions as Dramatised in *Sacrifice*". In *Rabindranath Tagore: American Interpretations*. Edited by Ira G. Zepp, Jr. Calcutta: Writers Workshop, 1981.

————. "Tagore's Critique of Saivite Traditions in the Drama, *Muktadhara*". *Kentucky Folklore Record* 27 (January 1981): 36–52.

Vasudev, Uma. "Theatre Couple: Interview with Sombhu & Tripti Mitra". *Natya: Theatre Arts Journal*, Tagore Centenary Number (1961), pp. 31–33.

Venkatesa Iyengar, Masti. *Rabindranath Tagore*. Bangalore: B.B.D. Power Press, 1946.

Verghese, C. Paul. *Problems of the Indian Creative Writer in English*. Bombay: Somaiya, 1971.

Verma, Rajendra. *Rabindranath Tagore; Prophet Against Totalitarianism*. Bombay: Asia, 1964.

Visva-Bharati News 1 (1932–33) to 7 (1938–39): passim.

X. "'Sannyasi' in China". *Modern Review* 37 (April 1925): 383–92.

Zbavitel, Dusan. "Rabindranath Tagore in 1887–1891". *Archiv Orientální* 24 (1956): 581–90.

———. "Rabindranath Tagore in 1891–1905". *Archiv Orientální* 25 (1957): 405–25.

———. "Rabindranath Tagore in 1905–1913". *Archiv Orientální* 26 (1958): 101–13.

———. "Rabindranath Tagore in 1913–1930". *Archiv Orientální* 26 (1958): 366–84.

———. "Rabindranath Tagore in 1930–1937". *Archiv Orientální* 27 (1959): 60–75.

Zepp, Ira G., Jr. "Tagore and Gandhi on Non-Violence: A Lover's Quarrel Represented by Dhananjaya". In *Rabindranath Tagore: American Interpretations*. Edited by Ira G. Zepp, Jr. Calcutta: Writers Workshop, 1981.

II. THESES AND DISSERTATIONS

Becker, Ann E. "Rabindranath Tagore as a Theater Artist". M.A. thesis, University of Oregon, 1958.

Chakraverty, Bishweshwar. "The Drama of Rabindranath Tagore". Ph.D. dissertation, University of Calcutta, 1961.

Chaudhery, Sumita Mitra. "William Butler Yeats and Rabindranath Tagore: A Comparative Study". Ph.D. dissertation, University of Michigan, 1973.

Dasgupta, Pranabendu. "The 'Subjective' Tradition: A Comparative Analysis of the Dramatic Motives in the Plays of W.B. Yeats and Rabindranath Tagore". Ph.D. dissertation, University of Minnesota, 1963.

Dev Sen, Nabaneeta. "The Reception of Rabindranath Tagore in England, France, Germany, and the United States". Ph.D. dissertation, Indiana University, 1964.

Haque, A.S.M. Zahurul. "Folklore in the Nationalist Thought and Literary Expression of Rabindranath Tagore". Ph.D. dissertation, Indiana University, 1967.

Hurwitz, Harold Marvin. "Rabindranath Tagore and England". Ph.D. dissertation, University of Illinois, 1959.

Mukerji, A.M. "The Dramas of Rabindranath Tagore Examined in the Light of Western Critical Theory". Ph.D. dissertation, University of Allahabad, 1950.

Mukherjee, Sujit Kumar. "Passage to America: The Reception of Rabindranath Tagore in the United States, 1912–1941". Ph.D. dissertation, University of Pennsylvania, 1963.

Sommerville, Marie. "The Writings of Rabindranath Tagore as a Bridge between East and West". Ph.D. dissertation, University of New Mexico, 1953.

III. ENGLISH AND AMERICAN REVIEWS CITED
(ARRANGED CHRONOLOGICALLY)

A. Book Reviews

1. *Chitra*

"Drama". *Athenaeum*, 17 January 1914, p. 99.

"From the Unreal to the Real". *Nation* (London), 24 January 1914, pp. 716–17.

De la Mare, Walter. "Poets from Afar". *Westminster Gazette*, 7 February 1914, p. 6.

"Tagore's Ideal Woman". *New York Times Review of Books*, 22 March 1914, p. 129.

"Plays and Books about the Drama". *American Review of Reviews* 49 (April 1914): 503.

Ficke, Arthur Davison. "A New-Old Tagore Play". *Little Review* 1 (April 1914): 33–35.

"East and West". *Times Literary Supplement*, 14 May 1914, p. 236.

"Drama". *Nation* (New York), 21 May 1914, pp. 611–12.

"Rabindranath Tagore, as a Playwright, Issues a Message to Women". *Current Opinion* 56 (May 1914): 358.

"Plays by Tagore". *Boston Evening Transcript*, 29 July 1914, p. 21.

Sinberg, Abraham E. "Rabindranath Tagore". *Colonnade* 8 (September 1914): 85–89.

Baerlein, Henry. "The Works of Tagore". *Bookman* 47 (December 1914): 100.

Forster, E.M. *Abinger Harvest*. New York: Harcourt, Brace, 1936.

2. *The Post Office*

"A Child Drama". *New York Times Review of Books*, 5 July 1914, p. 301.

"Plays by Tagore". *Boston Evening Transcript*, 29 July 1914, p. 21.

"'The Post Office'". *Times Literary Supplement*, 15 October 1914, p. 455.
"Drama". *Athenaeum*, 7 November 1914, p. 486.

3. *The King of the Dark Chamber*

"Mr. Tagore's New Play". *Times Literary Supplement*, 18 June 1914, p. 294.
"Drama". *Athenaeum*, 25 July 1914, p. 128.
"Rabindranath Tagore as Dramatist". *Guardian*, 17 September 1914, p. 1087.
G.C. "'The King of the Dark Chamber'". *Manchester Guardian*, 6 October
    1914, p. 4.
"Notes". *Nation*, 12 November 1914, p. 585.
"Books of the Autumn". *Independent*, 16 November 1914, p. 244.
Baerlein, Henry. "The Works of Tagore". *Bookman* 47 (December 1914): 100.
Henderson, Alice Corbin [A.C.H.]. "Two Kings". *Poetry* 5 (December 1914):
    133–34.
Woodbridge, Homer E. "Plays of To-day and Yesterday". *Dial*, 16 January
    1915, pp. 48–49.
Bullis, Helen. "Tagore and a Mystic". *New York Times Review of Books*, 14
    February 1915, pp. 49 + 51.
"'The King of the Dark Chamber'". *Dramatist* 6 (April 1915): 568–69.

4. The "Bolpur Edition"

"Tagore's Poems and Stories in English". *New York Times Review of Books*,
    10 December 1916, p. 541.

5. *The Cycle of Spring*

"'The Cycle of Spring'". *New York Times Review of Books*, 11 March 1917,
    pp. 87–88.
"Dramatists and the Drama". *American Review of Reviews* 55 (June 1917):
    663.
Buckley, Reginald R. "Tagore's New Books". *Bookman* 52 (July 1917): 120–
    21.
Firkins, O.W. "Verhaeren, Claudel, Cammaerts". *Nation*, 16 August 1917,
    p. 176.
"A Hindoo Drama". *Independent*, 29 September 1917, p. 512.
"New Books". *Catholic World* 106 (November 1917): 247.
"The Newly Published Plays". *Theatre Arts Magazine* 2 (December 1917): 62.

6. *"Sacrifice" and Other Plays*

"Recent Literature". *London Quarterly Review* 129 (January 1918): 136.
"The Play at Home and Abroad". *American Review of Reviews* 57 (January
    1918): 109.

"The Newly Published Plays". *Theatre Arts Magazine* 2 (February 1918): 116.
Colum, Padraic. "New Plays and a New Theory". *Dial*, 28 March 1918, p. 296.
Firkins, O.W. "Traditions and Modernities". *Nation*, 25 April 1918, p. 506.

7. *The Fugitive*

B.S. Review article. *Manchester Guardian*, 15 November 1921, p. 5.
"Moonshine from the East". *Saturday Review*, 19 November 1921, pp. 588–
    89.
E.S. "Two Eastern Singers". *Sunday Times*, 4 December 1921, p. 9.
Hyde, Fillmore. "Poetry in Prose". *Literary Review*, 10 December 1921,
    p. 255.
Le Gallienne, Richard. "Two Wise Men from the East". *New York Times
    Book Review and Magazine*, 11 December 1921, p. 3.
"Briefer Mention". *Dial* 72 (March 1922): 325.

8. *Red Oleanders*

"Drama". *Times Literary Supplement*, 9 July 1925, p. 465.
"The Bookman's Table". *Bookman* 69 (November 1925): 136.
Norwood, Gilbert. "Plays". *London Mercury* 14 (July 1926): 324–25.
"Drama". *Saturday Review of Literature*, 18 September 1926, p. 122.

9. *The Collected Poems and Plays*

Fausset, Hugh I'A. "Tagore's Poems and Plays". *London Mercury* 35 (December 1936): 206–7.
Engels, Vincent. "A Hindu Poet". *Commonweal*, 29 January 1937, pp. 391–
    92.
Parker, Barrett. "Rabindranath Tagore and His Poetry". *Boston Evening
    Transcript*, 30 January 1937, part 6, p. 3.
Keighton, Robert E. "Book Reviews". *Crozer Quarterly* 14 (April 1937):
    184–85.
"Theatre Arts Bookshelf". *Theatre Arts Monthly* 21 (April 1937): 331–32.

B. Play Reviews

1. *The Post Office* (1913)

"The Irish Players". *Times*, 11 July 1913, p. 8.
J.W. "Royal Court Theatre". *Westminster Gazette*, 11 July 1913, p. 3.
"An Indian Allegory". *Evening Standard*, 11 July 1913, p. 6.
"An Indian Play at the Court". *Globe*, 11 July 1913, p. 4.
"Indian Poet's Dream Play". *Standard*, 11 July 1913, p. 5.
"'The Post Office'". *Era*, 16 July 1913, p. 14.
"The Court". *Stage*, 17 July 1913, p. 20.

2. *The King and the Queen* (1919)

"The Union of East and West". *Era*, 19 February 1919, p. 12.
"The Comedy". *Stage*, 20 February 1919, p. 16.

3. *Sacrifice* and *Chitra* (1920)

"Prince of Wales Theatre". *Daily Telegraph*, 5 May 1920, p. 11.
"The Prince of Wales's". *Stage*, 6 May 1920, p. 16.
"Indian Art and Dramatic Society". *Observer*, 9 May 1920, p. 10.

4. *Sacrifice* and *The Post Office* (1920)

Woollcott, Alexander. "The Trials of Tagore". *New York Times*, 11 December 1920, p. 11.
Firkins, O.W. "Drama: St. John Ervine and Rabindranath Tagore". *Weekly Review*, 29 December 1920, p. 659.

5. Plays from *The Fugitive* (1924)

"Rabindranath Tagore's Plays in London". *Graphic*, 2 August 1924, p. 177.

6. *Sacrifice* and *The Post Office* (1952)

"Irving Theatre". *Times*, 15 May 1952, p. 8.

7. *The King of the Dark Chamber* (1961)

Taubman, Howard. "Tagore's 'King of Dark Chamber' Opens". *New York Times*, 10 February 1961, p. 21.
Balliett, Whitney. "Off Broadway". *New Yorker*, 18 February 1961, p. 93.
Brustein, Robert. "Off Broadway's Trials and Triumph". *New Republic*, 6 March 1961, pp. 21–22.
Lewis, Theophilus. "Theatre". *America*, 11 March 1961, p. 768.
Taubman, Howard. "Innocence of Spirit". *New York Times*, 9 April 1961, part 2, p. 1.
Driver, Tom F. "Revolutionless Worlds". *Christian Century*, 26 April 1961, pp. 535-37.
Pryce-Jones, Alan. "Alan Pryce-Jones at the Theatre". *Theatre Arts* 45 (April 1961): 68.
"An Offbeat Stage Hit on a Poet's Birthday". *Life*, 9 June 1961, p. 125.

IV. BENGALI WORKS CITED

Bandyopadhyay, Kanak. *Rabīndra Nāṭya Samīkshā*. Calcutta: A. Mukherjee, 1967.

———. *Rabīndranāther Tattva-nāṭak*. Calcutta: S. Banerjee, 1965.

Bandyopadhyay, Srikumar. *Rabīndra-Sṛishṭi-Samīkshā*. 2 vols. Calcutta: Satabdi, 1965; Orient Book, 1969.

Basu, Somendranath. *Rabīndra-nāṭake Ṭrājiḍī*. Calcutta: Tagore Research Institute, 1974.

Bhattacharya, Asutosh. *Rabīndra-Nāṭyadhārā*. Calcutta: Saṃskriti Prakasan, 1966.

Bhattacharya, Upendranath. *Rabīndra-Nāṭya-Parikramā*. Calcutta: Orient Book, 1960.

Bisi, Pramathanath. *Rabīndra-nāṭya-pravāha*. 2 vols. Calcutta: Orient Book, 1958–60.

Chaudhurani, Indira Devi. *Rabīndra-smṛiti*. Calcutta: Visvabharati, 1962.

Dasgupta, Santikumar. *Rabīndra-Nāṭya Parichay*. Calcutta: Bookland, 1963.

Datta, Harindranath. *Rabīndranāth o Sādhāraṇ Nāṭyaśālā*. Calcutta: Tagore Research Institute, 1983.

Ghosh, Sankha. *Kāler Mātrā o Rabīndra-nāṭak*. Calcutta: De's, 1978.

Ghosh, Santidev. *Gurudev Rabīndranāth o Ādhunik Bhāratīya Nṛitya*. Calcutta: Ananda, 1983.

———. *Rabīndra-saṅgīt*. Calcutta: Visvabharati, 1962.

———. *Rabīndra-saṅgīt Vichitrā*. Calcutta: Ananda, 1972.

Kundu, Pranaykumar. *Rabīndranāther Gītīnāṭya o Nṛityanāṭya*. Calcutta: Orient Book, 1965.

Mitra, Amal. *Kaviguru Rabīndranāth o Naṭarāj Śiśirkumār*. Calcutta: Tagore Research Institute. 1977.

Mukhopadhyay, Prabhatkumar. *Rabīndra-jīvanī o Rabīndra-sāhitya-Praveśak*. 4 vols. 4th ed. (vols. 1–2); 3rd ed. (vols. 3–4). Calcutta: Visvabharati, 1970–77 (vols. 1–2) and 1990–94 (vols. 3–4).

Nag, Kalidas. *Viśva-pathik Kālidās Nāg*. Calcutta: Writers Workshop, 1986.

Ray, Niharranjan. *Rabīndra-Sāhityer Bhūmikā*. Calcutta: New Age, 1962.

Saha, Gaurchandra. *Rabīndra-Patrāvalī: Tathyapañjī*. Calcutta: De's, 1984; Bolpur: Bolpur Pustakalay, 1984.

Sarkar, Pabitra. *Nāṭmañcha Nāṭyarūp*. Calcutta: Prama, 1981.

Sen, Asok. *Rabīndra-nāṭya-Parikramā*. Calcutta: A. Mukherjee, 1975.

Sen, Pulinbihari. *Rabīndra-grantha-pañjī*. Vol. 1. Calcutta: Visvabharati, 1973.

Sikdar, Asrukumar. *Rabīndra-nāṭye Rupāntar o Aikya*. Calcutta: Granthanilay, 1967.

Sita Devi. *Punya-smriti*. Calcutta: Maitri, 1964.

Thakur (Tagore), Abanindranath. *Abanindra Rachanāvalī*. 5 vols. Calcutta: Prakas Bhavan, 1973–83.

Thakur (Tagore), Rabindranath. *Chiṭhipatra*. 17 vols. Calcutta: Visvabharati, 1942–98.

———. Letter to Nirmalkumari Mahalanabis, 1 September 1929. In *Deś*, 6 May 1961, p. 22.

———. Letter to Nirmalkumari Mahalanabis, 21 March 1934. In *Deś*, 23 September 1961, p. 695.

———. Letter to Jagadananda Ray, 18 October 1912. In *Pravāsī*, Chaitra 1341, p. 752.

———. *Rabīndra-Rachanāvalī*. 26 vols. and 2 supplements. Calcutta: Visvabharati, 1939–48.

———. *Rabīndra Rachanāvalī*. 15 vols. Calcutta: Government of West Bengal, 1961–67.

———. *Svara-vitān*. 62 vols. Calcutta: Visvabharati, 1935–81.

V. UNPUBLISHED MATERIAL CONSULTED

Nag, Kalidas. Diaries.
Tagore, Amita. Interviewed by Shyamasree Lal. Calcutta, 15 March 1985.

VI. OTHER WORKS CITED

Arnott, Peter. "Greek Drama and the Modern Stage". In *The Craft and Context of Translation*. Edited by William Arrowsmith and Roger Shattuck. Austin: University of Texas, 1961.

"Arrangements for To-day". *Times*, 8 June 1915, p. 11.

Bentley, Eric. Introduction to *The Caucasian Chalk Circle*, by Bertolt Brecht. New York: Grove Press, 1966.

Bharucha, Rustom. *Rehearsals of Revolution: The Political Theater of Bengal*. Calcutta: Seagull, 1983.

Brockett, Oscar G. *History of the Theatre*. 4th ed. Boston: Allyn and Bacon, 1982.

Chislett, William. *Moderns and Near-Moderns*. New York: Grafton, 1928.

Cloyne, George. "Passages from India". *Times*, 23 February 1961, p. 15.

Dunbar, Olivia Howard. *A House in Chicago*. Chicago: University of Chicago, 1947.

Gazetteer of Kashmir and Ladak. Reprint ed. Delhi: Vivek, 1974.

Hartnoll, Phyllis, ed. *The Oxford Companion to the Theatre*. 4th ed. Oxford: University Press, 1983.

Haughton, John Alan. "Study India's Music, Tagore's Word to Western World". *Musical America*, 27 November 1920, p. 5.

Hochman, Stanley, ed. *McGraw-Hill Encyclopedia of World Drama*. 2nd ed. Vol. 5. New York: McGraw-Hill, 1984.

The Isa Upanisad. Translated by P. Lal. Calcutta: Writers Workshop, 1968.

Lévi, Sylvain. *The Theatre of India*. Translated by Narayan Mukherji. 2 vols. Calcutta: Writers Workshop, 1978.

Literatus. "Rabindranath Tagore in America". *Modern Review* 21 (May 1917): 549–53.

Millard, Bailey. "Rabindranath Tagore Discovers America". *Bookman* (New York) 44 (November 1916): 244–51.

Mitra, Rajendralala. *The Sanskrit Buddhist Literature of Nepal*. Reprint ed. Calcutta: Sanskrit Pustak Bhandar, 1971.

"Mr. Tagore's Poetry". *Times*, 10 May 1913, p. 8.

Nicoll, Allardyce. *English Drama 1900–1930: The Beginnings of the Modern Period*. Cambridge: University Press, 1973.

"Nobel Prize Given to a Hindu Poet". *New York Times*, 14 November 1913, p. 4.

Robinson, Lennox. *Ireland's Abbey Theatre: A History 1899–1951*. London: Sidgwick and Jackson, 1951.

Tagore, Rabindranath. *Gitanjali (Song Offerings)*. London: Macmillan, 1913.

———. *Selected Poems*. Translated by William Radice. Harmondsworth, Middlesex: Penguin, 1985.

"Topics of the Times: Our Case Isn't Desperate". *New York Times*, 15 November 1913, p. 10.

Vyāsa. *The Mahābhārata*. Translated by P. Lal. Vol. 21. Calcutta: Writers Workshop, 1970.

Wearing, J.P. *The London Stage 1910–1919: A Calendar of Plays and Players*. 2 vols. Metuchen, New Jersey: Scarecrow, 1982.

———. *The London Stage 1920–1929: A Calendar of Plays and Players*. 3 vols. Metuchen, New Jersey: Scarecrow, 1984.

Widgery, Robin Noel. "Survey of Asian Plays Produced in the United States from 1929 to 1966". *Afro-Asian Theatre Bulletin*, February 1967, pp. 5–10.

VII. ADDENDA TO SECOND EDITION

(ARRANGED CHRONOLOGICALLY)

A. Texts

Yogāyog. Edited by Jagadindra Bhaumik. Calcutta: Visvabharati, 1995.
Rakta-karavī. Edited by Pranaykumar Kundu. Calcutta: Visvabharati, 1998.

B. Translations

"Karna-Kunti Face-to-Face." Translated by Shyamasree Devi. In *Vyasa's Mahabharata: Creative Insights*. Edited by P. Lal. Calcutta: Writers Workshop, 1992.

The English Writings of Rabindranath Tagore. Edited by Sisir Kumar Das. Vol. 2. New Delhi: Sahitya Akademi, 1996.

The Post Office. Translated by William Radice. London: The Tagore Centre, 1996.

The Post Office. Translated by Krishna Dutta and Andrew Robinson. New York: St. Martin's Press, 1996.

C. Books in Bengali

Pal, Prasantakumar. *Rabī-jīvanī.* Vols. 1–8. Calcutta: Bhurjapatra (vols. 1–2) and Ananda (vols. 3–8), 1982–2001.

Chakrabarti, Rudraprasad. *Rangamancha o Rabīndranāth: Samakālīn Pratikriyā.* Calcutta: Ananda, 1995.

————. *Sādhāraṇ Rangālay o Rabīndranāth.* Calcutta: Visvabharati, 1999.

D. Books in English

Roy, R. N. *Rabindranath Tagore the Dramatist.* Calcutta: A. Mukherjee, 1992.

Roy, Supriya, compiler. *Tagoreana in "The Modern Review".* Santiniketan: Visva-Bharati, 1998.

Kundu, Kalyan; Bhattacharya, Sakti; and Sircar, Kalyan; eds. *Imagining Tagore: Rabindranath and the British Press (1912–1941).* Calcutta: Sahitya Samsad, 2000.

Chakraverty, Bishweshwar. *Tagore the Dramatist: A Critical Study.* Vols. 1–4. Delhi: B. R. Publishing, 2000.

E. Articles and Reviews in English

"Abbey Theatre". *Irish Times,* 19 May 1913, p. 9.

Colum, Padraic. "The Abbey Theatre". *Manchester Guardian,* 21 May 1913, p. 6.

"Another Tagore Play". *Observer,* 14 June 1914, p. 5.

"Mr. Tagore's Allegory". *Globe,* 15 June 1914, p. 3.

Littlewood, S. R. "A New Fairy-Teller". *Daily Chronicle,* 22 June 1914, p. 3.

"*The King of the Dark Chamber*". *Daily Express,* 2 July 1914, p. 7.

"Drama". *Illustrated London News,* 11 July 1914, p. 4.

"Three Poets". *Outlook,* 3 October 1914, pp. 434–35.

Review of *The Post Office. Nation* (London), 13 March 1915, pp. 756–58.

Sarkar, Jadunath. "*Chitra*". *Modern Review* 18 (October 1915): 431–32.

Dasgupta, Surendranath. "*The Post Office*". *Modern Review* 20 (September 1916):309–11.

C. H. H. "*The Cycle of Spring*". *Manchester Guardian,* 16 April 1917, p. 3.

J. D. "Literature in Drama". *Manchester Guardian,* 27 November 1917, p. 3.

"*Sacrifice*". *Christian Commonwealth,* 13 February 1918, p. 246.

"Union of East and West". *Morning Post,* 5 September 1921, p. 3.

"*The Fugitive*". *Observer,* 23 October 1921, p. 5.

"*Trial by Luck*". *Daily Chronicle,* 24 October 1921, p. 8.

"Two Indian Plays". *Daily Telegraph,* 24 October 1921, p. 4.

"Indian Plays at Cambridge". *Morning Post*, 2 November 1921, p. 11.

Steele, Drusie E. "Hindu Art Centre in Los Angeles". *Modern Review* 31 (January 1922):85–88.

"*Mukta-dhara*: A Berlin Review". *Modern Review* 32 (July 1922): 56–58.

"The Political Implications of Tagore's New Play". *Modern Review* 32 (September 1922):379–80.

"*Autumn Festival*". *Modern Review* 32 (October 1922):538.

Gillet, Louis. "Rabindranath Tagore's Plays". Translated by Mukund M. Desai. *Modern Review* 33 (February 1923):182–87.

Kramrisch, Stella [St. K.]. "The Visarjan Performance of the Visva-bharati". *Modern Review* 34 (October 1923):501–2.

"Tagore on the Moscow Stage". *Modern Review* 37 (January 1925): 119–20.

"Indian Theatre in Munich". *Modern Review* 49 (February 1931):260.

"Village Dramas and the Tagore Players". *Modern Review* 56 (November 1934):554–55.

Chatterjee, Kedar Nath [K. N. C.]. "Tagore's Play of Chitrangada in Dance and Music". *Modern Review* 59 (April 1936):450–51.

"Shoreham Church Pageant". *Sussex Daily News*, 6 July 1936, p. 3.

"Garden Play". *Evening News*, 29 July 1936, p. 6.

Datta, J. M. "Rabindra Nath Tagore in 1882". *Modern Review* 62 (November 1937):600–601.

"W. M. C. Theatre Group". *Westminster Chronicle*, 3 December 1937, p. 6.

"Tagore's Plays in Orissa, Germany and Czechoslovakia". *Modern Review* 63 (April 1938):482.

World Premieres Mondiales, October 1961, p. 2.

Petrovic, Sveto. "Tagore in Yugoslavia". *Indian Literature*, June 1970, pp. 5–29.

"Tagore Plays Abroad". In *Bilāti Yātrā theke Svadeśī Thiyeṭār*. Edited by Subir Raychaudhuri. Calcutta: Jadavpur University Department of Comparative Literature, 1972.

Bandyopadhyay, Sunil. "An Indian Princess in Munich". *Statesman* (Calcutta), 4 May 1987, p. 3.

Kampchen, Martin. "Rabindranath Tagore on the European Stage: A Reflection on Theatre and Cross-Cultural Experiments". *India International Centre Quarterly*, Spring 1997, pp. 1–12.

Glossary

This glossary lists terms and names of Indian origin that recur with some frequency in my translations of the plays. Each has been explained previously in the Notes, accompanying its first occurrence in the text. However, since they have not been annotated on subsequent appearances, I have extracted here in concise form their definitions from the Notes section. In a few cases I have indicated which specific note to refer to for more detailed information.

Agni: the god of fire. See *Tapati*, Note 55.

Ananga: "bodiless", one of the names of Kāma, god of love, because he was vapourised by a fiery flash from Siva's eye.

āñchal: the border or end of a sari draped over the left shoulder of an Indian woman.

bakul: often called the Indian Medlar, *Mimusops elengi*. An evergreen, it blooms in spring and summer, producing dull-white star-shaped scented flowers used in making garlands.

Bāul: a sect of itinerant minstrel-bards in Bengal who believe in a personal relationship with God and express their faith through devotional songs characterised by metaphysical themes and colloquial language.

Bhairav: Siva in his fearsome aspect as the Destroyer. Siva's violent traits are said to be emphasised in this manifestation.

chāmeli: the Spanish Jasmine, *Jasminum grandiflorum*, which bears very fragrant white flowers.

chhi: an interjection of contempt, reproach or disapproval.

devī: literally "goddess", this form of respectful address is directed to any venerable woman. Its closest English equivalent is "lady".

Dharma: Law or Justice personified. A relatively new god, his rise parallels the emphasis placed by later Hinduism on duty and virtue as the paths to salvation.

Dhruva: a prince who represents single-minded steadfastness and became immortalised as the pole star because of his constancy to Vishnu. A shrine to him adjoins the temple at Mārtanda.

Hari: one of the names of Vishnu. As an exclamation it expresses various emotions from amazement to disgust.

Indra: Vedic god of the atmosphere and sky, lord of rain. See *Red Oleander*, Note 72.

kali-yuga: the last and worst of the four ages (yugas) in Hinduism, known as an age of vice. See *Tapati*, Note 62.

Kandarpa: one of the names of Kāma, god of love.

kīrtan: a class of Vaishnava devotional songs in praise of and about Krishna and his love Rādhā. "Hymn" is a close equivalent.

Kurukshetra: site of the epic internecine battle that forms the core of the *Mahābhārata*. As a result the word has come to indicate any terrible battle or fight, or even a rowdy brawl.

mā: "mother", often used to address a girl or woman dear to the speaker, but also regularly applied to one of higher rank.

mādhavī: a climbing shrub, *Hiptage madablota*, bearing fragrant white blossoms tinged with yellow.

makar: mythical sea-monster, emblem of the god of love Kāma. See *Red Oleander*, Note 12.

Makar-ketan/Makar-ketu: "*makar*-bannered", two names for Kāma, god of love, whose flag displays the emblem of the aquatic creature, the *makar*.

mallikā: the Arabian Jasmine, *Jasminum sambac*, which bears very fragrant white flowers.

Mīnaketu: "fish-bannered", one of the names of Kāma, god of love, derived from the emblem of the *makar* on his flag.

Mrityuñjay: "conqueror of death", one of the names of Siva since he is regarded as immortal.

namaskār: the traditional Hindu method of greeting, with the palms of the hand joined together in front of the chest.

Naṭarāj: "king of dance", a name for Siva derived from his dance of destruction at the time of universal dissolution. Siva's dances — whether joyous or destructive — symbolise cosmic rhythm and the neverending cyclical movement of the universe.

Pañchasar: "five-arrowed", one of the names of Kāma, god of love, because he wields five arrows tipped with flowers.

Paush: ninth month of the Bengali calendar, corresponding to the second half of December and the first half of January.

Phālgun: eleventh month of the Bengali calendar, corresponding to the second half of February and the first half of March.

praṇām: the act of making obeisance to a god by lying prostrate, or the act of bending and touching another person's feet in reverence.

pūjā: the act of worshipping a god or goddess. "Worship" is the closest English replacement.

Pushpadhanu: "bow of flowers", one of the names of Kāma, god of love, alluding to the weapon that he carries.

rākshas: a category of evil demons. See *Red Oleander*, Note 25.

rasa: any liquid; the sap of plants; the marrow; the quintessence of the human body; the essence of something; enjoyment or pleasure; taste or flavour; and in Indian poetics, the aesthetic flavour of a work or the mood prevalent in it.

Rudra/Rudra-Bhairav: originally the Vedic god of storms, later one of Siva's commonly recognised forms. See *Tapati*, Note 18. Rudra-Bhairav is a compound of both names.

śāstra: any Hindu religious treatise or sacred book, or even the whole body of teaching on religion and mythology. "Scripture" is a suitable English replacement.

Satī: an incarnation of Durgā, Siva's consort. She put an end to herself by undergoing austerities because of an insult to Siva. See *Tapati*, Note 54.

satya-yuga: the first of the four ages in the history of the world according to Hindu myth, during which period everything was supposedly perfect, a veritable "Golden Age".

Sūrya: the sun-god, who formed with Indra and Agni the original Vedic triad. He lost his prominence in later mythology, but retained some honour as a benefactor of man.

tapasyā: devout and severe austerities, asceticism and self-discipline. See *Tapati*, Note 46.

thākur: literally "deity" or "lord", commonly used to address Brahmans respectfully. "Priest" may serve as an English substitute, though the Brahman thus addressed may or may not be a priest.

Yaksha: a class of demigods serving the god of wealth Kubera, appointed to guard the underground treasures of the earth. Although usually depicted as benign, sometimes they are portrayed as malevolent spirits, capable of causing demonic possession.

Yama: god of death and the underworld. See *Red Oleander*, Note 78.